117439

The signal call private K attached
rope to the starting derrick -
Ft Myer Va

Chas Taylor, Wilbur and Orville
Wright hooking the trigger rod to
the aeroplane at Ft Myer, Va

The Wright aeroplane

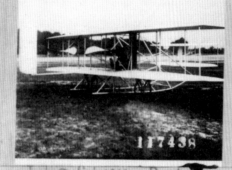

117436

117438

117435

A 3/4 front view of the
engine showing Orville
Wright in the seat

A 3/4 rear view of the Wright
aeroplane showing propeller
skids, etc

The Wright aeroplane with Orville
Wright in the seat leaving
starting rail for a short flight

117441

117435

117521

The Wright aeroplane leaving
the starting rail for a short
flight - Ft Myer Va

Orville Wright in Wright
aeroplane turning near
aeroplane shed

Removing the Wright aeroplane from
the shed - Wilbur Wright in

CONQUER THE SKY

CONQUER THE SKY

GREAT MOMENTS IN AVIATION

Featuring Photographs from Corbis-Bettmann

HAROLD RABINOWITZ

MetroBooks

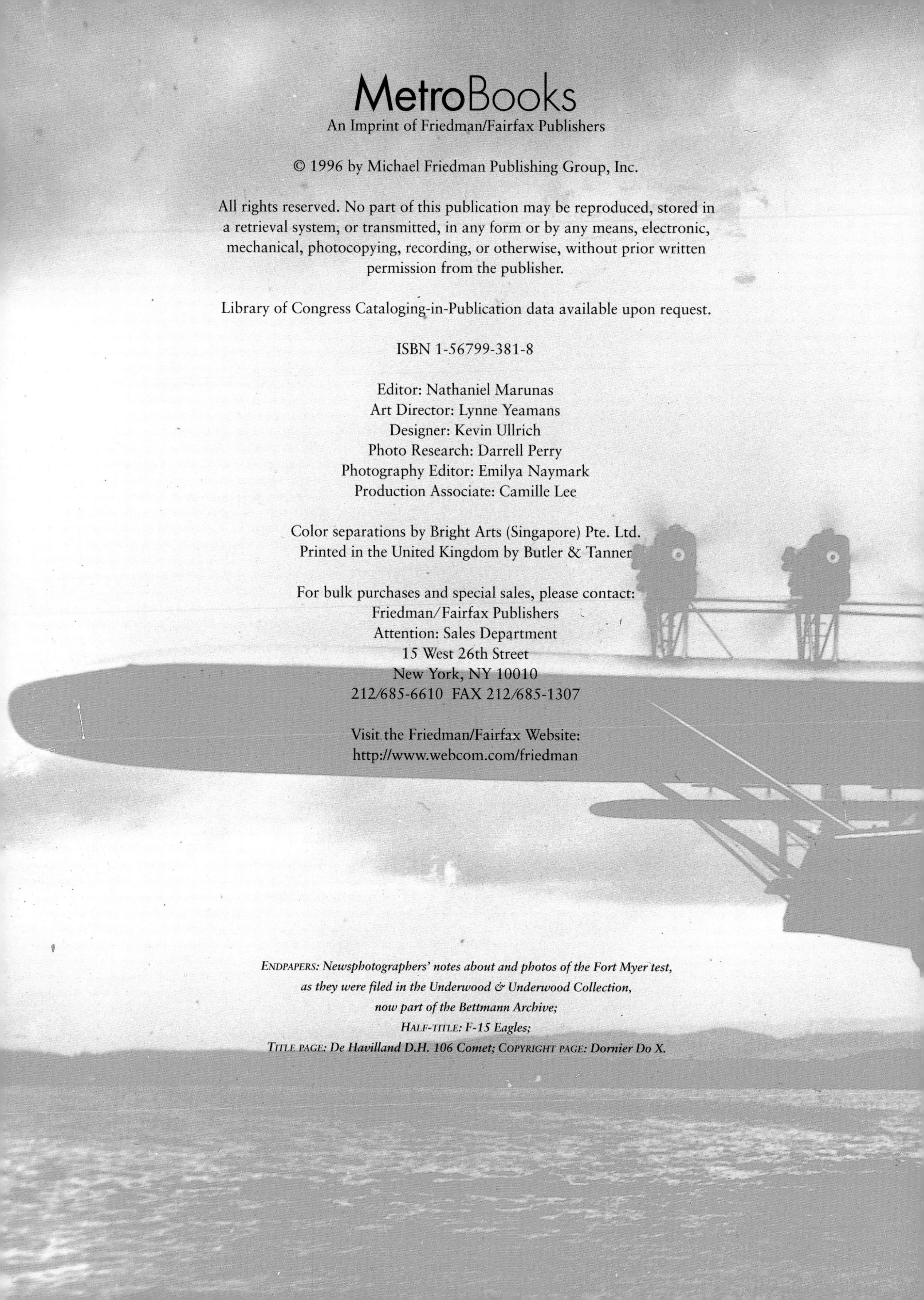

MetroBooks

An Imprint of Friedman/Fairfax Publishers

© 1996 by Michael Friedman Publishing Group, Inc.

Library of Congress Cataloging-in-Publication data available upon request.

ISBN 1-56799-381-8

Editor: Nathaniel Marunas
Art Director: Lynne Yeamans
Designer: Kevin Ullrich
Photo Research: Darrell Perry
Photography Editor: Emilya Naymark
Production Associate: Camille Lee

Color separations by Bright Arts (Singapore) Pte. Ltd.
Printed in the United Kingdom by Butler & Tanner

For bulk purchases and special sales, please contact:
Friedman/Fairfax Publishers
Attention: Sales Department
15 West 26th Street
New York, NY 10010
212/685-6610 FAX 212/685-1307

Visit the Friedman/Fairfax Website:
http://www.webcom.com/friedman

ENDPAPERS: *Newsphotographers' notes about and photos of the Fort Myer test,*
as they were filed in the Underwood & Underwood Collection,
now part of the Bettmann Archive;
HALF-TITLE: *F-15 Eagles;*
TITLE PAGE: *De Havilland D.H. 106 Comet;* COPYRIGHT PAGE: *Dornier Do X.*

Dedication

To Robert Wagner—
not the actor, not the mayor—
the teacher who first told me to go and
conquer the page.

Contents

Preface

Writing about the history of aviation has been an adventure in itself. It has only been in the last decade or so that the strictest standards of history have been applied to the history of aviation. Previously, accounts of episodes of aviation—even by eyewitnesses of important events or the participants themselves—have been written in a florid and romanticized style that, let's face it, may have sacrificed a fact or a truth to a turn of a phrase or a hyperbole. In almost every chapter of what follows, there are at least a half-dozen facts that are in dispute and, in some instances, fraught with political overtones. Who was, in fact, the first to fly? What exactly was the relationship between the Smithsonian and the Wright brothers? Why was Jack Northrop's Flying Wing discontinued when it was about to demonstrate the efficacy of the design? What was Billy Mitchell's motivation? What was Juan Trippe really up to in South America? And what really happened to the *Hindenburg*—or to Amelia Earhart?

In every one of these episodes, and in many more, I found a wide range of opinion even in the most reputable works, and sometimes, when I would consult with the authors of those very works, I would find a change of heart and a new approach to issues about which they had written. What this tells me is that the history of aviation is wrapped up in the adventurous personalities of the men and women who made that history, and there's just no pigeonholing such free and courageous spirits. There are many individuals in the history of aviation I wish I could talk to, but I have a feeling I would come away from such a meeting as perplexed as before, not knowing any more about what made these remarkable people tick than I do now.

I thank two people for providing invaluable guidance and inspiration over the years in this endeavor: Tom Crouch, a scholar of the highest caliber, at the Smithsonian's Air and Space Museum, and John Anderson, the United States' foremost aeronautical scientist and educator, at the University of Maryland. If this work does little more than encourage the reader to pick up and read the works by these distinguished men, I would consider the book a success.

In assembling the work, I received generous support and help from a remarkable group of professionals: Debbie Goodsite, photo archivist at the Bettmann Archive; Nathaniel Marunas, my ever-patient editor, Emilya Naymark, photo editor, and Kevin Ullrich, designer extraordinaire, at the Michael Friedman Publishing Group; and Daniel Vogel, my research assistant, who discovered that research can be backbreaking work when one has to rummage through hundreds of file cabinets in a photo archive. I am grateful to all of these talented and dedicated people.

I would finally like to thank my wife, Ilana, for reading text, evaluating issues, and generally being a sounding board and putting up with hours and hours of the most boring prattling she is ever likely to hear—at least until the next book.

—Harold Rabinowitz
New York City, 1996

Chapter 1
Dreams of Flight

Introduction

The history of flight is the history of a dream—human-kind's dream to soar through the sky like a bird. Birds seem to fly with so little effort that it was only natural that early attempts to fly would be attempts to emulate birds. Early myths about flight—and probably many early attempts—involved fashioning wings out of bird feathers. Since ancient times, however, it was suspected that the mechanism of bird flight was more complicated than it appeared to the naked eye. Although a clear understanding of bird flight was not attained until the twentieth century, the issue was considered settled with the posthumous publication in 1680 of Giovanni Alfonso Borelli's *De Motu Animalum*. Borelli described bird flight (erroneously, as it turned out) as the combined effect of the action of the individual feathers as they twist and turn during flight and the complex flapping of the wings, and claimed to prove that human musculature was far too weak to support a system of this kind.

Yet, birds are not the only creatures that fly. Bats, insects, and even some species of fish, fly without the complex structures of feathered wings, and virtually everyone has witnessed leaves, feathers, seeds, and what-not floating gently to the earth or being borne up by a gust of wind. It was also clear that heated air had the ability to carry things aloft, a phenomenon often observed in ovens and kilns throughout the Middle Ages. And even birds are often observed to be kept aloft without flapping their wings, not unlike the kite, a toy known since ancient times. It was just a short leap of imagination to envision a larger version of these flying objects with a person aboard. And imagination was in no short supply as intrepid (or perhaps foolhardy) would-be aeronauts

constructed and tested a wide variety of flying machines, often resulting in death or injury as they plummeted to earth. Yet, of the more than fifty documented instances of attempts to fly before 1800 that historian Clive Hart lists in his beautiful book, *The Prehistory of Flight*, about a dozen may have been brief instances of legitimate flight or gliding. One such attempt—by Besnier, a locksmith from Sable, France—involving a pair of wood-and-taffeta wings worn on the back and flapped by ropes attached to the hands and feet, became a celebrated instance of flight. And while there was always some doubt about Besnier's claims, believing them to be true only spurred the resolve of later experimenters.

Borelli's findings, and the many disastrous failures to "fly like a bird," soon made it apparent that the entire matter of human flight would have to be rethought if there was to be any progress. Several scientific findings of the seventeenth and eighteenth centuries laid the foundations for the science of flight: an appreciation of the fact that the air that surrounds us is a fluid and that it may exert forces in particular ways under the right conditions; that the forces required for flight can be separated, first conceptually and then practically; the development of the propeller as a by-product of the study of windmills and waterwheels by John Smeaton and the British engineers of the eighteenth century.

Amazingly, the theory of the airplane may be said to have been born by 1799—more than a century before the Wright brothers' achievements at Kitty Hawk—in the work of Sir George Cayley, an English baronet who worked on the problem from the 1790s until his death in 1857. Cayley understood the basic principles of flight and constructed working models, perhaps even one that carried a human being aloft, and for this reason he is known as "the father of aeronautics." But Cayley had a

This French engraving depicts Otto Lilienthal in a gliding mishap in 1894. The inclusion of the handy roof is a fanciful touch, but the thrill Lilienthal gave the public is accurately depicted.

long tradition on which to build, and in many ways his genius lay in being able to bring together well-established science with the legends and dreams of flight.

While the foundations of heavier-than-air flight were being laid, lighter-than-air flight was progressing through the late 1700s. The Montgolfier brothers (one of many brother teams to be found throughout the history of aviation) made their historic flight in 1783, and the balloon soon found a successful military application when it was used by the French at the Battle of Fleurus to defeat the Austrians. As thrilling as balloon flight was, its main contribution was to whet the appetite of the aerialists for real controlled flight, a dream that would not be realized for a century.

Ancient Myths

Nearly all ancient cultures contain myths about flying deities. The gods of ancient Egypt, Minoa, and Mesopotamia were often depicted as having magnificent wings, and the Persian god of gods, Ahura Mazda, is depicted in the Palace of Darius I at Susa (about 490 B.C.) as being nearly all wings. The ancient Hebrews had traditions of placing wings on the seraphim and on the cherubim that were on the Ark of the Covenant, but neither they nor the ancient Greeks and Romans saw wings as an absolute necessity for flight. Greek gods flew without any visible means and biblical descriptions of angels (such as those who visited Abraham or the one who wrestled with Jacob) are not depicted as winged. Wings on angels were not to become standard, in fact, until well into the Middle Ages.

To the people of ancient civilizations, flying was the province of the gods; humankind's place was on earth. For a human to don wings was an expression of the desire to become closer to the divine, but it was also seen

as arrogant, a mere mortal's attempt to usurp a prerogative of the gods. Two ancient myths demonstrate this ambivalence to flight: the tale of the Persian king Kai Kawus, who was said to have ruled around 1500 B.C., and the story of King Bladud of Britain (the supposed father of Shakespeare's King Lear), who is supposed to have ruled about 850 B.C.

According to a fable contained in the *Book of Kings*, composed by the poet Ferdowsi in A.D. 1000, king Kai Kawus was tempted by evil spirits to invade heaven with the help of a flying craft. This craft consisted of a throne to the corners of which were attached four long poles pointing upward. Pieces of meat were placed at the top of each pole and ravenous eagles were chained to the feet. As the eagles attempted to fly up to the meat, they carried the throne aloft. Inevitably, however, the eagles grew

The legend of Kai Kawus, the Persian king who was taken aloft on a throne lifted by eagles, was a favorite subject of folklore, as in this 1710 manuscript, in spite of the folly the king represented.

the aid of two large reed hats. Such hats are still worn in areas of China today and can be as much as three feet wide. Shun may well have been the first parachutist in history.

Analogous figures can be found in the mythology of nearly every ancient civilization. In Northern Europe Wayland the Smith was carried into the sky by a shirt made of feathers. In Africa Kibaga the warrior flew invisibly over his enemies and dropped rocks on them (the first mention of the possibility of aerial bombardment). He was finally killed when his adversaries simply shot their arrows blindly in the air. These fables were meant as warnings that humans should not attempt to penetrate the heavenly realms, literally or figuratively. No doubt these cautionary reminders fired the imagination of as many people as they intimidated.

Daedalus and Icarus

The Greek legend of Daedalus and Icarus is no doubt the most famous of the ancient legends of flight. Many aspects of the legend are worth considering since they certainly influenced later generations of experimenters. In Greek mythology, Daedalus (Greek for "cunning artificer") is an unusual figure: an Athenian architect and engineer with near-godlike intellectual powers. He is the mythical inventor of the axe and the saw, and was said by Plato to have constructed mechanical statues of the gods so lifelike that they perspired under the hot Aegean sun and had to be restrained lest they run away. Daedalus also invented various puzzles and gadgets that amazed onlookers, including a box that could be opened only by the sound of birdsong in perfect harmony.

In time, Daedalus moved to Crete with his son, Icarus, and became the resident architect and inventor for the wealthy King Minos. His greatest public achievement was the design and creation of the dreaded Labyrinth, a maze built in the city of Knossos and said to be so cleverly crafted that once one entered the maze it was impossible to find one's way out. In the center of the Labyrinth was the monstrous Minotaur, who was half-bull and half-man. Every year Minos sacrificed fourteen Athenian youths to this creature. Being an Athenian himself, this did not sit well with Daedalus. He supported Theseus, King of Attica, in his plot to overthrow Minos and shared with him the secret to finding one's way out of the Labyrinth. After Theseus killed the Minotaur, set fire to the palace, and escaped with the king's daughter, Ariadne, Daedalus' disloyalty was discovered and the king sent his soldiers to arrest him.

Years earlier Daedalus had witnessed the witch Medea take flight in a chariot drawn by fiery dragons; since then, he had secretly devoted himself to creating a mechanism that would allow him to fly. When he and Icarus arrived at Crete, they had set up a secret workshop in the

tired and the throne came crashing down. In Persian literature, Kai Kawus is known as "The Foolish King" (even though the legend has the eagle-propelled craft flying the king all the way to China).

King Bladud's motivation for attempting to fly seems to have been somewhat different: he was promoting magic and wizardry (and, perhaps, ingenuity) in the kingdom. Legend has it that the king donned large wings made of feathers and took flight over the city of Trinavantum (present-day London). As he twisted in the air, he lost his balance in mid-flight and came crashing down into the Temple of Apollo, in full view of his horrified subjects. Unlike Kai Kawus, however, Bladud remained a popular, if tragic, figure in British mythology.

In China, there are many legends of emperors flying in chariots or with the use of wings. As early as 2200 B.C., the emperor Shun is reported to have escaped a burning tower and later to have flown over his dominion with cliffs overlooking the sea. Daedalus spent many hours observing the silent gliding flight of the eagles that nested in the cliffs; he then experimented with many materials that might work for wings. Sail canvas was too heavy, silk and thin cloth were too weak. At last Daedalus came upon the obvious: why not construct the wings out of eagle feathers? The inventor was sad to be hunting the magnificent birds, but he soon collected enough feathers to fashion wings with beeswax.

Daedalus was about to begin testing his invention when word came that Minos' men were coming to arrest him. He and Icarus quickly repaired to their secret cliffside workshop and donned their untested wings. Dae-dalus instructed his son to fly at a middle altitude—high enough so that the ocean spray would not dampen the wings and make them too heavy; low enough so that the heat of the sun would not melt the wax that held the feathers together. With that they took off across the Aegean Sea, hoping to glide all the way to Sicily. The end of the story is well known to most Westerners. Icarus, intoxicated with the thrill of flying, flew too high. The wax melted, his wings came apart, and he plunged to his death in the sea, near an island that was later named Ikaria in his honor.

Crete does, in fact, have tall cliffs overlooking the sea, against which strong and persistent thermal updrafts are created by winds known as the Miltemi. Large gulls (the eagles, if there ever were any, are long gone) float and glide for long periods. Beginning with the excavations of Sir Arthur Evans in 1900, many of the details of the legend of King Minos and the Labyrinth have been confirmed, bit by bit, and some historians (no less a figure than H.G. Wells, for example) have come to believe that the legend of Daedalus and Icarus has some basis in fact.

The legend of Icarus was both a caution and an inspiration to those who dared to dream about flight. Some historians believe the legend may be based on a historical occurrence.

The Chinese and Their Rockets

Rocketry and space exploration are often included in histories of aviation, but there are only a few superficial points the two enterprises share. In both cases, a vehicle is used to transport a person or cargo above the surface of the earth. Sometimes vehicles that are rocket-propelled may also be airworthy, as in the case of the Space Shuttle. The skills and physical abilities of astronauts were, at least in the early stages of space flight, determined to be similar to those of test pilots. And NASA, the U.S. government agency that is responsible for the space program, grew directly out of NACA, the agency responsible for experimentation and research in atmospheric flight. But rocket flight is very different from aerial flight (different even from jet-propelled flight) and its place in the history of aviation is mainly in the early stages, when the distinction between the two was still blurred.

A rocket is simply a device in which an object—the payload—is propelled by the reactive effect of hot gasses exhausted in a specific direction. The faster the gas is spewed out in one direction, the heavier the payload can be and the faster it can be propelled in the opposite direction. The earliest rockets were almost certainly Chinese—there is little doubt that the Chinese first developed "black powder," the basic propellant used in rockets. The combination of saltpeter, charcoal, and sulphur was probably used in fireworks by the Chinese centuries before Christ lived, but the only written records available are dated well into the Middle Ages.

Mongols besieging the city of Kaifeng in 1232 used arrows propelled by rockets (though primarily as a psychological weapon). Knowledge about rocketry seems to have moved with the Mongol invasions—the Arabs are seen as having developed rockets by the thirteenth century and are reported as having used them against Saint Louis in the Seventh Crusade; the Italians were experimenting with rockets by the fifteenth century. A major refinement in the formula for black powder was made in the thirteenth century by Roger Bacon; this resulted in the creation of gunpowder. The British encounter with rockets in India led William Congreve to develop the Congreve rocket, the ancestor of the modern ballistic missile. The British used Congreve rockets during the War of 1812 (as "The Star-Spangled Banner" reminds us), and at the Battle of Waterloo.

BELOW: The ancient Chinese had the means of making a rocket-propelled chair, as in this depiction of the Emperor Wan-Hoo blasting off, but whether or not they actually attempted the feat is uncertain.

ABOVE: The military uses of rocket power are depicted in this fifteenth-century illustration of a blunderbuss, from the Bellifortis manuscript. BELOW: Roger Bacon, the thirteenth-century monk-theoretician.

What is strangest about rockets when considered from the perspective of aviation is that, even though rockets were used extensively throughout history all over the world—and soldiers in the field who were exposed to rockets conjectured about what it might be like to "ride" one or have one strapped to one's back—writers of fiction rarely used rockets as a means of transportation when they created stories about trips to the Moon or to outer space until well into the nineteenth century. Cyrano de Bergerac's *L'Autre Monde* (The Other World), completed in 1662, is a notable exception. In it, Cyrano is carried to the Moon by a ship fitted with many rockets. But virtually all other writers used every conceivable device—from geese to cannons to spheres filled with dew—except rockets. Even Jules Verne's *From the Earth to the Moon*, published in 1865, has space travelers flying to outer space in a capsule shot out of a cannon. This is why the remarkable 1881 drawings of Nikolai Kilbalchich of a crewed platform propelled by a battery of rockets, drawn literally moments before he was led to his execution for plotting against Tsar Alexander II (and thus not discovered until after the Russian Revolution in 1917), or Konstantin Tsiolkolvski's 1883 drawings (published in 1903) of staged rockets with a crewed cockpit in

the nose, were so revolutionary. Somehow, rockets drew people's attention skyward but failed to inspire dreams of flight until humankind looked to conquer the stars themselves.

The Middle Ages: Roger Bacon

The first individual to write in what we would consider a serious, scientific way about the possibility of flight was Roger Bacon, a Franciscan monk who lived from 1214 to 1292. Bacon was a prolific writer and devoted much energy to defending the power of reason and to ridiculing medieval scholasticism and the "magic" of alchemy. Those who followed him look upon Bacon as a critically important step in humankind's emergence from the ignorance of the Dark Ages; considering he had little support around him, he was probably one of the keenest minds of human history.

In 1260, Bacon wrote a work on the superiority of reason called *De Mirabili Potestate Artis et Naturae* (On the Marvelous Powers of Art and Nature). In it he suggests that human reason is so powerful that it could even manage to do something that seems utterly impossible, namely, build a machine that would enable a person to fly. The manuscript—which was not published for nearly three hundred years—then yields two incredible passages. The first outlines two possible ways in which a person might fly. One is a rough description of what was later to become known as an ornithopter. The other is a more detailed description of a globe filled with "ethereal air." Having demonstrated that air is a kind of fluid in which less dense objects might float like a ship floats on water, Bacon suggests methods of thinning the air in a globe that will give it buoyancy in air—more than five hundred years before lighter-than-air flight would become a reality.

The second remarkable section is even more intriguing, for in it Bacon claims, "There is an instrument to fly with, which I never saw, nor know any man that hath seen it, but I full well know by name the learned man who invented the same." It is possible that Bacon is referring to his fellow Englishman, Eilmer

Imagined flight, as in this illustration from Restiffe de la Bretonne's eighteenth-century fantasy about flying over the Australian wilderness, had not advanced much over two thousand years.

(also known as Oliver) of Malmesbury, a monk who was the first of the so-called tower-jumpers—people who tried to fly by jumping off a high place with winglike contraptions connected to their arms or body. Most of these attempts ended in the death of the jumper, but Eilmer, who jumped in about 1010, some 250 years before Bacon, was reported to have glided about 250 yards (228.5m) and survived a bumpy landing (though he broke both his legs). Eilmer is immortalized in a stained glass portrait in the Malmesbury Abbey, holding his batlike wings (perhaps pre-flight, since he is standing rather erect). If Bacon meant a device used in his own day that flew successfully, it was certainly the best kept secret of the Middle Ages.

Leonardo da Vinci: Forgotten Genius

It is not possible to write a history of aviation without mentioning Leonardo da Vinci, the Italian artist and scientist who lived and worked in Florence in the late fifteenth century, even though fate dictated that he would have virtually no impact whatever on the development of flight. In spite of his brilliance, the world knew nothing

of his theoretical work in aviation for the simple reason that nearly none of his notes were published (or even known about) until the late 1800s. Unlike Bacon, whose influence lay mainly in his efforts to dispel the human fear of flying as an impossible or demonic activity, Leonardo was very secretive about his aviation research, committing his drawings and notes to paper in a mirror writing that would conceal his findings from most observers. Leonardo discussed some things with his contemporaries (not many, since that could sometimes prove dangerous for a man like him), but it does not seem that anyone had any idea of his aeronautical musings.

In all, Leonardo left behind a large body of work about flight: more than five hundred sketches and thirty-five thousand words. Much of his work involved the careful study of birds and of batlike wing sections. He realized that human physiology was not capable of birdlike flight, but he designed many ornithopters that required coordinated pedaling of arms and feet. Most of his conclusions about how birds fly were wrong, and these errors rendered most of his aircraft useless. Recent models based on Leonardo's drawings have been built and flown for very short distances, but it is unlikely that the builders will be marketing kits very soon.

Two aspects of Leonardo's work are interesting, though. First, he did realize that an aircraft would require a tail section to stabilize the flight. And, second, he conceived of a proto-helicopter that used a wide screw to lift itself into the air. The principle behind this device, the Archimedean screw, was known since antiquity and was used to transport water uphill or up from a well. Leonardo seems to have been the first to apply the mechanism to aviation. Here, too, however, the power was to be provided by a human being, making it a hopeless enterprise.

Of his many designs, da Vinci made only one model: a miniature version of his helicopter. After he constructed the model, he wondered (in his notes) whether the machine would have to wait for the invention of a lighter power source than a human being to work. That no one tried anything remotely like any of the designs contained in his notebooks in the century after he died is evidence of how private this work was.

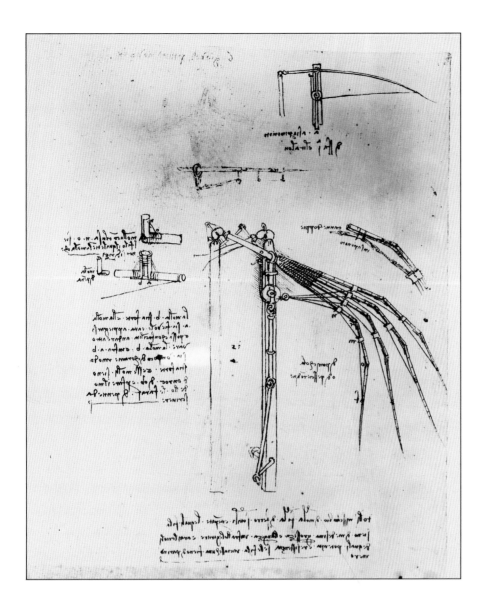

Balloons and the Montgolfier Brothers

While some were dreaming of flying like a bird, others preferred to take it one step at a time and simply try to lift into the air. The idea of using Archimedes' buoyancy principle to rise in the atmosphere by creating an object lighter than the air it displaces had been introduced in 1670 by a Jesuit priest, Father Francesco de Lana of Brescia, Italy. De Lana suggested (in print) that copper could be used to create spheres thin enough to be lightweight yet strong enough to be evacuated of all air, thereby making the total sphere lighter than the air the sphere displaced. The theory was sound, but producing sufficiently light spheres that would not collapse under the pressure of the air proved too difficult.

In 1766, the British scientist Henry Cavendish discovered hydrogen gas (as the product of mixing iron, tin, zinc shavings, and sulfuric acid) and found it to be one-tenth the weight of air. This should have stirred someone to realize that hydrogen gas could be used to fill a bal-

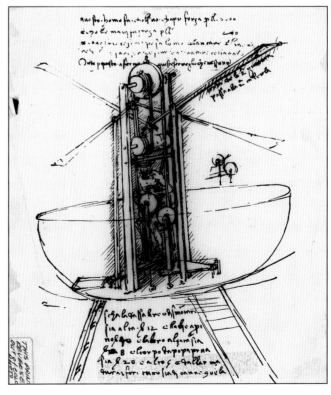

Barthelmy-Laurent de Gusman's flying boat, from a 1709 engraving. The craft was to be kept aloft by magnets in the two globes fore and aft. How this was to be accomplished was never explained.

first known date), and culminating in a public demonstration in the town square of Annonay on June 5.

Étienne was immediately summoned to Paris to address the Academy of Sciences about the brothers' invention. Even before Étienne arrived, the French physicist Jacques Charles, mistakenly believing the Montgolfiers had used hydrogen in their ascent, hastily constructed a balloon of varnished silk, filled it with hydrogen (an expensive chemical procedure on such a large scale), and launched it from the Champs de Mars, Paris, on August 27. It rose through heavy rains that fell that day and was carried away by the storm to the village of Gonesse some fifteen miles (24km) away, where it finally came to rest. The superstitious peasants of the village, believing the balloon to be a monster that was attacking them from the sky, proceeded to rip it to shreds with scythes and pitchforks. The flight of the first "Charliere," as hydrogen-filled balloons were to be called for many years afterwards, had therefore been a qualified success.

The Montgolfier brothers then built an even larger balloon—some seventy feet (21m) high—equipped with a circular gallery for the aeronauts. Two adventurers, Jean-Francois Pilatre de Rozier and Francois Laurent, Marquis d'Arandes, volunteered for the flight, which was prepared for and anticipated with the same nail-biting nervousness that characterized the first manned rocket launches of modern times. Tests were conducted with animals to determine what possible ill effects there might be on living beings, and then, beginning on October 15, tethered flights with humans were conducted from the courtyard of the Palace of Versailles. On November 21, the same pair made a free (untethered) flight in their Montgolfier, landing about ten miles (16km) away about twenty-three minutes after launching. That event is often considered the first time humankind flew.

loon and the result would be a lighter-than-air object. Inexplicably, it did not, and the first balloons to fly were filled with hot air.

In the mid-1770s, Joseph and Étienne Montgolfier, brothers who worked in their father's paper factory in Annonay in southeastern France, noted that paper rose in the updrafts of the factory's chimney, and occasionally a sheet would fold into a dome and continue rising even after leaving the immediate area of the chimney. They conducted some simple experiments with silk bags and soon became convinced that a large bag with heated air inside would rise. In actuality, this effect had already been demonstrated nearly seventy-five years earlier by the Brazilian priest Bartolomeu de Guasmao, who conducted a spectacular demonstration in the court of King John V in Lisbon, Portugal. But the Montgolfiers knew nothing of this demonstration, and they knew little about the reason their balloon rose into the air. They believed that the balloon was filled with a gas they called "Montgolfier gas" that had a special property they called "levity." They did not even associate heated air with Montgolfier gas—they believed that the levity was contained in the smoke.

Adding sulfuric acid to iron filings creates helium, as illustrated by this eighteenth-century drawing.

Still, the Montgolfiers conducted their experiments and trials with care and learned much from each trial run. After experimenting with smaller models, they constructed a large balloon of linen covered with stiff paper—prints of the time show a large blue ovoid, brightly decorated and held together with buttons—and conducted many trials, beginning on April 25, 1783 (the

On December 1, Charles and his associate, Nicolas Robert launched a new hydrogen balloon from the Tuileries Gardens. They landed twenty-seven miles (43.5km) away after a flight of two hours, and except for the fact that the balloon took off again with Charles when Robert abruptly jumped out of the gondola after their first landing (only to land several miles away), filling a balloon with hydrogen was quickly seen as the superior method: it did not require constant attention to a heat source to warm the air (and anyway, the heat source was a smoky mess since the Montgolfiers refused to accept Charles' instruction that it was merely the

LEFT: *The Charles hydrogen balloon, which was launched on August 27, 1783, was ripped to shreds by the fearful townsmen of Gonesse, where it landed.* RIGHT: *The throng that gathered to watch the historic flight of Montgolfier's crewed balloon on November 21 was less superstitious.*

heated air that was carrying their craft aloft and not the smoke). The explosive nature of hydrogen was not to become important until years later, when very large volumes of hydrogen were placed in close proximity to flames and sparks.

The French wasted no time exploiting the new technology. Eleven years later, in France's war with Austria, tethered balloons were used in the siege of Mainz and were decisive at the Battle of Fleurus. The captain of the Company of Aerostiers was a man named Coutelle, a shadowy figure who was ridiculed for espousing the use of balloons on the battlefield. After France's victory, he became a national hero. De Lana had foreseen the possible military uses of his flying evacuated copper globes, and feared flight for "the disturbance it would cause to the civil government of men." It took more than a century, but his words proved prophetic.

The Bernoullis and the Physics of Lift

Alexander McKee begins his fascinating book, *Great Mysteries of Aviation*, with the observation that the most puzzling mystery in the history of aviation is why it took so long for humankind to learn to fly. With so much intellectual and physical energy devoted to a single problem for so long, one might have expected someone to stumble on the secret, if only by accident, long ago. What was the obstacle?

The problem is that the physical principles that lie at the foundation of flight are counterintuitive; indeed, the mechanics of flight were ultimately revealed after some fancy manipulation of the physics and mathematics cre-

ated by Sir Isaac Newton in the late 1600s. Not only were the theories of Aristotle, Bacon, Leonardo, and the rest all wrong, but the true principles of flight, including how birds stay aloft, were simply unguessable and unobservable. It took several remarkable scientists, including members of a celebrated family of scientific giants, to piece together the puzzle. For all the triumphs of Newtonian physics—from explaining the tides to predicting comets—Newton had little success in applying his methods to fluids and fluid dynamics.

Along came the Bernoullis, a Swiss family among whom were some of the most important contributors to the development of mathematics and science in the seventeenth and eighteenth centuries. The two key figures in this family were Johann (1667–1748), who made the University of Basel in Switzerland the center of European science in its day, and his son Daniel (1700–1782). In 1725, Daniel accepted an appointment in St. Petersburg, Russia, where he stayed for eight years and did some of his most important work. He managed to take a friend with him: the great mathematician Leonhard Euler, who had been a student of Johann Bernoulli back in Basel.

In 1734, Daniel completed his famous work *Hydrodynamica*, which was not published until 1738. In addition to coining the word "hydrodynamics," Daniel laid out the basic principles of the new science, applying Newton's basic laws to simplified cases of fluid dynamics. Out of this work came Bernoulli's Principle (or Law), which Euler helped express as a mathematical equation known as Bernoulli's Equation.

What Bernoulli found boiled down to this: when a fluid is moving—through a pipe or conduit, or simply over any surface—it exerts pressure in all directions: against anything that is in the way of its flow, as well as against any surface it touches. For example, as water flows through a garden hose, you can feel the pressure of the water against the inner wall of the hose if you try to squeeze the hose. Now, if the fluid is noncompressible (meaning it can't be squeezed into a smaller volume, which is true of water, in most ordinary circumstances), and if there is no change in the amount of fluid flowing (meaning nothing is leaking out or coming in), then the faster the fluid is flowing, the *lower* its pressure against the surface it's flowing over will be. That means that when you pinch the garden hose slightly in the middle and the water keeps coming out of the end at the same rate, then the water must be traveling through the pinched portion a little faster (since the same amount of water is passing through that section of the hose as before). Our intuition is that faster water exerts greater pressure (and it does, but only in the direction of the flow), but the pressure of the faster water against the wall of the hose (which is perpendicular to the direction of the flow) is less—a total surprise. Euler gave Bernoulli's work mathematical form (with the help of the work of French mathematician Jean le Rond d'Alembert), and Johann, Daniel's father, made it intuitively palatable in his 1743 work, *Hydraulica* (which he tried to pass off as having been written in 1728).

Now, as to flying: if a sleek, symmetrical wing is in an air flow so that air is passing over it and under it, the flow can be considered noncompressible and a closed system—a few feet back (if the wing is sleek enough and the wind is not too strong), one wouldn't even know the air took a little detour around the wing. As the air flows over the wing's surface, it too exerts pressure in two directions—in the direction of its flow (that's the force of the wind) and perpendicular to its flow against the surface of the wing. But since the air has to travel a greater distance to flow around the wing, it speeds up, and by Bernoulli's Principle it exerts less pressure on the surface of the wing. Since the wing is symmetrical (a teardrop shape in cross-section), the reduced pressure is the same both above and below. Now what happens if we slice the wing in half, so that the lower surface is straight (and the air flows across it in a straight line), but the upper surface is curved (and the air speeds up only when flowing over that surface)? The pressure of the air on the upper surface drops, making the pressure of the air on the underside greater. The result is that there is a net force lifting the wing up, and so it rises. This differ-ence between the pressure upward on the underside of the wing and the force downward on the top surface is called "lift"; the curve of the top surface of a wing over its under surface is called its "camber." After centuries of believing the very reasonable notion that, like ships floating on the ocean, birds flew in a sea of air, and that a wing (of a bird or of a successful aircraft) would have a cross-section that, like a boat, would be curved on the bottom and flat on top, the exact opposite turned out to be the case. Flight is made possible by the lift created by the pressure difference resulting from air flowing over a wing with camber, and that's the secret of flight.

Ornithopters, Helicopters, and Kites

As the dream of flight lurched toward reality during the nineteenth century, two developments begun centuries earlier came to a climax. One was the failure of attempts to create an ornithopter—a flying machine that emulated birds by having flapping wings—and its cousin, the helicopter, and the other was the development of the kite, which had been around in some form or other for centuries.

In most minds, Italian theorist Giovanni Alfonso Borelli had laid the ornithopter question to rest, yet doubts persisted. New findings about bird flight were casting doubt on Borelli's conclusions, and new engineering techniques and designs were keeping the possibility of human-powered winged flight alive. One widely publicized plan was that of Frenchman Jean Pierre Blanchard, who later achieved fame as a balloonist. His machine consisted of an enclosed cabin in which a man's pedaling with both arms and legs would be amplified by gears and transferred to the flapping wings outside.

In 1809, it was widely reported that the Austrian Jacob Degen had successfully flown in an ornithopter. In fact, the reports and the illustrations that accompanied them neglected to mention that Degen and his contraption, an embellishment of Besnier's design, were tethered to a large hot-air balloon. Degen actually used his wings to provide him just enough lift to rise with the help of the balloon. In this manner, he went balloon-jumping in large leaps on a parade ground, to the delight of onlookers, but only the most gullible would take that for flying.

ABOVE: *The Bernoullis discovered the theoretical basis for lift produced by a rigid wing.* BACKGROUND: *This eighteenth-century drawing of kite-flying in Hai-Kwan, China, shows the Chinese having discovered the effect by trial and error centuries earlier.*

Still, Degen had made a contribution: unlike Blanchard and others, his design was actually built and offered some approximation of flight. It also spurred public interest in flight—Degen performed his "act" before appreciative crowds in Paris and Vienna sporadically from 1806 to 1817. Most importantly, however, reports of Degen's "flight" prompted Sir George Cayley to publish in 1809 the first of his monumental three-part treatise, *On Aerial Navigation*, a landmark in the history of flight.

In 1810, Thomas Walker's somewhat more practical design for an ornithopter of Thomas Walker appeared. Though streamlined and mindful of weight limitations, the craft had no chance of ever being airborne. Some elements of its design, however, caught the eye of experimenters in heavier-than-air flight. Although enough experimental and theoretical findings were published throughout the century to show that ornithopters were never going to be feasible flying machines, and the foundation for the airplane had already been laid early in the century, the 1800s saw an ever increasing number of ornithopter designs, particularly from American inventors. The reason for this was an odd policy of the U.S. Patent Office that granted a large number of patents for such devices; this policy existed because of an assumption that heavier-than-air flight was impossible. (European patent offices were more careful, thus discouraging a great many crackpot designs.) Inventors from weekend tinkerers to Thomas Edison offered a bewildering array of designs, and many were granted patents—but none of these machines flew.

A close relative of the ornithopter, the helicopter—a device in which blades rotate in a horizontal plane lifting the device—did see some success in the nineteenth century. As early as 1784, two Frenchmen, Launoy and Bienvenu, built a primitive helicopter powered by a tightly wound cord. Similar success was achieved by Vittorio Sarti in 1828, and by W. H. Phillips in 1842, both of whom used a steam engine as a power plant. These machines had no mechanism for control and were less maneuverable than balloons. Yet experimenters sensed that this, like the airplane, was an area of great potential.

Meanwhile, an age-old device known for centuries, the kite, also underwent some serious study and development. Kites had been used in China since several centuries before Christ, and Marco Polo reported in the

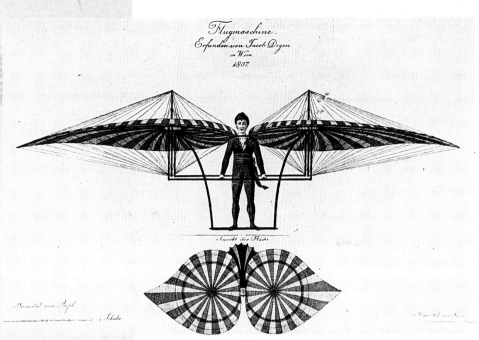

Front and aerial views of Jacob Degen's flying machine as it appeared in the early nineteenth century, but with one important element missing: the huge balloon that actually carried Degen aloft.

fourteenth century that the Chinese had developed kites powerful enough to carry a man aloft. The artistry of Chinese kites has been dazzling through the centuries, and their introduction into Europe by sailors and merchants who brought them back from the Orient delighted both adults and children. But the development of the kite into a device of interest to aeronautical researchers was the work of a remarkable Australian, Lawrence Hargrave, one of the many extraordinary figures in the early history of flight about whom very little is known.

From 1850 to 1915, Hargrave worked in New South Wales, Australia, on many aspects of flight. Far removed from aeronautical activity in Europe and America, and with only a rudimentary grasp of mathematics and physical science, he was a first-class draftsman and mechanic. In 1887, he invented the rotary engine that was later to become a standard design for aircraft power plants, and in 1893 he created the box kite, which was of even more immediate importance. In 1899, Hargrave attended a meeting of the Aeronautical Society in London and delivered a paper on the box kite. It was immediately obvious to all the attendees, as it had been to Hargrave, that the box kite design was highly adaptable to gliders and eventually to airplanes. Among those who attended was Percy Pilcher, who was later to achieve fame as a glider pilot using Hargrave's box kite design. In fact, the designs of early European—but not American—aircraft show the profound influence of Hargrave. The box kite design was eventually abandoned when it was realized that the configuration sacrificed too much maneuverability to aircraft stability (and as with the Wrights later, whom Hargrave resembled in many ways, stubborn adherence to principle prevented Hargrave from adapting to new forms, limiting his contribution to aviation history).

Flights of Imagination:
From Kepler to Wells

The meager literature of flight before the twentieth century dealt mostly with flight to other worlds. In the second century, the Greek philosopher Lucian wrote two works about people being transported (in one case by wings, in the other by a waterspout carrying a ship aloft) to the moon. After that, there was nothing until the late Middle Ages.

The first scientist to write about space travel was astronomer Johannes Kepler, in 1609. He wrote *Somnium seu Astronomia Lunari* (A Dream of Astronomy on the Moon) as an exercise when he came upon Plutarch's description of how the motion of the planets would appear to a hypothetical observer on the moon. Kepler knew exactly how Plutarch had erred (having discovered the laws of planetary motion), and wrote a more accurate description of how the planetary motions would appear to a lunar observer. To give the account some spice, he added a fanciful tale about how he managed to get to the moon, crediting spirits who were friends of his mother.

The *Somnium* was copied by many astronomers who, like Kepler, were interested only in the tables and the mathematics. But the next thing Kepler knew, his mother was being tried for witchcraft and threatened with torture and with being burned at the stake. He just managed to save her and the *Somnium* was not published until 1634, four years after Kepler died. In 1648, John Wilkins, Bishop of Chester and a founding member of the Royal Society of London for Improving Natural Knowledge, devoted a chapter of his book, *Mathematical Magic*, to flight. In it he made some extraordinarily perceptive predictions (amid a great deal of nonsense) about the future of flight. He believed that advances would have to be made in engines if flight was ever to become practical, and he supported the career of Robert Hooke, the outstanding mechanical engineer of his day. Hooke in turn reported on Besnier for a French journal (making larger claims than Besnier).

Cyrano de Bergerac's *A Voyage to the Moon* appeared in 1657 and his *Voyage to the Sun* in 1659. In the former, the author travels to the Moon in a sling attached to a network of rockets, the first Western instance of rockets used as a means of propulsion. Brief descriptions of explorers crossing the Australian wilderness in winged and parachute-like craft appeared in the writings of Restiffe de la Bretonne in the late eighteenth century, but it wasn't until Jules Verne came on the scene late in the nineteenth century that flight figured prominently in literature.

Verne was born in 1828 in the French river town of Nantes, and was headed for a career in law when he began writing travel stories. His writing was often criti-

cized for being nothing more than the pointless chronicles of people getting from here to there, but Verne injected a great deal of pathos and humor into his stories, and along the way made many remarkable predictions about future technology. Although he ascended in a balloon only once, he wrote several stories about balloon flight (*Around the World in Eighty Days* was the most famous) and about helicopter voyages and trips to the Moon. In *The Clipper of the Clouds*, published in 1886, a huge ship is carried aloft by thirty-seven helicopter blades powered by electricity.

The other great writer of flight fiction of the nineteenth century was H.G. Wells. Famous for his *War of the Worlds* (1898), a dour journalistic novel about an invasion of Martians that became a world classic, Wells published *When the Sleeper Awakes* the following year. In this book, a man kept in suspended animation for two hundred years awakens in the year 2100 to find that the trustees of his estate have, through their shrewd investments and cunning, taken over almost the entire world in his name. Much of the novel treats what Wells envisioned for the future of flight, by then a widely anticipated prospect whose accomplishment was considered to be just a matter of time.

The Great Leap:
Flying *Not* Like a Bird

In the late eighteenth century on a country estate in Yorkshire, England, a twenty-six-year-old English baronet took a blank silver disc about the size of a silver dollar and engraved on it something that looked like a shovel or some kind of grotesque bird. On the reverse side he etched a few lines—a right triangle, a diagonal, an arrow. He engraved his initials, "GC," and the year, 1799. This simple act might well be considered the birth of the modern concept of the airplane. The young man was George Cayley, and he is considered the father of the modern airplane.

George Cayley was born in Scarborough, Yorkshire, on December 27, 1773, at the family estate, Brompton Hall. He was a keen student of all manner of science and of mathematics, and became a devoted student of the accomplished engineer George Walker. He married Walker's daughter, Sarah, and settled down to a career of scientific and engineering pursuits at Brompton Hall. Sarah, as it turned out, was given to wild outbursts and fits of rage, and Cayley had to confine his work to times when Sarah went to London or abroad.

Cayley is credited with many engineering accomplishments—he invented the caterpillar tractor, forerunner of all modern tracked vehicles, in 1825—but he also pursued his interest in aeronautics for his entire professional life, and he lived to 1857. A calm, deliberate man, he was

Once flight was taken seriously, its use for purposes of war was all but inevitable. This 1908 illustration demonstrates this fact with its depiction of huge flying battleships.

intrigued by the balloon flights being conducted in France and he even dabbled for a while with ornithopter designs, but it soon became apparent that a new approach was required if flight were to be possible. Cayley soon turned his attention to fixed-wing flight.

The key was to separate into four components the forces involved when an aircraft is in flight. The downward weight of the craft had to be compensated for by an upward lift, and the resistance the craft would experience from the onrushing air—the "drag"—had to be compensated for by a forward "thrust." Cayley knew physics well enough to know that an aircraft in uniform level flight is experiencing a number of forces in various directions, but the total force on the aircraft is zero. All the forces cancel each other out, and that's why the aircraft doesn't accelerate in any direction. This is one of the difficult concepts to grasp about flight, especially when one thinks about all the power a jet aircraft is continually putting out to stay aloft, but when an aircraft is in stable flight—"in trim"—the sum of the forces on it are zero. This also means that the rotational forces (the "torques") balance out exactly, so that the aircraft doesn't spin end over end (pitch), rotate around its length (roll), or turn

from side to side (yaw). Cayley provided "control surfaces" in the form of a T-shaped tail section with surfaces that could be tilted up and down and sideways, so that all the rotational forces on the craft would cancel each other out.

Cayley applied Bernoulli's Principle and designed his aircraft with a cambered wing. When the craft thrust forward, the movement of the air over and under the wing, or the "airfoil," would, by virtue of the difference in the air pressures above and below, generate the lift required. All one had to worry about was providing thrust. Unfortunately, Cayley opted for a fishlike tail flapper and resisted propellers during all of his more than fifty years of research (even though he used propellers in his research in helicopter design). Still, the basics were sound, and Cayley, hearing about "successful" flights by Jacob Degen and fearing Degen's claims would prompt others to publish their research first, published his three-part paper, "On Aerial Navigation," in the November 1809 and February and March 1810 issues of English scientist and publisher William Nicholson's *Journal of Natural Philosophy*. The age of flight was conceived, but nearly a century would pass until it would be born.

The COMING MODE OF TRAVEL, PROF. HARRIMAN'S STEAM AIR SHIP.

Chapter 2

From Dream to Plan to Reality

Introduction

The nineteenth century saw the development of two things important for flight: the science of flying and the personality of the flier. Mastering the former was no mean feat. Objects hurtling through the air are not well behaved and don't conform nicely to the elegant diagrams of air flowing over an airfoil. All sorts of forces the Bernoullis never dreamed of can act to twist and turn the aircraft, and once a flier loses control and goes into a tailspin, it is very difficult to regain control and avoid crashing. Beginning with George Cayley and continuing through the Wright brothers, a great deal of testing and calculating was necessary—on paper and in test devices—if a feasible flying machine was going to be created.

But the people who were going to go up in those aircraft also had to undergo a transformation: they had to become fliers ("airmen," they called them). People had to gain experience riding the wind and adjusting—either their controls or their dangling weight—in order to maintain control of their aircraft. They had to be adept at reacting to the shifts in air pressure that might affect their aircraft. Flying an aircraft, some understood, was not like riding a wagon as a passenger; it was more like riding a temperamental horse. It required a bond and connection between flier, machine, and the sky itself.

Not everyone agreed with this assessment of the role of the pilot, and the question was one of the key issues among the community of experimenters. The active approach won out, but just barely. If Samuel Langley's machine had succeeded in flying when it was tested just a few days before the Wright brothers' landmark flight of December 17, 1903, the future course of aviation might have looked quite different and the active-flier concept

might be a relic of an idea instead of a fundamental of flight training and practice, as it has become.

If the proper approach to flight was discussed among experimenters and enthusiasts, the general public looked at the entire matter differently. Centuries of disappointment had created the impression that flight was just impossible and that anyone involved in any research or experiment related to flight must be a crackpot. Serious scientists or engineers who wrote about the subject rarely said openly that they were discussing flight—"aerial navigation" was the euphemism they used. When Langley's *Aerodrome* crashed into the Potomac on a cold December day in 1903, the report of the War Department, which had funded the project (and so must have had some hope that Langley would succeed), declared that "we are still far from the ultimate goal [of human flight]." Five days later, the Wright brothers proved them dead wrong.

George Cayley, Father of Flight

Many pioneers in the history of aviation who made landmark contributions soon faded into the background, sometimes embittered, as new visionaries rushed past them and pushed the frontiers of flight further. Although George Cayley had more than his share of frustration and disappointment, he remained a key figure in the history of aviation research for half a century.

The complexity of bird flight told Cayley that one might expect all sorts of forces around any airfoil in flight. Because of this, careful testing was required. He constructed a device on which an airfoil was swung in a circle at the end of a long arm, with the rotation powered by a falling weight pulling a string wound around the center pole. He observed the behavior of the airfoil and

Professor Harriman's steam-powered airship (1870s) was, if perhaps a little fanciful (note the resemblance to an enormous metallic butterfly), certainly ambitious in its scope. While the design does raise certain practical questions (about its tremendous weight, for instance), it also sports at least one useful feature: the forward bell, which no doubt was intended to alert the unwary of the craft's ponderous approach.

CAYLEY AND THE PARACHUTE

Sir George Cayley was interested in the design of parachutes and discussed the subject at length in his landmark paper, "On Aerial Navigation," published in 1809–1810. Cayley was particularly interested in England's first parachute jump, which was made in 1802 by Andres Jacques Garnerin. Garnerin used an umbrella-shaped parachute, and swayed violently during his descent. Cayley theorized that a cone-shaped parachute would be more stable. A reader of Cayley's paper who had also witnessed Gernerin's jump, artist Robert Cocking, decided he would attempt a jump using Cayley's design.

It was not until 1837 that Cocking had an opportunity to make his jump. He convinced the owners of a balloon, the *Royal Nassau*, that a parachute jump was just the sort of publicity they needed; it did not seem to bother them that Cocking had no experience whatever in parachuting or that he was sixty-one years old at the time. Cocking built a parachute in a funnel shape and attached a basket underneath in which he could ride. The balloon lifted the chute-and-basket combination, with Cocking in the basket, to an altitude of five thousand feet (1.5km) and released it. As soon as it was released, it was obvious that Cocking had neglected to take one thing into account: the weight of the parachute. The entire apparatus weighed 250 pounds (113.5kg), roughly ten times the weight of the modern parachute. The apparatus raced downward too quickly to suit the onlookers who had assembled below, and then the parachute came apart.

Cocking was killed in the crash, and a great deal of attention was given to determining what went wrong, with the possibility that Cayley's design was to blame casting a shadow on his entire work. It soon became clear (from tests made with dead weights) that the fault did not lie in Cayley's design (although he, in fact, did omit to discuss the weight requirements of the parachute), but was due to a combination of the weight and the flimsy stitching that held the strips of the parachute together.

measured the lift with a counterweight. The device proved somewhat useful in determining lift and in locating what was called the "center of pressure" of an airfoil—the point at which all rotational forces due to air pressure are balanced. This is important because the force of lift is not as "well behaved" a force as the force of gravity it is countering. Since the air pressure distributed over the surface of a wing depends on many factors—the direction of the wing in relation to the air flow (called the "angle of attack"), the details of the shape of the wing, the details of the eddies in the air flow—calculation is not enough (or even possible) in many cases. Testing was the only way to know how a wing would really perform in flight.

Cayley's whirling arm had its limitations, however: moving in a circle is not exactly the same as moving through the air in a straight line; the speed of the rotation was difficult to adjust and keep uniform; any experiment could be carried out for only short durations—until the weight hit the floor or the air around the device started rotating with it. So he turned to models, first a small model glider built in 1804, and later full-size kite gliders, in one of which a young boy made several gliding hops in 1809. The story is told that Cayley induced his elderly coachman into making a flight in his model glider in 1853, and the coachman threatened to quit when the flight ended with a bumpy landing. What glides or flights Cayley actually made are uncertain, and in any case they did not have much influence on other researchers. However, the mere fact that he was testing, designing, redesigning, and retesting established a methodology of aeronautical research that was to leave its mark on the history of flight for all time.

In 1852, when Cayley was seventy-nine, he published the next great paper summarizing his work, "Sir George Cayley's Governable Parachutes," in *Mechanics' Magazine*, a publication with a wide circulation. The aircraft described and pictured in the paper had two T-shaped tails for control, one of which responded to the pilot's controls; a boatlike pilot's undercarriage on wheels; a tri-wing airfoil assembly (so that the aircraft would stay aloft if one wing were damaged in flight); and, alas, flaps for propulsion. In many ways, it was a revolutionary design and should have excited other researchers and sparked public curiosity. It did none of those things; in fact, the article itself was forgotten until 1960, when it was rediscovered and republished by the great British aviation historian, Charles H. Gibbs-Smith.

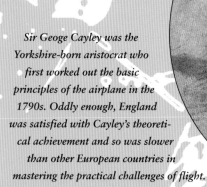

Sir Geoge Cayley was the Yorkshire-born aristocrat who first worked out the basic principles of the airplane in the 1790s. Oddly enough, England was satisfied with Cayley's theoretical achievement and so was slower than other European countries in mastering the practical challenges of flight.

All three of these nineteenth-century theoretical flying machines—designed by (FROM LEFT) Ritchell, Henry Badgley, and "The Flying Wanderer" (a character in a German fantasy of 1810), respectively—combine propeller propulsion and balloon lift.

One Englishman was paying attention to Cayley, however: William Samuel Henson. His designs, based on Cayley's work, were among the most widely known and most influential of the nineteenth century. Cayley died on December 15, 1857, and his work promptly sank into obscurity. Later historians are certain that, had researchers studied and remembered Cayley's work in the half-century following his death, powered flight would have been achieved a decade or two earlier.

A Short History of Thrust

After Cayley, the development of the airplane proceeded along two lines: one was to design a wing configuration that would permit controlled and sustained flight, and the other was to develop the means of providing an aircraft with thrust. Although propellers had been used successfully to propel balloons (and were an element in many of Cayley's designs), Cayley doggedly stuck to paddles and flaps, while others looked to propellers.

Propellers had appeared on hot-air balloons even before 1800, but these were all hand-driven and ineffective in providing control in even the slightest wind. In most instances, the propellers used were taken off ships and often looked like small windmills. A ship might go slower or faster depending on the efficiency of the propellers and the power of the engine, but a plane simply doesn't get off the ground until it is propelled at a sufficiently high speed. As with many elements of flight, the Wright brothers, expecting to use marine propellers and finding them inadequate, created the technology themselves.

One of the great achievements of the Wrights (mainly Wilbur), was to increase the efficiency of the propeller by fifty to seventy percent. The way they did it was to look at the propeller not merely as a device for blowing the air one way so that the propeller (and the craft attached to it) would move in the opposite direction, but to regard the propeller as an airfoil turned sideways. As the blades of the propeller turned, in addition to screwing into the air and moving it to the rear (from which the other name for a propeller—"airscrew"—derives), the blades may be cambered so that the air pressure in the rear is greater than that against the forward surface, resulting in a net force forward. The Wrights further refined the propeller by varying the camber—decreasing it toward the tip—so that the aerodynamic force on the faster-moving outer part of the propeller would be the same as on the slower inner part. This design was to influence all future propellers used on aircraft.

The engine—or "power plant"—was also some time in coming. Cayley considered the steam engine and rejected it as too heavy, but, unlike the stubborn blind spot he seemed to have had about propellers, he was very open-minded about engines, he considered using gunpowder and even attempted to construct an engine of his own that was a close relative of the internal combustion engine. Henson, on the other hand, believed that steam engines would improve and become lighter in time; the machines he designed were thus known as "aerial steam carriages."

The development of the internal combustion engine by Nikolaus August Otto in 1876 changed everything, and one of the first to realize this was Samuel Pierpont Langley, secretary of the Smithsonian Institution. In spite of a frustrating and controversial career in aviation, Langley was a sophisticated and perceptive researcher who saw the potential of the gasoline-burning engine. He tried to contract for an engine that would deliver 12 horsepower and weigh under one hundred pounds (45.5kg), but the manufacturer fell far short. Fortunately, Langley had as his assistant Charles Manly, an engineering student from Cornell. Using a radial engine similar to that designed by Lawrence Hargrave in 1887, he built a power plant that weighed 208 pounds (94.4kg) and produced an astonishing 52.4 horsepower.

The Wrights, also disappointed with available automobile engines, built their own engine with the help of their bicycle-shop mechanic, Charles Taylor. It was not nearly as well designed as Manly's; it produced only 12 horsepower and weighed one hundred pounds (45.5kg). It would not have been adequate for Langley's machine or even for the Wrights' had they not improved the efficiency of the propeller. Ignoring propeller design entirely, then, may have been the critical factor in Langley's losing the race to be the first to fly.

The English Channel crossing by Jean-Pierre Blanchard and John Jeffries marked the beginning of the Channel's place in aviation history and inspired the development of balloon-propeller systems.

Balloons and Airships of the Nineteenth Century

Meanwhile, following the flight of the Montgolfier in 1783, ballooning advanced throughout the 1800s, becoming popular worldwide by mid-century. Jean-Pierre Blanchard, unsuccessful in his ornithopter attempts, became famous for his balloon flights all over Europe and in America. He and John Jeffries, a Boston physician, crossed the English Channel on January 7, 1785, and Blanchard conducted an exhibition ascent in Philadelphia in 1793, with George Washington in attendance. He trained the first American balloonist, John Wise, who in turn trained many others and engendered enthusiasm for ballooning in the United States. Blanchard also conducted spectacular parachute experiments from his balloons; he died in a fall in 1809.

One of John Wise's students, Thaddeus Lowe, provided four balloons for the Union Army during the Civil War, and at critical points there was direct telegraph communication between the balloons and the White House. A balloonist alerted the Union of Lee's breaking camp in Rappahannock and setting out for Gettysburg. The Confederacy realized the usefulness of balloon reconnaissance and attempted to put together a program, but did not succeed in time to be effective.

Back in France, Felix Tournachon (also known as Nadar) developed the art of aerial photography from a balloon, at one point placing an entire photographic laboratory on board his huge balloon, *Le Géant*, in 1863. Nadar is also remembered for heroically ballooning mail and passengers out of Paris during the siege of 1870.

The nineteenth century ended with the ill-fated attempt by Salomon August Andree and two associates, Nils Strindberg and Knut Fraenkel, to balloon across the North Pole. The trio set out from the island of Spitzbergen on July 11, 1897; they soon drifted into the fog and vanished. In 1930, a Norwegian expedition discovered their frozen bodies, Andree's journal, and even some photographic plates. The balloon had crashed in the frozen wastes and all three explorers died trying to walk back to civilization.

The advantage of placing a propelling mechanism on a balloon, making it capable of controlled, directed flight, was immediately apparent to everyone, and many designs came off the drawing boards of nineteenth-century engineers, including George Cayley. The first successful flight of a steerable airship—or "dirigible"—occurred on

Der Ballon beim Aufstieg zur grossen Fahrt.

Der Ballon nach der Katastrophe.

Dr. ing. Graf Zeppelin.

September 24, 1852, in Paris, with Henri Giffard using a cigar-shaped, hydrogen-filled balloon driven by a 3-horse-power steam engine and using a design inspired by Cayley and others. The average speed for the flight was only 5 miles (8km) per hour, and the craft was clearly carried much of the way by the wind, but the day is often cited as the date of the first practical conquest of the skies.

By the late 1880s, many successful dirigible flights had taken place and serious thought was being given to using the airship as a means of transportation, particularly in Germany. Two experimental models, one using a gasoline engine and the other covered with a thin layer of alu-minum sheeting, crashed during test flights in 1897. But Ferdinand von Zeppelin, a German army general who witnessed the use of balloons in the American Civil War and followed airship research for the next thirty years, created his own company in 1893 and with his chief engineer, Ludwig Durr, was preparing to test a 420-foot (128m) -long airship as a first step in creating a fleet of ships capable of transporting sizable numbers of people. The close of the nineteenth century also saw the arrival on the French aviation scene of a diminutive Brazilian, Alberto Santos-Dumont, who would become one in the most colorful figures of the early years of modern flight.

Henson and Stringfellow: The Dream Takes Shape

Born in 1812, William Samuel Henson was, like his father, a successful industrialist in the lacemaking business in Somerset, England. In 1840, under the influence of Cayley's early writings, Henson and an engineer who also worked in the lacemaking industry, John Stringfellow, designed a steam-driven airplane they called an "aerial steam carriage." There were many elements of the design of the *Ariel* (as Henson called it) that proved to be prophetic of later aircraft, and a simple glance at the design makes one feel as if one is looking at a cartoon prototype of the modern airliner.

In fact, Henson and Stringfellow planned to create an international airline, the Aerial Transit Company, and proceeded to raise investment capital. They embarked on a massive publicity campaign that involved illustrations of the *Ariel* in flight over London and exotic settings in Egypt, India, and China. They hoped that the illustrations would make people believe the aircraft was an established fact. These illustrations appeared in newspapers, magazines, on handkerchiefs, trays, wall tapestries, and lace-frilled placemats. The public was caught unprepared for this barrage, and instead of taking to the idea, investors who might have supported it withdrew.

Henson then appealed to George Cayley, who declined to invest (or even to endorse the idea until they built a working model of the *Ariel*). The pair built a model in 1847, but the steam engine Stringfellow had designed was simply not powerful enough. Finally, Henson abandoned the entire project and emigrated to the United States, but Stringfellow stayed on and in 1848 tried once more to fly a model with an improved steam engine. The results were disappointing—nothing more than a short, uncontrolled hop. At this point, Stringfellow also gave up, and the entire episode was forgotten.

But the *Ariel* did have some positive effects: its design prompted Cayley to rethink wing configuration and come up with the multiple-wing design, a feature of nearly all the early successful aircraft. The plane itself was logically designed and inspired many later builders. In spite of the scorn heaped on Henson and Stringfellow's outrageous publicity, the many illustrations that found their way all over the world placed the issue of aviation and the possibility of comfortable flight to faraway places squarely before the popular consciousness.

The Tragic Case of Alphonse Penaud

When the Wright brothers conducted their exhaustive study of everything that had been done in aeronautics and aviation until their day, they paid particular attention to the work of two men: George Cayley and Alphonse Penaud. Penaud, trained as a marine engineer, applied his training to the field of aeronautics. In 1870, at the age of twenty, he became famous as the inventor of a helicopter toy powered by a twisted rubber band. In 1871, he used the same mechanism to power a twenty-inch (51cm) monoplane (single-wing aircraft) that he called a "planophore."

Penaud's model incorporated many elements of Cayley's designs, but with some subtle differences. Some

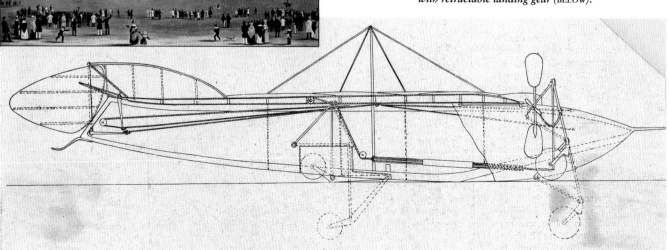

Visionary designs of the nineteenth century: Henson's Aerial Steam Carriage (LEFT) and Penaud's incredible 1876 design for a seaplane with retractable landing gear (BELOW).

distance behind the wings, Penaud placed a tail section: a vertical rudder and two small wings called "elevators" tilted at a downward angle. This counteracted all the destabilizing forces on the aircraft. Penaud's tail assembly did not just change the direction of the aircraft as it flew, which was all Cayley had attempted to do, but succeeded in making the aircraft stable in flight. The tests of his model represented the first flight of an inherently stable aircraft.

In 1876, Penaud patented a design for a large amphibious aircraft with such innovative features as retractable wheels, a glass-enclosed cockpit, a single-lever control for both the rudders and the elevators (the first "joy stick"), and twin propellers driven by an engine concealed in the fuselage. The design was amazingly ahead of its time, so much so that no engine existed that could drive such an aircraft and make it fly. Unable to raise money to build his design, in failing health and discouraged by jealous criticism of his work, Penaud committed suicide in 1880, when he was but thirty years of age. Next to Cayley, he ranks as the most significant aerodynamical theorist of the nineteenth century.

Francis Wenham and the Short-Hoppers

The latter decades of the nineteenth century saw a great increase in aviation activity. In 1866, the Aeronautical Society of Great Britain was founded. This organization attracted some of the most outstanding engineers and scientists of the day. At the first meeting of the society, an engineer, Francis Herbert Wenham, delivered a paper, "Aerial Locomotion," which became an aviation classic. Wenham described his research into lift and airfoils and drew the conclusion that, since most of the lift of an airfoil is contributed by the forward section of the wing, long narrow wings would be more efficient than short stubby ones. The ratio of the length of a wing to its width is called its "aspect ratio," and Wenham had discovered the advantages of high-aspect-ratio airfoils. What made Wenham's findings so important is that he had measured them in his new invention, the wind tunnel, which he built in 1871 with John Browning. Crude by today's standards (and even when compared to the

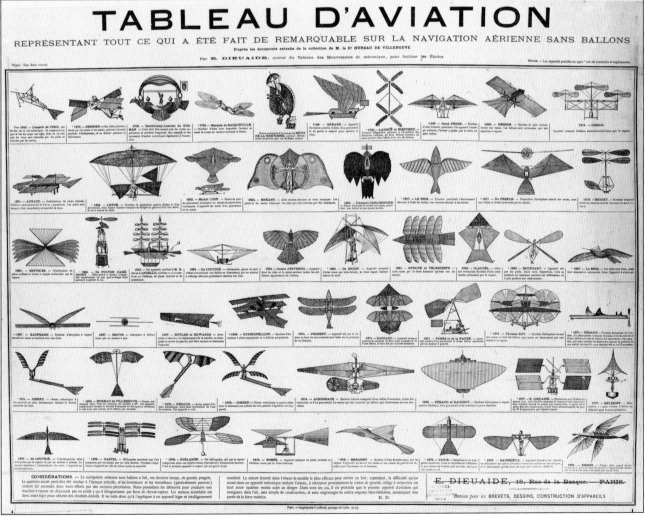

French experimenter E. Dieuaide's Tableau D'Aviation, c. 1881, summarized four centuries of heavier-than-air ("sans ballons") flight, from da Vinci to Thomas Edison. There was then no obvious way of distinguishing the sound designs (like Penaud et Gauchet's, 1878) from the unsound (like Breant's, 1854, and Dieuaide's, 1877).

version the Wright brothers constructed), Wenham's wind tunnel set the stage for all aerodynamic research for well over the next century.

Wenham built a model of a five-wing aircraft that he did not manage to fly successfully, but his lecture brought John Stringfellow out of retirement to redesign Henson's *Ariel* as a tri-wing airplane. The plane was part of the world's first aviation exhibit at London's Crystal Palace in 1868, and this time, the more modest presentation commanded the public's respect and attention (even though none of the Aerial Steam Carriage's original problems had been solved).

In the coming years, a number of experimenters built and tested powered aircraft inspired by the Henson-Stringfellow model or by the designs of Cayley or Penaud. These aircraft made short hops and glided for the most part uncontrolled and unsustained, but these were necessary steps on the way to legitimate flight.

The earliest of the short-hoppers included Jean-Marie Le Bris, a French sailor inspired by his observations of albatrosses at sea. His 1857 glider—which was pulled by a horse down a track and then, once aloft, allowed to glide—looked like a large bird. On his second glide, Le Bris crashed and broke his leg. In 1868, another version of his "artificial bird" (as he called it) was tested unmanned. This time the craft simply crashed and was

The inventive genius unleashed in the early days of flight was remarkable, but there was little to distinguish the serious researcher from the eccentric. The most serious experimenter in this group of photographs was August Herring (TOP), whose design was later used by French-born American experimenter Octave Chanute. The feathered approach (SECOND FROM TOP) proved a dead end, as did Le Sauteral's 1923 pedal-powered machine (THIRD FROM TOP, built in 1923) and the 1910 design (BELOW), which was based on a discarded (but theoretically feasible) Cayley idea.

destroyed. A more serious effort was made by the French engineer Felix Du Temple and his brother Louis in 1857. Du Temple flew a model aircraft of his own design—powered by a spring-driven clockwork mechanism and with unusual forward-swept wings (instead of wings that stuck straight out or were swept back). In 1874, a larger version, powered by an unknown kind of engine, was flown for a short, uncontrolled hop by a sailor hired by Du Temple. Similarly, a steam-powered hop in a piloted aircraft occurred in 1884 in Russia, in a plane built by Alexander F. Mozhaiski after a design derived directly from Stringfellow's 1868 effort.

Two other experimenters who made short hops were Clement Ader and Hiram Maxim. Ader was a distinguished French inventor who made important contributions to the development of the telephone. After some experiments with tethered gliders, in 1882 he built and tested an ungainly aircraft, the *Éole*. On October 9, powered by a steam engine and weighing a light 653 pounds (296.5kg)—with pilot—the *Éole* lumbered forward and rose about eight inches (20cm) off the ground for a "flight" of about 165 feet (50m). Ader seemed to think he had been the first to fly, but those seriously involved in the field would say only that this had marked the first take-off of a heavier-than-air craft moving under its own power, but it was not sustained and controlled flight.

Ader retracted some of his boastful claims, possibly so that he could obtain further funding for airplane development from the French government. His second aircraft, the *Avion III*, did not even match the performance of the *Éole*, and the French government cut off his funding. Ader was to become a controversial figure in the history of flight because of the claims he made in 1904 (belied by his own notebooks) that his 1890 flight was every bit as deserving of the accolades then being accorded Santos-Dumont and the Wrights.

Hiram Maxim was born in Maine in 1840 and became an accomplished draftsman and machinist. In the late 1870s, he invented the machine gun and tried to sell it to the U.S. government. The War Department found his invention impractical and turned him down, but he found a sympathetic ear at the British War Office, so he settled in England in 1881. With British support, he developed a machine gun that could shoot six hundred rounds per minute, making it a formidable weapon. He became wealthy from the invention, which allowed him to turn his attention to a childhood passion—aeronautics.

Maxim was adept at building lightweight steam engines, including one that produced 180 horsepower. He constructed a test track that would allow an aircraft to take off but would then keep it close to the track. The aircraft he built was huge—two hundred feet (61m) long with a wingspan of 107 feet (32.5m) and a wing surface of four hundred square feet (157 sq m)—and weighed eight thousand pounds (3,632kg); it was driven by propellers that measured eighteen feet (5.5m) in diameter. Observers from the British Aeronautical Society were certain that the craft was capable of flight and had indeed flown off the track. More than one observer urged Maxim to unleash his machine, but Maxim, with an ebullience some of the British found charming and others found annoying, insisted that he had paid no attention to stability and that all he had wanted to demonstrate was that powered lift was possible with existing engines.

Otto Lilienthal: First Man in the Air

One of the points Francis Wenham made in his landmark 1866 paper was that as much work needed to be done in unpowered gliding as in engine-driven powered flight. The short-hoppers, all versed in some aspect of engine technology, concentrated on the latter, but one man, Otto Lilienthal (along with his brother), paid close attention to

Two machines that might have flown were Clement Ader's Avion *(LEFT), grounded when funding was quickly withdrawn after a failed test in 1897, and Hiram Maxim's* Giant *(RIGHT), which strained against the rail restraint that kept it from flying. In this artist's version, the machine is breaking through the rail, but is it aloft?*

the engineering problems posed by glider flight. In any discussion about the history of flight, Lilienthal deserves to be mentioned alongside Cayley and the Wrights.

Otto Lilienthal was born on May 23, 1848, in Anklam, Prussia, near the Baltic Sea. As children, he and his brother Gustav would watch in wonder the gliding flight of storks at the shores of the Baltic, noticing for themselves what was already known—namely, that the storks gliding in circles as they search for fish rise when they circle into the wind (and not with the wind, as one might expect). Otto was trained as a mechanical engineer at the Berlin Technical Academy, graduating in 1870, and he set up a factory in Berlin manufacturing steam engines and the like. In his spare time, he pursued his aeronautical interests (sometimes with Gustav, now an accomplished architect) outside Berlin, and later in the Rhinower Hills near Stollen.

Lilienthal built rigid fixed wing gliders—more than eighteen distinct designs—and made more than two thousand glides, many longer than eight hundred feet (244m). His approach was markedly different from that of most experimenters of the day. He believed that the best way to learn to fly was to get into the air and experience flight for oneself. Whereas the others rode the machines they created, Lilienthal flew his, learning the feel of the air and the response of the aircraft. "The manner in which we have to meet the irregularities of the wind," he wrote, "...is by being in the air itself." It was thus necessary, he believed, to gain experience in flying an unpowered version of an aircraft before adding a propulsion system to it. Lilienthal was planning to add a propulsion system to his gliders, thereby adding "powered" and "sustained" to his accomplishment of controlled flight. Others scoffed at his feats—Maxim derisively called him a flying squirrel.

These photos of Lilienthal show three of the many designs he used to make more than two thousand glides. Lilienthal, a mechanical engineer by training, had developed the bi-wing design so he could install a motor that would power propellers. It was in such a glider (without the safety bar in the top left design) that he fell to his death in 1896.

But improvements in photography and printing resulted in pictures and accounts of Lilienthal's feats appearing in newspapers all over the world, including in Dayton, Ohio, where they came to the attention of the Wright brothers.

Although his work in airfoil design was groundbreaking, Lilienthal's method of control—swinging his legs and torso in order to shift the craft's center of gravity—was limited and difficult, certainly not a method that would become practical for anyone other than a circus acrobat. Having studied birds so carefully (his 1889 book *Bird Flight as the Basis of Aviation*, was an instant aviation classic), he looked to ornithopter-like systems or engines that would, in emulation of birds, flap narrow slats at the wingtips, as methods of propulsion. Later tests showed that these would never have worked (so that claims that Lilienthal would have flown before the Wrights had he lived longer are doubtful). But Lilienthal never had the chance to test them.

On Sunday, August 9, 1896, during a glide, a gust of wind turned Lilienthal and his glider upward and the aircraft stalled. (A stall is what happens when the wing cuts though the air at an angle so large that the airflow over the top surface separates from the wing. The wing becomes an obstacle to the wind and there are no longer two smooth layers of airflow creating lift. When an aircraft stalls, it suddenly loses lift and falls). Lilienthal's glider crashed and he died at the Bergmann Clinic in Berlin the next day. Over the centuries, many had died leaping from towers and attempting to fly, but Lilienthal's death was the first death of a man actually flying. When people had pointed out the dangers of gliding to Lilienthal, he often said, "Sacrifices must be made." This was the epitaph that was carved (in German) on his gravestone.

Octave Chanute in the 1890s.

Pilcher and Chanute: Gliding into History

By the turn of the century, interest in flight was too great to be set back by the death of Lilienthal. One individual upon whom Lilienthal had a profound effect was Percy Sinclair Pilcher, a lecturer in naval architecture and marine engineering at the University of Glasgow. Lilienthal was generous in his support of Pilcher, allowing the latter to gain flight experience with Lilienthal's gliders in preparation for flying his own. Pilcher's glider, the *Bat*, which was built in 1895 and similar in design to Lilienthal's but without a tail assembly, was less dramatic in its appearance but more aerodynamically efficient.

With the flight experience gained on Lilienthal's glider, Pilcher built several others, including the *Hawk*, which included a tail unit with a hinged surface controlled by the pilot and a wheeled undercarriage with dampening springs to absorb landing shock. Pilcher then turned his attention to propulsion and calculated that an engine weighing forty pounds (18kg) and generating 4 horsepower (not yet in existence, but within reach) could keep his aircraft in flight although it would be insufficient for an unassisted take-off. Pilcher never got to test his aircraft engine. In an effort to generate interest and gain investors, he exhibited the unpowered *Hawk* in Leicestershire, England, on September 30, 1899. In flight, the tail assembly broke, and the craft crashed. Like Lilienthal, Pilcher died a day after crashing; he was thirty-two.

During the nineteenth century, while aviation research was pushing forward in Europe, nearly nothing constructive was happening in this area in the United States. Although there was interest in flying, and patent offices in the United States and around the world were swamped by fanciful designs for flying machines, very little in the way of research and experimentation was going on. The country was still expanding to fill its borders, securing its footing in the community of nations, and lunging toward industrialization. However, in the 1890s, this situation turned itself so completely around that in 1892 the French-Egyptian experimenter Louis Mouillard commented, "You Americans are clearly in the lead in the aviation movement."

Chanute poses with William Avery's model of the Katydid, *one of three designs tested near Lake Michigan in the summer of 1896. These tests showed that the increased lift provided by multiple wings was offset by the weight of the structure required for stability.*

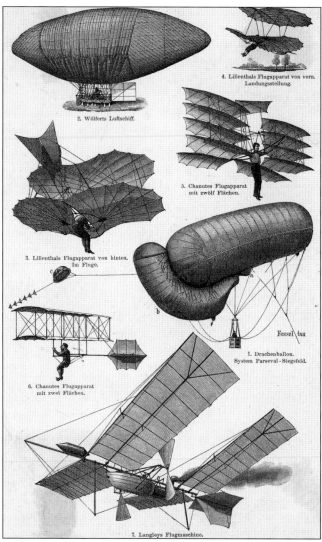

At the turn of the century, it was clear from such surveys of the state of flight what the expectations were for the competing designs: the multi-winged machines of Lilienthal and Chanute were more exciting than the airship designs of the day, but Langley's powered machines (BOTTOM) showed the most promise.

Credit for this leap goes largely to two men working quietly and independently: Octave Chanute and Samuel Pierpont Langley. Octave Chanute (born Chanut, but he Americanized the pronunciation of his name by adding the e) was born in France, but the family emigrated to the United States in 1838. Octave joined a railroad crew where he apprenticed himself to Henry Gardner, the engineer for the Hudson River Railroad, and in a few years developed a reputation as an outstanding engineer in his own right. He served as president of the fledgling American Society of Civil Engineers and chaired a committee that devised a rapid-transit rail system for New York City. The political pressures with which Chanute had to contend, following on the heels of his heroic but frustrated efforts to improve the scandal-ridden Erie Railroad, caused him to enter a period of depression and exhaustion. This prompted him to tour Europe, where he could relax, and it was on this tour that he was exposed to the work being done there in aviation.

Flight was never more than a hobby for Chanute, but his interest was to remain avid for the rest of his life and he was among the first to think seriously about the aerodynamic effects of wind on roofs, bridges, and railroad locomotives. Upon his return to the United States, he moved to Chicago and continued his engineering work. Chanute was continually recognized as making important contributions to the country's westward expansion, so when his history of flight, *Progress in Flying Machines* (based on articles he had written for the *Railroad Engineering Journal*), was published in 1894, it was widely read and considered a serious work. In this work, Chanute summarized all aviation efforts to that time and made some pointed suggestions as to the avenues along which serious experimenters might proceed. *Progress in Flying Machines*, along with Lilienthal's work, was studied carefully by the Wrights, whose respect for Chanute, based on this work, was so great that the brothers corresponded with Chanute and later they became friends.

At the age of sixty-two, Chanute decided to take his interest one step further and experiment with building and flying gliders himself. Too old to fly himself, he sought out young men with engineering talent and assembled a team consisting of August M. Herring, a New Yorker who had already built several moderately successful Lilienthal-type gliders; William Avery, a Chicago carpenter who was building a glider to Chanute's specifications; and William Paul Botusov, a Russian immigrant who claimed to have built a successful glider along the lines of Le Bris's artificial birds.

In June of 1896, Chanute set up camp along the duned southern shore of Lake Michigan, east of Chicago, and that summer his group tested a number of gliders (under the full view of reporters who filed almost daily reports on the group's progress). First they tested a glider Herring had already constructed—with financial backing from Chanute—on the Lilienthal model. However, they found it difficult to fly and capable of only short hops of no more than 116 feet (35m). In the meantime, Avery's workshop back in Chicago had completed a multi-wing glider, the *Katydid*, so named because of its insect-like appearance, and brought it to the test site. The craft had six pairs of wings, arranged on a central frame and pivoted so that the wings could adjust and bring the aircraft back into trim no matter what the wind conditions. Experimental glides with the wings in different configurations resulted in a craft that was safe, stable, and manageable even in winds of twenty miles per hour (32kph), though not capable of longer glides than Herring's machine. On July 4, the group disbanded and returned to Avery's workshop to use what they had learned to build three gliders: a version of Butusov's glider (dubbed the *Albatross*), an improved version of the *Katydid*, and a new craft designed by Chanute and Herring. At the end of August, the group returned to the testing site with all three machines.

The *Katydid* and the *Albatross* performed well, but not significantly better than the machines used in the earlier trials. The third machine, however, represented a vast improvement and a major step forward. Chanute used a bridge-building device, Pratt trusses—crossed wires bracing vertical struts evenly spaced between upper and lower wings—to give the rigid wings more structural stability, and added a cruciform tail section and a seat for the pilot. This machine made many flights at over 350 feet (106.5m) and was remarkably stable and easy to fly. It also had the characteristic wing shape that the Wrights were later to adopt. Chanute ended the trial in late September.

In the summer of 1896, Herring conducted further tests with this glider. On October 11, 1898, using a two-cylinder compressed-air engine, Herring conducted a powered glide of about fifty feet (15m). Though Herring was convinced this feat had made him the first to fly, Chanute realized that what the young man had actually accomplished was to come closer to the goal of powered, controlled flight than anyone had before, but that they were still not there.

Samuel P. Langley and the *Aerodrome*

While Chanute's group was hard at work on the banks of Lake Michigan, America's other pre-Wright aviation researcher was also closing in on the prize of being the first to fly. Samuel Pierpont Langley was appointed Secretary of the Smithsonian Institution in 1887 after a distinguished career as an astronomer and professor of physics at the Western University of Pennsylvania (later called the University of Pittsburgh) and director of the Allegheny Observatory at Pittsburgh—all without any formal education beyond high school. Langley was a self-taught scientist whose work displayed the highest standards of scientific rigor, yet he was capable of making elementary mistakes and relied heavily on the work of his assistants.

At the Allegheny Observatory, Langley built a whirling arm to test airfoils as George Cayley had done, but his machine was driven by a steam engine that whirled an arm seventy feet (21m) long and attained speeds (measured by electrical trip circuits) at the tip of seventy miles per hour (112.5kph). Once at the Smithsonian, he began building models powered by rubber bands. Realizing the limitation of this kind of power source, he adapted steam engines to the models and tested them carefully on many configurations, leaving behind careful records in his *Memoir*.

ABOVE: *Langley's* Aerodrome *is poised atop a houseboat, ready for launching, on October 7, 1903.* TOP: *Langley conferred with his assistant, Mathews Manly, days before the test, but was not present for the launch. Assistant secretary of the Smithsonian Cyrus Adler (right) looks on.*

In the period between 1894 and 1896, several large model aircraft that Langley called "Aerodromes" were launched by a catapult device from atop a houseboat on the Potomac River near Washington, D.C. Several test flights were observed by Alexander Graham Bell, himself a flight enthusiast (as we will see later), and by 1896 Langley's *Aerodrome No. 6* made a stable flight of forty-two hundred feet (1,280m) in one minute, forty-five seconds, landing gently on the waters of the Potomac.

Langley was inclined to let the matter rest there, but two events made him press on: America's involvement in the Spanish-American War, and the rise of Charles Matthews Manly, a recent graduate of Cornell, to the position of Langley's principal assistant. Hoping to create a military device that would assist the United States in the war, President McKinley and the War Department had enticed Langley to Washington with a generous fifty-thousand-dollar grant to develop the airplane.

Manly's contribution of a gasoline engine that weighed 187 pounds (85kg) and produced more than 50 horse-power solved the power plant problem. Tests on a quar-ter-scale model in August 1903 were successful. Aware that they were in a race against other experimenters (and pressed by the War Department), Langley and Manly went directly to a full-sized craft, abandoning Langley's long-established practice of careful, piecemeal experimen-

RIGHT: Glenn Curtiss in a significantly modified version of Langley's Aerodrome. BELOW: Curtiss flew the craft on May 28, 1914, in Hammondsport, New York, in an effort to invalidate the Wright patent. Although it seems that several other machines could have flown as much as fifty years earlier, the Wright Flyer was the one that did fly. The Wrights prevailed (as Curtiss knew they would), but they were diverted from developing their invention further by the court battles initiated by Curtiss for just that purpose.

tation. They constructed a full-scale model, making modifications they could not test, and adapting the catapult mechanism in ways that were, they knew, unpredictable. Langley was justifiably apprehensive.

Manly piloted the *Aerodrome* on its first test flight on October 7, 1903; the test ended in seconds with the craft falling into the water ("like a handful of mortar," the *Washington Post* reported the next day) and Manly having to be fished out. Langley and Manly were not certain what had gone wrong. They reviewed the catapult atop the houseboat and examined the *Aerodrome* itself, but they could not ascertain what had caused the crash. Ordinarily, Langley would have investigated the matter at length, but he knew that if he did not make a test flight soon he would have to wait until spring, and the War Department was getting impatient. On December 8, another test was run with the same result; this time Manly was just barely rescued.

The reports in the press created a public outcry, and speeches lampooning Langley were delivered on the floor of Congress. (A secretary position at the Smithsonian Institution was looked upon as nearly a cabinet-level post—a kind of Secretary of Education—so that his failure presented a political opportunity to the opposition party.) Langley was deeply hurt by these attacks and withdrew from active research entirely. He died a broken man in February 1906.

Throughout his life, Langley blamed the catapult mechanism for the failure of the *Aerodrome*, but later analysis revealed that many elements of the craft were deeply flawed. First, the stress on a machine cannot be accurately measured by a smaller model, and simply multiplying the proportions of the model's dimensions does not result in a structurally sound machine. Langley made no attempt to have a pilot learn the feel of the aircraft in gliding experiments; Manly was not so much a pilot as cargo unable to control the performance of the machine. Also, the idea of bringing a full-sized aircraft to flight speed in just seventy feet (21m) by catapulting it into the air was unsound on the face of it.

All these flaws became apparent when, in 1914, Glenn Curtiss borrowed the original *Aerodrome*, modified it significantly, and flew it over Lake Keuka in New York, all in an effort to challenge the Wright brothers' patents. The modifications Curtiss made only highlighted the fact that, as originally conceived and constructed, the *Aerodrome* was not an airworthy craft. The conflict between the Smithsonian and the Wrights (fueled by Curtiss) lasted for many years and resulted in the original Wright *Flyer*'s being exhibited in London rather than in the United States. Not until Orville had passed on in 1948 (the then-Secretary of the Smithsonian having already offered a formal apology acknowledging the priority of the Wrights) was the *Flyer* returned to the United States and exhibited in the Smithsonian.

Enter (From Out of Nowhere) the Wright Brothers

By the first decade of the twentieth century, interest and work in the field of flight had reached a fever pitch. As highly publicized efforts by engineers and scientists to develop an airplane capable of carrying a person were underway in Europe and America, two brothers from Dayton, Ohio, were quietly, doggedly, and methodically teaching themselves everything there was to know about flying, and inventing all the rest as the need arose. What exactly drove the Wright brothers to embark on the odyssey that led them to Kitty Hawk is not at all clear, and even definitive biographies like Tom Crouch's *The Bishop's Boys* have trouble penetrating those two inscrutable minds. And that's just the way they would have wanted it.

Wilbur was born in 1867, and Orville four years later, the third and sixth of seven children born to Milton and Susan Koerner Wright. Milton was a minister in the United Brethren Church, an evangelical Protestant denomination, and the family moved frequently until Milton was named a bishop in the church and the family settled in Dayton, Ohio. In childhood and throughout their lives, Orville and Wilbur were constant companions

Wilbur (RIGHT) and Orville Wright were photographed by the French aviator Léon Bollée in May 1909. Their triumphs and travails were as much consequences of their approach to life as of their approach to the problems of flight.

TOP: *This 1900 glider, in a wind from the left, was moored by a wire below and raised or lowered by a wire (not visible in the photo) that pulled the forward elevator up or down.* CENTER: *With a pilot (in this case, Orville) warping the wing, the glider banked as expected, but would "slip" to the side and invariably crash sideways into the sand.* BOTTOM: *The solution was to place a double rudder in the rear so the glider would "bite" the wind when it banked into a turn, as it does here as Wilbur banks the glider in the 1902 tests. The pilot is still lying down in order to cut down wind resistance ("drag").*

(in Wilbur's words, the brothers "lived together, played together, worked together, and, in fact, thought together") and displayed many of the Yankee characteristics of their parents and forebears: an inner-directed spartan strength and a clear-eyed, determined outlook on the world and on life. Neither brother finished high school, though they were both insatiable readers and tinkerers.

The Wright brothers tried their hand at several enterprises, including publishing newspapers and running a printing shop, but without success. In 1892, America was in the midst of a bicycle craze and the brothers established a bicycle shop in Dayton that proved financially successful. They manufactured some bicycles under their own brand name, including one they called the *Flyer*.

Around 1896, the Wrights read about the death of Otto Lilienthal and they became intensely interested in the question of flight. They collected all existing information on flight, writing to Octave Chanute and Samuel Langley at the Smithsonian, beginning an active correspondence with these men that was to last for years. Chanute (who regarded himself as a kind of international clearinghouse of information about flight) was particularly generous. The Wrights designed a glider, strongly influenced by Chanute's design, and decided that their aircraft would not be as difficult to fly as Lilienthal's glider, but neither were they going to be passive passengers on an inherently stable aircraft. They devised a method to control an aircraft in flight that involved twisting a Chanute design in a technique called "wing warping." There are many stories about how the Wrights came upon wing warping, but the fact is that the technique was not new, and at least one American experimenter, E. F. Gallaudet, made use of it in kite tests near New Haven, Connecticut, in 1898.

With their customary thoroughness, the Wrights also wrote to the U.S. Weather Bureau to find out the best place to test aircraft. On the basis of that information, they selected the Kill Devil Hills sand dunes outside Kitty Hawk, North Carolina, a fishing village on the Outer Banks, a thin peninsula that jutted out into the Atlantic and enjoyed strong and relatively constant winds. In 1899, they tested a scale model of a glider in Dayton, and by the late summer of 1901 they were ready to test-fly their first full-size glider at Kitty Hawk.

The trips to Kitty Hawk were arduous; a great deal of material had to be brought along, some in pieces that would be reassembled on site. The conditions were difficult and the pair's resolve and fortitude were tested to the limit by heat, mosquitoes, storms, cold gale-force winds, and isolation. The locals liked the Wrights and the Wrights liked them, but the brothers' natural reticence caused some people to regard them as secretive—some believed that was why Kitty Hawk was chosen as a test site in the first place. But at this stage, the Wrights were not at all hesitant to share their findings with fellow researchers. In fact, in the midst of their experiments, Wilbur accepted an invitation from Chanute to report on his and his brother's experiments at a meeting of the Western Society of Engineers in Chicago, and many of the people Chanute kept bringing to Kitty Hawk to assist them were, the Wrights well knew, doing research of their own.

The craft "flew" (it actually glided) well enough, but with thirty percent less lift than the Wrights had calculated. They returned to Dayton and built a larger craft with a front horizontal rudder (called a "canard"), and returned to Kitty Hawk in July 1901 to test it. The performance was improved and the control bugs were worked out, but the Wrights were perplexed about why their calculations were still off. Their response to this was unique and would be reason enough to regard the Wrights as the first to fly. They constructed a wind tunnel in the rear of their bicycle shop and conducted precise tests of different wing sections. The tunnel was only six feet (2m) long by sixteen inches (40.5cm) square, with a glass window in the top panel to allow observation. A steady fan driven by a small gas engine blew air through the box at a steady twenty-seven miles per hour (43.5kph), and inside, balance and spring scales measured lift and pressure on a variety of airfoils. In these experiments, the Wrights raised aviation experimentation to the level of serious engineering (and were thus more

firmly in the tradition of Cayley and Langley than anyone else had been for over a century).

These tests were made in November and December 1901; they collectively represent one of the most important phases in the early history of flight. The Wrights discovered that much of the published data on airfoils was incorrect or had ignored important elements of an airfoil in flight. They arrived at a clear idea of how the center of pressure moves about an airfoil in relation to the angle of attack and as a function of the camber. And they knew what the control surfaces would need to be able to do if the flight was to be controlled by the pilot.

After testing two hundred different wing surfaces, the brothers used their newly gained information to design Glider Number 3. It was equipped with a forward elevator wing and a rear fixed double fin that was later made adjustable, with its controls connected to the wing-warping controls for the main biplane wing section. They returned to Kitty Hawk in September and tested their new machine in more than one thousand glides. It not only performed well, it performed as predicted. It was only now that the Wrights felt they were on the verge of succeeding in creating a powered airplane. They filed for a patent in March 1903, and turned their attention to the last hurdle: turning their glider into a flier.

ABOVE: *This photograph shows the 1902 glider being tested in October 1903, ready for the engine and propellers. The Wrights' camp is visible on the desolate dunes below, and off in the distance is the Atlantic Ocean.* BACKGROUND: *The glider is being launched in October 1902 by Wilbur (left) and Dan Tate, with Orville piloting.*

FROM DREAM TO PLAN TO REALITY

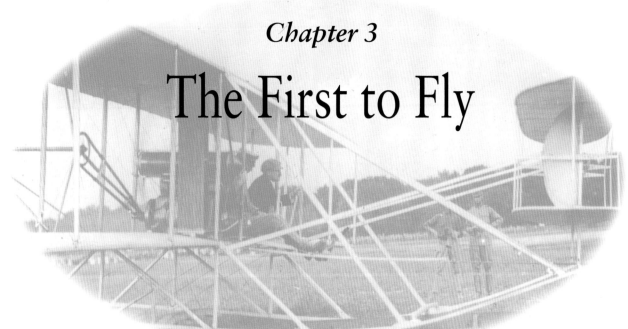

Chapter 3

The First to Fly

Introduction

The decade from the December 1903 flight of the *Flyer* at Kitty Hawk to the outbreak of World War I in August 1914 was an extraordinarily busy one in the development of aviation. Looking at the aircraft being built in 1913 and comparing them to those built in 1904, it is difficult to believe that only a decade had passed. Airplanes like Louis Bechereau's Deperdussin Racer and Geoffrey de Havilland's B.S.1, both produced in 1913, were built with enclosed, metal fuselages that used "monocoque" design: instead of just the frame, the entire fuselage supported the plane's load. These planes are recognizable early versions of planes produced thirty and forty years later, while the spindly frames of the Wrights' airplanes and the early flying machines were by that time only relics. The Wright brothers had clearly uncorked a torrent of industry and creativity that had simply been waiting for some indication that the prospect of flight was not hopeless.

But if the Wrights were the spark that ignited the enterprise, there were other forces at work that drove it to a fever pitch. One was the giddy optimism that characterized the opening of the new century. True, the twentieth century's ambivalence about technology was born in its very first decade, but in the face of the many advances from 1900 to 1914, it really began to look as if technology could and would make just about anything possible. The Wrights played a large part in the forming of this attitude: the remoteness of their experiments gave fuel to the claims made by such prestigious publications as *The New York Times* and *Scientific American* that their flights were a hoax. One can imagine these publications being much more careful afterward in their skepticism about any scientific and technological claims.

Yet, there was the equally powerful sense that a war was coming, and that one result of the industrialization of Europe would be an improved ability to conduct armed conflict. What role aviation would play in the theater of war was not clear even to the most visionary planner, but there was no doubt that aircraft (both heavier and lighter than air) would be exploited by combatants to the fullest and that command of the sky could possibly be a decisive factor in any war. Military strategists who prepared for possible invasions across natural barriers such as the English Channel or the Alpine mountains had to rethink their defenses in the light of aerial warfare of unknown effectiveness. Behind all the hoopla of the races, the feats, the records, the stunts, the glamour and derring-do—all the romance of early aviation—were calculating minds fully aware (or aware enough to take anxious notice) of the military potential of flight.

In the decade between Kitty Hawk and the outbreak of World War I, one can summarize the history of aviation very simply: while the Wrights and Curtiss were slugging each other senseless in court, the Europeans slowly took the lead in aviation. The Wrights won many of their court battles, but lost the war for supremacy in the air. They enjoyed two crowning moments in the decade following Kitty Hawk: their exhibition in France and their test for the Army at Ft. Myer. But they allowed many opportunities to slip by: while Curtiss was winning prizes for aviation feats he was performing years after the Wrights had passed that level of technology, the brothers were too proud or secretive to claim any prize; while Curtiss was winning races that the Wrights could have won handily, the brothers would not consent to enter any contests; while Curtiss was gaining fame participating in aerial exhibitions and air shows, the Wrights regarded them as circuses unworthy of their talents; while Curtiss

Wilbur Wright before a 1908 flight in France in 1908; photograph by James H. Hare.

was forming productive and useful alliances with a wide range of people—from Bell and the Smithsonian to August Herring, Octave Chanute's old assistant to Henry Ford and his high-priced patent lawyers—the Wrights steadfastly rebuffed any offer of collegiality (including from Curtiss) and preferred to go it alone; while Curtiss developed new technology as quickly as it became available—he abandoned wing warping when it became clear ailerons were a superior means of lateral control; he developed wheeled undercarriages when they were shown to be preferable to skids; and he experimented with different engines and configurations—the Wrights never strayed far from the basic design configuration they inherited from Chanute; and while Curtiss developed the entire field of naval aviation, developing seaplanes that could consider attempting to cross the Atlantic Ocean, the Wrights entered the field belatedly and half-heartedly.

But for a moment, the Wrights were alone at the pinnacle of the mountain, and their country and the world paid them homage. Wilbur died of typhoid fever in 1912, but Orville lived until 1947. Orville was honored late in his life for the contribution he and his brother had made to flight, but he certainly must have wondered what might have been had Wilbur lived. Publicly he blamed Curtiss and the Smithsonian for everything (even Wilbur's death), but Curtiss retired from active involvement in aviation in 1921 and turned to real estate speculation in Florida until his death after an appendectomy in 1930. So it was hardly the case that it was all Curtiss' fault. Typically, Orville never voiced any regrets for letting the dominion of flight slip through his fingers. Still, one wonders.

The Wrights are captured here in an uncharacteristically casual (and derbyless) pose, on the back porch of 7 Hawthorn Street, in June 1909. Wilbur's dark suit, high button shoes, and pained expression (left) contrasts with Orville's wingtips, argyle socks, dapper light-colored suit, and pleasant countenance.

Kill Devil Hill, December 17, 1903

After the Wright brothers' successful glides in the summer of 1902, it was time to add an engine and propellers to the machine. Typically, however, the Wrights did not simply add a power plant to their glider; they redesigned the entire machine and integrated the propulsion system in a technically well-designed machine. The added weight of an engine meant they could increase the camber (which would result in the center of pressure behaving about the same as it did for the glider), and enlarge the wing to a forty-foot (12m) wingspan and a surface area of 510 square feet (47.5 sq m) for the two wings combined. The machine—which they called the *Flyer I* (only later was its name changed to the *Kitty Hawk*)—retained the glider's front canard-design elevator and the movable rear rudder.

The plan was to place the engine on the lower wing, next to the pilot who would, as was the case with the gliders, lie prone on the lower wing. The propellers would be "pusher" (meaning, pushing the machine from behind the wing, as opposed to "tractor," which means pulling the machine in front of the wing) and would turn

in counter-directions. As they had done with the wings, the Wrights had tested and perfected the propellers in their wind tunnel and greatly improved their efficiency. Unlike the gliders, the *Flyer* could not be launched by leaping from a dune or by running down a hill; it would then be only a powered glide and not a real flight. They designed a launch mechanism that consisted of a single track on which ran a simple flat car that the aircraft was placed upon. The car would be propelled by the aircraft's propellers, and when take-off speed was attained, the airplane would simply lift off. The Wrights calculated that they would need sixty feet (18m) of track (and that is what they brought).

The Wrights had put off the question of the engine, hoping that the strides being made in the automotive industry would produce a light and powerful engine they could use. But no such engine was forthcoming and finally they attacked the problem head-on and designed their own engine with the help of their machinist, Charles Taylor. The engine just barely met their specifications, but they decided not to postpone testing it. They did not arrive at Kitty Hawk that year until September 26 and were not ready to test their machine until winter was already setting in. It was too cold even for Chanute, who had waited patiently as long as he could. After many delays and repairs, on December 14 the *Flyer* seemed ready. The brothers, aware that they were about to make history, tossed a coin to see who would have the honor of the first flight. Wilbur won. On the first attempt, however, the elevator was set low and the craft plowed into the sand at the end of the track, damaging the aircraft.

After three days of frantic repairs and threatening weather, the Wrights were ready for a second try. They raised a flag signaling the crew of the lifesaving station that they were ready, and when a small group arrived, Orville took his turn on the lower wing. At 10:35 A.M. on December 17, before several witnesses from the weather station, the *Flyer* took off into a twenty-one-mile-per-hour (34kph) wind. Wilbur ran alongside the aircraft, keeping the right wing from dragging in the sand but being careful not to assist the plane down the track; they wanted this to be an unassisted take-off. Sensing that they would be successful on this day, they had set up their cumbersome glass-plate camera and aimed it at the end of the track. They instructed one of the witnesses, John T. Daniels, to snap the shutter as the plane left the end of the track. Daniels took one of the most famous photographs in the history of aviation, possibly in the history of all of technology. It shows the *Flyer* lifting off with Orville aboard, and Wilbur off to the side having just run down the track

TWO WHO JUST MISSED BEATING THE WRIGHTS

In the first years of the century, the only serious flight experimenter in Europe was French army captain Ferdinand Ferber, who wrote articles praising both Otto Lilienthal and Octave Chanute. Ferber contacted Chanute in 1901 and through him became acquainted with the work of the Wrights. He attempted to build a glider along the lines of the Wrights' design, but he had no understanding of the principle behind wing-warping, so his machine had no means of controlling flight. To test his glider, Ferber built a fifty-foot (15m) crane near Nice, equipped with a balance arm from which he suspended the glider. He attached a large set of propellers and tested the air-worthiness of the machine. The tests were disappointing, and when the Wrights were conducting their flights at Kitty Hawk in the fall of 1903 Ferber was trying once again to get the hang of wing warping.

A serious claim to have beaten the Wrights into the air was made by supporters of a German immigrant living in Connecticut, Gustave Whitehead. An accomplished mechanic, Whitehead claimed to have flown as early as 1901, in fields near Bridgeport, Connecticut, and over Long Island Sound. Reports of Whitehead's flights appeared in the New York *Herald*, though never by reporters who were eyewitnesses and never with any photographs of the machine in flight. Several photographs are extant showing Whitehead with a glider-like wing structure and no visible source of power for the windmill-design twin propellers. In over half a century of controversy and investigation, no aeronautical engineer investigating the Whitehead claims has suggested that the machine pictured in the photographs had the slightest possibility of flying.

Whether or not any of the Whitehead claims were true, his experiments had no influence whatever on the development of aviation, and Whitehead has rarely been mentioned in all the disputes regarding whether the Wrights were beaten by Clement Ader or Hiram Maxim. Nevertheless, in 1964, the Governor of Connecticut, acting on the basis of signed statements by some of the original witnesses (who had been children at the time) to Whitehead's exploits, declared Whitehead the "father of Connecticut aviation."

Wilbur is seen here aboard the Flyer *(now outfitted with motor and propellers) as it dips and runs aground on takeoff during its first test on December 14, 1903. The damaged elevator required three days to repair.*

alongside. The *Flyer* flew for twelve seconds and landed in the sand 120 feet (36.5m) away.

The brothers quickly placed the *Flyer* on the launching car for another flight. This time Wilbur piloted the craft and it flew almost two hundred feet (61m) before landing gently in the sand. In all, they conducted four flights, alternating as pilots, with the best flight the fourth: 852 feet (260m) in fifty-nine seconds. After the fourth flight, a gust of wind overturned the aircraft and damaged it beyond quick repair. The brothers knew they would be returning to Dayton. They ate a leisurely lunch, then went into Kitty Hawk, called a few friends to report on their success, and sent a telegram to their father: "Success four flights Thursday morning all against twenty one mile [34km] wind started from Level with engine power alone average speed through air thirty one miles [50km] longest 57 seconds inform Press home Christmas. (signed) Orvelle [sic] Wright."

Contrary to legend, the reaction of the press to the historic flight was not a deafening silence. *The Dayton*

TOP: *The most famous photo in aviation history shows the first flight of the* Flyer*, with Orville aboard and Wilbur running alongside (keeping the right wing from dragging in the sand); it was taken by John T. Daniels at 10:35 A.M. on December 17, 1903.*
ABOVE: *The first man to fly was Orville Wright.*

Evening Herald reported the flight the next day on the front page, and the *Virginian-Pilot* was careful to point out in a sub-headline that no balloon had been attached to the aircraft. Garbled accounts appeared on the front page of the New York *Herald*, but there was little follow-up and many of the sporadic reports that appeared during the first two years after Kitty Hawk ridiculed the Wrights' claim by adding facetious exaggerations to the account. The first full, serious, and accurate account of the Wrights in flight appeared in the January 1, 1905, issue of *Gleanings in Bee Culture*, an apiary journal, written by the publisher, Amos I. Root.

But the Wrights were not people to waste time. On their return to Dayton, they immediately set to work on the next aircraft, the *Flyer 2*, incorporating all that they had learned in the Carolina dunes. It looked like the first machine, but had a smaller wing surface and a gentler camber. Most importantly, it had a more powerful engine. The brothers rented a ninety-acre (36ha) farm outside of Dayton that became known as "Huffman

Prairie" (after the owner) and tested their new machine there. On September 20, 1904, Wilbur flew the *Flyer 2* in a complete circle and returned to his starting point and landed. This was the flight Root witnessed and described, and in the minds of some aviation historians, this flight and the others conducted at Huffman (and not the four Kitty Hawk flights) deserve to be considered the beginning of the age of flight. (Others point out, however, that these take-offs were not unassisted: to compensate for the lighter winds, the Wrights launched their aircraft at Huffman with a weight-and-derrick launcher.) The best flight of the season, four circles of the field, lasted over five minutes.

In the summer of 1905, the Wrights tested an even more improved machine, *Flyer 3*, as always, in full view of onlookers and inviting the press to important tests, which they rarely attended. The aircraft had an even smaller wing surface but the same camber as the 1903 machine. This time the machine flew beautifully, and many of the more than forty flights conducted were limited only by the amount of fuel the aircraft could carry. The plane could take off and land with minimal adjustment, and the elevator and rear rudder, pushed out farther from the wings, gave the pilot almost complete control of the aircraft in flight. The longest flight of that summer was over a half hour, and the aircraft could circle and fly figure eights easily. This aircraft, the *Flyer 3*, is often referred to as the first practical aircraft in history.

In 1905, the brothers sensed trouble when their patent application of two years earlier was delayed. The U.S. War Department was unenthusiastic about their proposal to build airplanes for the Signal Corps, and they kept hearing rumors that competitors were copying their designs. The patent (for wing warping) was granted eventually in 1906, and the U.S. government eventually came around, but the challenge from rivals—one in particular: Glenn Curtiss—proved to be one hurdle too many.

Glenn Curtiss—Hot on Their Heels

Glenn Hammond Curtiss was born on May 21, 1878, in Hammondsport, New York, near Keuka Lake, one of the Finger Lakes in upstate New York. He received little formal education and his father died when Glenn was only five years old. The family made a meager living from the vineyard they cultivated in their front yard. In 1900, he took over a bicycle repair shop (ironically, just the profession the Wrights had chosen), and he soon established a reputation as a speedster. Speed, in fact, was to become an obsession for Curtiss all his life. He was a champion cyclist in 1900, and in 1901 he added a motor to the bicycle and became a champion motorcyclist. By 1902, he was being asked to design motorcycles and engines for other racers, and in 1903 he opened a factory in Hammondsport, producing motorcycles and engines

acknowledged to be the best—meaning, with the highest power-to-weight ratio. In 1904, Curtiss raced one of his machines at Ormond Beach, Florida, and established a land speed record of sixty-seven miles per hour (108kph) over a ten-mile (16km) course, a record that stood for seven years. (In 1907, he set an unofficial world speed record on a motorcycle—136 miles per hour [219kph], a speed then unimaginable to most people.)

Initially, Curtiss had little interest in aviation. His first foray into the field was as the provider of engines for dirigibles built by Thomas Scott Baldwin. In 1904, a Baldwin dirigible, the *California Arrow*, became the first American dirigible to complete a circular course, and by 1906 Curtiss-powered Baldwin dirigibles were in demand across the country. Dirigibles were too slow to interest Curtiss, but he developed a lifelong friendship with Baldwin and had his first taste of flight piloting a Baldwin balloon.

In August of 1906, a fateful meeting took place between Curtiss and the Wrights. Curtiss had accompanied Baldwin to the Dayton Fair to help him demonstrate his dirigibles; the Wrights also attended (and on one occasion even helped retrieve a dirigible that went astray). Baldwin and Curtiss visited the Wright bicycle repair shop. By this time, the Wrights had become secretive as they awaited the protection of a patent. They would not show their visitors their airplane, but, regarding the pair as mere balloonists with no interest in airplanes, they were very forthcoming with information about their work and discussed aeronautics at length with the visitors.

What the Wrights did not realize at the time was that Curtiss had already delivered an engine to Alexander Graham Bell, the famous inventor of the telephone, and

Glenn Curtiss at the controls of an experimental aircraft. His experience racing motorcycles helped him improve on the efficiency of aircraft design and propulsion systems.

that plans were afoot to marry Curtiss' engine-building abilities with the others' aeronautic talents to create airplanes. In the legal wranglings that subsequently arose between the Wrights and Curtiss, these August 1906 conversations were pointed to as the source of Curtiss' work in aviation and formed the basis of the Wrights' suit for patent infringement. (Interestingly, an almost identical set of circumstances lay at the heart of the patent suit over electronic computers brought by John Atanasoff against John Mauchly and J. Presper Ecker, and won by Atanasoff for the same reasons in 1973.)

Curtiss was a complex individual, and it is difficult to determine his attitude completely. Sometimes he seemed to be trying to avoid confrontation with the Wrights or provoking them; at other times he seemed bent on keeping them busy with litigation while he moved on to other areas of aviation. Curtiss' failed 1914 attempt to prove that Langley's *Aerodrome* was really the first machine capable of flight probably precluded any possibility of reconciliation. In 1915, Orville sold his share of the Wright company, and though the new owners continued the litigation, in 1917, after the United States entered World War I, the government created a patent pool for all aircraft devices created to that time, making the entire question an academic one.

Alexander Graham Bell and the AEA

The Scottish-born inventor of the telephone, Alexander Graham Bell, who had grown rich from his 1876 invention, had been present for some of the failed tests of Langley's *Aerodrome*. Bell was interested not just because he was a friend of Langley's, but because he had dabbled with the question of flight and had experimented with kites made of many pyramidlike cells (sometimes as many as three thousand). He called these "tetrahedral kites," and their aerodynamics were similar to the box kite. The sight of a large complex structure flying in the wind was certainly impressive and gave Bell the idea that the tetrahedral kite could be used as the basis for a heavier-than-air craft.

At the insistence of his wife, Mabel, and with her financial support, Bell assembled a small group and formed the Aerial Experiment Association (AEA) in the summer of 1907. The group met first at the Bell summer home at Baddeck, Nova Scotia, and in 1908 moved to Hammondsport to be near Curtiss' shop and Keuka Lake. The group—known as "Bell's Boys"—consisted of two Canadian engineers, John A.D. McCurdy and Frederick W. "Casey" Baldwin (not related to Curtiss' balloonist friend); a U.S. Army officer, Lieutenant Thomas Selfridge, assigned by the War Department at Bell's request; and Glenn Curtiss, who at that time had

nearly no involvement in aviation outside of providing engines for Thomas Baldwin's dirigibles. Curtiss quickly became the driving force of the AEA, being designated director of experiments and given the largest stipend of the group.

The strategy of the AEA was reminiscent of Chanute's approach a decade earlier—each of the members would design an aircraft that would be outfitted with a Curtiss engine and tested, in the hope that five different approaches would yield the best possible airplane. The group started with one of Bell's kites, the *Cygnet I*, tested on December 6, 1907, and piloted by Selfridge. It was clear that this design was not going to yield a controllable aircraft. Bell, now sixty, accepted this disappointment and, to his credit, continued his support of the AEA.

The next aircraft tested was a Selfridge design called the *Red Wing* (because of its bright red wing fabric)—it was piloted by Baldwin and flown over frozen Keuka Lake on March 12, 1908, before a huddled audience. The aircraft flew some 320 feet (97.5m) at an altitude of about twenty feet (6m) for approximately twenty seconds, and then crashed onto its wing. Baldwin was unhurt and the AEA was able to claim its first success. The public reports of the *Red Wing*'s success were particularly galling to the Wrights since Selfridge had written to them asking specific questions about design, giving the brothers the impression that he was inquiring as an official of the U.S. Army.

The AEA next experimented with a design of Baldwin's dubbed the *White Wing*. This aircraft used triangular wing-tip ailerons at the ends of both wings to control the aircraft, and performed excellently when flown on May 18 by Selfridge, and then by Curtiss. Selfridge's report to the Associated Press made it clear that the AEA airplane had the ability to land and take off immediately on its wheeled undercarriage, dispensing with the Wrights' derrick catapulting method and landing skids. The group believed that their problems with the Wright brothers' patents were finally over with this, the first successful use of ailerons in the United States. Unfortunately, on May 20, with an inexperienced McCurdy piloting the *White Wing*, the plane crashed.

The AEA now turned to its crowning achievement: the Curtiss-designed *June Bug*, which incorporated all that was learned from the previous two efforts. The airplane was controlled in flight by the wing-tip ailerons and had a wheeled undercarriage (and raised skids in case a hard landing crushed the wheels). Most important, it used a wing design that had been inadvertent in the earlier *Red Wing* and *White Wing* but which was discovered to boost stability and control. The earlier aircraft had been built with their lower wings curved upward to prevent them from bumping on the ice and slowing down the plane. (Recall that at Kitty Hawk Wilbur had to run alongside the *Flyer* to keep the wingtip from dragging in the sand.) The only way this could be accomplished with wings so light was to curve the upper wing downward. The result was a double-wing configuration that made the plane look like a narrow eye when viewed head-on.

When wings are slanted upward from the horizontal plane, that is known as "dihedral"; this configuration keeps the aircraft locked when it banks into a turn and prevents it from slipping sideways. Wings slanted downward are called "anhedral"; this gives an aircraft more vertical control. The combination of dihedral and anhedral wing design gave the aileroned *June Bug* control that rivaled the Wright *Flyer*. The aerodynamics of this configuration were not well understood in 1909, certainly not by the courts that heard the Wright patent suit. A better understanding might have vindicated the AEA design as an alternative means of airplane control, putting an end to the litigation that hurt the Wrights.

Less than a month after the crash of the *White Wing*, the *June Bug* was ready. Curtiss entered it in a competition sponsored by the magazine *Scientific American*, which offered a trophy and a twenty-five-hundred-dollar cash award for the first public flight over a 0.6-mile (1km) straight course. The entire competition had been the brainchild of the magazine's publisher, Charles A. Munn, who felt bad about how his magazine had treated the early reports about the Wright brothers and who was making virtually a gift of the prize and the money to the Wrights. All they had to do was step forward and claim it. The Wrights steadfastly refused (even declining the written pleas of Munn), claiming that their plane did not meet the qualification of taking off unassisted. Wilbur was off to France to demonstrate their *Model A*, and Orville was too busy preparing for the trials at Fort Myer, Virginia, to make the necessary modifications. But the truth was that the Wrights were not so easily placated and would probably have turned Munn down anyway.

This left the field open for the AEA, and on July 4 Curtiss flew his craft over the prescribed course at Stony Brook Farm, Hammondsport, and claimed the prize,

BELOW: Glenn Curtiss and the AEA team are seen here on the morning of March 12, 1908, at the first flight of the June Bug. In the background, Curtiss is at the controls of the rebuilt Langley Aerodrome. It was Curtiss who first had the pilot seated instead of lying prone. BOTTOM: Alexander Graham Bell's Cygnet II was a tetrahedral kite (the craft had to be towed to become airborne), one of many constructed and tested.

much to the embarrassment of Munn. The event was widely covered in the press and bolstered the impression that the AEA was a worthy rival of the Wrights. The AEA tested one more plane, John McCurdy's *Silver Dart*, which, on February 23, 1909, became the first plane to fly in Canada.

When Bell disbanded the AEA in March 1909, he pointed to the death of Selfridge in the Fort Myer accident (described below) and the loss of Curtiss, who went off to market his aircraft, as the reasons. More than likely, Bell had continuing doubts about what the outcome of a patent fight with the Wrights would be and he wanted no part of being on the losing side. (The fact is, he did have his lawyers inspect the *June Bug* for possible patents and received a discouraging report.) And Bell may have gradually lost interest once it was clear his tetrahedral kites were not to be a part of aviation's future.

In the summer of 1908, Orville Wright was preparing to test his airplane for the Army and a great deal hung in the balance. The successes of the AEA that spring and summer had cast some doubt as to whether the Wrights were the best airplane manufacturers available, especially when it was reported that the AEA was preparing to sell their planes at one-fifth the Wrights' price. Orville's consternation must have strained even his stolid character when he discovered that the military observer who was to evaluate the plane and actually go up as a passenger was none other than Thomas Selfridge, who had come to the trials in the company of Curtiss himself.

Triumph and Tragedy at Fort Myer

The trials began on September 3 in an atmosphere of suspicion and acrimony. Orville put the *Model A* through its paces and it performed beautifully, soaring, banking, and turning sharply and seemingly effortlessly in the air. (The

Wrights had prepared for both the U.S. and the French exhibitions by practicing their flying at Kitty Hawk earlier in the summer.) Orville made four flights of more than one hour each and took up a passenger on three of the flights (both had been conditions set forth by the government for any plane it would consider purchasing). There was simply no question in the Army's mind (or in Curtiss' or Selfridge's) that the Wright *Model A* represented the cutting edge of flying machines.

On September 17, Orville planned one more test, this one with Selfridge aboard. Hoping to impress Selfridge with additional speed (or possibly because Selfridge himself was heftier than the other passengers he had taken up), Orville replaced the original propellers with longer ones. Selfridge climbed aboard and sat in the cushioned seat (aviators did not yet wear seatbelts) and looked forward to an exciting flight. The airplane circled the field three times at an altitude of about 150 feet (45.5m). On the fourth lap, one of the propellers cracked along its length. The difference in thrust between the two pro-

In representations of the accident (such as in Gallieni's painting, LEFT), Selfridge (BELOW, LEFT) is often depicted falling out of the Model A, while in fact he stayed with the craft and was injured, along with Orville, in the crash. BELOW, RIGHT: Selfridge has been taken off to the right, outside camera range (he was to die not long after), while Orville is still being removed from the wreckage.

pellers created a vibration that loosened the shaft of the other propeller, which spun wildly and soon cut a wire that controlled the rudder. At that point, Orville lost control of the plane and it headed to the ground nose first.

The plane crashed and raised a cloud of dust that made it difficult for the first rescuers on the scene to find either Orville or Selfridge. The first to spot the aviators as the smoke cleared was W.S. Clime, a photographer. Orville was hanging from the plane's mangled wires; Selfridge had struck the ground and lay motionless. Orville left the field conscious, recuperated in a hospital, and returned to Dayton in a wheelchair six weeks later. He eventually recovered and with typical Wright grit, he forced himself to walk without a limp, though his hip and leg bothered him the rest of his life. But Selfridge was declared dead the next day and became the first casualty of the age of flight (and the fourth to die in pursuit of the dream of flight).

News of both Orville's triumph and the tragedy of Selfridge's death spread throughout the world and moved

even the most intrepid flyers. The trials were called off (mainly because of Orville's injury), but it was clear that the Army was going to buy the Wright planes. When the Wrights founded their flying school in Montgomery, Alabama, and in Pau, France, their announced reason for doing so was to enable them to enter their own planes, flown by their own pilots, in competitions, but in reality they created these schools because they were aware that the planes they would be selling to governments would require trained pilots and instructors.

The trials were not resumed until July 27, 1909, when Orville again put the *Model A* through its paces. This time, President Taft was among the spectators and Lieutenant Frank Lahm, Commander of the Army Signal Corps, rode as a passenger—and neither would have occurred had there been any doubt about the success of the trial. The army bought one plane, but there were clear indications that others would be ordered later. The amount paid was thirty thousand dollars, five thousand of which was a bonus for exceeding the speed requirements.

Wilbur Wright in France

If the Wrights looked upon Curtiss as a usurper, the Wrights themselves were regarded in much the same way by the entire French nation. Since the Montgolfiers, the French regarded flight as a particularly French province. Even in the area of heavier-than-air flight the French believed they were preeminent, based on the questionable claims of Clement Ader. After the humiliating failure of Ader's *Avion III* in 1897, however, the French focused their attention on balloons and dirigibles as the most promising avenue of flight.

At the turn of the century, one man, Ferdinand Ferber, a captain in the French artillery, himself a bit clumsy, pompous-looking, and nearsighted (he once failed to see, and so failed to salute, the French Minister of War and was passed over for promotion), kept the dream of heavier-than-air flight alive in France. Ferber conducted a lively correspondence, first with Octave Chanute, and then with the Wrights themselves, and wrote articles for French magazines about the goings-on in America under the pseudonym Monsieur de Rue.

One of Ferber's most avid readers was an Irish-born Frenchman, Ernest Archdeacon (pronounced "arsh-deck"), an influential lawyer interested in all forms of transportation. Archdeacon helped found the Aéro Club of France, soon to become the hub of aviation activity in all of Europe, and he donated his own money (twenty-five thousand francs), matched by a donation from the French oil magnate Henry Deutsch, to create the Grand Prix d'Aviation (known as the Archdeacon-Deutsch Prize), to be given to the first aviator to complete a flight around a measured course of 0.6 mile (1km). This was in 1904; the prize was still unclaimed in 1905, long after the Wrights had far surpassed this distance in the air. The Aero Club received reports of the Wrights' accomplishments and tried to entice the brothers to exhibit the *Flyer* in France with the fifty thousand-franc prize (about ten thousand dollars), but the Wrights, now in their secretive phase, did not even respond to the invitation.

From 1903 to 1906, the French made very little progress in airplane development, in spite of the fact that French journals contained much information about the Wright machines and experiments. Chanute himself had lectured in France in 1903 and all but gave away the Wrights' secret, and the entire Wright patent was published once it was granted in 1906—still nothing. Only a solitary French engineer, Robert Esnault-Pelterie, made any progress, developing a successful radial engine and developing ailerons: hinged surfaces attached to wings that provided better lateral control than the Wrights' wing warping. The French were simply unwilling to experiment painstakingly and to develop the technology step by step, piece by piece.

What is amazing is that France had an airplane manufacturing industry thriving before it had any aviators flying. The brothers Gabriel and Charles Voisin had set up a shop to produce gliders for Archdeacon and the Aéro

ABOVE: *Wilbur at the controls of the Model A in France in 1908.*
For all their skepticism about the Americans, the French had never seen an aircraft so large, sleek, or sturdy.
LEFT: *The French were ecstatic about Henry Farman (*INSET*, in a picture taken just before his death in 1958) completing the first European closed-circuit kilometer flight at Issy-Les-Moulineaux, although the feat was not accomplished until January 1909.*
BACKGROUND: *Meanwhile, Orville's trial flights at Fort Myer were a triumph.*

Club, and orders soon came in from all over Europe for Voisin machines, to be built to the specifications of the customer and each with the customer's name emblazoned on the tail (over the more discreet name of the manufacturer). Having been designed by people with little knowledge of aerodynamics, none of these machines had any chance of getting off the ground. The Voisins were not entirely blameless in this self-deception; they were perfectly aware of the shortcoming of the designs their customers sent in and they had boasted that their basic model was easy to fly. Their basic model, in fact, was based on the design of the *14-bis*, the machine Alberto Santos-Dumont had just barely flown on November 12, 1906. The aircraft was a canard ("duck") design—with the elevator and tail section in front, looking like a duck in flight—and clearly inspired by Lawrence Hargrave's box kites. The Voisin craft did not reach the point of development where it could even attempt the modest flight required to capture the Archdeacon-Deutsch Prize until a young art student and son of an English newspaper correspondent, Henry Farman, ambled into the Voisin factory and ordered an aircraft. Farman was British by birth and had only recently come to France, but he was so taken with all things French that he usually spelled his first name "Henri" in the French manner and spoke with a thick French accent even when speaking English. Farman had an instinctive grasp of the fundamentals of flight and an uncanny ability to anticipate how design changes would affect an aircraft's flight. He worked with the Voisins to produce an aircraft that would fulfill the Archdeacon-Deutsch requirements. On January 13, 1908, Farman flew his plane, the *I-bis*, in a wide flat circle of 0.6 mile (1km) at Issy-les-Moulineaux field outside of Paris, winning the Grand Prix d'Aviation and becoming the toast of France.

Heady with his accomplishment, Farman issued a challenge to the Wrights, offering a five thousand-dollar purse for a speed and distance contest to be held in France. By this time, the U.S. War Department had responded positively to the Wrights, offering to allow them to display their airplane, the *Model A*, as part of a sales agreement. The Wrights were still not certain of American interest and decided an exhibition in Europe might spur overseas sales of their plane, as well as light a fire under the War Department. (In fact, the Wrights had had an offer from French businessmen in 1907 to manufacture Wright planes if one of the brothers would

Huge crowds gathered to witness Wilbur's flying demonstrations throughout Europe in 1909. Here he flies with aviator Paul Tissandier at a January exhibition at Pau, France, while the horses drawing the carriages of dignitaries have to be calmed below. The Wrights were hailed as masters of flight on both sides of the Atlantic.

demonstrate the craft. It seems, however, that the Wrights did not consider this prospect seriously until 1908.) Orville was to demonstrate the Wright plane for the U.S. Army at Fort Myer, Virginia, while Wilbur would take up Farman's challenge in France.

Wilbur's reception in France was none too warm: the aircraft they had sent over in 1907 was still tied up in customs in June 1908. When Wilbur finally freed the crates from the customs house in Le Havre, he discovered that the craft had been virtually destroyed during a French customs "inspection" (Wilbur naively blamed Orville for poor packing). The newspaper reports heaped derision and scorn on the Wrights, openly calling them liars and frauds. The test was to take place at the race track at Le Mans, where Wilbur set up a tent workshop and patiently and stoically proceeded to put the aircraft back together. Wilbur's reserve and taciturn nature drove the demonstrative French insane and the crowd that assembled on the afternoon of August 8 was expecting (and hoping for) something akin to a beheading.

Wilbur seated himself in the pilot's seat (no longer was the pilot to lie prone on the wing) and signaled the workers to drop the weight atop the derrick that would launch the aircraft. The aircraft took off and for one minute and forty-five seconds, Wilbur put the *Model A* through its paces, flying in circles, making sharp turns, and landing precisely, all over the heads of a crowd stunned into silence. When Wilbur landed, the crowd erupted. Léon Delagrange, a pilot who was Farman's chief rival, put it simply: "*Eh bien, nous sommes battus. Nous n'existons pas!*" ("Well, we are beaten. We do not exist!") In the ensuing weeks, Wilbur moved the test site to Camp d'Auvours and conducted more flights, culminating in a world-record flight of one hour, thirty-one minutes, and twenty-five seconds on September 21.

The flight of the *Model A* in France resulted in the licensing of Wright manufacturing plants in France, Germany, and England—a greater windfall than the Wrights could have expected—but it also set the Europeans on the right track. Farman, who had missed the Le Mans event (he was in America observing the Fort Myer trials), returned to discover the pandemonium Wilbur's flight had caused, and immediately adapted Wright technology to his Voisin-built aircraft. The year 1909 began with the announcement that the London *Daily Mail* was offering a prize of five thousand dollars to anyone who could fly over the English Channel between sunrise and sunset in a heavier-than-air machine. When asked if he intended to compete, Wilbur responded that he saw no benefit to a distance flight over water that could not be derived from a less risky flight over land. He was alone among aviators in thinking this.

Wilbur was joined in January 1909 by Orville, who was still recovering from the accident at Fort Myer the previous September, and by their sister Katherine. The trio toured Europe and were feted wherever they went, received and praised by royalty and admired by everyone. Even Katherine, who dressed with the characteristic Wright dowdiness, became the most admired and emulated woman in Europe. When they returned to the United States, they were received by President Taft and given a gold medal by Congress. Even Dayton, which had forgotten them after Kitty Hawk, declared a two-day holiday and honored them with parades.

By the time the Wrights returned to the United States, their chief rival, Glenn Curtiss, had left the Aerial Experiment Association and the group had disbanded. Amid the euphoria, the Wrights may have felt secure, but news that Curtiss had joined forces with August Herring and was selling a version of the *June Bug* called the *Golden Flyer*, and that he intended to enter the aerial contest at Rheims in August, convinced the Wrights that Curtiss had commercial intentions all along. It was at this point, after all the threats and accusations, that the Wright brothers filed suit to prevent Curtiss from selling or exhibiting his aircraft. Curtiss had his sights set on Rheims.

The Dirigibles Keep Coming

Once balloons were outfitted with propulsion devices and thus became dirigibles (or airships), unpowered balloons were used primarily for upper atmosphere research. In July 1901, two ambitious German physicists, Berson and Surring, established an impressive altitude record of thirty-five thousand feet (10,668km) that was to stand for some thirty years.

In the early decade of the twentieth century, airships developed along three lines: those that consisted of a balloon from which the power plant and the crew quarters dangled were known as nonrigid; airships with a skeletal structure encasing a balloon and to which a crew compartment and propulsion system were attached were called semirigid; and airships that were made of a solid outer shell, with the passenger and crew compartments attached and which had balloons inflated inside, were known as rigid.

LEFT: Alberto Santos-Dumont in his signature floppy hat (portrait by Trojano Dias). RIGHT: The Brazilian aeronaut created a sensation with his 1901 flight around the Eiffel Tower, depicted in an imaginary aerial view by Eugene Grasset.

In the first decade of the twentieth century, experimenters in flight investigated both heavier- and lighter-than-air machines. Thomas Baldwin and Glenn Curtiss test a Baldwin dirigible (ABOVE) at Fort Myer on August 18, 1908.

Prior to 1904, when he turned his attention to airplanes, the preeminent builder of nonrigid airships was Alberto Santos-Dumont. His flights over Paris delighted the citizenry, particularly when a malfunction would result in a crash, from which the diminutive Brazilian was lucky to survive. He created a sensation in Paris (and entered aviation history) when he flew around the Eiffel Tower in his *No. 6* and claimed the Deutsch de la Meurthe Prize established in 1900. Santos-Dumont used his *No. 14* airship to test his aircraft before his historic flight of 1906.

In the United States, the nonrigid airships being constructed by Thomas Baldwin were all the rage. The first aircraft purchased by the U.S. military was a Baldwin dirigible known as the SC-1. Equipped with a Curtiss motorcycle engine, these machines were easy to transport. They found great use during World War I when they were used extensively by the British and French for offshore antisubmarine patrol.

Semirigid airships replaced nonrigid ones with the improvement of motors and propellers, and a streamlined design boosted speed. Several successful semirigid airships were built by Paul and Pierre Lebaudy before 1910, and they performed so well that several governments ordered them for their fleets. A typical Lebaudy airship might be two hundred feet (61m) long and thirty feet (9m) in diameter, powered by engines of 70 to 100 horsepower, carrying a crew of four, and capable of covering distances of several hundred miles at a clip of forty-five to fifty miles per hour (72.5–80.5kph). In England, the flamboyant American aerial showman Samuel F. Cody teamed up with aerialist Colonel J.E. Capper to build the

Nulli Secundus ("Second to None"), a semirigid airship that amazed Londoners in flights on October 5, 1907, and became a popular attraction when exhibited at the Crystal Palace. (The airship was torn apart just five days into the exhibit, however.) The semirigid airships were abandoned after 1911, but only because German rigid airships performed so much better.

In the United States, semirigid airships did not fare so well: The *America*, a semirigid dirigible built by Walter Wellman, made two failed attempts to reach the North Pole and went down in the ocean during a 1906 attempt to cross the Atlantic. The crew was rescued, but one of them, Melville Vaniman, decided to try again. His ship, the *Akron*, caught fire and crashed off the coast of Atlantic City, New Jersey, on July 2, 1912, killing Vaniman and his crew of four.

The era of the rigid airships is easy to pinpoint: it begins on July 2, 1900, with the flight of the *Luftschiff Zeppelin 1* (*LZ 1*), over Lake Constance, Germany, and it ends with the *Hindenburg* disaster on May 5, 1937. Count Ferdinand Graf von Zeppelin had been an observer of the use of military balloons during the American Civil War, and soon became convinced that large dirigibles would be an effective means of air transportation. The *LZ 1*, designed by chief engineer Ludwig Durr, was 420 feet (128m) long and thirty-eight feet (11.5m) in diameter, with sixteen internal cells for lifting gas encased in a shell of aluminum and cotton. The dirigibles built by Zeppelin's company, DELAG, from *LZ 1* to *LZ 129* (the *Hindenburg*) varied in details, but they were all modeled on the principles established by the first one.

In the years prior to World War I, five DELAG Zeppelins (for by now the name had become synonymous with the aircraft) carried some thirty-five thousand passengers over long distances without mishap. The only fatalities were incurred in late 1913 when the two airships were on military missions. During World War I, Germany built more than one hundred airships for the purpose of bombing London, but these were no match even for the primitive fighters the British sent up against them. It was just as well, then, that the British rigid airship program never got off the ground. Its one attempt, the *Vickers Mayfly*, designed to be the largest then aloft (at 510 feet [155.5m] long), was torn apart by a strong wind as it was taken out of its hangar for a test flight.

Blériot Crosses the English Channel

By now, flight attracted all sorts of people, including possibly more than its share of eccentrics and droll characters. Arguably, the best example of this is Louis Blériot, who went from a national joke to a national hero in the space of the thirty-seven minutes it took him to fly across the English Channel. Blériot had made a fortune manufacturing gadgetry for the booming automobile market. He had an engineering degree, but his reputation was that he was clumsy and erratic, a charming walrus-mustached bear of a man, quick to anger, and just as quick to be gripped by some half-baked notion and run off with a gleam in his eye and a mutter on his lips.

The airship met with disaster after disaster. After it crashed near a farmhouse (in which a petrified family cowered) in Essex, England, in 1916, the L33 *was destroyed by its captain, who feared that the craft might fall into the hands of the English.*

Of all the avocations Blériot might have considered, aviation should have been last: he was a dreadful pilot, he did not seem to grasp aéronautics at even the most basic level, and he had an uncanny knack of being present when machines went wrong in extraordinary ways (Americans would call Blériot a "jinx"). None of the mishaps he endured or caused, and none of the designs he kept ordering and crashing, deterred him from his goal of one day being hailed as a great aviator. They also failed to teach him much about aéronautics or aviation.

Many of Blériot's aircraft were built by the Voisins, who knew better and tried to dissuade him from some of his notions. Most of the time they were not successful, and some of the designs are among the most misguided in the early history of flight. On one occasion, Blériot and Gabriel Voisin took one of their designs to the Bagatelle, a field in the Bois de Boulogne park in the middle of Paris. The aircraft had a tubular tail and looked like a beer barrel with wings. The aircraft was never tested since it fell apart while it was taxiing to the starting line. This was probably fortunate since it spared Blériot the pain of a crash. But on the same field that afternoon, November 12, 1906, the spectators who had gathered to watch Blériot still managed to witness history in the making, as Alberto Santos-Dumont flew his *14-bis* on its historic first flight in Europe, to the cheers and huzzahs of nearly everyone in the crowd. (Of all the luck!)

With nearly all his fortune squandered, Blériot used a last-minute loan to enter the competition for Lord Northcliffe's *Daily Mail* prize to the first to cross the Channel. It was, he realized, his last chance. Blériot faced stiff competition—men and planes that brought a great deal to the race. One pilot was the popular young aviator Hubert Latham, a sophisticated Frenchman of English ancestry, suave, debonair, and already a record holder for endurance flying. His airplane was an Antoinette IV, an elegant tractor monoplane (in fact, with both engine and propeller in front) with an effective wing-warping system of control (though Latham was more comfortable with the ailerons with which the Antoinette was usually fitted), and with the Antoinette engine as the power plant. The plane and the engine were the work of a burly red-bearded engineer, Léon

Levavasseur. The engine was a water-cooled V-8, meticulously crafted and able to produce 50 horsepower with a power-to-weight ratio of 1 to 4. It was already being widely used by European aviators. It had one fault, however: it had a tendency to cut out.

The other competitor was Count Charles de Lambert, the first European trained to fly by the Wrights, who brought two Wright-built airplanes to Sangette, down the coast from Calais and the starting point for the competition. The Wright planes were considered in a class by themselves, the best in the world, but during a test run,

de Lambert crashed one of the planes and decided to drop out of the race rather than risk the other plane.

Everything about Latham's effort was first class—the ground crew, the hangars, the landing site—in marked contrast to Blériot. Blériot's plane, the *Blériot XI*, was smaller and less powerful than the Latham craft, used an untested wing-warping system for control, and was barely fully constructed, with no instruments of any kind. To make matters worse, Blériot had been badly burned in a recent racing accident and could barely walk, let alone fly a plane as rickety as the *Blériot XI*. Worst of all, the engine was a homemade product of a coarse Italian motorcyclist named Alessandro Anzani. It was crude and sputtered hot oil and smoke on the pilot (something the injured Blériot did not need), but it nearly never faltered. Blériot calculated that its meager 25 horsepower would be enough if the engine would run for the half-hour he needed.

On July 19, Latham took off from Sangette and headed toward Dover. Seven and a half miles out, the engine failed and Latham landed on the sea, smoking a cigarette while he waited to be rescued. On land he shrugged off the failure and declared that he would try again and that he would succeed. The Latham camp did not give Blériot much of a chance, and with de Lambert out of the race, believed they had the field to themselves. The Channel weather remained blustery for the next five days, but on the evening of July 24, the evening was calm and the next day promised to be clear. Latham went to bed and left instructions that if the weather was good, he was to be awakened at 3:30 A.M. (The flight had to take place in daylight; the *Daily Mail* was not interested in a night flight, when no photographs could be taken.)

But 3:30 came and went, and no one woke Latham up. As the dawn neared, it became obvious that the weather was going to be clear. A car was sent to Calais for Blériot; he had to be coaxed into going (as he was probably fighting off an infection from the burn injury). He finally roused himself, went to the hangar and, after seeing his wife onto a destroyer escort, donned his ridiculous aviator cap and boarded his plane. The flag signal-

Blériot's crossing of the English Channel in 1909 gave a boost to French aviation. In reality, Blériot did not fly over the Cliffs of Dover, but through a gap in the cliff wall.

ing sunrise went up at 4:41 A.M. on the morning of July 25, 1909. Blériot took off and headed into the dark western sky.

In mid-flight, with not so much as a compass to guide him, Blériot flew on. Believing that he had been blown north, when he spotted some boats heading south, he guessed they were headed for Dover, so he followed them. He soon came upon the cliffs and searched for the pass through them to the field where Charles Fontaine, a newsman, was waiting for him. For once, luck was with Blériot—he found Fontaine waving a French flag in Northfall Meadow near Dover Castle, just as the newsman had said he would do. Blériot cut the engine and thumped into the field, crushing the landing gear and the propeller. It was only a thirty-seven-minute flight, and in many ways Wilbur Wright had been correct: it did not prove much. But Blériot had done it; he had beaten Latham and had been the first to cross the English Channel.

The effect Blériot's achievement had on his own fortunes were immense. Orders for his Blériot airplane came pouring in and he was honored everywhere with parades, banquets, and medals. The effect of the flight on the British was considerable as well. It drove home the point that Britain was vulnerable to attack from the air and that the English Channel would not provide the buffer it had in the past. Baron de Forest promptly offered a four-thousand-pound prize to the flier who crossed the

Channel in the other direction, hoping to remind the Europeans that invasion was possible from either side. Hubert Latham attempted a crossing the next day anyway, but failed again when the engine cut out within sight of Dover.

The Antoinette Company eventually failed and Latham retired from aviation, only to be trampled to death in 1912 while on safari in Africa. The only thing not affected by Blériot's feat was Blériot's flying. After he lost by a hair to Glenn Curtiss at Rheims, he crashed his plane during a flight in Turkey later that year, sustaining a serious injury that took him out of flying. He died of a heart attack in 1936, after predictably squandering his second fortune.

Rheims: Race to Glory

Blériot's feat excited Europe about flight as nothing else had. The city of Rheims and the French vintners of the Champagne region decided to sponsor a week of aviation exhibition and competition, putting up large purses in prize money, the most prestigious being the International Aviation Cup, known as the Gordon Bennett Trophy, after its sponsor, James Gordon Bennett, the flamboyant American publisher of the New York *Herald* and the Paris *Herald*. The meet attracted the cream of European society, from royalty and generals to ambassadors and the merely wealthy, to the Betheny Plain outside Rheims from August 22 to 29, 1909. While there were to be many other such meets before and after World War I, none would match Rheims for grandeur and elegance or for sheer excitement.

The major European manufacturers, all French, entered various events—there were planes by Blériot, Voisin, Antoinette, and Farman, and even several French-built Wrights. The Wrights themselves had passed on an invitation to race at Rheims, which was awkward since the Gordon Bennett Trophy was crowned with a large replica of a Wright *Flyer*. The Aéro Club of America, which had sponsored the *Scientific American* trophy won by Curtiss a year earlier, turned to Curtiss. Curtiss' *June Bug* was not as well developed a plane as the Wright machines (and possibly the Wrights were hoping to drive this point home if Curtiss failed at Rheims) and while it was more maneuverable than the European planes, it was not nearly as fast.

Curtiss worked feverishly to produce a more powerful engine and stripped down his airplane to give it greater speed. The result was the *Golden Flyer*, which was a light version of his earlier planes and had a 50-horsepower water-cooled engine. With virtually no time to test the engine or the airplane, Curtiss packed and was off to Rheims. When he arrived, he found that the accommodations for the aviators set up by their manufacturers were as extravagant as those of the spectators. Elaborate cook-

ing facilities, decorated hangars, fully stocked machine shops, trunks brimming with clothing, spare parts and backup planes, and a retinue of mechanics and helpers, all floated on an ebullient sea of champagne provided by the sponsors. Curtiss' spartan approach—a simple tent, a single plane, and two scruffily dressed mechanics—so surprised the French that he instantly became a favorite.

A brief but heavy rain on the first day turned the field into a muddy plain that was to affect take-offs throughout the meet. But there were so many aircraft, built by every major manufacturer and flown by every famous aviator, that the crowd was kept enthralled for the entire week. The early winners included Farman, flying one of his own planes equipped with the newly designed Gnome rotary engine, just beating Latham (flying an Antoinette) and Louis Paulhan (flying a Voisin) for the endurance championship; Latham, who won the altitude championship handily; and Eugene Lefebvre, flying a Wright *Model A*, who had the best qualifying round for the Gordon Bennett Trophy. Curtiss, aware that he had only one plane and precious few replacement parts, held back and worked on his aircraft in secret, trying to lighten it and squeeze out more power from the engine. He knew that his plane was not as fast on the straightaway as the light, single-winged Blériot XII, which was outfitted with a new 80-horsepower engine, but he had won many a motorcycle race on the turns with inferior machines.

On the last day of the meet, the race was held for the Gordon Bennett Trophy. It came down to a contest among Lefebvre, Latham, Blériot, George Cockburn (a Scott flying a Farman plane), and Curtiss, now flying a machine he called the *Rheims Racer*, which was in fact a further stripped-down model of the *Golden Flyer*. The course consisted of two six-mile (10km) circuits around tall towers, with each plane flying alone and timed. Cockburn was the only entrant who failed to finish, his aircraft crashing into a haystack after a single lap. The others thrilled the crowd with their sharp turns and with the drama of the race.

During tests, Curtiss noticed that the field, drenched by the rains earlier in the week but now drying, had pockets of updrafts that tossed his lighter plane violently. He guessed (blindly, but correctly) that these updrafts would increase the efficiency of his propellers and could help carry him forward and keep him steady on the

The pusher (propeller in the rear) was the design of choice as long as the pilot was exposed to the wind. The Voisin airplane of 1909 (TOP, becoming the Farman of 1910) was slow and sluggish; Geoffrey de Havilland's No. 2 (CENTER) was nimble, but slow; the Curtiss Rheims Racer (BOTTOM) combined power and agility, winning the Gordon Bennett Cup of 1909 by 5.8 seconds.

turns. He abruptly notified the judges that he was going to race (fearing the updrafts would wane as the day grew hotter) and took off. His flight was a bumpy one as he bobbed up and down trying to catch the updrafts while keeping his plane under control and taking the sharp turns. It was an extraordinary feat of piloting, because when he landed, he had been timed at fifteen minutes and 50.4 seconds. Lefebvre and Latham did not come close to that time, so French hopes rested with Blériot, who decided to pilot his own plane, replacing Léon Delagrange, the lighter man who had flown Blériot's planes throughout the meet. Delagrange had not flown well and had nearly had a mid-air collision with Paulhan the day before.

The powerful *Blériot XII* streaked straight across the sky and completed the first lap ten seconds faster than Curtiss, who watched from the sidelines, anticipating a second-place finish. But Blériot took the turn clumsily and swung wider than necessary. He cruised to a perfect landing and the crowd, judging the French aviator's speed only on the straightaway, was certain he had won. But his time was fifteen minutes and 56.2 seconds, 5.8 seconds longer than Curtiss. Blériot was left to wonder if his added weight was responsible for those extra 5.8 seconds, while Curtiss was hailed as "Champion Aviator of the World" in headlines from Paris to Dayton.

The Baroness Raymonde de Laroche, the world's leading woman aviator, was killed in an airplane accident at Croydon Airdrome in July 1919.

Raymonde de Laroche and the First Women Fliers

At the Rheims meet of 1909, many reputations were made as the best known pilots competed with unknowns on an equal footing. This meant, however, that many of the pilots were novices; it was nothing short of miraculous that no pilot or spectator was killed during the many crashes that week. Of the newcomers, one commanded special attention, since she was the only woman pilot in the meet—Elise Deroche. She had received basic instruction on flight from Charles Voisin (though at the time, until she suddenly pushed down on the throttle, Voisin thought he was just showing his aircraft to a young woman admirer). She purchased a Voisin and entered the Rheims meet, scoring high on the endurance competition.

On the basis of her strong showing at Rheims, the Aéro Club of France allowed Deroche to take its qualifying tests and, on March 8, 1910, issued her the first pilot license to a woman anywhere in the world. By this time, she was using the name Baroness Raymonde de Laroche. In July of that year, de Laroche was competing on an equal footing with the likes of Blériot and Latham. In 1913 she won the Coupe Femina, a prize for women aviators given by a French magazine. De Laroche became the most celebrated of the early women aviators, in part because of the reports of her spunky eloquence regarding

flight and the role of women in the sky, but she certainly was not the first woman aloft. In the early 1800s, Sophie Blanchard, widow of a noted French balloonist, became a sensation as a solo balloonist throughout Europe and was appointed official "Aeronaut of the Empire" by Napoleon. By 1834, women were ascending in balloons all over Europe, the most celebrated being Margaret Graham, whose career spanned thirty years. During the 1880s, an American woman balloonist, Mary Myers, set new altitude records (four miles up, and without oxygen equipment) and achieved fame under the name Carlotta, the Lady Aerialist. Just before the Wrights flew at Kitty Hawk in December 1903, Aida de Acosta made one of the first flights of a dirigible over Paris.

Just weeks before Wilbur Wright flew at Le Mans in 1908, Thérèse Peltier became the first woman passenger, flying with Léon Delagrange in Milan. By 1909, photos appeared in many periodicals showing famous aviators (including the likes of Wilbur Wright!) giving rides to women. There were likely many assisted and solo flights by women in the early days of aviation that went unrecorded, but women fliers were considered something of an oddity for many years, and as late as the 1930s articles were still appearing questioning whether women "ought" to fly.

After de Laroche, however, there could be little doubt that women were every bit as capable of flying as men (though the novelty, it seems, has never worn off). Almost as celebrated as de Laroche was Hélène Dutrieu,

Belgium's first licensed woman aviator. Following several solo flights that astounded Europeans and earned her the title "The Girl Hawk of Aviation," she entered a field of fifteen fliers, all men, competing in Florence for the coveted King's Cup in May 1911. Her victory assured her place in aviation history and she went on to set many records for endurance and speed. In 1913, she was awarded France's Legion of Honor. Unfortunately, the world press never failed to point out that Dutrieu flew without a corset, and she became almost as famous for this as for her flying.

In America, two women blazed the trail into the sky: Blanche Stuart Scott and Bessica Medlar Raiche. In 1910, at the age of twenty, Scott had demonstrated the ease of driving an Overland car by driving it from New York to San Francisco, and this gave the manager of Glenn Curtiss' exhibition company the idea that a woman flier on the team might be a powerful draw. Curtiss himself had to be talked into it, and by September Scott was flying with the Curtiss team and became known to the press as the "Tomboy of the Air."

Whether or not Blanche Scott made the first solo flight in the United States is in doubt, but she certainly was close to doing so. This is because Bessica Medlar Raiche, a native of Wisconsin who studied in France just when de Laroche was at the height of her fame, had made a halting solo flight on September 16, 1910, flying a machine she and her husband built in the backyard of their Mineola, New York, home. Bessica Raiche was recognized by the Aeronautical Society—although perhaps incorrectly—as the "First Woman Aviator of America." She and her French husband, François, created the unsuccessful French-American Aeroplane Company, which produced more of the same aircraft, virtually in their living room.

But Blanche Scott remained with the Curtiss team until 1916 and was one of the most celebrated aerobatic fliers in the country. She performed a dazzling array of stunts, some not to be duplicated by any other flier for years, and she earned five thousand dollars a week as the star of the troupe. Long frustrated, however, with her inability to break into the community of mechanics,

LEFT: *French pilot Hélène Dutrieu sits at the controls of a plane, having just joined the air scouts of the French Aviation Corps.* BELOW: *Blanche Scott test-flies the Baldwin Red Devil, which featured an innovative welded construction, at Mineola, New York, in 1911.*

engineers, or manufacturers—or even of conventional fliers who did not have to risk their lives each time they took off—she suddenly quit.

The most celebrated woman aviator of this period was an American, Harriet Quimby, a woman of mysterious origins who was alternately from a wealthy family and at other times raised in poverty, from New England or from California—the fashioning of her origins probably owed as much to her background as a drama critic for *Leslie's Weekly* as to the truth. She was intrigued by flight when she witnessed John Moisant's flight around the Statue of Liberty as part of the Belmont Park Air Race of 1910. When Moisant was killed in a crash a short time later, Quimby prevailed on his brother, Alfred, to teach her to fly at the Moisants' Flying School in Hempstead, in New York. She became a close friend of Alfred's sister, Matilde, and the two became the first and second women to receive pilot's licenses in the United States.

Quimby and Matilde joined the Moisant International Aviators flying troupe, and by 1911 Quimby was drawing crowds in the thousands. She combined a perky smile and a stylish outfit with her trademark monk's hood that accentuated her good looks. That same year, she wrote articles on flying for *Leslie's Weekly* that were wildly popular. Toward the end of the year, she began thinking about a solo flight across the English Channel. Blériot and Jacques de Lesseps had already made their historic flights, and her inspiration, John Moisant, had made a historic flight from London to Paris fifteen months earlier. By March 1912, she had the sponsorship of the *Daily Mirror* and borrowed a Blériot monoplane, which she had shipped to Dover.

On the morning of April 16, 1912, Quimby took off over the Channel in rough weather. A British aviator, Gustav Hamel, had instructed her on the plane, and emphasized that even a small navigation error would put her into the North Sea, which would mean certain death.

Hamel had even offered to make the flight instead of Quimby, wearing her suit for photographers and then changing places with her when he landed in France; Quimby would not hear of it. As it turned out, she missed Calais and landed twenty-five miles (40km) south in the fishing village of Hardelot. She became an international celebrity and the foremost woman aviator in the world.

Harriet Quimby did not live very long after that historic flight. Three months later, she was performing a routine maneuver during the June 1912 Harvard-Boston meet when her plane suddenly plummeted earthward. Two aviators who would become celebrated in the years to come, Ruth Law and Blanche Scott, watched for a few anxious seconds as it seemed Quimby was managing to pull the plane out of the dive. But then she was thrown from her seat (fliers did not wear seatbelts at that time) and into the shallow waters of Dorchester Harbor. A similar crash had happened to Matilde Moisant just a few weeks earlier. She had survived, though, and decided to retire while she still could (she died in 1964). Quimby was not as fortunate. In eulogizing her, the *Boston Post* wrote, "She took her chances like a man and died like one."

Three other women paved the way for women fliers in later years by creating schools and instructing women (and, for that matter, men) in the art of flying: Lidia Zvereva, a Russian aviator who soloed in 1911 and then taught Russian women to fly so well that, when the Lindberghs visited Russia in the 1930s, they found virtual parity between men and women in the Russian air force; Melli Beese, a particularly brave aviator who gained her German aviator's license in spite of her airplane's being sabotaged by resentful men, and who went on to train many men pilots at her Berlin school; and Hilda B. Hewlett, the first English-woman to hold a pilot's license and instructor of many of the pilots who flew in World War I.

In the area of airplane building, Blanche Scott certainly had a point: women were simply excluded from the fraternity. The only significant pre–World War I woman airplane builder was Lilian Bland, who built and flew Ireland's first airplane. Her craft, the *Mayfly*, flew in early 1911 using some parts purchased from A.V. Roe, the airplane manufacturer of Manchester, England. The year 1911 also saw the first fatality of a woman aviator when Denise Moore crashed her Farman on July 21. The Baroness Raymonde de Laroche's life also ended in a crash on July 18, 1919, just six days after she had set a women's altitude record. Ironically, she was not at the controls at the time, but was hurled out of the passenger's seat. Her death finally prompted designers to take a serious look at outfitting their planes with seatbelts and other safety features.

While Europe developed land-based planes for possible military use, the American designer Glenn Curtiss, with U.S. Navy support, was developing aircraft that could land on and take off from water.

Europe Takes the Lead and Prepares for War

In 1908, the British writer H.G. Wells published *War in the Air*, a fantasy that depicted with frightening clarity the possibility of cities being bombarded from aircraft and wars being determined by air battles. As Europe felt itself lurching closer and closer to a major war, each of the possible combatants took stock of their preparedness in all areas of warfare, including air power. Even strategists who believed aviation in the decade before World War I was the province of cranks and adventurers, or useful only for reconnaissance, speculated on what role an air force might play in a war and how they would fare against an airborne enemy.

In the years 1910 to 1914, the French were certainly the most advanced in aviation of all the European nations. The International Exposition of Aerial Locomotion (known as the Aéro Exhibition) at the Grand Palais in Paris in October 1909, just weeks after the spectacle at Rheims, made this abundantly clear. Organized by Robert Esnault-Pelterie, 333 exhibitors displayed their wares and aircraft, everything from balloons to airplanes to clothes and accessories; 318 of the exhibitors were French. On display were the Blériot plane that had made history and Ader's *Avion* of 1897 (which had not); Henry Farman's aileron-equipped biplane; Santos-Dumont's lightweight *Demoiselle 20*; and (in the most prominent position in the hall) Esnault-Pelterie's *R.E.P.*, with its revolutionary internally braced wing (doing away with the need for guide wires) and the first fully enclosed fuselage.

The French believed that their planes had developed nicely—the monoplanes they preferred were lighter and faster than the American biplanes. The Gnome engine, developed by the brothers Louis and Laurent Seguin in 1909, was quickly developing into the prototype of the next generation of airplane power plants, and between 1911 and 1913, French aviators owned virtually every aviation record on the books. The two areas in which the French believed there was room for improvement were raw speed and maneuverability; the Wright aircraft had excelled in both these aspects of flight at Le Mans and even at Rheims, and these were factors that would be important in military situations.

The French answer in the first area was to develop flying techniques that took full advantage of Farman's ailerons. In September 1913, one of Blériot's test pilots, twenty-three-year-old Adolphe Pegoud, a flier so reckless the press nicknamed him "the fool," demonstrated

In spite of the technical achievements of the Americans, the French influenced aircraft design profoundly. The graceful and elegant lines of the Levasseur-designed Antoinette *and the* Blériot *planes (such as the* Blériot XI *shown here) set the course for future design and spelled the end of the Chanute-Wright box kite approach.*

maneuvers that took flying to an entirely new level. His techniques allowed him to fly upside-down and to perform all manner of loops, rolls, and turns that were thought to be impossible. One maneuver had the aircraft climb steeply until it stalled, then drop backwards tail-first, then recover and dive, and then level off, with the plane describing a *Z* in the sky. Pegoud became a celebrated flier in World War I and was shot down in 1915 after a flying career of only three years. Fighter pilots on both sides during the war openly acknowledged their debt to Pegoud.

The response to the speed question was to develop a new kind of airplane construction: the monocoque fuselage. "Monocoque" means "single shell" and refers to the fact that the stresses on the wings and fuselage of an airplane can be borne by the entire shell of the aircraft instead of by support struts and guy wires, as they were in the earlier airplanes. The result is a lighter plane with greater strength and structural integrity. The trail was blazed by two planes: the *Deperdussin*, designed by Louis Bechereau and built by the industrialist Armand Deperdussin; and the *Nieuport*, brainchild of engineer Edouard Nieuport.

The *Deperdussin*, unveiled in 1912, was a sleek aircraft with a single tractor propeller and was the first plane to have a monocoque fuselage. The *Nieuport* might be looked at as the step between the Blériot-Voisin planes and the *Deperdussin*: it did not use monocoque construction, but it was designed to have a streamlined, fully enclosed fuselage and a revolutionary "cowling" or (the

cover that enclosed the engine). These features, plus a flatter wing camber, gave the aircraft speed and permitted it to set a world speed record when introduced in 1911. The superiority of the *Deperdussin* was believed demonstrated in a race known as the Circuit of Anjou (after the county in which it was held), held in June 1912. However, the victory of the *Deperdussin* had more to do with the determination of its pilot, Roland Garros, to fly in stormy weather than with the quality of the aircraft.

In England, aviation had a slow start. The earliest British planes were built and flown by an expatriate American, Samuel F. Cody, who seemed for some years to be the only one in England interested in developing a home-grown airplane. The British were content to rely on the Wright brothers' invention, taking pride that it was based on the pioneering work of Sir George Cayley, an Englishman. The Short brothers, Oswald, Horace, and Eustace, became licensees of the Wright patents, and were soon the major supplier of Wright aircraft to Europe.

Meanwhile, after a brief stint flying man-carrying kites and dirigibles, "Papa" Cody, as he was called in the British press (when he first flew in 1908, he was forty-seven years old), turned to aircraft. Cody was a showman in the tradition of Buffalo Bill Cody (to whom he was not related), Texas-born and bred and, to all appearances, a cowboy in a traveling rodeo show. Yet Cody had an instinctive feel for airplane design and, with virtually no schooling, he designed some of England's first flying machines. The first flight of an airplane in England was made in his British Army Airplane No. 1 on October 16, 1908. Ever the showman, Cody's airplanes were huge for their time; they were called "Flying Cathedrals" because of their large wing spans and their angular shape and pointed canard elevator wing.

Largely at the insistence of hawkish politicians like Winston Churchill, the British army finally held trials in April 1912 at Larkhill for the purpose of evaluating and commissioning military aircraft. In spite of the fact that several designers and builders were already producing noteworthy aircraft, Cody's Flying Cathedrals won handily and were the first planes to be produced at the Royal Aircraft Factory (formerly a balloon factory) at Farnborough. Samuel Cody died in a crash on August 7, 1913, while testing one of his planes. Britain had lost someone as important in promoting flight in England as Ferber had been in France.

Between 1907 and the outbreak of World War I in 1914, three Englishmen entered the field of aviation, working in relative obscurity, but catching up year by year to the French and the Americans, and ultimately playing a vital role in both British aviation and the history of flight. In 1907, Alliot Verdon Roe (or A.V. Roe, as he was known) began building small motorized model airplanes, and by 1909 he had built the first aircraft made entirely in England (that is, without French engines in American designs), the *Avroplane*, a lightweight triplane that barely flew, powered by a 9-horsepower engine. (At this time, the Wrights were delivering planes to the U.S. Army that could fly ten miles [16km] and were powered by 32-horsepower engines.) In 1912, Roe introduced the Avro Type F, the first aircraft with a fully enclosed cockpit (an advance in design, but not a factor in World War I), and in 1913 he introduced the first of a series of staggered biplanes (where the upper wing is forward of the lower wing, streamlining the plane further as it flies) that led to the Avro 504, one of the most popular and durable planes of World War I. (Some ten thousand 504s were built and many remained in service till the mid-1930s.)

ABOVE: Völlmöller's Taube, though it finished second in the German Circuit, was clearly a plane Germany would use if war broke out.
BACKGROUND: Soldiers at Camp Logan, Texas, test a French monoplane during World War I.

Two builders who worked independently before 1912, but who made important design contributions at Farnborough, were Geoffrey de Havilland and Thomas Sopwith. De Havilland was a designer of buses when he turned to aviation. With the help of his brother-in-law, engineer Frank Hearle, and his grandfather's fortune, de Havilland built and tested his first plane in 1909—it crashed—and the *No. 2* in 1910, which flew well enough to interest the British War Office in 1911. The plane was renamed the *F.E.1*, for "Farman Experimental 1" because it resembled a Farman biplane. De Havilland adopted this practice of naming his plane after its inspiration when he designed the *B.E.1*, which stood for "Blériot Experimental 1" and which led to the *B.S.1* (the *Blériot Scout 1*), a staggered-wing biplane with a monocoque fuselage and powered by a 90-horsepower Gnome engine. The *B.S.1* became an important fighter in the war and inspired the design of another classic fighter plane, Tom Sopwith's Tabloid, which in turn led to the design of the legendary Sopwith Camel.

By 1910, Germany was convinced that it had made a terrible mistake in directing all its energies toward the development of airships at the expense of airplanes. As it turned out, airships played a more significant tactical role in World War I than airplanes, and the absence of native design and building talent made the Germans more prone to investigate and adapt foreign expertise—and this resulted in the Germans being very successful in its wartime air campaigns. The first heavier-than-air flight in Germany was made by a visiting Dane, J.C. Ellehammer, and Anthony Fokker. Fokker, who was to become a central figure in German wartime aviation, was Dutch and had offered his services to the British first. The Germans hastily organized an aeronautics industry and produced airplanes that owed a great deal (if not everything) to French planes. The one prewar aircraft the Germans built and looked upon as their own was the *Taube* (German for "dove"), a 1910 monoplane designed and built by an Austrian, Igo Etrich, and originally used by Italy against the Ottoman Turks in Libya. The plane had a hopelessly outdated birdlike design with a complex wing-warping system of control. The *Taube* was clearly not going to lead to other, more advanced aircraft and was considered an interim solution at best. Yet the *Taube*, outfitted with a Daimler-Mercedes engine, was light and allowed pilots to hone their flying skills, which would be tested in the war.

In Russia, Igor Sikorsky, a naval academy graduate, designed, built, and tested the world's first practical four-engine airplanes, culminating in the *Ilya Mouremetz*, a biplane with an enormous wingspan of 113 feet (34.5m), a fully equipped and heated enclosed passenger cabin, and an odd but usable promenade deck. Eighty planes built along these lines were proud elements of Czar Nicholas II's air force and were the basis for the Vityaz bombers, which were among the largest used in the war.

RIGHT: Eugene Ely, a Curtiss exhibition pilot, makes the first take-off from the deck of the U.S.S. Birmingham *on November 14, 1910. BELOW: Ely's first take-off from and landing on the deck of a ship (the U.S.S.* Pennsylvania*) took place at the San Francisco Air Meet on January 18, 1911. ABOVE: Meanwhile, the Russians were hard at work developing large bombers. Sikorsky (right, behind the searchlight) stands atop the observation deck of the* Ilya Mouremetz.

The situation in the United States at this time was, to say the least, paradoxical. On the one hand, flight had been developed by Americans to a very advanced stage by the Wright brothers and Glenn Curtiss, and there was a clear notion among military leaders that this was a technology the country had to develop for the sake of national security. More than ever before, America felt a greater connection to the rest of the world, particularly to its own western states and Europe, and flight offered the best prospect of transporting people across oceans and continents. (And the entire rambunctious ethos of flight was perfectly suited to the American mentality and Yankee ingenuity.)

THE FIRST TO FLY

On the other hand, President Wilson was determined to keep America out of the war, and one element in the strategy to do so was to keep American forces—forces that could be used to provoke America into entering the conflict—at minimum strength. The only branch of the American armed forces that was enlarged for defensive purposes was the navy. (Ironically, it was the sinking of a ship, the *Lusitania*, by a German U-boat, that brought America into war.)

While the U.S. government could control procurement and development, it could not halt progress in design and aviation. American planes developed, particularly seaplanes, which would play an important role both in the postwar development of civil aviation and in naval aviation, particularly in the development of the aircraft carrier, which would prove critical in World War II. American inventors created the first bombsight (Riley Scott in 1911) and adapted the gyroscope to airplane stability (Lawrence Sperry installed the gyroscope developed by his father, Elmer, in a Curtiss seaplane in 1914). Americans had been first to use radio to communicate with the ground from an airplane (Baldwin and McCurdy in 1910), accumulating more experience than anyone else in using radio communication in flight. And Americans had done the most testing of aerial bombing and reconnaissance, beginning with Glenn Curtiss' display on June 30, 1910, of the successful "sinking" of a dummy battleship on Lake Keuka by dummy chalk bombs (scoring fifteen direct hits out of seventeen passes).

It was clear as early as 1911 that, while Europe might momentarily take the lead in aviation, being confronted directly with the war, America was going to develop the airplane and its military capabilities at its own pace, to be used when necessary, either in this war or the next.

The Colorful Career of Alberto Santos-Dumont

Historians of aviation are not certain what to make of Alberto Santos-Dumont; no one ever was. He was a hero, a genius, and a visionary to some, and to others he was a laughable character who was only accidentally more than a footnote in the history of flight. Peter Wykeham's biography of the man presents a complex picture of a man who persevered over terrific odds—thrown at him by the world and his own demons—and who "forced history to be made by sheer will."

Santos (as he was known) came to France from Brazil in 1891. He was the eighteen-year-old son of a wealthy coffee plantation owner, and showed mechanical adroitness even as a child. An inveterate gadgeteer, he soaked up French culture insatiably and regarded himself a son of France, even after his return to Brazil in 1928. Santos was short and frail—about five feet tall and weighing no more than ninety pounds (41kg)—and his attempts to compensate for this by wearing high collars, tall floppy hats, and pinstripe suits made him appear like a caricature of a dandy. Soon after arriving in Paris, he became intoxicated with the idea of flight and with all the activity he found all around him in the area of dirigibles and heavier-than-air aircraft.

Santos made his first flight in Paris in a dirigible of his own design in 1898, and though he crashed Parisians learned something about Santos that would be true of him his entire life: crashing never deterred Alberto Santos-Dumont. He parked his aircraft near his Champs Elysees apartment and was frequently seen gliding around Paris to the delight of children, visitors, and the press. Officialdom looked at these exploits with nervous amusement, particularly when his dirigibles would occasionally appear at an official function uninvited and unannounced.

When, in 1900, the financier Henri Deutsch offered a prize of 100,000 francs to the first aeronaut to fly the seven miles (11km) from the Aéro Club de France's headquarters in Saint-Cloud to the Eiffel Tower, the Paris press felt that the two leading contenders were Count Ferdinand Graf von Zeppelin and their adopted son Santos. Santos made two attempts that ended in spectacular crashes—one on the estate of Baron Rothschild, the other in the courtyard of the Trocadero Hotel, both in full view of onlookers and in both cases with Santos barely escaping with his life—and then, on October 19, 1900, he completed the course, adding a flourish by circling the Eiffel Tower and returning to Saint-Cloud. This extra maneuver almost cost him the prize because the judges claimed that the contest required that the flight be considered over by the securing of the guide rope (to differentiate the flight from an unpowered balloon flight). Popular sentiment was so behind Santos, however, that the judges relented and awarded him the prize. With typical magnanimity, Santos announced that he would give seventy-five thousand francs to charity and to volunteers who had helped him (though Brazil, eager to reclaim its native son, matched the French prize with one of its own).

In 1904, Santos experimented with gliders and helicopters, producing a machine of silk and bamboo. It did not fly, though it tossed Santos about. He went back to the drawing board and emerged in 1906 with a machine that looked like several box kites haphazardly put together. He called it the *14-bis* (14-encore) because it was to be carried aloft by his No. 14 dirigible. On July 23, 1906, in a procession that looked like a major parade and included Ernest Archdeacon and other members of the Aéro Club, Santos brought his No. 14 and the *14-bis* to the Bagatelle for testing. Noticing that the aircraft had been damaged during the procession, the unflappable Santos announced that the test was off and sent everyone home. He tried again on July 29, this time using a donkey (named Kuigno) to pull the aircraft-dirigible combination.

RIGHT: *A frequent sight on the streets of Paris in 1909: Santos-Dumont driving his* Demoiselle *to Saint Cyr airfield for testing.* BELOW: *Compare the* Demoiselle's *size to the* 14-bis, *the plane in which Santos-Dumont made his historic 1907 flight.*

Santos continued to test the aircraft, soon coming to the conclusion that the dirigible was not necessary. On September 13, the *14-bis* took a short hop of from twenty to forty feet (6 to 12m); on October 23 it flew a full 197 feet (60m); and on November 12 it went 722 feet (220m) in a flight lasting twenty-one seconds. All of Europe was electrified by this, the first heavier-than-air flight by a European. Octave Chanute reported back to the Wrights that, while Santos-Dumont had indeed flown, he had no means of controlling the aircraft except by shifting his weight, and even that was difficult because the pilot stood in a narrow wicker basket.

Santos' next airplane, the *No. 15*, equipped with a makeshift wing-warping mechanism, broke up while taxiing for a take-off in March 1907. By this time, Santos had seen several Blériot aircraft in flight and had decided to construct a monoplane. The result was the *Demoiselle No. 19*, an ultra-light tractor monoplane made of bamboo and silk and weighing only about 153 pounds. The *Demoiselle* (nicknamed the *Grasshopper*) became a sensation all over

Europe and was sold by the thousands, introducing an entirely new generation to the thrill of flight for less than five hundred francs. Many designers regarded the *Demoiselle* as an oddity, but the aircraft had a clear impact on many designers and its image can be seen lurking in the lines of Anthony Fokker's first aircraft, the *Spinne* (Spider) of 1912 and in light aircraft of the post-war period.

In 1910, Santos-Dumont was diagnosed with multiple sclerosis. He went into retirement, though he followed aviation developments throughout the war. In 1928, he returned to Brazil and was given a hero's welcome. As his ship was docking, a sea plane carrying six prominent Brazilians who wished to greet him crashed and all six were lost. Santos, by this time quite frail, asked that all ceremonies and events honoring him be canceled. On July 23, 1932, Alberto Santos-Dumont committed suicide. In his final years, he had become despondent about the destructive uses to which nations had put aviation, and about his role as a pioneer of flight.

Chapter 4

World War I: The Airplane Goes to War

Introduction

The Great War that engulfed Europe from August 1914 to November 1918—World War I—exacted a human cost that was staggering. Of the sixty-three million combatants mobilized by all participants, 8.3 million were killed or missing in action, and twenty-one million were wounded or taken prisoner—which means nearly half of all the soldiers sent to battle were casualties. The civilian toll was just as horrifying: eight million dead; 19.5 million wounded. Though a war later in the century would revise even this gruesome calculus, the result of "The War to End All Wars" was the wiping out of a generation on the European continent. As if to punctuate this calamity, nature outdid the human carnage with some carnage of its own. A Spanish influenza epidemic killed twenty million people across Europe and Asia in 1918, unchallenged by the world's health and medical facilities, by then stretched to the breaking point by the war.

The total number of fliers killed in World War I was less than one-third of one percent of the total military fatalities: the British, French, and Germans lost fewer than ten thousand each, and the Americans lost 237 airmen in battle, for a total toll to all air forces in the war of just under thirty thousand. Yet the exploits of the fighter pilots of World War I have been glorified and romanticized to this day, far beyond their importance to the war effort and in morbid disproportion to the sacrifices made in the trenches below. The high command on both sides recognized this and feared that the glorification of the "ace" would lead to lower morale on the ground. But with both sides dug in for a war of attrition that the Central Powers, surrounded and embargoed by the Allies, had little hope of winning, the air was the only battlefield on which there could still be winners and losers.

Until the very end of the war, when air power was used in coordination with ground attack by Billy Mitchell at St. Mihiel, air power did not tip the balance in any battle or result in either side's having a tactical advantage. Much of the contribution of aviators in the war was as the eyes of the military, first as eyewitnesses of troop deployments, and later as bearers of reconnaissance cameras that could record enemy positions and allow for patient interpretation back at base. Some strategists even referred to this phase as the "war of lenses," and each side was forced to respond by developing new techniques of camouflage and night maneuvers.

Realizing that the war was going to last a long time, both sides turned to their aviators for some heroic victory, however symbolic, that would maintain morale at home. The fliers on both sides were cut from the stuff heroes are made of: generous helpings of derring-do, bravado, foolhardiness, recklessness, fearlessness, and an overwhelming desire for adventure and glory. Some of the best pilots might be described as a bit unbalanced; many were the pampered, college-educated sons of prominent families. The stark contrast between American ace Eddie Rickenbacker, a race car driver from a poor, working class background, and the other fliers in the American corps, scions of aristocratic families, only highlighted the social origins of most fliers.

As the war progressed, a paradoxical situation developed: the fliers became more important psychologically to boost morale at home and in the trenches, and so became less expendable, which in turn forced their commanders to restrict them from venturing into enemy territory where, without cover from the fighters on the ground, the risk of being shot down was very great.

The famed 85th Squadron mainly featured S.E.5 fighter planes, which were designed by H. P. Folland of the Royal Aircraft Factory. The American pilots of this squadron were under the command of Colonel Bishop and Major Mannock.

Thus, reconnaissance aircraft had little chance of ever returning from sorties with information. So the very celebrity that turned the fliers on both sides into legends served to limit their effectiveness.

But though the planes did not have an essential impact on the outcome of World War I, aviation took two important steps during the war: First, the war showed that while the planes may fly through the air, the industry floats on a sea of money. Bond issues and appropriations in the European nations before the war took the entire airplane industry out of the hands of the tinkerers and put it in the hands of industrialists. Most companies passed into the hands of auto manufacturers, who had experience in mass-production techniques, and to people who were comfortable in the world of corporate finance. The Wrights, Blériot, and Curtiss did not belong to this world; Fokker, Saulnier, and Martin did.

Second, the war only whetted the appetite of many military strategists for a time when the full potential of air power could be applied to conflict. The requirements for effective aerial bombing, for instance, turned out to be much more stringent than those for close fighter combat. Bombers have to carry larger payloads, have greater range, fly faster and higher, and be better armored than fighters. World War I saw two cycles begin that were to become perennial parts of the future of aviation. One cycle was the parry-and-thrust between adversaries, as one side gained an advantage that required better planes from the other side as a counter; the other cycle was the same sort of competition between the makers of fighters and the makers of bombers. Better fighters created the need for better bombers, which in turn created a need for better fighters, and so on. As terrible a war as the Great War was, it is fortunate that it ended when it did, because both sides had already produced the beginnings of a fleet of advanced bombers that would have decimated cities and resulted in even greater civilian deaths across Europe.

A common sight along the Western Front throughout France: a German plane brought down by ground fire.

Roland Garros and the First Aces

At the opening of the war, France held the lead in the air with the most aircraft and the most experienced pilots. Aircraft were used mainly for reconnaissance, but in the early days of 1914 aerial reconnaissance reports (such as those detailing the German advance through Belgium as General von Moltke outflanked the French and British armies) were ignored. The Allies were just barely able to recoup and, this time believing aerial reports, halted the German advance at the Marne River, along which both sides dug in for a long standoff.

At first, spotters who rode as passengers waved to enemy aircraft; soon they used pistols and rifles to try and shoot down their adversaries. This was totally ineffective given all the buffeting and vibrations the spotter would experience even in a smooth flight. (The rotary Gnome engines were highly efficient and reliable, but the fact that the entire engine rotated with the propeller meant the aircraft experienced a great deal of vibration.)

The solution was thought to be machine guns. The French Hotchkiss, the Belgian Lewis, the British Vickers, and the German Spandau and Parabellum were all well-crafted weapons that allowed gunners to spray the enemy with a barrage of fire, increasing the chance of a hit. But this was a very limited solution, first, because the gunner was at the mercy of the pilot's sudden maneuvering, and second, because a very important target area right in front of the plane was eliminated from the gunner's field of fire. Some work had been done before the war in developing a mechanism that would allow the pilot to aim a machine gun through the whirling blade of a propeller without destroying it, but it had proven unreliable.

The solution to the problem came about as a result of a collaboration between the French aircraft designer-builder Raymond Saulnier of the Morane-Saulnier firm and the world-famous aviator Roland Garros, who had been the first to fly solo across the Mediterranean

Top: By 1915 Curtiss Jenny Trainers were outfitted with synchronized machine guns, but they were not as reliable as Fokker planes. Above left: The Morane-Saulnier Type N planes were equipped with deflector plates. Above right: The British were already advanced in machine gun technology thanks to Maxim. Eventually, the Lewis gun gave airplane gunners lethal range and flexibility.

in 1913, using a Morane-Saulnier Parasol. These two men developed a deflector shield for the propeller blade that would deflect rounds. Garros tested the device on a Parasol airplane against four German fighters on April 1, 1915. The German fliers were stunned by Garros' ability to simply aim his aircraft and fire in a direct line to wherever he was pointing. An added feature incorporated the firing mechanism onto the joystick, giving the pilot easy control of both the flight and the shooting. On April 19, Garros' plane was forced down behind enemy lines and he was captured before he could destroy it. The Germans were now in possession of the secret, but there was no need to copy it, thanks to a capable airplane builder and

entrepreneur named Anthony Fokker, with a lethal secret of his own.

The first "aces" (an unofficial title given to fighter pilots who had shot down five enemy aircraft) were Garros and Adolphe Pegoud, the aerobatic pilot who had demonstrated loops and dives before the war. Garros escaped in 1918 and returned to service, only to be shot down and killed later that year. Pegoud died on August 15, 1918, while on a reconnaissance mission.

The only German aviator in the early stages of the war was Ernst Udet, later to become the second highest rated German ace. Udet began the war in an Aviatik B, used mainly for spotting, and then flew the faster "D" planes built by Siemens-Schuckert. (Udet committed suicide in 1941 rather than continue as a spokesman for the Luftwaffe.) The only British aviator to emerge at this stage was Lanoe Hawker, winner of the Victoria Cross for defeating three German aircraft from his Bristol Scout. Hawker was to become an important architect of Allied air power, but at this stage there was little a plane could do other than bombing and bringing down the airships ("sausages") the Germans used to guide artillery fire, and a plane could do this only while heavily protected by ground-based anti-aircraft fire ("Archie") and by fiery artillery shells ("flaming onions").

The Fokker Scourge

Anthony Fokker was born in Java on April 6, 1890, to Dutch parents. He learned the basics of aeronautics at a technical school in Mainz and built his first plane in 1910. By 1913, he had established a small factory and a successful flight school at Schwerin, one hundred miles (161km) northwest of Berlin. He was to become one of the most interesting and controversial figures in the history of aviation. Fokker's career in aeronautics lasted until his death in New York City on December 23, 1939.

Fokker was accused of copying the designs of others; in fact, he was an admirer of Morane-Saulnier planes and based many of his aircraft on their lines. His Oberursel engine in his planes was a virtual copy of the French Gnome engine. He was accused of fabricating tall tales, such as the story he told about taking the propeller off Garros' captured plane and singlehandedly concocting the mechanism of his landmark Eindekker (single wing) E.I in a marathon forty-eight-hour session of frantic engineering. The fact was that he and engineer Heinrich Luebbe had already designed a mechanism that successfully synchronized the propeller with the firing of a machine gun, and had installed it on one of his aircraft. His mechanism had nothing whatever to do with the Garros-Saulnier device, and Fokker promoted the tall tale to hide the fact that he had also offered his invention to the Allies (who turned him down). Fokker produced forty different types of aircraft during the war (all designed by a team led by his chief engineer, Reinhold Platz), and after the war produced the planes that formed the basis of the commercial aviation industry of the 1920s and 1930s.

The first Fokker E.Is reached the front in the summer of 1915, and two fliers in particular showed a facility in handling the new system: Oswald Boelcke, a flier whose

Max Immelmann is pictured here in front of the Fokker E.I Eindekker, a plane that was not particularly fast or maneuverable, but had the distinction of having the first synchronized machine gun and propeller. In Immelmann's hands, the Eindekker outclassed anything in the sky.

exploits as a reconnaissance aviator in an Albatross spotter plane had already earned him the Iron Cross; and Max Immelmann, known as "The Eagle of Lille," after the town in northern France over which he often prowled. He was a husky, athletic man who could barely fit in the E.I's pilot's seat. These two men formed the core of the squadron Jagdstaffel (fighter-squadron) Nr. 2 (contracted to Jasta 2), and became the most celebrated aces in the last six months of 1915, during which the Fokker planes had unchallenged control of the skies.

Boelcke and Immelmann often flew together, displaying an uncanny coordination. Yet they were very different people. Immelmann was a loner, moody and given to fits of anger, brooding and undisciplined. He sometimes used aerobatic turns to outflank an enemy flier. One such maneuver, a combination loop and half-roll that gives the pilot a quick second pass at a target, is called the "Immelmann turn" (though he never mentioned the maneuver in any of his letters and the turn was already a staple among stunt fliers before the war).

Boelcke was a teacher before the war and, though he thought of himself as a lone knight, he also understood the importance of coordinated and disciplined attack. He was an outgoing leader of men, a bon vivant who often took young women for rides in his airplane and who enjoyed the finer things. Boelcke shared his knowledge and experience, and trained many of the fliers who were to become aces later in the war. Yet, Boelcke and Immelmann were like-minded in their beliefs about how the Fokker planes should be used. They took an aggressive approach, ignoring directives that forbade them from chasing Allied planes across battle lines.

For their leadership in clearing the skies of Allied planes, Boelcke and Immelmann were awarded the Ordre Pour le Merite, a medal that became known as the Blue Max (after Immelmann), Germany's highest military honor, established by Frederick the Great in 1740 (when French was the language of the court) and previously awarded only to generals responsible for winning wars. By the end of the war, eighty-one fliers were awarded the Blue Max (much to the consternation of the highest ranking generals or the far fewer prewar recipients still living at the time), making the flier the most glorified soldier since the Middle Ages. Boelcke and Immelmann died during in-flight accidents in 1916, and both received funerals fit for a Wagnerian hero.

By the summer of 1915, German control of the skies allowed its ground forces to fend off every Allied offensive and to mount the assault on Verdun in February 1916, exacting a great toll in Allied casualties and throwing the Allies into disarray. Continued Allied efforts to duplicate the Fokker firing mechanism proved difficult, and by the time better-performing Allied planes came off the production lines, the German aces had accumulated valuable combat experience—and an invaluable psychological edge.

Anthony Fokker (TOP) looked even younger than twenty-five, his age when he rose to the top of Germany's military aircraft program—and he was not German. The executives and engineers at Albatross had to swallow hard taking orders from the young upstart. But the key to Fokker's success was that he sought the advice and friendship of the aces who flew the planes, including Oswald Boelcke (ABOVE), a master flier and tactician of the World War I air war.

The Allied Response

The Allies had ample opportunity to copy the Fokker mechanism from captured Eindekkers, but for reasons not clear to this day, they did not even attempt it. Instead, they rose to the Fokker challenge in a number of ways that eventually proved effective and swung the balance momentarily in their favor. The strategy was designed by the commander of the Allied air operations, Brigadier General Hugh Montague "Boom" Trenchard of the Royal Flying Corps (RFC), a man whose features and British resolve were both chiseled out of granite, and carried out by the French field commander, Jean Du Peuty, and his British counterpart, Lanoe Hawker. Trenchard's simple strategy called for systematically upgrading each element of the air campaign and exploiting the few limitations of the German Jastas.

The strategy had four main components: create better performing planes (even if they did not have synchronized forward gunning); train a larger corps of highly qualified pilots; develop coordinated formation flying that made best use of the Allied numerical advantage; and most important, take the air war to the Germans—pursue them relentlessly and clear the skies at any cost. In order to give the Allied pilot the same facility with a forward-shooting machine gun that the Germans had, it was necessary to create either pusher planes (with the propeller in the rear) that could perform as well as the tractor aircraft or to place the gun on the top wing (out of the propeller's disc). The de Havilland D.H. 2 was of

Top: Ace Charles Nungesser is pictured here aboard the Nieuport 17. On the side of the fuselage is portrayed a braying mule, one of the hundreds of colorful emblems used by Allied fliers in the war. Above: The SPAD XIII was the plane flown by Eddie Rickenbacker and René Fonck for most of their kills. The SPAD XIII dove better than any other World War I fighter, which made it effective over Allied lines and in the afternoon, when it could attack from above, swooping out of the sun.

the first kind; the Nieuport 17, the Bebe, was of the second—both were equipped with powerful engines that allowed the planes to outperform the German planes. By mid-1916, they were joined by three additional aircraft, which were fitted (at long last) with synchronized forward-shooting Vickers machine guns and were to become legendary fighters: the SPAD VII (built by the Societe pour l'Aviation et ses Derives), which developed into the SPAD XIII, considered the finest fighter the Allies pro-

duced in the war; and two planes produced by Tom Sopwith: the Pup, a biplane that responded quickly to the pilot's controls, and its descendant, the Camel, a biplane named after the hump over its gun casing and so maneuverable that fliers considered it just a step removed from having wings attached to one's body.

The next piece of Trenchard's plan was training, and this was turned over to Robert Smith Barry, a flight instructor for the RFC. Smith Barry made a study of possible training aircraft and selected the Avro 504, a two-seater airplane known for its speed and responsiveness, neither of which was sacrificed with an instructor aboard. (The 504 remained the main trainer until the early 1930s.) The instructor in the rear seat spoke to the student through "Gotsport tubes" (named after the airfield in England that was Smith Barry's base of operations) and the focus of instruction was on mastering the skills of organized formation flying and coordinated attack. The program did not begin until 1916, but by the end of the year, following the resurgence of the Allies at the end of 1916 and the deadly command of the air by the Germans in early 1917, the dividends of the new kind of flight training were beginning to pay off.

In the meantime, with the Allies repelling the surge at Verdun and mounting a push of their own at the equally gruesome Battle of the Somme, a new crop of celebrated fliers piloted the new planes and added their names to the role of the immortal aces. They were concentrated in a particular squadron of escadrilles (squadron groups) known as *Les Cigognes*—"The Storks." (The stork had long been a good luck symbol among aviators.)

Three aces who emerged from this group became legendary figures in aviation history, and two of them established in the popular mind (the world over) the image of the World War I ace as a tireless, suave, devil-may-care iconoclast who scoffed at orders and convention as easily as he did at enemy fire and impossible odds. Jean Navarre became famous patrolling the skies over Verdun in 1916, garnering twelve kills—tops among Allied pilots at the time—before crashing in the Argonne forest and being too injured to fly for the remainder of the war. (Navarre died in a crash while practicing a flying stunt for a 1919 victory parade.) His flying partner, Charles Nungesser, was, like Navarre, an athlete and a scholar who could cavort in the local tavern all night and then fly for hours hunting and shooting down enemy aircraft the next day. Nungesser was injured many times and never allowed himself the luxury of a full convalescence. As a result, he spent much of the war and his postwar years in constant, excruciating pain. Nonetheless, by the end of the war, he had amassed forty-five confirmed kills, third among French aces in the war, and a countrysideful of tales of his larger-than-life exploits. Bored with being an idol of Parisian society after the war, he set out in 1927 to cross the Atlantic and was lost at sea.

The third ace, Geoges Guynemer, replaced Navarre in 1916, at the age of 22, after only a year of flying but with eight victories under his belt. He was a very different sort of young man from his boisterous predecessors. A pale and delicate youth with a modest, romantic gaze, Guynemer traced his ancestry to a soldier who fought with Charlemagne, and it seemed fitting somehow that he had been born on Christmas Eve. He was widely quoted saying the sort of things Joan of Arc might have said ("I owe myself to my country"). In December 1915, Guynemer began flying Nieuports, and his score soared: by January

1917 he had accumulated thirty victories, and by May of that year (now flying the newest SPAD models), he had reached Nungesser's total of forty-five. He was shot down seven times and injured each time, but he kept flying. By September 11, 1917, with fifty-four confirmed victories (second highest among French fliers), he flew a mission over Poelcapelle and disappeared without a trace. The nation mourned as it did for no other fallen flier.

By mid-1916 Trenchard's strategy was working and the Allies had control of the skies. The Germans, in an effort to create a coordinated flying strategy, devised some common-sense rules (*Dikta*) for air attack calculated to rein in the individuality of their fliers. They did little good. It was not until the quality of the planes was once again raised by the Germans and put in the hands of a fresh group of intrepid fliers that the balance shifted.

The British, pleased with the development of their program, still hoped for a British ace who could bolster morale at home and in the field. Such a man emerged in the summer of 1916: Albert Ball. Ball's entire career in the air spanned only sixteen months, from February 1916 to May 1917, yet he became the most celebrated British flier of the war—up to that time, and possibly even for the entire war, surpassing in fame fliers with many more victories. Ball was the personification of British grit, charging any number of enemy aircraft without a thought of the odds or the dangers. He developed a unique fighting style, shooting at all angles, being especially successful shooting down enemy aircraft while climbing from below. His style was perfectly suited to the Nieuport and later to the new aircraft produced in Farnborough, the S.E. 5 and 5a, the biplane that was to represent the technical limit of Allied aircraft performance.

In the opening months of 1917, two great British fliers were lost—Lanoe Hawker and Albert Ball—to fire from German aircraft piloted by two brothers: Manfred and Lothar von Richthofen. It marked yet another shift in balance, this time to a period when the previous exploits of pilots on either side paled. It began with the delivery of new aircraft from the Fokker factories in October of 1916. During the training with the new aircraft, a new sense of cohesiveness grew and a leader emerged: Manfred von Richthofen, the legendary "Red Baron."

The Red Baron and His Flying Circus

The planes Anthony Fokker delivered to the front at the end of 1916 looked very familiar to the airmen. Fokker never made a secret of the fact that he used downed aircraft as models and improved on designs the Allies had been kind enough to test in the field. Out of his factory came the new crop of such aircraft and they were among the best and most advanced to fly in the war.

Flying aces of World War I were lionized by both sides, but in different ways. TOP: *In order to humanize him, British ace Albert Ball was pictured with his family; British military leaders feared that idolizing air aces would lower the morale of the soldiers in the trenches.* ABOVE: *In contrast, the Germans portrayed such heroes as Baron Manfred von Richthofen as larger than life. This photo and others like it could be found in nearly every German home during the war.*

The first plane the new crop of fliers were given was not a Fokker (though by this time, Anthony Fokker had become a virtual minister of aircraft procurement in the government), but the Albatross D II (later to evolve into the D III), a lightweight plywood-frame biplane fighter with a powerful 160-horsepower Mercedes engine and two Spandau machine guns. (At the beginning of the war, Albatross was the largest German aircraft builder, supplying 60 percent of the entire air force. By the war's end, it could barely field a few fighters, and after the war the company disappeared, appearing briefly in a failed 1919 attempt at commercial aviation.) The German fliers were convinced that these were the finest machines either side had produced—or could produce—until they received the new planes from Fokker.

The first was the Fokker Dr I, a triplane modeled after the Sopwith Triplane (made famous by British ace Raymond Collishaw, whose plane was called *Black Maria*), but including features of the Sopwith Camel, and equipped with an additional wing on the undercarriage for more maneuverability. The Dr I was compact and agile, presenting a small target that was almost impossible to hit: a length of less than nineteen feet (6m), a wingspan of less than twenty-four feet (7m), and a top speed of 103 miles per hour (166kph), which was not the fastest in the sky, but more than enough to evade virtually any attack run. It was flying this plane that one ace

TOP: *Richthofen and his Flying Circus became famous flying the Fokker Dr I, a triplane that borrowed heavily from the Sopwith Triplane. The Dr I could be controlled by only the best pilots, which limited its deployment. In the hands of Richthofen, the Dr I could zigzag like a large fly, eluding faster planes.* ABOVE: *The cockpit was sparse—it sported only a tachometer, a fuel gauge, an oil gauge, and a compass—and the controls simple: joystick and stirrup pedals.*

in particular, Manfred von Richthofen, became a legend and one of the most famous fliers in history.

Manfred von Richthofen was born on May 2, 1892, to an aristocratic Silesian family. He grew up to be a handsome young man with a proud, piercing stare and steely nerves, and soon came to the attention of Oswald Boelcke, who made him the commander of Jasta 2, renamed Jagdstaffel Boelcke after the great ace's death. Von Richthofen extended Boelcke's ideas of teamwork and fostered a unity in the corps that allowed it to function as a single-minded and single-willed unit. Von Richthofen was still flying an Albatross D II when he won his Blue Max after his eighth kill in November 1916 and when he downed Lanoe Hawker (sometimes called "the British Boelcke") on November 23. It was this engagement that convinced von Richthofen that he needed a fighter with more agility, even at the expense of speed. By the end of 1916, von Richthofen had acquired the new Fokker Dr I and he flew both it and the Albatross D III, as the situation warranted.

After he learned that he had shot down Hawker, von Richthofen painted his plane red out of joy, giving rise to a new epithet, the "Red Baron." He created a new squadron consisting of the best fliers in Germany, Jasta 11, and the planes began their operations in earnest in January of 1917. In order to camouflage which plane was his, all the planes of Jasta 11 were brightly colored with much red, though it was clear to most ground observers which airplane was almost entirely red. (The Germans learned that the bright colors of the planes had a disorienting effect on gunners and, far from offering a better target as was feared, gave the pilots a tactical advantage.) In order to be close to the front, and as mobile as possible to avoid Allied bombing, Jasta 11 (men and planes) were quartered in tents, giving rise to a nickname for the squadron: "the Flying Circus."

The Red Baron often landed near the crash site of a fallen enemy to retrieve a memento. Of all the aces of the war, von Richthofen may lay claim to having been the most complex, the most troubled by the war, and the most uncertain of his role in it. He fought severe headaches and bouts of depression, and recognized more than most the disparity between how the war was going in the air and how Germany was faring on the ground.

ABOVE LEFT: Baron von Richthofen's Albatross D III is the second in line in this 1917 photo of Jasta 11 at the Douai airfield. These planes were responsible for eighty-three kills in a single month, a period dubbed "Bloody April" by the British. ABOVE RIGHT: Fighter pilots on both sides recognized the special camaraderie among aces of the same squadron. Instead of a family photo, downed airmen were often found with photos of their fellow pilots, such as these (above and background) of von Richthofen and his Jasta.

By the end of March, the fliers of Jasta 11 were tested and hardened into a cohesive unit that was invincible in the sky. The month of April 1917 was one of the worst for Allied airmen, as Jasta 11 alone accounted for eighty-three victories and 316 lost airmen. The month became known as "Bloody April" and the Germans were uncontested in the skies over the Somme battlefields below. But on the ground the Germans called 1917 "the turnip year," as the embargo of the continent by the British continued to strangle the Central Powers. It seemed to all that 1918 might be the fateful year in which the war would end.

In 1918 Fokker created one more plane, taking the basic design of the Nieuports and creating the D VII, a biplane thought today to be the finest all-around fighter of the war, and the only plane the Allies insisted the Germans relinquish as a condition of the armistice. But the crash program to turn out these planes came too late to affect the outcome of the war. By 1918 the Allies had recovered from Bloody April and even von Richthofen's talents could not overcome the plodding, methodical, piecemeal conquest of the skies by the Allies.

Manfred von Richthofen met his end in battle on April 21, 1918, probably at the hands of a Canadian pilot of a Sopwith Camel, Captain A. Roy Brown, though questions persisted as to exactly how the Red Baron died. Richtofen, chasing the plane piloted by Captain Brown and being pursued by a plane piloted by another Canadian, Lieutenant Wilford May, was caught by a bullet fired by one or the other of his assailants as he stood and turned to check the tail of his plane. Having fallen in Allied territory, the Red Baron was taken from his plane and given a funeral by the Allies worthy of one of their own fallen aces—the pallbearers were all captains and squadron commanders, as Richthofen himself had been.

American aviators flew in the service of France as the Lafayette Escadrille until the United States entered the war. Pictured here with their lion cub mascots, Whiskey and Soda (which soon grew to full size), is the squadron commanded by French captain Georges Thenault and his American lieutenant, William Thaw (seated, third and fourth from left, respectively). The squadron boasted French, Russian, and American fliers and a French chaplain, Ammonier Meyer (to Thaw's left).

The Lafayette Escadrille— Americans Prepare to Enter the Air War

American fliers had wanted to see action in the war from the very first and, as fliers, they were not likely to be content with only reading about the exploits of their European colleagues. Ever since American mercenary fliers flew for the rebels in Mexico in 1913, Americans could be counted on to go wherever their flying services were needed. At the outbreak of World War I, Americans petitioned to be allowed to volunteer for service with the Allies, and permission was granted after a year. The corps of American fliers was formed in April 1916, at first under the name the *Escadrille Americaine* (AEF), but after the German ambassador complained about so partisan an involvement, the name was changed to the Lafayette Escadrille, after the French naval hero who fought with Washington.

The group did not have a great impact on the war effort, but it did cement the relationship between the Americans and the Allied aviators, particularly the French, who still remembered the impression the Wrights and Glenn Curtiss had made just a few years earlier. The French also liked the free-wheeling and generous nature of the Americans and were welcoming of one in particular, Raoul Lufbery, an American of French lineage who had served in China and the French Foreign Legion before coming to Europe. In 1914 Lufbery was servicing airplanes for the Stork Squadron and taking flight training on the side.

The most celebrated aviator of the Lafayette Escadrille, Raoul Lufbery, commander of the 94th "Hat-in-the-Ring" Squadron, is pictured here in Paris in July 1917. Although he had made only seventeen kills, his death in the spring of 1918 was widely mourned by the Allies.

The Lafayette Escadrille did not form until two Harvard graduates—Norman Prince, a student pilot who came to Paris for the express purpose of forming the volunteer squadron, and Victor Chapman, doing graduate work in Paris when the war began—and William Thaw, a Legion volunteer from a wealthy Pittsburgh family, teamed up with an influential American in Paris, Dr. Edmund Gros, a leader of the volunteer American medical and ambulance corps serving in France. Together, the four allayed the French fears about spies in the American group and convinced them to supply planes for combat and reconnaissance.

All through 1916 and 1917, Prince and Chapman did aerial combat with Germany's best fliers, and they and the rest of the corps accumulated some respectable kill totals. Prince downed five planes before being shot down in 1916; Chapman was praised by the French for his bravery, but was killed fighting Fokkers that same year, as was Thaw. The only ace to come out of the Lafayette Escadrille was Lufbery, who had seventeen confirmed victories, as both volunteer and then as part of the AEF. In the AEF, Lufbery commanded the 94th Air Squadron, which included Eddie Rickenbacker, America's top ace in the war. The "Hat-in-the-Ring" squadron, as it was

called (after its insignia) became the elite American air fighting unit under Lufbery's command and allowed Billy Mitchell, commander of the entire American air forces in Europe, to contemplate and then launch aerial assaults that would determine the outcome of battles. Lufbery died in combat in June 1918, in full view of Mitchell, who was observing on the ground.

In all, some two hundred fliers flew in the Lafayette Escadrille. They supported tank movements and protected certain targets that they believed held special psychological significance, such as the great cathedral at Rheims, a frequent target of the German bombers. Camped in their barracks at Chaudun, the Americans were famous for keeping two lion cubs, Whiskey and Soda, and were looked upon hopefully as an advance guard for the entry of the Yanks into the field of battle.

America Enters the War

America finally declared war on Germany on April 6, 1917. American soldiers did not see any combat action at the front lines until October of that year, and American-made armaments, and especially air materials, did not reach the front lines until well into 1918, just a few months before the war ended. The Germans, who sued for a separate peace with Russia so they could eliminate one front, stepped up their industrial program and struck out with bold last-ditch military offenses, hoping to redraw the map of Europe before the Americans even arrived.

America added just enough weight to tip the balance in favor of the Allies. This was no less true in the air war than on the ground. The Americans barely had enough time to have a few flying aces, but like the aces of an earlier time, they were cut from a different cloth and they were worshipped as heroes. Five Allied aces closed out the era of the World War I aviator, and while they were brave and gifted fliers, they operated largely in an arena that was not nearly as challenging or dangerous as that of their predecessors. With the German air force in shambles and the German army in retreat, many of the final victories were against little or no resistance.

France's last great ace, and on paper its greatest, was René Paul Fonck, a flier and marksman of incomparable skill, but a man of such annoying social qualities that he became something of an embarrassment to the French. He is credited with seventy-five confirmed victories, many using a hand-held rifle with which he was a deadly marksman. He may have had as many as twenty-five more victories that were unconfirmed, because he also had a knack for flying damaged planes back to base after solitary encounters with lone, renegade enemy planes. (Before 1918, the Germans did not allow isolated plane-to-plane engagements.) He may well have been the best technical pilot-marksman to fly in World War I. The problem was that Fonck was the loudest at trumpeting his own accomplishments, which was considered bad form in the fighter ace fraternity. Fonck died peacefully in 1953 at the age of fifty-nine in his Paris home, having been honored by France and the world of aviation (if perhaps not to the degree that Fonck thought he deserved).

The British produced two aces: the Canadian William Avery Bishop and the Irishman Edward Mannock. Billy Bishop (as he was known) had lightning-quick reflexes that gave him the ability to shoot down planes as they were getting into position to engage him (and even as they were taking off!). Bishop's total was the second-highest number of British air victories at seventy-two, which is amazing when one considers that he flew for little more than a year, from March 1917 to June 1918. (After the war, Bishop became a promoter of Canadian aviation; he died in Florida in 1956.)

Britain's most successful ace, at seventy-three confirmed kills, was not lionized until years after the war, mainly because his reputation rested more on his leadership and tactics than on his individual exploits. Edward "Mick" Mannock was born in Belfast, Ireland, but was working on the Turkish telegraph system in

Three celebrated Allied aces: Canadian William Avery Bishop (ABOVE LEFT, in front of his Nieuport 17), who once shot down twelve enemy aircraft in three days; French sharpshooter René Paul Fonck (ABOVE RIGHT), one of the very few fliers who could shoot enemy pilots out of their cockpits with a sidearm, was credited with seventy-five kills, but may have wounded or neutralized many more pilots; and American Eddie Rickenbacker (BELOW, with his SPAD), who devised the strategy that many able pilots used against the Fokkers.

The Sopwith Camel, Britain's superlative World War I fighter. With most of its weight compressed in a seven-foot (2.1m) span between its two (not three, as erroneously depicted in the comics) wings under a hump (from which it received its name), the Camel could use the torque of the rotary engine to make hairpin turns—but only to the right, a weakness the Central Powers never discovered.

Constantinople when war broke out. He was arrested and treated so badly in prison that he was repatriated in 1915 because of his poor health. Mannock was consumed with a bitter hatred for the Central Powers, which inspired him to lead violent and reckless sorties against German aircraft, showing neither fear nor mercy for enemy fliers. At first, he flew Nieuports, but eventually Mannock commanded a squadron of the advanced S.E. 5a planes known as the "Tiger Squadron." From January to July 26, 1918, this squadron grew to have the same mastery of the skies that the Flying Circus of Baron von Richthofen had enjoyed a year earlier. It was said that Mannock's sorties were so well planned that his Tiger Squadron was never surprised, but this may also be testimony to the enfeebled state of the German air defenses in the last months of the war. Mick Mannock was killed when a stray bullet, shot up from the trenches, hit his fuel tank and his plane exploded.

The two most celebrated American aces in the latter stages of the war (besides Lufbery, who was considered French) were anything but typical of the Americans who flew in the Lafayette Escadrille and in the America Corps. Eddie Rickenbacker was considered old at twenty-seven when he entered flight training, and he and Frank Luke were coarse young men from common backgrounds and with little formal education. Edward Vernon Rickenbacker was born in Columbus, Ohio, in 1890, and was intensely interested in motors and car racing since childhood. Between 1910 and 1917, Rickenbacker gained a reputation as an outstanding race car driver. He had retained the old German spelling of his name—Rickenbacher—and raced in England under the title of

the "Wild Teuton." He was detained several times on suspicion of being a spy, causing him to change the spelling to "Rickenbacker," which he thought sounded less Germanic.

When America entered the war, he returned to the States and went to Washington to lobby for a squadron composed of race car drivers, arguing that such men would be mechanically adept and accustomed to high speeds. He was turned down, but allowed to enlist. For many years, the story had it that he was General Pershing's chauffeur and that Pershing pulled strings to get Eddie into flight school. Rickenbacker never denied the story even though it wasn't quite true: it was Colonel Billy Mitchell for whom he drove and who arranged his flight training at Tours.

Rickenbacker did not fit in at all with the Ivy Leaguers at flight school. He was tough and given to the profane language of the racetrack, and he would not spend time cavorting with the fellows in the local towns. He spent all his time practicing flying Nieuports and studying their mechanisms. He remained a loner throughout the war, focused on the techniques of air combat. Rickenbacker developed a unique fighting style: he would fly high into enemy territory before sunrise and then, when he was about twenty miles (32km) away from the front, turn around as the sun rose and head toward the lines. He used clouds as cover or he would glide some of the way, waiting for German aircraft to take off. Once in the air, the Germans would suddenly find themselves under attack from a plane diving down at them out of the sun or shooting at them from directly behind their tail. This tactic would have been impossible earlier in the war, when his pre-dawn flight would have been challenged near the front.

Rickenbacker flew high and selected his targets carefully, and, with the guidance of Lufbery, commander of the 94th, and flying the latest aircraft, the SPAD XIII, he became the most decorated and most successful ace (twenty-six victories) of the war. He went on to have a distinguished career in aviation, becoming the driving force behind Eastern Airlines.

The second most successful American ace of the war was Frank Luke, Jr., a quiet young loner from Phoenix, Arizona, who had spent his youth working in the copper mines of Arizona and was said to be a first-rate shot with a rifle and a roughneck. Luke gained fame as a crack "balloon buster"—destroyer of observation and spotter balloons—a duty hated by other fliers because of the intense ground fire that protected the blimps. Luke joined

Lieutenant Joe Wehner (also a loner) to become a lethal team in clearing the skies of the Zeppelin aircraft. Flying the newest SPAD XIII, Luke would brave the ground fire to get close enough to shoot or to drop a bomb, while Wehner guarded Luke's plane from rear attack by German fighters.

In September 1918, Wehner went down in combat. Luke was crushed, and on September 29 he set out for what amounted to a suicide mission: to bring down a series of balloons along the front. Knowing Luke was despondent about his friend's death, his commander grounded him. Luke defied the order and took off in another pilot's SPAD. The arrest order followed him up the line as he shot down balloons or stopped to refuel or apprise aviators of what he saw in the air. He was finally forced down in Marvaux behind enemy lines and died with pistol in hand defending his plane from German troops. Luke's final total has never been clear, since he made many kills on unauthorized flights. The official total stands at eighteen. He was posthumously awarded the Congressional Medal of Honor, the only man to receive that medal for actions performed while under house arrest.

The Bombers of World War I

Bombing did not play much of a role in World War I, though the attempt to build planes capable of carrying large loads did advance aviation technology, particularly toward the end of the war. The earliest bombs used in the war weren't bombs at all, but thin steel darts called fléchettes, dropped over soldiers in trenches or on enemy aircraft. The Germans used the Zeppelin effectively in bombing Paris in 1914 (though more as a psychological weapon), and attempted to use Zeppelins to bomb London in May 1915, but the ships were so easy to spot

and bring down, and so costly when lost, that the bombing soon stopped. (In fact, the British had successfully bombed the Zeppelin sheds at Friedrichshafen, but soon determined that it was better to allow the airships to cross the Channel and be shot down over British soil.)

In 1914 the two nations who had the most experience in building the large planes that would be necessary for aerial bombing were Italy and Russia. The Italians had used bombing against the Turks in Libya in 1912 and 1913, and developed the multi-engine twin-fuselage Caproni Ca series, the Ca 45 being the most effective (in part because it was fitted with America's Liberty 400-horsepower engines). The Russians had built huge enclosed-cockpit planes before the war, and some eighty planes of the *Ilya Mouremetz* type flew missions on the Eastern Front.

The British took a dual approach to bombing: they concentrated on increasing their fighter capabilities, hoping to develop a small bomber that had the ability to fend off fighter attack, and they patiently developed larger planes capable of carrying large loads and flying at high altitudes and for long distances. It took a few years, but the British succeeded in both goals.

The de Havilland D.H. 4 was a light bomber that also served as a fighter plane at various stages of the war. It may not have been as agile as the smaller fighters, but with a top speed of 143 miles per hour (230kph) it could hold its own against anything the Germans had and carry a significant bomb load as well. The D.H. 4 was eventually outfitted with the American-made Liberty engine—the plane was even known as the "Liberty Plane"—which enhanced its effectiveness. (The British attempted to

The 11th Squadron—with its famous emblem of the bomb-toting financier on the side of every plane—is pictured here at Maulan, France, in 1918. The 11th Squadron featured the D.H. 4, a medium-range bomber-reconnaissance plane that was dubbed the "Liberty Plane" because it used the 400-hp Liberty engine. The only plane with a U.S.-made engine to enter service, the D.H. 4 was noted for the reliability of its engine and was deployed in overwhelming numbers.

De Havilland D.H. 4

Farman MF 40

Le Pere-Lusac II

Breguet Br 14

SPAD Two-Seater

Caproni Ca 30

create versions of the aircraft that would not take a Liberty engine, but the result, the D.H. 9, was not nearly as powerful or versatile an aircraft as the D.H. 4.)

Toward the end of the war, in retaliation for the desperate German bombing of Paris and London, the British deployed their largest airplane of the war, the Handley Page 0/100, known as the "Bloody Paralyzer." It had a one-hundred-foot (30.5m) wingspan but was easy to transport to forward combat positions because the wings folded easily. It could carry over a ton of bombs, including a single bomb of over sixteen hundred pounds (726.5kg) that could devastate an entire factory. The bombing of Kaiserslautern in October of 1918 and the raids against industrial targets in the Ruhr Valley and the Saarland with very large bombs (convincing the Germans that the planes could carry many such bombs), had a devastating effect on the already crumbling German morale.

The French were also eager to retaliate against the Germans for the bombing of Paris in April 1918. However, the best French bomber, the Breguet 14.B2, could carry only a limited load and was designed to drop its bombs at low speeds, which improved accuracy but made the plane vulnerable to fighter attack. The requirements of a bomber—being able to fly long distances, high and fast enough to evade fighter aircraft yet able to carry a significant bomb load, and reliable enough to go on many bombing missions without significant maintenance—was a tall order for the airplane technology of the day, then only fifteen years old.

But for the Germans, developing a bombing capability was a life-and-death issue. It was the only answer the Germans had to the British command of the high seas and the Allied stranglehold on Europe. If the sky could be used to deprive the British and the French of resources and materials through bombing, the way battleships deprived the continent, the contest would be more even, perhaps even winnable. The prewar development of the Zeppelins had been carried out with this in mind, and

By the end of World War I, airplanes had developed from spindly, haphazardly designed novelties to solid, reliable craft designed for specific mission profiles. FROM TOP TO BOTTOM: The de Havilland D.H. 4 pioneered the practice of building a frame to fit the specifications of an independently designed engine; Farman kept developing wide wingspans to increase the ceiling of reconnaissance aircraft—the MF 40 had a ceiling of ten thousand feet; the Packard Le Pere-Lusac II was the most advanced fighter designed in the war, but of the 4,500 ordered only 27 were built and just 2 deployed before the armistice; the Breguet Br 14 was the first to standardize the use of duralumin in the airframe; the SPAD design team of Bechereau and Birkigt tested a series of variations on the basic S-series design, sometimes improving performance, and sometimes not; the Caproni Ca 30 bomber was one of a large variety of configurations tested (this one featuring a combination tractor-pusher propulsion system that did not work) to improve bombload, accuracy, and armament.

realizing that the strategy was not going to work out must have been one of the most disappointing discoveries in the annals of military history.

As early as the summer of 1915, the Allgemeine Electizitats Gesellschaft (AEG) G-II, a twin-engine biplane, made its first bombing run. The Germans kept developing bomber aircraft throughout the war (while continuing to develop Zeppelins, hoping to come up with a formula or strategy that would make them effective once again). They created the Gotha series of planes, beginning with the the Gotha G.I in 1915 and culminating in the G.IV, the plane that was used in the raids against England and France in 1917. The Gotha G.IV was powered by two Mercedes 260-hp engines and was a remarkably nimble and fast aircraft for its size. The bombing raids on cities in England and France were meant to have a terrorizing and demoralizing effect on the civilian population, but many strategists believed it backfired by hardening citizen resolve.

The Gothas spurred the British into developing the S.E. 5a, the only plane that could climb with the G.IV and fight it on its own terms. The most important and lasting effect of the Gothas, however, was to force the British into creating an independent air force—the Royal Air Force, or the RAF—on April 1, 1918, a date many historians mark as the real beginning of aerial warfare.

The RAF is Born

When the announcement of the formation of the Royal Air Force was made on April 1, 1918, an explanation was given that All Fool's Day was selected as a wry joke on the military leaders who maintained that air power should play a strictly supporting role in connection with ground and naval actions. But the attacks on London were increasing and taking their toll, and the German strategy of countering British naval power with supremacy in the air had become clear. Countering the Gothas and Zeppelins and delivering a retaliatory blow to the Germans both involved air operations away from the theater of battle in France, so no cooperation with infantry movements was possible.

A secret report submitted in October 1917 by General Jan Smuts, military chief of British Union of South Africa, supported the notion of consolidating the various air forces and squadrons of England and forming a single air force operating independently under a cabinet ministry. Almost before anyone could object, the Air Ministry was formed in January 1918, with Lord Rothermere as Secretary of State for Air and General Hugh Trenchard as Chief of the Air Staff. Meetings of the General Staff now included Trenchard, and the air needs of the Empire were as important as its naval or infantry requirements. The announcement of the formation of the RAF was thus a validation of what had already taken place with little

public scrutiny, though the move was greeted happily by a public looking for relief from the threat of German bombing.

The transition did not go smoothly. Rothermere kept trying to placate the generals (mainly Pershing), and Trenchard resigned when his demands for complete independence were brushed aside. He was sent to France to command the Independent Air Force, which combined all Allied air resources under one command (nominally Trenchard's, but actually Pershing's) for the purpose of "carrying the war to the Germans" in a vigorous bombing campaign. Rothermere resigned a few days later, and the two British air services—the Royal Flying Corps (RFC) and the Royal Naval Air Service (RNAS)—which were supposedly consolidated into a single branch of the service on April 1, continued to operate independently.

Back in England, RFC squadrons cleared the skies of German bombers and made preparations for the postwar development of British air power (in terms of flight training facilities, experimental stations, research, development, and testing facilities, etc.). Eager to prove its usefulness, the RFC, now in a transition mode toward consolidation and operating as the RAF, was instrumental in preparing for airmail service between England and the continent, and stepped up its involvement in the Middle East, providing air support to General Allenby in his march to Damascus in September 1918.

The RNAS continued to operate independently as well, launching an attack on the airship hangars at Tondern with Sopwith Camels that took off from the deck of HMS *Furious* in the North Sea on July 19. Yet this service also realized the fundamental soundness of Smuts' proposal and prepared for consolidation. The matter was settled in January 1919, when a strong advocate of air power and consolidation, Winston Churchill, was appointed Air Minister.

THE WOMEN'S ROYAL AIR FORCE

In spite of Ruth Law's disappointment in not being allowed to fly combat missions in World War I, the British actively recruited women into the WRAF: the Women's Royal Air Force. Most of the work required of the volunteers to the WRAF involved the traditional work asked of women—typing, cooking, etc.—yet many women were given duties in the repair and production of aircraft, and in the maintenance of training aircraft (although they received half the pay of men doing the same work). Women seamstresses were particularly important in the manufacture of the linen-covered surfaces of the airplanes.

The WRAF recruited twenty-five thousand women during the war, an important factor in the rise of plane production from 150 to two thousand per month. Although not a single WRAF volunteer flew, the positive experience paved the way for women to take a more active role in aviation in World War II.

Billy Mitchell and the St. Mihiel Offensive

General Pershing had strict principles of command that precluded Trenchard's notions about launching independent assaults on the Germans. Pershing insisted that air operations be directed by him and his air chief, Brigadier General Billy Mitchell. Pershing had few doubts about the potential of air power; if he had, it's doubtful that Mitchell would have risen to the rank of general (through two promotions by Pershing) or that he would have been given the go-ahead for the most ambitious air operation of the war: the September 12–15, 1918, air assault on St. Mihiel.

The importance of St. Mihiel was clear to both sides. It was the southernmost salient of the German advance and it protected the rear flank of Verdun. A break in the Hindenburg line here, and Verdun would be unprotected and the entire Allied defenses would unravel. Knowing this, the Germans amassed significant forces there. Pershing saw that a full-scale Allied assault on St. Mihiel would push through the lines, and that a similar assault farther north would accomplish the same thing. A two-pronged attack—one to the north and the other at St. Mihiel—would break the line and fracture the German army. But could he afford to divide his forces? Mitchell convinced Pershing that air power could make the difference and that a smaller AEF force could take St. Mihiel if he launched a full-scale aerial attack at the same time.

With detailed planning that was to become his hallmark, Mitchell assembled fifteen hundred aircraft, drawn from every Allied air service, and made careful plans for the division of responsibilities in the assault and the objectives of each sortie. Gone was the attitude of simply flying up to meet whatever was waiting. For the first

time, air operations had sequential objectives and fliers had to discipline themselves not to chase solitary German fighters, no matter how tempting. Supply lines were cut, bridges in the rear were blown up, armories were bombed, stables were strafed, artillery emplacements were wiped out, barracks were hit, and key trench nests were eliminated. Soldiers on the ground were now locked in mortal (almost hand-to-hand) combat with the flying machines.

In a four-day operation in which one out five aircraft was used to monitor the progress of the others and direct responses to enemy actions, thirty-three hundred sorties were flown and more than 150,000 pounds (68,100kg) of explosives were dropped. The assault succeeded beyond Mitchell's (and Pershing's) wildest expectations, and the German army was in full retreat even before the Allied ground forces attacked. The British broke through at St. Quentin to the north a few days later (with many more casualties)—and it was over. The war officially ended six weeks later.

Two men observed the Mitchell operation and were to remember it for a long time. One was a good friend of Mitchell's, Lieutenant Colonel George Patton, who drove his tank into St. Mihiel after the third day of the operation, ahead of his own troops, and was amazed and delighted to discover the place virtually deserted, the Germans in full flight. The other was the man who had taken over command of the Flying Circus after Richthofen's death, a flier with twenty-two kills to his credit and a recipient of the Blue Max who would, in 1935, become the chief of the German Luftwaffe under the Nazis: Hermann Göring.

The Fokker Dr I and the Sopwith Camel: Studies in Elegance and Limits

The two planes that to many had the greatest impact in World War I were the Sopwith Camel and the Fokker Dr I. The names and images of these planes are virtually emblematic of World War I aviation. It is interesting to note that they were both the product of one mind: Thomas Sopwith. (The Dr I was copied very liberally from the design features of the Sopwith Triplane, a fact that Anthony Fokker never denied.)

What was so special about these planes? Both were quite small and compact, and both were extremely unstable in flight, requiring constant vigilance on the part of the pilot. It would have been impossible for a pilot to operate both the controls of the plane and a machine gun without Fokker's interrupter mechanism. In this sense, the planes were a vindication of the approach created by Otto Lilienthal and championed by the Wright brothers: that the pilot must actively fly an airplane and not simply ride it as a passenger.

The Camel's secret was in the way Sopwith crammed all the weight of the plane in as small a space as possible. The hump was not an accident; it was necessary to allow the pilot to bend his knees so he could put his feet on the rudder bar, and still keep the gun, the ammunition, and the engine all within a volume of only a few cubic feet. About fifty-five hundred Camels were built, bringing down 2,790 enemy aircraft, the best such ratio of any plane in the war. The Camel was often described as "inelegant" because of its hump, but watching a Camel in flight, as it responded to the controls as if reading the pilot's mind, it is no wonder that it is considered by fliers the most graceful plane ever built.

The Fokker Dr I was, of course, the plane made famous by Manfred von Richthofen, the Red Baron. Both sides in the war had experimented with multi-wing planes because the configuration offered the promise of great control with short wingspan, a definite plus for a fighter.

The problem was how to make such an aircraft structurally sound: the wings had to be kept in rigid relationship with one another or the plane would respond wildly and unpredictably to the controls. Sopwith availed himself of the standard solution, namely securing the wings with wires. He also staggered the wings to maximize lift.

Fokker copied the lines of the Sopwith plane, but then added an important innovation: he relied on cantilevered wings—meaning wings supported in flight entirely by their structural connection to the fuselage—and a single steel vertical strut to keep the wings together. The Dr I was thus one of the first planes to dispense entirely with guy wires and cross struts, which is why it has an astonishingly clean and modern look. In the hands of a capable pilot, the Dr I was as agile as any plane of the war, perhaps of all time (at that speed, one must add). The Dr I, especially the version delivered to Richthofen, was also one of the most difficult planes to master. These had a fourth airfoil in the undercarriage that helped the aircraft climb, but also added a number of ways for going into a tailspin. Not surprisingly, only about 320 were built.

The two planes illustrate a problem in airplane design that was to crop up again and again throughout the century (and is every bit as much a concern today): how to keep the performance capabilities of an aircraft within the limits of a pilot's flying skills. There is little point in designing airplanes that no one can fly; in the most advanced modern fighter aircraft, the forces on a pilot during certain maneuvers are deadly. For quite a few years after the war, the Camel and the Dr I were considered to have performed in the greatest harmony with the limits of pilot skill—to some people, that never stopped being the case.

This photograph shows the Fokker Dr I triplane and the Sopwith Camel. For many, these planes represented the ultimate combat aircraft, the piloting of which was the perfect blend of human skill and machine capabilities.

Chapter 5

Barnstormers, Trailblazers, and Daredevils

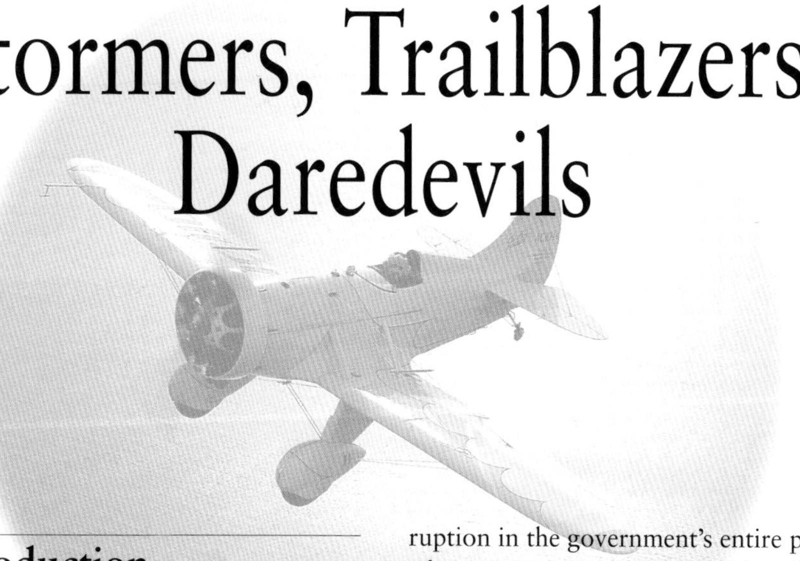

Introduction

The twenty years from 1919 to 1939 are known as the Golden Years of aviation. These two decades constituted the period of the great flights, the great races, the great heroes, and the great tragedies. Designers and builders set out to create planes that could perform better than the one they had created the night before; aviators climbed aboard and set out to cross oceans, set records, or win trophies, even after somebody else beat them to it; and entrepreneurs set out to turn flying into a profitable industry, even after it was clear there was no end to the ocean of red ink they were flying over. Through it all, however—and this is perhaps why the age deserves to be called "golden"—people were never satisfied to let things be; they were not satisfied with what they had accomplished. Through the 1920s, when the world thought all things might be possible, and through the 1930s, when the world shuddered in fear at what might yet be possible, the men and women of flight never gave up, never called it a day.

After the Great War ended, Europe and America stepped back and gasped at the human toll the war had taken. Nearly every country was depleted of resources; people turned away in anger and disgust from everything military, including aviation. Factories shut down and a great many workers sought other jobs, many in the growing automobile industry. The air services were cut back to skeleton strength, and governments made a sober determination that aviation had made a minimal contribution to the war effort, certainly not warranting the kind of money spent. To make matters worse, a congressional investigation after the war into why America contributed so little (and so late) to the air war exposed rampant cor-

ruption in the government's entire procurement and manufacturing apparatus—something the public was in no mood for. In the eyes of many, aviation was cast right back to where it had been a decade earlier.

But a number of factors helped pull aviation out of these dog days. First, there were a great many planes around. In the United States alone, the Curtiss Company had produced ten thousand JN-4s and JN-4Ds, known as "Jennies" (or "Canucks" if manufactured in Canada), all paid for by the U.S. government and now idle in storage hangars all over the country. These planes were not great performing aircraft and were shoddily put together, but they were cheap (especially when new ones were sold as war surplus) and parts were available (from cannibalized models, if need be). Similar numbers of aircraft were strewn all over Europe—many German fliers had simply been given the planes they were flying at the time of the armistice, and England had been in the middle of a major bomber-building program when the war ended.

Along with the undeployed planes were the unemployed fliers. Since it was difficult to know if a flier had the skill and nerve it took to be an ace until he was tested in battle, both sides had ambitious training programs in full swing when the war abruptly ended. Tens of thousands of young fliers were produced, and were now never going to be assigned to an air squadron. For many, this was good news and they joyously returned home. But for quite a few others, once having tasted the thrill of flying, they were simply unable to return home to their humdrum jobs.

Finally, public sentiment notwithstanding, the major nations knew that air power was not something to be ignored. The armistice expressly forbade Germany from certain kinds of aviation activity, but the enthusiasm with which the Germans pursued the flying allowed them

Glenn Curtiss understood the promotional benefits offered by stunt fliers, and as a result had a crew of brave pilots to barnstorm around the country. The survivor of numerous crashes, Charles "Daredevil" Hamilton, pictured here at the wheel of his plane, was one of these aerial acrobats.

made it clear that Germany had every intention of building an air force when (not "if") it rearmed. Some important theoretical aerodynamics had come out of Germany, prompting England and the United States to increase their research and experimentation budgets.

In the last year of the war, the first unsteady steps were taken to make some practical non-military use of the airplane. The U.S. Post Office carried mail, first between Washington, Philadelphia, and New York in May 1918, then to Chicago a year later, and on to California by September 1920. Similar operations got underway in Europe as soon as the war was over. Passenger flights (mainly for diplomats at first) began between European capitals, and the first commercial flights were already up and running by mid-1919, spearheaded by the Germans. The governments of England and Germany (and, to a lesser extent, Russia) all looked to convert the large bombers they never got to deploy into passenger aircraft and thereby recoup some of the cost of developing and building them.

But these benefits would not have captured public interest, and flying as a viable means of public transportation would not have been taken seriously for decades, had it not been for a strange breed of flier: the barnstormers and daredevils who dotted the landscape of America and Europe giving many thousands of people their first experience with flying and keeping the public enthralled with the magic of flight. Out of the actions of these self-admitted lunatics came the impetus for the great distance and endurance flights of the era, the celebrated races that engaged the best engineering talents of many nations, and most important, the willingness on the part of an ordinary person to pay for a ticket, step onto an airplane, and fly somewhere.

Ormer Locklear and the "Lunatics"

Aerobatics were a part of flying from the start: they were certainly an important element of Lilienthal's career. The Wrights indulged in aerobatics, though they probably would have bristled at the suggestion that they were having any fun at it. Curtiss, a seasoned racer, understood the entertainment potential of flying and fielded an exhibition team around 1909. One of his fliers, Charles "Daredevil" Hamilton, survived sixty-three crashes, only to die in bed of tuberculosis in 1914 at the age of twenty-eight. (Hamilton's observations about his 1911 flights in Mexico with Roland Garros and the Moisant Brothers first alerted tacticians to the military uses of airplanes.)

Before the war, planes were limited in the maneuvers they could perform and fliers were still grappling with the basics of flying. The feats of Adolphe Pegoud captured the imagination of many young fliers and spurred them on to try stunts neither they nor the planes were prepared to do. One such flier was Lincoln Beachey, a member of

the Curtiss team whose stubborn determination made him the most daring and celebrated of the prewar fliers. Beachey is credited with dispensing once and for all with the forward elevators of the Curtiss planes; he once set an altitude record (of 11,642 feet [3,548.5m]) by simply climbing until he ran out of fuel and then gliding back to the ground with a dead engine. His stubbornness resulted in many crashes, and he must have had a very high threshold for pain to have survived some of them.

Dressed in a pinstripe suit, a high collar, and fancy tie, and wearing a large golf cap turned backwards, Beachey would fly close to the ground, let go of the controls and wave to the crowd; he would loop over and over, getting closer to the grandstands with each loop; or fly under, through, or around bridges, streets, hangars open at both ends, and even inside large exhibition halls. His most famous stunt was to fly over Niagara Falls, dive down toward the foam below and pull up in the mist just as he was about to crash into the river, then fly under a bridge and land, dripping wet and smiling to the crowd of 150,000. In 1914, after a brief retirement, Beachey toured the country racing autoracer Barney Oldfield ("The Daredevil of the Air" vs. "The Demon of the Ground") in front of large audiences. Beachey died on March 14, 1915, performing a stunt near the San Francisco pier as part of the Panama-Pacific Exposition.

After World War I, aviators were to be found almost everywhere in the American countryside. These young fliers often slept out in the field under the wings of their machines, and frequently they would offer a ride in return for a meal or enough gasoline to get them to the next town. They had to learn how to fix their own machines, and they frequently came up with novel solutions to problems. They performed ever more complex

Lincoln Beachey in his signature flying attire.

and dangerous stunts because the jaded public demanded it. Some barnstormers traveled with an ambulance that would simply drive through the town with its siren blaring, leading customers to the airfield.

In time, fliers pooled their resources and formed little troupes, and sometimes the best partnerships were formed when a flier and a talented promoter joined forces. One such team became the most successful barnstorming act of the postwar period—the flier Ormer Leslie Locklear and the promoter William Pickens. Locklear had been trained at the Army Air Service flight school at Barron Field, near Fort Worth, Texas, and was performing stunts on the wings of his Jenny even while in the service. Wingwalking was not new in 1918; it was not unheard of that a pilot or passenger would (if he absolutely had to) climb out onto a wing to make a timely repair or pry loose a stubborn control surface. But Locklear took the practice to new levels, devising new stunts that seemed aimed at nothing less than tempting fate. He perfected the use of the over-wing struts on the Jenny as a brace for wingwalking; spectators who never noticed the structures before thought they were made specifically for Locklear.

When Locklear met Pickens in 1919, the promoter already had a great deal of experience promoting barnstormers like Lincoln Beachey and some postwar fliers, but from the very beginning Pickens knew he was going to have his greatest success with Locklear. Jumping from one plane to another was Locklear's trademark stunt, and then, when the public tired of that, he worked on jumping from a car to a plane and from a plane to car. Locklear was severely injured in some of the earlier attempts of this stunt, but Pickens used that (and exaggerated bandages) to heighten the drama and stir public interest. One stunt of Locklear's, the "Dance of Death," is difficult to believe and is probably the most thrilling aerial stunt ever performed. Locklear would pilot one plane and fly right next to a second plane, with the two aircraft almost touching wings. At a signal, with the con-

trols locked in place, the two pilots would change places, passing each other as they scampered across the wings!

Locklear and Pickens became wealthy and lived in high style, in contrast to the poverty of most other barnstormers. They became even more successful when they brought the act to Los Angeles and came to the attention of the movie-making community. After several highly publicized exhibitions at an airfield owned by Sydney Chaplin, Charlie Chaplin's brother, Pickens arranged for Locklear to appear as a stunt man in Universal's *The Great Air Robbery* in 1920, and an offer was made by Twentieth Century Fox for a feature film, *The Skywayman*. Locklear took to Hollywood very well. He became a hit. Buzzing the lot, he perfected a maneuver in which he ricocheted off the roof of the sound stages, calling it the "Locklear Bounce," and he romanced a rising young actress at Metro, Viola Dana (though he had a wife back in Texas).

During the filming of *The Skywayman*, Locklear insisted on performing his stunts as realistically as possible, including those scripted to take place at night (and forgoing the device of using filters to make daytime scenes appear as though shot at night). On August 2, 1920, while filming one of the night scenes, Locklear was apparently blinded by a spotlight; the Jenny went into a tailspin and crashed. Locklear received what might be called a gala Hollywood funeral (complete with Viola weeping, alone in her limousine).

Locklear had made the entire enterprise respectable and profitable, and with the help of the hundreds of fliers who flew for meal money, he rekindled the nation's interest in flying. After January 1920, however, many fliers moved south and saw their fortunes take an immediate turn for the better. The passage of the Eighteenth Amendment—Prohibition—had provided them with a new source of income: using their planes to smuggle liquor from Mexico into the United States. One barnstorming troupe operated out of Dallas, Texas, under the name "The Lunatics of Love Field," managed by the irrepressible Floyd "Slats" Rogers. Rogers would conduct air shows in the afternoon and send one of the planes across the border for a shipment of whiskey. If Slats suspected a government agent was in the crowd, he would have the plane smuggling in the contraband join the stunt or formation as if it had been stunt-flying all along.

The Lunatics operated successfully until Congress passed the Air Commerce Act of 1926. The law called for the licensing of aircraft and pilots, and laid down strict rules about the kinds of stunts fliers could perform. Ironically, the law was passed at the insistence of the fledgling air transport industry, who saw the barnstormers as fostering the idea that flying was dangerous and difficult—which, of course, is the whole idea behind barnstorming in the first place.

The Mad (and Organized) Science of Wingwalking

The Air Commerce Act thinned out the ranks of barnstormers, but it did not eliminate the profession. In fact, the regulations forced fliers to join together to form "flying circuses" that could manage the aircraft and comply with regulations. This meant that barnstorming could become a business with its own political clout.

One of the more successful flying circuses was operated by Major Ivan Gates, a World War I veteran (but not, as he claimed, of the Air Service). Gates had a temper of mammoth proportions—he was prone to simply punching people in the jaw if he disagreed with anything they said. Gates had been running a flying circus based at Teterboro Airport in New Jersey, close to the plants that manufactured Fokker aircraft and Whirlwind engines. In addition to Jennies, he used planes manufactured by the Standard Aircraft Company of Plainfield, New Jersey. He fancied himself the P.T. Barnum of flying and sought the sponsorship of different aircraft companies, not realizing that they looked askance at his entire operation. He finally struck a deal with the Texas Company to receive free fuel in return for painting TEXACO on the wings and fuselages of his airplanes. (There were periods when the company withdrew its sponsorship, but Gates astutely kept the brand name on the planes to give him a big-business appearance.)

Gates faced only one problem: how to keep pilots from walking out on him. The answer was Clyde Edward

Mabel Cody, niece of Wild West showman Buffalo Bill Cody, became an international celebrity when—on her 113th attempt—she leaped from an airborne glider being towed by a speedboat to a ladder dangling from the bottom of an airplane flown by A.B. McMullen.

Pangborn, whom Gates met in 1922. Pangborn was the exact opposite of Gates—reserved, dignified, and professional. He had worked as an engineer in Idaho when he entered the Army in the war and became a flight instructor in Texas. He performed stunts along the Pacific Coast, but his total inability to promote himself resulted in thin crowds and meager receipts. Gates heard about a stunt Pangborn had attempted involving jumping from a speeding car to a ladder dangling from a plane. The stunt went badly and Pangborn was seriously injured when he missed the ladder. After rolling and bouncing on the ground, obviously seriously hurt, Pangborn leapt to his feet and bowed grandly to the crowd—then he collapsed and spent the next two months in the hospital. If this wasn't just the sort of man Gates was looking for, who was?

Pangborn's specialty was flying upside down—he went by the name "Upside Down Pangborn." Performing stunts from a Jenny flying in this odd position was particularly difficult because the plane had a tendency to cut out when upside down. Pangborn's feats became more and more complex, and more expensive to perform, and of greater interest to fliers and aircraft people than to the thrill-seeking public. But Gates never objected, because by 1924 Pangborn was a full partner in the circus, and because he realized that it was only the respect the pilots had for Pangborn that prevented them from bolting.

The Gates Circus spawned many others that crisscrossed the country through the late 1920s and into the 1930s. Competing against the Gates Circus was never easy, however, and some of the stunts involved near-suicidal pyrotechnics, in-flight explosives, or headlong crashes into burning buildings. Many featured women fliers: the Doug Davis Baby Ruth Flying Circus (sponsored by the candy bar) featured Mabel Cody, a niece of the famed Buffalo Bill Cody and an accomplished stuntwoman; the

LEFT: *Clyde Pangborn began as a daredevil and barnstormer, but eventually made several pioneering flights, such as the first trans-Pacific flight, from Japan to the United States, in October 1931.* RIGHT: *Meanwhile, daredevil wingwalkers (like Ivan Unger and Gladys Roy of the Flying Black Hats, shown playing tennis on a wing in 1925) had to keep coming up with new stunts to satisfy their public.* BACKGROUND: *Al Wilson and Virginia Brown Fair are "spooning on a wing" in a 1924 stunt.*

Ruth Law Flying Circus featured the famed woman aviator standing erect on the top wing, her arms akimbo, while the airplane performed a loop. (As was the case with other wingwalkers who performed this striking stunt, she was fixed to the wing by wires that ran up her pant legs.) An all-black flying circus, the Five Blackbirds, headed by "Colonel" Hubert Julian, toured the West and Southwest in the early 1930s. A group of Hollywood stunt fliers banded together in 1925 and performed under the name The 13 Black Cats and performed to large crowds for nearly four years.

The Gates Circus reached its pinnacle in 1928 with the addition of Aaron Krantz, who first flew under the name Diavalo, a generic name Gates had given fliers other than Pangborn (to save him the expense of reprinting fliers when a named flier was injured or died), and then under the name A.F. Krantz, the Master Daredevil. In Krantz's case, this was not an exaggeration. Krantz did trapeze stunts dangling from the bottom of the plane, hung by his teeth and twirled, and brought the art of wingwalking to new heights.

The government targeted the flying circuses (and the Gates Circus in particular), viewing them as public hazards and obstacles to the development of commercial aviation. But the flying circuses served to advance aviation as well: they were the training ground for the next generation of fliers—both Charles Lindbergh and Wiley Post flew in the flying circus, Lindbergh being personally trained by Pangborn (and flying for Gates under the name The Flying Fool). A number of flying techniques were pioneered by stunt fliers—the first in-flight refueling was performed by barnstormer Frank Hawks in 1921. And an engineer or designer could count on a barn-

stormer to test most any newfangled device in return for a few parts or a repair.

Gates did everything he could to prove to the government inspectors that his planes were safe and his pilots were competent. He even had Charles H. Day, designer of the Standard, vouch for him. But the commission was adamant and the inspectors closed down many Gates performances, sometimes with large angry crowds of ticket-holders waiting at the gate. When, after a wildly successful tour in 1928, Texaco was pressured to withdraw its sponsorship (and insisted that its name be taken off the planes), the Gates Circus was doomed. Pangborn decided to throw in the towel and became a commercial pilot, entering the limelight again in historic crossings of the Pacific Ocean. The Gates Circus closed down in 1928; four years later, a broke and broken Ivan Gates committed suicide, leaping to his death from a New York apartment window.

In 1929 the government confiscated all Jennies and destroyed them, and declared most Standards unfit to fly (whether they were or not). A few flying circuses operated between 1929 and 1938, but the regulations for them were so harsh and limitations on the stunts so severe, that only a few could operate legally and at a profit. The most successful circus of this period was The Flying Aces Air Circus, operated by Jimmie and Jessie Woods and featuring a daredevil race car driver named Rocky Moran. The aerial stunts involved maneuvers of a trimotor airplane—either the Ford "Tin Goose" or the Fokker Trimotor—and while these planes were excellent flying machines, they did not dip and turn with the same excitement as the old Jennies. (For one thing, they flew faster, so turns were wider, higher, and more difficult to follow; and wingwalking had to be performed too high to be appreciated or even seen.)

The Civil Aeronautics Act of 1938 put an end to the flying circus for good. The airlines and manufacturers had had their say, but there could be little doubt that the barnstormers and the circuses had made their contribution. The nation had clearly taken flying back to its bosom, and this reacquaintance was responsible for several successful major motion pictures being made with spectacular flight sequences. The first Academy Award for Best Picture had been won in 1927 by *Wings*, a tale of World War I fighter aviation. It would have been more than fitting if the recipient of that Oscar had thanked the barnstormers of the 1920s.

Saner Uses for an Aircraft: Gliding and Soaring

Ironically, the attempts of the Allies to eliminate the threat of a rebuilt German air force by outlawing anything resembling fighter aircraft development had the effect of helping Germany to advance in aviation and to prepare for the next air war. Deprived of using power plants on their aircraft, the Germans turned to gliding and took the science of aerodynamics to new heights. Many of the pilots and designers of fighters used in World War II had their initiation into flight through gliders. In just the same way as the restrictions of the Schneider Cup races of the mid-1920s forced builders to push the performance of their planes to new levels, the need to deal with the special problems of gliding allowed the Germans to develop the science of aerodynamics and the new technology, all of which would be put to military use sooner or later.

The leading German theoretician in the postwar period was Ludwig Prandtl, a physicist who created an entire school for aerodynamic research at Gottingen that served as the center of theoretical aerodynamics for thirty years after World War I. Prandtl developed a theory that described the aerodynamics of the wing more accurately than ever before. This theory was named after two prewar scientists, the German Wilhelm Kutta and the Russian Nikolai Jukowski, but Prandtl's initiation into the theory was from a British scientist, Frederick W. Lanchester, who visited Gottingen in 1908 and spoke to Prandtl at length about his theory of aerodynamics.

Lanchester's work had grown out of the work of Francis Wenham, a mid-nineteenth-century theoretician who is credited with the invention of the wind tunnel. Lanchester's work was published in 1907, but it was presented in so complex a manner that it was ignored (just as Cayley's had been a century before). Fortunately, when Lanchester spoke to Prandtl, he used Prandtl's student, Theodore von Karman, as interpreter. Von Karman was

to become the leading theoretician in the United States for decades following his emigration in 1926; he knew firsthand exactly what level German aerodynamic science had reached and how the gliders being experimented with could yield results useful for the design of military aircraft. By the mid-1930s, the United States could do nothing to stop the German effort, but instead embarked on a research program of its own. When the Nazis announced in 1935 that they were rebuilding an air force and that they would catch up to the United States and England in two months, the general public pooh-poohed the claim and ascribed it to Nazi propaganda, but insiders knew that all the work done in gliding (and in commercial aircraft development) had been aimed from the start at rebuilding the Luftwaffe, and that the boast was not an idle one.

Top designers applied the theory known in Germany as the Kutta-Jukowski theory and in England as the Lanchester-Prandtl theory to the gliders, and devised new structures and configurations for airfoils. It was as if the days of Percy Pilcher and the Wright brothers had returned. It was out of glider design theory that Alexander Lippish discovered the advantages of the delta wing and the flying wing, configurations that would play an important role in jet-age aircraft design. An entire generation of pilots and designers was learning the vagaries of the wind and air currents in gliders light enough to respond to up- and downdrafts. Willy Messerschmitt began his career in aviation as a glider pilot-designer, adapting glider flight technology readily to fighter aircraft.

The hub of German glider activity was Mount Wasserkuppe in the Rhone Mountains, which from 1920 on was spearheaded by Oscar Ursinus, an aviation magazine editor, and builder-pilot Wolfgang Klemperer (called the "father of modern soaring"). Meets and races were held at Wasserkuppe, and records seemed to be shattered on an almost daily basis. To get an idea of the intensity of this activity, in 1918 the record glider flight was still the nine minutes and forty-five seconds of Orville Wright's 1911 glide at Kitty Hawk; by 1922, record glides had passed the three-hour mark and the record distance stood at 313 miles (503.5km). (In the thirties, gliders were required to carry passports before taking off, since there was no telling how far and across which borders they would sail.) The glider fad became an absolute frenzy and German obsession in 1926, when pilot Max Kegel discovered that flying into a cumulus cloud would propel the craft upward through the cloud. As long as the glider was sturdy enough to hold together through the turbulence, the pilot could "soar" over virtually limitless distances. Flying the *Darmstadt*, designed by Professor Walter Georgii (who managed a permanent laboratory atop Mount Wasserkuppe), much-celebrated Austrian glider pilot Robert Kronfeld captured the *Daily Mail* prize for the first glider crossing of the English Channel in 1931.

In the United States, gliding was not pursued until 1928, when J.C. Penney, Jr., son of the chain-store tycoon, sponsored an exhibition at Corn Hill near Provincetown on Cape Cod, where conditions were similar to those in the Rhone Mountains. The Department of Commerce, then in the middle of its war on the barnstormers, issued a long list of regulations regarding soaring and the structure of gliders, but these turned out to be unnecessary. The enthusiasts of gliding were of a different breed, interested primarily in the joy and freedom of flying and not in aerobatics. Major aircraft manufacturers supported glider meets and manufacture, and the foremost aviators and builders—Earhart, Rickenbacker, Fokker, Moffett—lent their support to the sport. The outstanding glider in the United States was Hawley Bowlus, a former mechanic at the Ryan Aviation Company who had supervised the building of *The Spirit of St. Louis,* Charles Lindbergh's historic airplane. Bowlus flew on the West Coast and got the Lindberghs interested in gliding, which did much to popularize the sport.

In 1930 Wolfgang Klemperer, a recent emigré to the United States who worked in Akron for the Goodyear Zeppelin Corporation, was asked to help organize a gliding and soaring exhibition and to choose the best site for it. With the help of his protégé, Jack O'Meara, Klemperer selected a site in the Chemung River Valley near Elmira, New York. Thanks in part to many corporate sponsorships, the annual glider exhibitions drew large crowds who came to see such well-known fliers and barnstormers as Frank Hawks and Charles "Casey" Jones put the silent aircraft through their paces. The sport was further boosted when another young millionaire, Richard C. DuPont, entered the sport and convinced his family to put up large prizes for soaring events. DuPont teamed up with Bowlus to form a company that built gliders, and out of it came a series of aircraft with a distinctive, compact design that influenced all future gliders built in the United States. (DuPont was killed in 1939 in a crash of a glider he was flying for the U.S. Air Corps in preparation for use in World War II.)

The Germans never lost their supremacy in glider flight in the years before World War II, but their designs and exhibition flights were more and more geared to eventual military application. The gliders built in the United States, especially the all-metal gliders built by the Schweizer brothers in their Elmira factory, were

For some, Robert Kronfeld, given to toying with storm fronts and thunder clouds in a glider, was the most daring flier since Lilienthal. Here he stands next to the glider in which he won the Daily Mail *prize in 1931 for the first glider crossing of the English Channel. Because there were reports that an unofficial glider pilot had beat him to the punch by a few hours, Kronfeld crossed the channel twice in the same day for good measure.*

BARNSTORMERS, TRAILBLAZERS, AND DAREDEVILS

to become the standard for decades of glider design. Through the thirties, Western Europe watched Germany with apprehension, uneasily suspecting that its scattered aviation program would come together in some deadly way. Meanwhile, an estimated 200,000 glider pilots were registered in Germany when Hitler came to power. They would prove to be a deadly and valuable resource for the Nazis in the next war.

The Airplane Sets Out to Sea— The Schneider Cup

Jacques Schneider, the son of a French arms manufacturer, became infected with the flying bug around 1910 and became one of the officials in the French government responsible for the development of aviation. Schneider decided that since so much of the earth was covered with water, and major cities were located on ocean shores or along rivers, airplanes should develop the ability to land on water, on pontoons (seaplanes) or on hulled fuselages (flying boats).

In order to move aviation in this direction, Schneider created an international competition—the Coupe d'Aviation Maritime Jacques Schneider, or the Schneider Cup (actually a silver trophy and not a cup). The rules of the Schneider competition reflected his intent, although in a sometimes bizarre way: planes had to float on the water for six hours and prove their seaworthiness by traveling a distance of about 550 yards (503m) on water. Twice during the flight portion, planes had to land on the water (or "come in contact with" the water, the wording of which stipulation gave rise to a bouncing maneuver invented by Pixton in 1919 that cut time from the race). If the pontoons took on water, the planes had to continue the flight portion with the added weight. The rules called for the trophy to go permanently to the country that won three consecutive competitions; each competition was to be held in and managed by the country currently holding the trophy.

Two contests were held before World War I—in 1913 and 1914—both off the coast of Monaco. The planes raced in these years were land planes fitted with clumsy pontoons haphazardly attached to the underside of the fuselage. Maurice Prevost, the French pilot who won the first race in a Deperdussin, was the only pilot to finish, his pontoons heavy with water by the time he crossed the finish line. The following year, Tom Sopwith and Harry Hawker brought to the race a Tabloid plane equipped with pontoons and piloted by Howard Pixton. Pixton's bounce won the race for the British, though the French were quick to point out that the Tabloid used a French-built Gnome engine and that Pixton's bounce maneuver was largely responsible for his nearly halving the previous year's time.

The sleek lines of the British Supermarine S5 (ABOVE) and of the other 1927 Schneider Cup planes (BACKGROUND) make it apparent how much the war had accelerated aircraft design. Unfortunately, the planes did not taxi well on water and had to be towed by boat to the starting line.

The race was suspended during the war and resumed in 1919 at Bournemouth near the Isle of Wight off the English coast. The race was a fiasco—the facilities were inadequate, and a British ploy that confused the Italian entrant into flying the wrong course resulted in the lone finisher, the Italian Guido Janello, being disqualified. The International Aeronautic Federation (FAI—for Fédération Aéronautique Internationale), the French administrators of the competition, appeased the incensed Italians and moved the race to Venice in 1920. The Italians had their revenge by pressing the FAI to add a weight requirement on the planes. By this time, the Italians had developed powerful (but slow) flying boats and a weight requirement favored their aircraft. They won handily in 1920 and 1921 against a thin field.

The 1921 race was held at Naples, and the French and British fielded several teams, determined to prevent an Italian victory. The winner was Henri Biard of England, flying the Supermarine *Sea Lion II*, a flying boat that had crashed in the 1919 race. The race was a close one, and the pilot of the technologically inferior British plane (in spite of some inspired modifications by R.J. Mitchell) won by sheer piloting skill. Reports of the race were followed around the world and the Schneider Trophy was once again the premier aviation competition.

The average speed for the race had climbed from eighty-six miles per hour (138.5kph) in 1914 to 106 miles per hour (170.5kph) in 1920 to 146 miles per hour (235kph) in 1922. It was not fully appreciated at the time, but the obstacles and hardships of the Schneider races actually helped rather than hindered the development of faster aircraft. The mere fact that a more powerful engine was required to overcome the handicap of the pontoons made for designs that would, when adapted to land, allow for the setting of new speed records. The very long take-off afforded by the water allowed for smaller wings and thus less drag. And pilots flying over water were more daring and more prone to push their aircraft to its limits, being able to ditch in the sea in the event of trouble.

The 1923 race was won by Lieutenant David Rittenhouse of the United States, flying a Curtiss CR-3. Several new elements had entered the race. The Americans were now supported by the U.S Army and Navy, who saw the race as an opportunity to test and develop aircraft. The entire atmosphere of the race became more professional and the American team trained long and hard on a variety of aircraft. But the most important change was in the plane itself. The engine used in the Curtiss CR-3 was a newly developed CD-12 (for "Curtiss Direct Drive"), which used a cooling system invented by Charles B. Kirkham, employing a technology developed by the Swiss engineer Mark Birkigt. Instead of cooling the engine with an independent cooling system of tubes that carried heat away from areas remote from the sleeves that generated the heat, Kirkham created an engine out of a solid block of metal that allowed the

coolant to flow onto the sleeves directly. This was known as the wetsleeve-monobloc engine, and it was to revolutionize aircraft design. The power-to-weight ratio went from 1:2 for the most efficient previous engines to an astounding 1:1.5. It also took up less space, which allowed a sleeker design. Rittenhouse won his race at a record average speed of 177 miles per hour (285kph), yet anyone feeling his radiator would have discovered that it was stone cold—the cooling system had kept the engine running virtually at the ambient temperature.

The United States agreed to cancel the 1924 race (to give the competition a chance to further advance their designs) and hosted the 1925 race off Baltimore. The Italians brought a flying boat, hoping the choppy seas of Chesapeake Bay would damage the lighter seaplanes, and the British brought monoplanes using the cantilevered designs pioneered by the German aircraft builder Hugo Junkers in a plane designed by Reginald J. Mitchell—the Supermarine S4. The European planes had the edge technologically on the American planes (even after the S4 crashed in the prerace trials), but the hairpin turns and expert flying of Lieutenant James Harold "Jimmy" Doolittle gave the United States its second win, with an average speed of 232.6 miles per hour (374kph).

Both the British and the Italians were determined to prevent a third American victory; by now they had discovered the secret of the wetsleeve-monobloc and had abandoned flying boats for sleek single-wing seaplanes. In 1926 Mario de Bernardi of Italy won, flying a Macchi M39 with a Fiat engine and averaging 246.5 miles per hour (396.5kph). The M39 was the brainchild of the great designer Mario Castoldi, who left a sickbed (some

The requirement that the Schneider planes be seaworthy (BELOW, 1929 Italian entries undergo tests at sea) was viewed by the British as having great military significance. The Supermarine S6 (LEFT) was the plane in which Henry Waghorn broke the 300 mile-per-hour (480kph) mark in 1929, establishing British domination of the competition.

reports had it that he was forced out by Mussolini, who was intent on winning the race) to design the plane. The plane incorporated all the engine and design features of previous planes, and added unequaled aerodynamic sleekness to the fuselage and the pontoons. The plane and the win bolstered Italy's prestige in the aviation community, and it also meant that the race would continue.

The 1927, 1929, and 1931 races (now officially made biannual) were won by the British, who thus captured permanent possession of the trophy. The planes that won were all Supermarines—the S5, S6, and S6B, respectively—designed by Mitchell and equipped with "R" engines that were developed by Sir Henry Royce of Rolls-Royce and were capable of delivering 1,500 horsepower. The average speeds of the final three British wins—281.6, 328.6, and 340 miles per hour (453, 528, and 547kph)— shows clearly enough how fast planes had become and how far aviation had come since the war.

Mario Castaldi's planes performed excellently in the 1927 and 1929 races; a crash in the testing of the Castaldi plane that was to race in 1931 left the British unopposed, and by this point the FAI did not want to postpone the race. In pretrial flights, the Macchi M-planes consistently set new speed records, culminating in 1934 when a Castoldi-designed MC72 set a record of an astonishing 440.68 miles per hour (705kph). The universal opinion was that the Schneider competition had compressed twenty years of aircraft research into only six. Reginald Mitchell spent the last years of his life (he discovered in 1935 that he had cancer and only a few months to live) heroically cajoling the British government into using what had been learned in the Schneider races and adapting the basic design of the Supermarine in order to create one of the most important fighter planes of World War II, the Spitfire. Jacques Schneider had in the meantime died (in 1928). His family's arms business had

been driven into bankruptcy and he died flat broke, leaving behind only the name of the most important aviation competition of the interwar period.

The Great Races

In the United States, racing began with the Los Angeles meet of January 1910, in which Glenn Curtiss and Louis Paulhan were the big winners. Paulhan was again victorious in the grueling London-to-Manchester race in which he beat a heroic effort by the British aviator Claude Grahame-White. It seemed, in fact, that Grahame-White made more capital out of losing than Paulhan did winning. Although he was a relative newcomer, Grahame-White won the Gordon-Bennett trophy at Belmont Park, Long Island, in October 1910, making him an international celebrity.

After Rheims, a series of races were held across Europe—Paris to Rome; and circuits in France-Belgium and in England—pitting, for the most part, Andre Beaumont against Roland Garros. Here, too, Garros seemed to make more out of losing each time than Beaumont did winning. Garros finally won the races held in Monaco in August 1914, a year after the first Schneider Cup event, and then went on to be first to cross the Mediterranean.

The war curtailed racing in Europe, and in the United States the vigorous litigation by the Wrights against anyone they thought was infringing on their patents put a damper on racing and on flying in general. After World War I, the sons of newspaper tycoon Joseph Pulitzer established the Pulitzer Trophy races in 1920. The huge turnout at Mitchell Field, New York, proved that interest was still there. A crowded field—thirty-seven planes staggered just two minutes apart, which meant nearly all of

Glenn Curtiss continued designing and building planes in the 1920s for racing and exploring. The Oriole, among the most popular, was a versatile and inexpensive plane that could fly a good race one day, deliver mail the next, and fly the Arctic the day after.

them were on the 116-mile (186.5km) course at the same time during most of the race—circled the course three times, with the winner, Corliss C. Mosley, in a Verville-Packard biplane.

The first man to congratulate Mosley was Billy Mitchell, now a hero of the war and at this point still highly respected in military aviation circles. Mitchell sold the armed services on the value of the Pulitzer (and other races) as a means of improving aircraft design and flying technique. During much of the twenties, the army and navy participated extensively in racing, and they often flew Curtiss racing planes, which became a profitable portion of Curtiss' business.

The next Pulitzer races were held in 1921 in Omaha, and the event was part of a larger cavalcade of aviation races and displays called the National Air Congress. These meets developed into annual events that eventually came to be called the National Air Races. Many design innovations had their first testing at the Nationals, and some of the better aircraft went on to race in the Schneider or in other races. The Curtiss R3C-2 racer that Jimmy Doolittle flew to victory at the Schneider races in 1925 had been flown (minus the pontoons) at the 1924 Nationals by Cyrus Bettis, who walked off with the Pulitzer that year.

Along with the planes, many a flier's reputation was made at these events and many pilots became household names of the period. Bert Acosta, a Curtiss test pilot, became famous for winning the 1921 Pulitzer in record time (177 mph), and the 1922 races saw the introduction of the Thomas-More monoplane, the first all-metal plane constructed in the United States (though the race was won by Russell Maughan flying a Curtiss racer and setting another world speed record of 220 miles per hour [354kph]). Two well-known former barnstormers, Casey Jones flying his trademark Curtiss Oriole, and Charles "Speed" Holman flying a Laird biplane, became even more famous for winning the 1924 and 1927 cross-country "derby" races to the site of the nationals.

From 1928 to 1932, the National Air Races were directed by Clifford Henderson, a dapper and dashing figure who was a master at promotion and organization. A healthy rivalry developed between the army and the navy, and between civilian aircraft and the government planes, a rivalry that Henderson exploited to the fullest. Henderson's extravaganzas were filled with constant action, dignitaries and celebrities, and music and spectacle. (None other than Charles Lindbergh flew in a stunt-flying act at the 1929 Nationals, when one of the fliers was killed in an accident!) The early races held in Cleveland went so well that all but two held in the 1930s were in Cleveland and the city became the air-racing capital of the United States. In 1929 Henderson introduced the first women's race, the Women's Air Derby (which Will Rogers later dubbed the "Powder Puff Derby"), and "race horse" starts, in which planes began all at once

Wiley Post is seen here with Winnie Mae, *the Lockheed Vega aircraft in which he made his legendary round-the-world flights. Air races (such as the 1925 Army-Navy contest at Mitchell Field,* BACKGROUND) *tested planes of many designs and capabilities with a clear view to eventual military application.*

from a starting line instead of racing against the times of their competitors flying separately. The race gave rise to the sport-within-a-sport of "pylon polishing" (seeing who could fly closest to the pylon on the turn without hitting it), which the crowd found nearly as enthralling as the race. Being a pylon judge was definitely not a job for the squeamish.

In 1929 Henderson also convinced manufacturer Charles E. Thompson to sponsor a new Trophy event—a fifty-mile (80.5km) race open to all aircraft. The Thompson Trophy became the premier air-racing event of the 1930s, bringing a whole new cast of intriguing dark horses into the spotlight, all trying to beat the army and navy planes. The 1929 Thompson race was won by Douglas Davis, flying a Travel Air "Mystery" plane. (The mystery turned out to be that the plane had a Whirlwind engine, thought to be too bulky for racing.) The big news coming out of the race was that for the first time a civilian plane had beaten a government plane in a race. To make matters worse, the third-place finisher was also a civilian: Roscoe Turner flying a Lockheed Vega.

The 1930 Thompson Trophy introduced the aviation world to Benjamin O. "Benny" Howard, an airmail flier who built his own aircraft, a racer marked DGA-3 (which Howard said stood for "Damn Good Airplane") and which Howard called *Pete*. Howard and *Pete* would become fixtures at the Nationals throughout the 1930s, though Howard never won a trophy. The year 1930 also saw the debut of an unknown barnstormer with a patch over one eye, Wiley Post, who flew a Lockheed Vega called *Winnie Mae*. The field that year was rich in planes and pilots that would ultimately become legendary in aviation history: Speed Holman flying Emil "Matty" Laird's *Solution* (which had not been completed until hours before the start of the race, and had been test-flown for all of ten minutes), Frank Hawks in one of two Travel

The Gee Bee R2 (LEFT) in which Jimmy Doolittle won the Thompson Trophy in 1932 (BELOW), with a record speed of 296 miles per hour (474kph). Doolittle then quit racing, claiming the Gee Bee was too dangerous to fly. (Later analysis showed that the odd weight distribution made it virtually impossible to control the plane once it went into any sort of roll.)

Air "Mystery" planes built by Walter Beech, and several others. The favorite plane that year was a Navy Curtiss Sea Hawk, with a 700-horsepower Curtiss Conqueror engine. However, the navy plane crashed and Holman won the race. (In 1931, Holman was killed in a crash while stunting in Omaha.)

The 1931 Thompson competition saw the unveiling of one of the most unusual aircraft ever to fly: the Gee Bee. The name stood for the Granville Brothers, a small airplane manufacturer in Springfield, Massachusetts. The designer, Bob Hall, had no experience designing racing planes, and the final design looked like a bad drafting mistake—as if someone had forgotten to draw in the back half of the aircraft. Amazingly, the Gee Bee flown by Lowell Bayles beat Jimmy Doolittle flying a Laird Super-Solution and took the Thompson home. Doolittle was impressed, and the next year he flew a Gee Bee and won the Thompson. The experience must have been a harrowing one, though, because not only did Doolittle never again fly a Gee Bee, but he also became a staunch opponent of air racing and testified before Congress to have it banned.

In truth, the Gee Bee was configured as it was because it housed an enormous Pratt & Whitney Wasp engine. The plane was notoriously unstable and structurally fickle; every Gee Bee ever built crashed sooner or later. Bayles, the 1931 Thompson winner, crashed after the competition trying to set a land speed record in the aircraft (which is how Doolittle got to fly the plane in the

ABOVE: Roscoe Turner accepting his third Thompson Trophy in 1939. Though he became a showman and a flamboyant businessman, the Thompson victories attested to his great skill as an aviator.

first place). And in 1934, Zantford "Granny" Granville died when a Gee Bee he was flying to a customer crashed. That's when Edward Granville discontinued the line.

In 1931, a fourth major race, the Bendix Trophy, joined the Schneider, Pulitzer, and Thompson as the prestige races of the period. The Bendix was no more than the cross-country race to the Nationals that was held informally every year. The big winners of the Bendix included Benny Howard, who won it and the Thompson

Jimmy Doolittle on a pontoon of the plane in which he won the 1925 Schneider Cup. The Curtiss Racer set new standards for clean, sleek lines and for speed, beating its nearest competitor by over 32 miles per hour (52kph).

in 1935, his banner year; Jimmy Doolittle; and Roscoe Turner, ever the showman, winning it flying with his pet lion cub.

The Bendix was taken very seriously because it was a race that related directly to the desire to use aviation to traverse the vast distances of the United States. It encouraged cross-country speed flights by non-contestants that extended the capabilities of long-distance flight. Frank Hawks and the Lindberghs established cross-country records in the early 1930s, the latter proving in their Lockheed Sirius that airplanes could fly best high over storms in the rarefied atmosphere above fifteen thousand feet (4,572m). All these records were to fall, however, when a brash young movie producer named Howard Hughes, flying an open-cockpit Northrop Gamma H-1 mail plane (which he had personally enhanced by installing a powerful Wasp engine), established records on an almost yearly basis in the early to mid-1930s, culminating in his January 1937 flight from Los Angeles to Newark in seven hours, twenty-eight minutes, and twenty-five seconds.

The Women Who Dared the Skies

During World War I, some flight schools discovered something that has been noted by air force training programs throughout the century: women make exceptional flight instructors, particularly for male pilots. (The theory is that the cockier male pilots are less stubborn and confrontational with a woman instructor, and are more receptive to criticism and instruction from her than from a man.) The Stinson family of San Antonio, Texas, were all fliers and the flying school they founded there trained many Canadian pilots who went on to serve in the British Royal Flying Corps. Marjorie took care of the school

(becoming a legendary flight instructor), while Katherine supported the school with stunt flying. Both sisters toured the country, flying in exhibitions for Liberty Bonds and the Red Cross, and Katherine was sent on a goodwill tour of Japan and China, where she stunned men and women alike with her stunt flying and her liberal attitudes. Katherine's flight from San Diego to San Francisco in 1917 set a nonstop long-distance record—for men or women—of 610 miles (981.5km). The Stinson sisters retired from aviation shortly after the war, but their brother Eddie continued flying and became a builder of airplanes that were widely used in the airmail service in the interwar period.

The other great woman aviator of the war years was Ruth Law, also from a family of aviators. Law was a very competitive individual, likely to try anything just because someone told her she couldn't do it. Just such a dare was responsible for her being the first woman to perform a loop in 1915. She competed in several altitude and distance events, sometimes winning and setting records, but always being greeted by adoring crowds and always demanding that she be evaluated on the same basis as male fliers. At America's entry into World War I, Law applied to the United States Army to fly combat missions. She bristled when she was turned down and wrote an article for *Air Travel* ("Let Women Fly!") that inspired many future women aviators. After the war, Ruth Law formed a flying circus and became one of the most successful barnstormers of the 1920s. She retired from flying after one of her women stunt flyers, Laura Bromwell, was killed in a stunt.

One of the women inspired by Law was Pheobe Omlie, who became one of the greatest barnstormers of the postwar period and was the first woman awarded a pilot's license. Omlie crusaded for safety markers to assist aerial navigation and, with the help of fliers Blanche Noyes and Louise Thade, flew around the country identifying the best locations for directional markers. Omlie was appointed by President Roosevelt to the National Advisory Committee for Aeronautics (NACA), making her the first woman to hold a government post in the field of aviation.

A Frenchwoman named Adrienne Bolland was the first to fly a plane from Argentina to Peru across the treacherous Andes Mountains in 1921. It would be seven years before anything comparable was attempted by women aviators. Many of the women who performed great feats of flying and who won races against all competitors resented being singled out as women and being praised for flying so well "for a woman."

This attitude is evident in the reaction of women fliers to the career of Ruth Elder. Elder was a capable flier who placed high in the competitive Women's Air Derby of 1929. In 1927 she announced that she would attempt a crossing of the Atlantic with her flight instructor, George Haldeman. The feat was clearly a publicity stunt (as much for the Stinson Detroiter aircraft they were flying as for Elder) and she named the airplane *American Girl.* In the eyes of other women fliers, the photos and the entire project were a throwback to the days when women were thought to be incapable of flying. At the urging of many women aviators, a second woman flier, Frances Grayson, entered the field, flying a Sikorsky amphibian, *Dawn.* But the aircraft of 1927 were not prepared for such a trip—something the extraordinary flight of Lindbergh earlier only highlighted—and Elder and Halderman were forced to ditch their Stinson short of the Azores, near a tanker that rescued them. Grayson, who insisted on taking the North Atlantic route instead of the longer but safer South Atlantic course to Europe, was not as fortunate. She took off from the coast of Newfoundland on December 23 and was never heard from again.

A similar conflict surrounded the career of Elinor Smith, an outstanding flier by any standards, who broke records both individually and with her fellow woman flier, Evelyn "Bobbi" Trout. The two fliers teamed up in 1929 and became well-known for establishing an endurance record and for performing the first in-flight refueling by women fliers. In the thirties, Smith billed herself as the "Flying Flapper" and was widely photographed by newspapers modeling clothes near airplanes. This did not sit well with other women aviators.

One prominent barnstormer of the early 1920s was confronted with an additional barrier: race. Bessie Coleman was born in 1893 in Texas to a poor black family, but managed to enter college. When she could

no longer afford to stay in college, she moved to Chicago and decided to try to learn to fly. After asking virtually every flight instructor in the country and being turned down (and having built a successful business in Chicago), she went to France and earned a pilot's license. She returned to the United States and began a barnstorming career that spread her fame throughout the Midwest. Coleman purposely flew a Nieuport (a military plane) and wore military clothes to emphasize that she could fly a plane as well as any military pilot.

The participation of the preeminent women aviators in the 1929 Women's Air Derby, held at that year's Nationals, advanced the cause of women's aviation. The contestants were all accomplished fliers and record holders: Amelia Earhart; Ruth Elder; Marvel Crosson (sister of the famed Arctic flier Joe Crosson and the only fatality of the race); Blanche Noyes; Thea Rasche, the famed German woman aviator; Bobbi Trout; Florence "Pancho" Barnes, acknowledged to be one of the greatest Hollywood stunt pilots and speed racers, male or female, of the day; Ruth Nichols; and the Australian long-distance flier Jesse Miller. The course was a long and hard one, and there was evidence that resentful individuals had tampered with some of the equipment. The winner, Louise (McPhetridge) Thaden, already a simultaneous holder of speed, altitude, and endurance records for women fliers, was now catapulted into the public spotlight and became a hero to women everywhere.

Another positive result of the Women's Air Derby was the formation of an association of women fliers called the Ninety-Nines (after the number of charter members) which had Amelia Earhart as its first president. The Ninety-Nines promoted women's aviation by lobbying for women to be allowed to enter air races (women had been barred in 1930 because of the death of Crosson, but were allowed back the following year), and by publishing

Some great women of flight (FROM LEFT): *Katherine Stinson in 1916; Ruth Law, the woman who came closest to flying combat missions for the Allies in World War I, in 1919; and Elinor Smith, an endurance champ who flew out of Roosevelt Field, New York, in 1929.* BACKGROUND: *"Ninety-Nines" gather to applaud Amelia Earhart's successful 1935 flight across the Pacific.*

BARNSTORMERS, TRAILBLAZERS, AND DAREDEVILS

Louise Thadden (ABOVE) was among the most accomplished aviators of her day, wining the 1936 Bendix Trophy in a Beechcraft Model 17 Staggerwing. Ruth Nichols (ABOVE RIGHT) seems overdressed to pilot her Vega for a 1931 test flight, but she was as rugged and determined as any flier of the period. Bessie Coleman (RIGHT, in a 1923 photo) became the first black woman aviator, but she had to go to England to get her license.

The 99-er, a magazine highlighting the latest developments in aviation and the careers of women fliers.

Probably the greatest triumph in aviation for women during this period—even more important than the exploits of the great long-distance fliers—was the victory of Louise Thaden and Blanche Noyes in winning the Bendix Trophy in 1936. The pair flew a new design from Beechcraft, the Model 17 Staggerwing, a biplane with the lower wing forward of the upper wing (instead of the other way around, as was the case with most biplanes). They completed the course hours before their nearest competitor. The victory had an electrifying effect on women's aviation; the victory of Jacqueline Cochran in the 1938 Bendix race was possible only because of the Thaden-Noyes victory two years earlier.

One could get a rousing argument going about who was the best woman flier of the Golden Age, but there wouldn't be much disagreement about who was the grittiest: that would be Ruth Nichols. Nichols was born into a wealthy family and attended the finest schools; she was expected to enter high society and take her place in the Social Register. Because of her blue-blood background,

she was called the "Flying Debutante" by the press, a name she hated.

As a graduation present, her stockbroker father treated her to a ride in a barnstormer's airplane, and as she would write years later, "I haven't come down to earth since." While vacationing in Florida during a break from her studies at Wellesley, she took lessons from a barnstormer named Harry Rogers, and she soon abandoned plans to enter medical school and took up flying. Her big break came when Rogers asked her to be his copilot in an attempt at a record-setting run from New York to Miami in 1928. She was instantly propelled into the spotlight and was able to dedicate herself to flying full-time. She became a spokesperson for the Fairchild Airplane and Engine Company and toured the country in her trademark custom-made purple leather flight suit and helmet.

With a Lockheed Vega borrowed from radio manufacturer Powel Crosley, and coached by Charles Chamberlain, the noted test pilot for Whirlwind, Nichols set several records in cross-country flying and altitude in preparation for a solo flight to Paris along Lindbergh's route. Naming the plane the *Akita* (an Indian word meaning "to explore"), she took off from New York on June 22, 1931, to cross the Atlantic. Instead of stopping to refuel in Portland, Maine, she went to an alternate site, St. John, New Brunswick, with which she was unfamiliar. The runway was too short for so fast a plane and the Lockheed plowed into the forest at the end of the field. Nichols was badly injured—she cracked five vertebrae— and was told it would be a year before she could fly again, and even then only with a thick steel body brace.

But only a month later, Nichols was supervising the repairs to the *Akita* and, still in her plaster cast, preparing to take another run at the Atlantic. The weather would not cooperate and, after a month's delay, she decided instead to try to beat the nonstop solo overland distance record of 1,849 miles (2,958.4km) set by French flier Maryse Bastie. This time, there would be nothing left to chance. She flew from New York to California, stopping at each potential landing site along the way to become familiar with the runways and the terrain. She took off from Oakland and made it as far as Louisville, Kentucky, short of her goal but still just breaking Bastie's record. As she took off to finish her journey, a leaking valve caught fire. Nichols managed to land the plane and, now in her heavy and cumbersome steel body brace, to climb out and leap clear just as the plane exploded. The *Akita* was demolished, and thus ended Nichols' plans to cross the Atlantic.

"Putty" and "Nancy"—Albert Read and the Flight of the NC-4

World War I put many aviation plans on hold, which was probably just as well. Had it not been for the war, many more fliers would have tried crossing the Atlantic and would have been claimed by its icy waters. The planes of 1913 were not capable of the nearly nineteen-hundred-mile (3,057km) flight between Newfoundland and Ireland, the shortest route across the Atlantic, nor of the twenty to thirty hours of reliable continuous operation that would be required by any engine that would power such a plane.

In England, Alfred, Lord Northcliffe, publisher of the London *Daily Mail*, had offered a prize in 1913 of fifty thousand dollars to the first aviator to cross the Atlantic. Northcliffe had offered other prizes—it was in pursuit of Northcliffe prizes that Blériot had crossed the English Channel and Paulhan had flown from London to Manchester—but this was considered the ultimate prize, and almost as soon as it was announced, various groups in different countries prepared to try for it. Northcliffe

realized how difficult this feat would be in 1913. In the original rules, the plane making the Atlantic crossing was allowed to land on the water along the way, could be refueled in the Azores, and even towed for repairs, as long as the flight continued from the point of touch-down. The only plane with any real chance of making the flight would have to be a seaplane, and at that time the best seaplanes were being manufactured by Glenn Curtiss.

While in England looking for buyers of his planes, Curtiss met British naval commander John Cyril Porte, who apprised him of the Northcliffe challenge and even found him a financial backer in Rodman Wanamaker, the Philadelphia merchant millionaire. (Porte, who was stricken with tuberculosis and didn't expect to live very long, even offered to fly the plane across the Atlantic!) Curtiss began testing his seaboat designs back on Keuka Lake and by February 1914 had a gangly-looking aircraft that he calculated would be able (just) to make the crossing.

The aircraft was one of the largest built to that time, with a forty-five-foot (13.5m) podlike hull, 126-foot (38.5m) bi-wings, and three large engines, the entire aircraft weighed more than twenty-eight thousand pounds (12,712kg). Curtiss built two models and prepared to fly one, dubbed *America*, to Newfoundland for the trans-Atlantic launching, which after many delays was set for August 15, 1914. The outbreak of war on August 4 made the flight of the *America* impossible, but the British Admiralty was so impressed with the performance of the planes that it ordered sixty of them for submarine patrol.

By the end of the war, several things had changed. Curtiss was now building planes in partnership with the U.S. Navy—the planes were thus designated NC for "Navy-Curtiss" and soon came to be called "Nancies"—in a larger plant in Buffalo, New York. The planes were now outfitted with four powerful Liberty engines, the only advance made in American aviation during the war. And Curtiss and navy engineers, under the supervision of G.C. Westervelt, designed a stronger, lighter, more

Curtiss was triumphant again in December 1918, when the U.S. Navy unveiled the NC seaplane. With a wingspan of 125 feet (38.1m), it was among the most formidable planes then in the air.

streamlined hull. In 1919 the *Daily Mail* renewed the prize, though it changed some of the rules (to eliminate, it seemed to many, the NC planes from contention.) Now the flight had to be nonstop and without refueling or landing on water or at the Azores. The navy decided (with strenuous lobbying by Assistant Secretary of the Navy Franklin Roosevelt) to attempt the trans-Atlantic flight anyway "for scientific purposes."

A squadron of three Nancies took off from Rockaway, New York, for the first leg of the trip to Trepassey Bay, Newfoundland, on May 8, 1919. The lead craft, NC-3, was piloted by a crew of six commanded by John H. Towers, a famous Curtiss-trained Navy flier who had been scheduled to fly the *America* in 1913. The NC-1 was commanded by Patrick N.L. Bellinger, also a famous flier, and the NC-4 was commanded by Albert C. "Putty" Read. (The NC-2 had been used for spare parts for the other three ships.) Read, a quiet New Englander who earned his nickname because his face rarely showed any emotion, was, at five-foot-four, the most unlikely looking hero of the group and was not expected to finish.

In fact, the NC-4 went down eighty miles (128.5km) off the Massachusetts coast with a broken connecting rod and had to taxi through the night to the naval station at Chatham. It took six days for the repairs to be completed and for Read to resume the flight, but he still managed to catch up to Towers and Bellinger, who had been fogged in, and the three planes took off on May 16 in *V* forma-

tion. The route was marked by a string of twenty-five navy destroyers spaced fifty miles (80.5km) apart. Problems plagued the NC-1 and the NC-3 almost from the start and, at one point, with both their radios unable to transmit and the fog making navigation all but impossible, both Towers and Bellinger decided to put down to get their bearing and attempt repairs.

Both aircraft were badly damaged in landing and for them the flight was over. The crew of the NC-1 was picked up by a Greek freighter, but Towers and the NC-3 were not spotted and the plane drifted for nearly three days. Fighting sixty-mile-per-hour (96.5kph) gales and rough seas, hoping that as they were floating backward they were being blown toward the Azores, and requiring a crew member to climb out to the end of a wing and hang on for most of the sixty-hour ordeal in order to balance the craft after a portion of the wing on the other side broke off, the NC-3 finally limped into Horta Harbor in the Azores. (Ironically, the element of the entire mission that drew the most notice from aviators was Towers' seamanship and not Read's airmanship. Far more powerful land-planes were already in existence and in just a few weeks, one would complete a nonstop crossing of the Atlantic. But Towers had shown that the sea could be counted on as a safety buffer for a plane that went down over the ocean. It led to the rise of the great flying boats as the primary intercontinental transport aircraft of the 1930s.)

Meanwhile, Read and his crew flew the NC-4 to the Azores, arriving on May 17. They waited there anxiously for the NC-3 as they repaired the NC-4 and prepared for the next leg of the trip to Lisbon, Portugal. Read knew that word of his success would reach two crews back in Newfoundland who would race to launch their aircraft and still beat him to England—although not by air—(demonstrating that the *Daily Mail* money was not all

that important to the aviators.) One was the Sopwith team, flying a biplane called *Atlantic*, and piloted by Harry Hawker and Kenneth Mackenzie Grieve; the other, the Martinside team of Frederick P. Raynham and William Morgan, flying a biplane called the *Raymor* (a combination of the aviators' names).

The *Atlantic* took off first on May 18 and the *Raymor* followed two hours later. The *Raymor* never made it aloft; a gust tipped the overloaded aircraft on takeoff, crushing a wheel, and the plane dug nose-first into a bog, a total loss. The *Atlantic* did little better: the radiator clogged and the engine started overheating over the mid-Atlantic. An hour into the flight, Hawker knew he wasn't going to make it. In a bit of inspired airmanship, Hawker headed south toward the shipping lanes, hoping to spot a freighter he could ditch near, while he bobbed up and down trying to air-cool the engine. He spotted a ship that turned out to be a Danish freighter with no radio and he put the *Atlantic* down. Hawker and Grieve were rescued (and, amazingly, so was the floating *Atlantic* a few days later), but there was no way of getting word to England until the ship reached British waters on May 25. Hawker and Grieve arrived in London just as the memorial ceremony honoring their martyrdom was concluding.

With both challengers out of the running, Read took his time and set out for Lisbon on May 25. He landed on May 27, completing the first crossing of the Atlantic by an airplane. Two days later, Read took off again (Towers refused to relieve Read of command of the NC-4, even though navy protocol would have allowed him to do so) and landed in Plymouth, England, on May 31. The success of Read and the NC-4 was hailed by the British and the French no less than by the Americans. All three countries, in fact, heaped medals and accolades on the crew of the NC-4. What puzzled Read, though, was that he arrived in England in the middle of a similar celebration of the accomplishment of Hawker and Grieve. (Read had to ask several times to make sure he got it right, that the pair had failed to cross the Atlantic by air. What made

matters even more confusing was that the *Daily Mail* awarded the pair a twenty-five-thousand-dollar consolation prize; Read and his crew were offered nothing.)

The flight of the NC-4 was quickly forgotten: a nonstop flight across the Atlantic was only a few weeks away and the great flights of the next decade eclipsed the accomplishment of Read and his crew. Even at the time, few newspapers covered the flight (admittedly difficult for reporters to keep up with), and the most extensive reporting on the operation was filed by a Yale undergraduate for the *Yale Graphic*. The reporter was named Juan Terry Trippe, and he would later become the creator of Pan American Airways and pioneer the great flights of the clipper flying boats to South America. For many years, the NC-4 was stored in a forgotten hangar and gathered dust; it was even broken up into several pieces and stored in a number of places. Read died in relative obscurity in 1967 near Washington, D.C., but he lived long enough to see the NC-4 restored after World War II, and to see his contribution to aviation history remembered and acknowledged.

Alcock and Brown Take the Atlantic

Back in Newfoundland, two teams worked feverishly to finish assembling their planes and testing their equipment in preparation for what they considered the ultimate prize: the still unclaimed *Daily Mail* prize of fifty thousand dollars for the first nonstop crossing of the Atlantic. One team had a clear head start: the Handley Page team headed by Admiral Mark Kerr. The Handley Page V/1500 "Berlin Bomber" was the largest aircraft built by the Allies during the war, and was equipped with four powerful Rolls-Royce engines. The plane and crew were making preparations to fly the Atlantic almost from the beginning. They watched Hawker and Grieve begin their ill-fated trans-Atlantic flight; Alcock and Brown had also heard about the failed attempt of the *Shamrock*, which had gone down while crossing from England to Ireland in the first stage of an east-to-west crossing; and they had been there when the navy group passed through on their way to the successful crossing (with stops) of the Atlantic. The plane enjoyed the best airfield and the best accommodations, and for some of the time, had the only fuel on the island. Afterward, Handley Page executives would wonder what had kept their plane on the ground.

By the time the final plane and its crew arrived in Newfoundland on May 26, the Handley Page had been tested and repaired many times. In what might be considered typical of the naval approach, Admiral Kerr seemed determined not to attempt the flight until his plane was in perfect condition. The last plane to arrive was the *Vickers Vimy*, a night bomber built too late to be used in the war. The Vickers engineers replaced the bombs with fuel tanks, quickly disassembled the plane, and shipped it to Newfoundland. The crew for the flight was headed by Captain John Alcock of the Royal Air Force, and the navigator was Lieutenant Arthur Whitten Brown of the Royal Flying Service. Both men had spent the last years of the war in a German prison camp and had very limited flying experience, especially with so large a plane. (Brown, as it turned out, had been an observer when he was shot down, and had taught himself aerial navigation while a prisoner. He had almost no experience as a navigator before the flight of the *Vimy*.)

The *Vimy* was assembled in an open field (there was no available hangar big enough) in cold and often rainy weather. Miraculously (and with the help of a gifted local mechanic named Lester), the plane was ready after only fourteen days—Kerr was waiting for a new radiator to replace one on the Handley Page that "wasn't quite up to snuff." What Kerr did not know, but Alcock realized, was that the problem was not with the radiator, but with the water. Using local water, the Handley Page radiator kept clogging—which was exactly what had brought Harry Hawker down—because of the heavy mineral content and sediment. To counter this, Alcock had the water filtered several times and boiled (and then cooled), so that the radiator would not clog. On the morning of June 14, while the Handley Page team was preparing for yet another test, Alcock and Brown took off.

The flight of the *Vimy* was a difficult one. Brown had to climb out onto the wings six times during the flight to chip off ice that formed there. Several times, Alcock had to fly precariously close to the ocean, hoping that the warmer air of the lower altitude would melt the ice that kept clogging the engine. And on at least two occasions, Brown made what he thought would be a last entry into the flight log and stuffed it into his shirt, hoping his experience would be of use to later aviators if his body were ever found.

Sixteen and a half hours later, on the morning of June 15, the *Vimy* landed in a bog near the installation at Clifden, in Ireland. People on the ground tried to wave them off from the bog and direct them to a landing field that was prepared for aircraft; Alcock and Brown just waved cheerfully back. Before taking off, Brown had removed a front nose wheel from the plane in the hopes of reducing weight and drag. Now, without the front wheel, the *Vimy* landed in the bog and simply plowed its nose into the soft mud. Local people and soldiers ran up to the plane and asked Alcock where he had flown from. When he said they had flown across the Atlantic, the crowd broke out in laughter.

Alcock and Brown's historic 1919 flight ended ingloriously, as the Vimy *plowed into an Irish bog—its front landing gear had been removed before the flight. The first people to greet the aviators thought they were joking when they claimed they had just flown across the Atlantic.*

The outgoing John Alcock (RIGHT) and the diffident Arthur Whitten Brown—both of Manchester, England—had the right combination of skills to win the Daily Mail *prize for the first flight across the Atlantic, outclassing better-funded teams.*

England erupted in celebration. Alcock and Brown were knighted by King George V and awarded the Northcliffe prize by the Secretary of State for War and Air, Winston Churchill. Alcock and Brown toured England and were praised from banquet to banquet. But Alcock was killed in a crash in December 1919, and Brown never flew again (though he lived till after World War II). Back in Newfoundland, Kerr decided he would attempt some sort of land record instead and flew to the United States. The Handley Page crashed near Cleveland, Ohio, and while the crew survived, the Berlin Bomber was a total loss, marking the end of Admiral Kerr's brief career in aviation.

Alcock and Brown's crossing of the Atlantic was to have a profound effect on two men who up to this point had not done much flying. One was a navy lieutenant named Richard E. Byrd, a dashing young flier trained at the navy's Pensacola Flight School. During the war, Byrd had volunteered to fly bombers built in the United States to England, and when the war ended, before any such ferrying could take place, he formally requested to be part of the crew that would fly a Nancy across the Atlantic. Byrd could not know that such plans were already afoot, so when he was called to Washington he was disappointed to discover that he was not being asked to fly the planes, but to take command of the naval air station in Nova Scotia to scout out a suitable stop for a possible trans-Atlantic flight by the U.S. Navy. Later he

discovered that foreign service (even in Canada) disqualified him from being a member of the NC crews.

The other man was a Frenchman who had worked his way up from being a shepherd in France to being a waiter to, by 1919, being the owner of two fashionable Manhattan hotels. His name was Raymond Orteig, and he had no connection to the world of aviation. But watching the prizes of postwar aviation being garnered by England and the United States, and seeing France fall by the wayside, he sent a letter to the president of the Aero Club of America, dated May 22, 1919: "Gentlemen: As a stimulus to the courageous aviators, I desire to offer, through the auspices and regulations of the Aero Club of America, a prize of twenty-five thousand dollars to the first aviator of any Allied country crossing the Atlantic in one flight, from Paris to New York or New York to Paris, all other details in your care. Yours very sincerely, [signed] Raymond Orteig."

Orteig made no secret of his motive: he hoped the prize would prove an incentive to French fliers and would lead to France's once again being a first-rank nation in aviation. In the original rules, a five-year limit was set (it was later extended), and there was no stipulation that it had to be a solo flight—that was Lindbergh's idea (as a way of lightening the load).

The year 1919 saw yet a third crossing of the Atlantic, this one in July by a British dirigible, the R.34, a virtual carbon copy of a captured German Zeppelin (called, as it happened, the L.33). The crossing was, in fact, a two-way transatlantic flight, making the R.34 the first aircraft to cross the Atlantic both ways. The flight from Scotland to New York was not without its harrowing moments. The weather was bad the entire trip over, and at one point a crew member had to parachute out of the airship to direct the ground crew. But the airship created a sensation in New York and heralded the beginning of regular airship service over the Atlantic. (The crossing back to Europe took only three days.)

The Atlantic Strikes Back

During the five years of Raymond Orteig's challenge, there were no serious contenders for the prize, so he renewed the challenge for another five years. The first serious entrants into the contest (fliers wishing to be considered had to first register with the Aero Club of America) were, as Orteig had hoped, French. Two veterans of the war wounded in action, French ace Paul Tarascon and François Coli, outfitted a Poletz biplane for the flight during the summer of 1925. They planned to drop the wheeled undercarriage after taking off and land on skids on a golf course in Rye, just north of New York City. Racing against them was another French team flying a Farman Goliath bomber that had set an endurance record of forty hours in the air. The Poletz, trying to duplicate the endurance record of the Goliath, crashed and exploded; the crew just barely escaped with their lives.

In the United States, a captain of the Air Service Reserve, Homer M. Berry, decided he would take a crack at the prize, and he organized a company for that purpose, Argonauts, Inc., with the help of New Hampshire paper magnate Robert Jackson. Berry and Jackson then contracted with the recent emigré Igor Sikorsky to build a plane that could make the trans-Atlantic flight. Sikorsky had just fled the Russian Revolution and, with the help of some illustrious refugees (like Sergei Rachmaninoff), was establishing an aircraft manufacturing business on American soil. By the end of 1925, Sikorsky had constructed for the Argonauts the S-35, a huge biplane with a 101-foot (31m) wingspan and weighing nine tons (8t) when fully fueled (but without crew and cargo); it was

at first powered by two Liberty engines, then by three Gnome-Rhone Jupiter 450-hp engines.

Sikorsky built and serviced the plane—now named *New York-Paris*—at Roosevelt Field on Long Island, New York, and all of New York (it seemed), including the flamboyant mayor, Jimmy Walker, came out to watch the plane put through its paces. Berry no doubt thought that he would pilot the plane, but late in 1925 the legendary French ace René Fonck visited the hangar where the S-35 was being built. He made it clear to the Argonauts that he would welcome an invitation to fly the plane, and the Argonauts happily obliged, making Berry the copilot. Fonck made all sorts of demands on the design of the plane itself, including insisting that the fifteen-foot (4.5m) cabin be decorated in red satin, gold fittings, and mahogany and leather paneling. All this irked Sikorsky, who was depending on the S-35 to make

TOP RIGHT: The favorites to win the Orteig Prize in 1926 were Igor Sikorsky (far left) and Captain René Fonck (far right), who are seen here being visited by the assistant secretaries of war, Trubie Danison and (to his left) William McCracken. TOP LEFT: Fonck was frequently photographed in the cockpit of the S-35 wearing anything but flying togs. ABOVE: The S-35 was among the most advanced aircraft of its day, and in the opinion of most experts would be able to make the trans-Atlantic flight to Paris with little difficulty. And yet....

his reputation, but Fonck, aside from being a hero of the war, had been instrumental in procuring the Jupiter engines. The crew had grown to five, and at the last minute Berry was forced out in favor of a navigator supplied by the U.S. Navy.

Finally, after anticipation had risen to a fever pitch, the date for the take-off was set for September 21, 1926, if weather permitted. Thousands of New Yorkers lined the field to witness this historic moment. Fonck led the grand procession to the plane, and all the crew had baggage and gifts loaded onto the plane. Fonck was given a basket of croissants by Orteig, which he cheerfully tossed into the cabin. Sikorsky watched nervously and estimated that the gross weight of the plane was well over fourteen tons (12.5t)—more than ten thousand pounds (4,540kg) over specifications. Later there would be some question whether Sikorsky said anything to Fonck, but at the time it probably would not have mattered. Fonck and the others were completely caught up in the moment.

During take-off, a wheel on the undercarriage came loose when the plane passed over a rough service road that crossed the runway. Jacob Islamov, a friend of Sikorsky and the plane's mechanic, was in charge of releasing part of the landing gear once the plane was airborne (to reduce the load). Thinking the entire plane would roll over, Islamov released the landing gear, sending the plane hurtling over the hill at the end of the runway. The crowd watched in horror as the plane disappeared silently over the hill; then a great explosion erupted and shook the ground and lit up the sky. Sikorsky ran the length of the field and found Fonck and another crewman crawling away from the burning wreckage; Islamov and the radio man were trapped inside. Fonck stood dazed, watching the fire and the frantic, but futile, efforts of rescuers. "It is the fortunes of the air," he pronounced, and Sikorsky eyed him poisonously.

At the inquest, Fonck was accused by many (including, naturally, Berry) of not being competent to fly so large a plane and of not aborting the take-off when the wheel fell off. Sikorsky was mildly reprimanded for not carrying out the complete regimen of flight tests with full loads (though the problem, it was determined, had not been with the plane, but with the runway and undercarriage), and the navy man, a former aide to Admiral Moffett, vouched for Fonck's abilities. The coroner, possibly bowing to political pressure, exonerated Fonck and ruled the crash "an unfortunate accident." Most amazing of all,

Pictured here is Captain Homer M. Berry, a respected World War I flier who was first on, then off, the crew of the S-35 that made the ill-fated attempt at a trans-Atlantic flight in September 1926.

perhaps, is that after the inquest Sikorsky and Fonck announced that they would build a new plane and try again the next year.

The S-35 was only the first casualty to be claimed by the Atlantic; before Lindbergh's flight, there would be others. Following his successful flight over the North Pole, Richard Byrd persuaded a young Norwegian flier, Bernt Balchen, to join him, Floyd Bennett, and George Noville, as a ground-crew member in an attempt to cross the Atlantic. Byrd placed his plane, the *Josephine Ford*, on display in department stores owned by Rodman Wanamaker, which led to Wanamaker's enthusiastic backing of the trans-Atlantic flight. Byrd ordered a new Fokker Trimotor, and Wanamaker sentimentally named it the *America* (after the Curtiss boatplane he financed before the war for a trans-Atlantic flight). During a test flight in Teterboro, New Jersey, with Fokker himself at the controls and the three crew members aboard, the plane flipped over during landing. Byrd had a broken arm, Bennett a fractured leg, and Noville was most seriously hurt with internal injuries; only Anthony Fokker walked away from the crash unhurt. The flight of the *America* would be delayed until craft and crew mended.

Another entrant was Noel Davis, commander of the Naval Reserve Station in Boston, who had tried to get support since 1925 for a try at the Orteig prize. In January 1927, he filed that he would be flying a tri-motor manufactured by the Keystone Aircraft Corporation. Keystone called the model the *Pathfinder* (only one was built), but he called the plane the *American Legion* because most of the funding was coming from the Legion, which hoped that a successful flight would publicize the convention it was having in Paris that summer. During trials out of Langley Field, Virginia, in April 1927, the plane lost power and dove into a marsh, killing Davis and Stanton Wooster, his copilot.

Meanwhile, the French made another attempt at the prize. Charles Nungesser, France's second highest ranked war ace (second only to Fonck, and considered a better flier), teamed up with François Coli and the two prevailed upon the airplane builder Pierre Levasseur (of Antoinette fame) to equip a plane he was building for the French Navy for a trans-Atlantic flight. The plane, the PL-8, was an open-cockpit biplane with a detachable undercarriage and a watertight fuselage that could float on water. It was Nungesser's plan to eject the undercarriage after takeoff and land in New York Harbor on the

Top: Seen here in 1926 is Floyd Bennett, pilot of Commander Richard E. Byrd's Josephine Ford, *a Fokker triplane, which flew over the North Pole. Above: Charles Nungesser, heroic aviator of World War I, was known as the "Prince of Pilots." His disappearance over the Atlantic was a tragedy that was deeply felt by the entire aviation community.*

fuselage. Nungesser painted the plane white and called it *L'Oiseau Blanc* (The White Bird), putting his trademark skull-and-crossbones-in-a-black-heart emblem on the side of the plane.

Nungesser and Coli took off from Le Bourget Field (they claimed they were flying the more difficult east-west direction out of patriotism, but the simple fact was that they had no money to transport the plane to New York) on May 8, 1927, Joan of Arc Day and the anniversary of the beginning of the flight of the NC boats. Candles were lit all over France and prayers were uttered in churches as the entire nation turned out to watch the plane fly over the coast of Normandy toward America. The weather reports were discouraging—at Roosevelt Field, Clarence Chamberlin, engineer of the Wright engines, heard reports of Nungesser's takeoff and of the weather over the Atlantic, and muttered, "I don't see how Nungesser can make it."

A report was sent to Paris, resulting in a detailed front-page story, that Nungesser and Coli had landed safely near the Statue of Liberty. France erupted in joyous celebration, but the report proved false, which made the later disappointment even greater. The White Bird was never seen again, and it was all the U.S. State Department could do to dispel rumors that American weatherman had withheld weather information that would have delayed the flight. No part of the wreckage of the White Bird has ever been found.

The deaths did not end even after Lindbergh's flight in May 1927. Before the end of the year, three other planes set out to cross the Atlantic and did not make it. The first, an east-west flight in a single engine Fokker called the *St. Raphael*, took off from England on August 31, bound for Ottawa. The plane was piloted by two experienced RAF pilots, Leslie Hamilton and Fred Minchin, and had an illustrious passenger: Princess Anne Lowenstein-Wertheim. Wertheim was well known as an intrepid aviator with several records to her credit. She kept her involvement in the flight secret (mainly because of her aristocratic family's objections to her flying career) until just before boarding. The plane was spotted en route by an oil tanker, and then disappeared into the Newfoundland fog. For years, searchers combed the Canadian wilderness for wreckage, but found nothing.

On September 6, a Fokker single-engine called *Old Glory* took off from Old Orchard Beach, Maine, for Rome, attempting the first nonstop U.S.–Rome flight. The plane was sponsored by William Randolph Hearst, who, ever sensitive to publicity, had Philip Payne, editor of the New York *Daily Mirror*, one of his newspapers, go along on the flight to drop a wreath over the Atlantic that read, "Nungesser and Coli: You showed the way. We followed. (Lloyd) Bertaud and Payne and (James D.) Hill." The next day, an SOS was received and rescue ships raced to the spot 600 miles (960km) off the Newfoundland coast. They found the plane bobbing in the water, but there were no bodies and no indication of what had happened. Even before the wreckage of the *Old Glory* was found, another plane took off to cross the Atlantic, the *Sir John Carling*, with a British crew of two. It disappeared without a trace over the Atlantic, without so much as an SOS. On September 9, 1927, the U.S. Department of State and the Navy, in response to public revulsion at all the lost fliers, called a halt to further transoceanic attempts.

Chapter 6

The Pathfinders:
Aviators of Flight's Golden Age

Introduction: Two Ways to Circle the Globe

In the years following World War I, aviators looked at the globe and saw an opportunity in every corner to set a record and gain a place in history. The flights they contemplated and completed may not have been the kind of nonstop flights that immortalized Lindbergh, but each one opened new airways between different and remote parts of the world and shrank the globe step by step. For every flight that brought glory to a flier or aircraft, there were many other attempts that ultimately went awry and some that proved fatal for the pilots.

The routes were well known and the news media followed each one as teams and nations set out to fly them: the South Atlantic; the overland air route from England to Australia; the southern route from England to South Africa; the trans-Pacific routes; and, finally, the Arctic and Antarctic. England had a special interest in setting these long-distance records because of the ties it wished to maintain with British colonies and Commonwealth members. The United States, emerging after the war as a military power relatively unscathed by the devastation of battle, saw long-distance flights as a way of extending its military and political influence beyond its borders. The French invested their aviators with the pride and honor of the nation; Germany had nothing at stake, being taken out of the entire enterprise of aviation development (at least overtly) by the Treaty of Versailles. As a result, the French took every failure to heart and eventually became demoralized and disenchanted with flying; the Germans went on to take complete control of commercial aviation in Europe.

This difference in motives was translated directly into the very style of the record-setting attempts: The Americans who flew the NC aircraft across the Atlantic gave no thought to national honor or prize money (again, not overtly). The same attitude marked Richard Byrd's attempt to fly the first solo flight from New York to Paris. He did not even register for the Orteig prize, claiming to be on a "purely scientific exercise." The British, by contrast, set out to connect their territories and aimed their flights at British possessions. The flight from London to Delhi, India, in late 1918 by A.E. Borton and Ross Smith; the twenty-seven-day, seventy-two-stop flight of the Smith brothers in 1919 from England to Australia; Bert Hinkler's solo flight along the same route a year later; and the 1920 flight of Van Ryneveld and Brand from London to Capetown—all these ocean-crossing feats of aviation clearly bespoke an agenda of connecting the many colonies of the British Empire more firmly to Mother England.

In most instances, the competition to be the first to fly from England to a remote place had many contenders, but rarely did American and British fliers find themselves going head to head. The exception was the attempt by both countries to circumnavigate the globe in 1924, and the contrast in the manner that each country carried out its plan is striking. In the early 1920s, no fewer than eight groups set out to circle the globe. Each had to arrange for landing sites and supply stations with fuel and provisions along the way for its fliers, so it was not possible that such an attempt could be prepared for in secret. A 1922 British attempt ended before it began when Ross Smith crashed a Vickers Viking and was killed; a second attempt later that year headed by Norman Macmillan got as far as the Bay of Bengal before going down.

This photograph of The Spirit of St. Louis *being flown over Paris by Charles Lindbergh was probably taken on May 28, 1927 (a week after the historic flight), when Lindbergh flew to Brussels to begin the return trip.*

BELOW: *Four Douglas World Cruisers, parked at Clover Field near the Douglas plant in Santa Monica, California, on March 25, 1924, before taking off for the official start of the round-the-world flight in Seattle.* RIGHT: *Donald W. Douglas (under the propeller, in a suit), who conceived the feat and designed the planes, poses with six of the aviators who piloted the planes.*

Hearing that the U.S. Army Air Service was looking into sponsoring a round-the-world flight, Macmillan organized a new attempt, this time trying to keep the preparations quiet. He had the amphibian aircraft designed for the flight constructed in secret (his earlier flight had taught him the importance of the aircraft being seaworthy in rough seas) and sent out yachts with supplies to forty stations along the route. Whether the U.S. Army knew what Macmillan was up to or not is uncertain, but the U.S. Treasury agents who raided the yacht docked in the harbor of San Pedro, California, were interested only in enforcing the Prohibition laws. They confiscated 65 gallons of Scotch whiskey and attached the boat. The British accused the Americans of using the Volstead Act as a pretext for sabotaging their planned flight. The delay forced Macmillan to abandon the flight. In retaliation, when the American group was flying across the lower rim of Asia, the British denied them permission to fly over India.

While the British approached the challenge in very individualistic terms, filming the project and placing their hopes on a single plane (with spare parts and alternate planes to be used as needed along the way), the Americans created a squadron of four planes, built for the U.S. Navy by Donald Douglas, who at the time was building planes in an old movie studio in Santa Monica, California. The four "Douglas World Cruisers," as they were called, were named *Seattle, Boston, Chicago,* and *New Orleans*—after four American cities—and the four commanders were navy fliers. Two of the planes went down during the

flight, including the flagship plane flown by the group leader Frederick L. Martin. As had been the case in the trans-Atlantic flight of the NC planes, the other planes continued with their original crews. This would have been unthinkable for the British flight, even if multiple planes had been used. The commanders of the planes that finished the circuit, Lowell H. Smith and Erik H. Nelson, were simple soldiers who did not present larger-than-life images, in spite of the fact that they were lionized when they completed the flight successfully. The Americans brought two kinds of landing gear with them—pontoons and a wheeled undercarriage—and changed the landing gear configuration according to what they anticipated they would find at the next landing site. The British decided not to waste time doing this and relied instead on an experimental retractable landing gear that would allow the Vickers Vulture they were flying to land either on land or on water.

The course and direction chosen by the American fliers were dictated by simple weather considerations. Although flying eastward took best advantage of the prevailing winds, flying westward would allow the squadron to avoid the four main weather hazards: the Alaskan fogs; the typhoons of the China Sea; the monsoons of Southeast Asia; and the winter storms of the North Atlantic. The British chose the opposite direction, opting, over safety, for the flashier route and (if luck was with them) the faster one.

On March 25, 1924, the British plane took off, under the command of RAF squadron leader A. Stuart MacLaren. The Douglas World Cruisers took off from Santa Monica for Seattle for the official start of the journey on April 6. MacLaren's flight was plagued with bad luck almost from the start, and he ran into (as predicted) virtually every weather obstacle the sky had to offer.

Then, in the middle of the flight, MacLaren found himself in Burma with a disabled plane and no way to have the spare plane in Japan delivered to him. In a remarkable act of generosity, Lowell Smith arranged for a U.S. Navy destroyer to deliver the plane to MacLaren so he could continue the flight. This act of magnanimity turned the British attitude around instantly.

The three American planes (one crashed off the coast of Iceland, after completing nineteen thousand miles [30,571km] of the total 26,000-mile [41,834km] trip, but was replaced by a fifth plane Donald Douglas had built during the summer) were cheered in Paris and London. In crossing the Atlantic, the Americans were joined by an Italian Dornier Wals boatplane piloted by Antonio Locatelli. The Italian plane followed behind the Americans, using them as a navigation guide, and then, once reaching Iceland, raced ahead. Such behavior would have outraged the British. But the Americans thought nothing of it, and even defended Locatelli's actions. When they discovered on reaching Labrador that Locatelli had not arrived, they realized he must have been forced down at sea and U.S. naval vessels were sent to rescue him.

The fliers landed on American soil on September 6, and were greeted three days later in Washington by President Calvin Coolidge, who waited in the rain for three hours for the planes to arrive. On September 28, 175 days and seventy-two stops after the flight began, the planes reached Seattle. Smith, who was weak from dysentery contracted en route, had to be held up to acknowledge the cheers of the crowd.

Following are the stories of a dozen or so of the most celebrated fliers of the Golden Age of Aviation. We begin with Calbraith Rodgers, even though he made his historic flight in 1911 and died in 1912, because his flight set the tone for the pathfinding flights of the post–World War I aviators. All of these men and women were famous in almost every corner of the globe; they were hailed as heroes and role models, and many were idolized and romanticized by young and old. Each was admired almost as much for his or her style and persona as for the feat or record that made the flier famous in the first place. Many of them were hardly perfect people and their personal lives were frequently a shambles. But together, they represented a branching out into the unknown reaches of the planet and of human accomplishment and, as such, they were an inspiration to an age. In the period between the wars, there was arguably no single endeavor that yielded as many worldwide heroes and legends as aviation.

Calbraith Rodgers

Before 1911 Calbraith P. Rodgers was not well known in aviation circles and, if the truth be known, he was never considered a very accomplished flier. When he took off from Sheepshead Bay, New York, attempting to fly to the California coast in thirty days, aiming to win a prize of fifty thousand dollars offered by William Randolph Hearst, few people gave him much chance of even completing the flight, let alone doing so in the stipulated time.

He flew a Baby Wright plane that was prone to stalling even in the hands of a good pilot. The plane was called the *Vin Fiz*, after the grape-flavored soft drink produced by the Armour Company, which sponsored the flight. Rodgers' route took him from New York to Chicago, then down to San Antonio, Texas, and finally along the southern border of the United States to Long Beach, California. This allowed him to avoid the mountains entirely, a barrier Rodgers was not equipped (by machinery or skill) to hurdle.

During the flight, Rodgers made sixty-nine stops, sixteen of which were crash landings. (Rodgers refused to admit it, but there was no question that he had trouble landing.) Each crash landing necessitated repairs, and the

Miraculously to the many people following the around-the-world progress of the Douglas World Cruisers, three of the planes approached San Francisco on September 29, after more than 170 days and twenty-five thousand miles (40,000km) of flight.

Army fliers McCready and Kelly established a new endurance record by staying aloft for thirty-eight hours in a Fokker monoplane, flying near San Diego, from October 14 to 15, 1922.

Alan Cobham and Bert Hinkler

Born on May 6, 1894, Alan Cobham came from a simple English farm family and did not particularly distinguish himself as a member of the Royal Flying Corps in World War I. After the war, he became a test pilot for de Havilland and promoted the line of light D.H. planes that culminated in the famous de Havilland Moth models. It was in a precursor of the Moth (a D.H. 50J) that he made a flight from London to Cape Town in November 1925, and then from London to Melbourne and back between June 30 and October 1, 1926, a flight that covered nearly twenty-seven thousand miles (43,443km). Cobham returned to London amid cheering crowds, dramatically landing his seaplane on the Thames next to Parliament.

Neither the flight to Cape Town nor the one to Australia were the first of their kind, but they were impressive because they demonstrated the reliability of airplane transportation and the effectiveness of careful planning. Neither the London–Australia flight of the Smith brothers in 1919 nor the London–Cape Town flight of Van Ryneveld and Brand in 1920 convinced governments or airlines that routine air transportation between these points was feasible. Cobham's flights accomplished this, and serious international flights over long distance (in many countries, not just from England) began after Cobham's flights.

The flight to Australia had been anything but routine. While flying over Iraq, a sandstorm forced Cobham to fly low. Bedouins, probably seeing their first airplane, shot at it and hit Arthur Elliott, Cobham's copilot and long-time friend. Cobham made an emergency landing in Basra and Elliott was taken to a hospital, but he died the next day. This incident underscored the dangers of flying over unknown territory; that Cobham's flight was able to convince people that flying was practical in spite of Elliott's death was a tribute to Cobham's planning and perseverance.

Cobham's next project was to survey the coast of Africa from the air (filming from an open cockpit) in preparation for commercial flights to African, Asian, and South American destinations. He then toured England, sponsoring National Aviation Day exhibitions that entertained and informed the public on the benefits of air transportation. Cobham became a proponent of in-flight refueling, founding a company that became the world leader in the development of that technology. He died in 1973 at the age of seventy-nine, after a distinguished career in aviation.

From the close of the war right through Cobham's flight, one man was determined to fly solo from England to Australia, but no one seemed of a mind to let him. He was a short Australian named Bert Hinkler and he had served in the Royal Naval Air Service during the war.

times he landed without crashing, people flocked to the plane and grabbed a souvenir, usually a vital piece of the aircraft. Fortunately, Rodgers was not alone. He followed railroad tracks and below him was a private train paid for by Armour, on which were machinists, Rodgers' wife and mother, and enough spare parts to build four complete airplanes just like the *Vin Fiz*. It turned out that he needed those parts, because only two parts of the original plane he took off in were still on the craft he flew into Long Beach on November 5.

Rodgers completed the four thousand-mile (6,436km) flight in fifty days, too late to win the Hearst money, but Armour rewarded him with a prize of their own of more than twenty thousand dollars. He became celebrated through the posters and advertisements Armour produced commemorating the flight, but the most remarkable aspect of it, aside from his perseverance, may have been simply his having lived though all those crashes. In April of 1912, Rodgers died in a crash as the plane he was flying in an air show plunged into the Pacific off the coast of Long Beach. Observers thought he may have been attempting to land when the crash occurred.

Rodgers paved the way for the first nonstop coast-to-coast flight, made on May 2 to 3, 1923. Flying a single-engine Fokker T-2, powered by a Liberty engine, the U.S. Army Air Service team of Oakley G. Kelly and John A. MacReady made the 2,650-mile (4,264km) trip in just under twenty-seven hours. They flew from Roosevelt Field on Long Island, New York, diagonally across the country, skirting below the Rocky Mountains and landing at Rockwell Field near San Diego. Although they arrived after midnight, a large crowd turned out to greet them and newspapers across the country hailed the feat as the beginning of a new era. The most direct consequence of the flight was that it prompted the U.S. government to prepare for a transcontinental airmail service, inaugurated in July 1924.

ABOVE: *One of the great pathfinding aviators, Alan Cobham (wearing a white flight suit, flanked by his mechanics), completed several historic long-distance flights in the 1920s that made him a household name in England. TOP: Cobham is shown here returning to London from one such historical flight, to Australia and back. Another of his flights was to Cape Town, South Africa.*

When flying to Australia became an official challenge sponsored by the Australian government and supervised by the Royal Aero Club, Hinkler proposed to make the flight solo in a Sopwith Dove biplane he convinced the Sopwith Company to lend him. The Aero Club sanctioned some attempts—and eventually the Smiths claimed the prize amid fierce competition—but two fliers were not accepted as entrants: Bert Hinkler, because the Club did not believe it possible to make the long flight solo; and Charles Kingsford-Smith, because he proposed to reach Australia by crossing the Pacific, and the Aero Club did not believe that possible either.

Sopwith withdrew the plane when Hinkler did not qualify, so the Australian flier spent the next few years test flying Avro planes and eventually saved up enough to buy an Avro Baby, a small plane with a 35-horsepower engine. He attempted his solo flight to Australia in May 1920, but had to abandon his plan in Italy because hostilities in the Middle East made that part of the world unpassable. Four years later, Hinkler, now considered an accomplished aerobatic flier and racer, bought an Avro Avian, a slightly larger plane (still less than half a ton unfueled) that could be outfitted with extra fuel tanks. Knowing his solo run to Australia would not be sanctioned (or even permitted), Hinkler took off from Croydon, England, on the morning of February 7, 1928, virtually in secret. His wife, an Avro executive, and two passersby were the only witnesses.

Hinkler made the London-to-Rome flight in record time—thirteen hours—but was arrested when he mistakenly landed at a military air field. Bailed out by the British Consul, he continued the next morning, stopping in Malta, Libya, India, Burma, and Singapore, and establishing speed records between London and all those destinations along the way. (It was a great feat of flying stamina and navigation, but Hinkler would always claim, ingenuously, that his most important piece of equipment was his alarm clock.) By the time he reached Southeast Asia, news had spread of Hinkler's flight and a huge throng was waiting in Darwin to greet him. He reached Australia in fifteen days, nearly halving the time it had taken the Smiths (along essentially the same route). He was paraded through the streets of Darwin and Brisbane, and awarded medals and cash by the Australian govern-

ment. The flight had proved to be more than a stunt. It showed that a carefully laid-out plan and solid technical flying could put the Australian continent within two to three weeks from England, a short jaunt in that era.

Hinkler, by nature a shy man, became an international celebrity, inspiring fashions, dishes, and even dance steps. He hit the headlines again in 1931 when he flew a de Havilland Puss Moth in the first solo flight across the South Atlantic and the first east-west crossing from Brazil to Senegal, West Africa. Again, he kept his intentions secret (and again he was detained by authorities, this time the Brazilians, who found his papers not in order). Hinkler died in January 1933 in Italy while attempting to set a new England–Australia speed record.

Richard Byrd and Floyd Bennett

Exploration of the uncharted areas of the globe by airplane and airship became very active in the 1920s for a variety of reasons. Looking forward to the establishment of aerial transportation from continent to continent, it was necessary to know what aircraft were capable of, whether aerial navigation techniques were adequate, and whether or not ground support could be provided en route. These reasons, combined with the general adventurousness that pervaded the 1920s, led to many pathfinding flights across oceans and continents, but an additional set of reasons came into play in motivating aerial exploration of the Arctic and Antarctic regions.

In the late twentieth century, it is difficult to believe that as late as the mid-1920s there was thought to be land north of the Alaska in the middle of the Arctic Ocean, in an area known as the "blind spot," in the middle of which was the "Pole of Inaccessibility," a point equidistant from all land masses and about four hundred miles (643.5km) south of the North Pole. On official

TOP: *Bert Hinkler poses in front of his famous Avro Avian.*
ABOVE: *Three aviators pose at a dinner in their honor at New York's McAlpin Hotel. Known as "the three B's of aviation," they are Commander Richard E. Byrd (left) and Floyd Bennett (right) in their dress-white uniforms and Captain Homer M. Berry (center), who was already being feted as the pilot of the first New York-to-Paris nonstop flight, scheduled to take place some months in the future. Berry was a respected air hero of World War I, and there was little doubt that he would be the winner of the Orteig challenge. As it turned out, however, he was soon thereafter replaced as the pilot and the aircraft crashed on take-off.*

BEN EILSON AND THE GREAT TRADITION OF ARCTIC AVIATION

As difficult as flying was everywhere in the world during the 1920s and 1930s, the difficulty reached a peak in the Arctic areas, and some of the greatest pilots ever to fly negotiated this treacherous area. Landmarks were few and the shifting glaciers sometimes changed the landscape from season to season. Compasses were practically useless because of mineral deposits that affected them and because the position of the magnetic north pole shifted in relation to the flight path. Furthermore, the extreme cold made engine stalls likely and, with virtually no areas on which to land, if a crash landing was somehow survived the extreme cold made rescue a virtual impossibility.

The bush pilots of the Arctic are now legendary names in Alaska and northern Canada. Punch Dickins became famous for mapping the Canadian Barrens in 1928. Air mail service to the Yukon was inaugurated in 1932 by Grant McConachie, who became a hero when he swooped down on a wilderness camp set ablaze by a gas explosion and rescued the survivors. The year 1929 saw several landmark Arctic flights: Wop May conducted the first winter flight over the Arctic Ocean, opening up a mail route to one of the most isolated places on earth. Pat Reid opened the air route across the Northwest Passage, setting up a systematic search-and-rescue operation. Rescue was also the objective of Herbert Hollick-Kenyon, who went searching for the lost MacAlpine Expedition, finding them near Cambridge Bay after they had been missing for two months.

Alaska's premier bush pilot, however, was certainly Ben Eilson. Born in North Dakota, Eilson flew an open-cockpit Jenny, introducing flight to Alaska, where he had gone to teach math and science. He convinced the Post Office in 1924 to buy him a de Havilland D.H.4 so that he could fly the mail from Fairbanks to McGrath, Alaska, 280 miles (450.5km) away. Eilson's plane crash-landed a few times and the Post Office canceled the contract, but other aviators began offering their services, and since the terrain was so difficult to traverse even in good weather, fliers had many passengers and delivery contracts.

Eilson returned to Alaskan aviation and piloted several historic flights in 1928. In November 1929 Eilson and his mechanic, Earl Borland, were lost near North Cape on the northern coast of Siberia. They had been on their way to an ice-bound schooner, the *Nanuk*, to pick up some furs when they encountered another great danger of Arctic aviation: a sudden storm that seemed to come out of nowhere. The search subsequently conducted for Eilson and Borland involved American, Canadian, and Russian fliers, with the entire world on the edge of their seats awaiting news. On February 16, 1930, Borland's body was found near the wreckage of their plane; two days later the rescue party found Eilson. Both men had been thrown clear of the plane when it crashed and had been killed instantly. On March 4, 1930, Eilson and Borland were buried in coffins draped with American flags sewn by Siberian Eskimo women.

---

charts, it was called Crocker Land or Keenan Land, and appeared with question marks and purported outlines, arrived at from unreliable sightings and calculations based on measured anomalies of the currents passing through the Bering Strait.

Three teams were deeply involved in the aerial exploration of the Arctic: the Norwegians, led by the famed explorer Roald Amundsen, who had reached the South Pole over land in 1912; an American team headed by Richard E. Byrd, a lieutenant commander in the U.S. Navy; and a group led by the Australian George H. Wilkins, who sought and accepted help from many sources. First out of the gate was Amundsen. After being forced into bankruptcy in 1924 through mismanagement on the part of a ship broker who had failed to purchase planes for a flight over the North Pole (after all other provisions for the flight were bought and paid for), he teamed up with a wealthy American who simply called him in his New York hotel room and offered to finance the expedition to the North Pole, if he could come along.

Seen here is Lincoln Ellsworth, one of the great aviators in the grand tradition of Arctic (specifically Alaskan) aviation.

This was how Lincoln Ellsworth, by then a man of over forty and with virtually no connection to flying (he had flown some in the war) and no Arctic experience, entered the annals of Arctic aerial exploration.

Amundsen had the resources now to purchase the planes he needed. He and Ellsworth acquired two Dornier-Wal all-metal boat planes with two powerful Rolls-Royce engines arranged in tandem atop the wing. Amundsen and Ellsworth took off in May 1925 in two planes, the N-24 and the N-25, each with a crew of three, from King's Bay, Spitsbergen. Both planes were forced down short of the Pole. In one of the most dramatic feats of perseverance and survival on record, all six crew members managed to survive for three weeks, repair one of the planes (the N-25), and make it back to Spitsbergen on June 15.

Amundsen and Ellsworth were determined to try for the Pole again, and in 1926 they purchased a semirigid dirigible, the N-1, from the Italian designer Umberto Nobile. While they were preparing the dirigible—renamed

the *Detroiter*, and a single-engine Fokker called the *Alaskan*. He too had a talented pilot at his disposal, a North Dakotan named Carl Ben Eilson who had become the foremost Alaskan bush pilot. Wilkins was more interested in exploring the "blind spot" than in making an over-the-pole flight, but the newspaper publishers who were his backers insisted that he try for being the first to fly over the pole. Thus, as May 1926 dawned, the three teams preparing to fly into the Arctic region were not really competing with one another. The *Detroiter* was soon out of commission after its landing gear collapsed, and the *Alaskan*, considered a hard-luck ship because a reporter had been decapitated accidentally by the propeller, was not powerful enough to make a polar flight. That left the field to Amundsen and Byrd.

ABOVE: Flying over the Arctic was a treacherous and dangerous undertaking. Here, Amundsen (right) inspects the monoplane in which he plans to attempt a flyover of the North Pole; on the wing is his mechanic, Oskar Omdal. RIGHT: After the successful flight of Byrd and Bennett over the Pole in 1926, the pair teamed up to cross the Atlantic, but Bennett was injured in the last test flight before the planned attempt. Bennett (on crutches) is greeted by Byrd in front of the America.

the *Norge* (or "Norway"), much to the consternation of the Italians—for flight, an American team arrived at King's Bay. The Americans had tried an over-the-pole flight two years earlier, using three Loening amphibian biplanes with open cockpits. The team, headed by Captain Donald P. MacMillan and Richard E. Byrd, was sent by the navy to find Crocker Land (or whatever was out there) and to perform a flying feat that could diminish some of the lustre of the army's Douglas World Cruisers. It was clear from the start that the planes were not nearly durable enough, especially not their landing gear, and MacMillan abandoned the project. But Byrd and his very able pilot, Floyd Bennett, sought private funding for another try. With the help of Edsel Ford, Byrd purchased a Fokker Trimotor and named it the *Josephine Ford* (much to Anthony Fokker's consternation).

The third group to arrive in 1926 was headed by George Hubert Wilkins, flying a Fokker Trimotor called

The newspapers promoted the notion that a race was underway, but in fact, the two teams assisted one another throughout the preparations. Bernt Balchen, a Norwegian flier who had been sent to search for Amundsen back in 1925 and who had become a close friend of Amundsen and a valuable member of his crew, gave Byrd much advice (with Amundsen's blessing) on the best construction of landing gear for the Arctic. Balchen would later be invited by Byrd to join him in subsequent history-making flights. (After Byrd's death in 1957, Balchen claimed that Byrd had not flown to the North Pole, but this claim was never substantiated.)

At 12:37 A.M. on May 9, 1926, Byrd and Bennett took off in the *Josephine Ford* and flew toward the North Pole. They reached the Pole (by Byrd's calculations) at 9:02 and circled for fifteen minutes taking pictures. They had intended to return by way of Cape Morris Jesup on the northwestern corner of Greenland, but an oil leak prompted them to take no chances and they returned directly to Spitsbergen, arriving to cheering Norwegians (and an uncharacteristically effusive Amundsen) at 4:07 P.M.

The *Norge* took off two days later, and while it passed over the Pole and made it to Teller, Alaska, in just under seventy-one hours, the flight was a torture to both Amundsen and Nobile. The two men were determined not to let their countries be deprived of the honor that was due to the nation that sponsored the first crossing of the Arctic Ocean. Amundsen, a stoic, imperious-looking figure (but by all accounts a man of great warmth and humor), irritated the excitable Nobile at every opportunity. None of the crew of sixteen (and one dog) slept for the three-day flight—the cabin was simply too cramped—but Amundsen insisted on sitting in the only chair and mercilessly needled Nobile and his Italian crew (who in truth knew much more about dirigible flying than the Norwegians), believing there was little point in even making the flight now that Byrd and Bennett had reached the Pole. It was considered the height of irony when, in June 1928, Amundsen perished while flying a rescue plane in search of Nobile and the *Italia*, a refitted version of the *Norge*.

Wilkins and Eilson returned to Alaska in the spring of 1927 with two Stinson biplanes and attempted to cross the Arctic from Point Barrow to King's Bay. They landed successfully and took off on the polar ice, the first time an airplane had managed that feat, but they crash-landed only sixty-five miles (104.5km) out of Barrow. The fliers trekked over treacherous ice for more than thirteen days, racing not only the cold, but the frostbite that had set in to Eilson's fingers and threatened to take his entire arm if they did not reach help soon. They soon made it to Beachey Point, an Eskimo trading post east of Barrow, where Eilson was rushed to the hospital. (He lost only one finger to the ordeal.)

A year later, Wilkins and Eilson were back for another try. This time they flew one of the first Lockheed Vegas produced. The plane performed excellently and the flight, which began on April 15 and ended six days later because of a five-day storm that the fliers waited out on the ground, was hailed as one of the great Arctic flights of the period. Wilkins was knighted and the pair became international celebrities. Their flight had accomplished a number of things. It demonstrated the capabilities of the Vega, a plane that was to become a favorite of long-distance fliers for years to come. It put to rest once and for all the notion that there was any land mass between Alaska and the North Pole. And it

demonstrated that trans-Arctic flights might not be as dangerous as once thought, which meant that great circle air routes from North America to Europe and Asia should be seriously considered for commercial aviation when planes improved.

Byrd received the Congressional Medal of Honor for his Arctic flight (which makes Balchen's later claim all the more curious). Just as he had assisted the NC aircraft crews and Alcock and Brown in their trans-Atlantic flights, he provided navigational assistance to Lindbergh for his historic 1927 flight. After a June 1927 flight across the Atlantic with Balchen (Bennett was nursing a broken leg at the time), Byrd turned his attention to the Antarctic. By now an admiral and an international celebrity, Byrd raised private funds with the help of Edsel Ford and John D. Rockefeller, Jr., and began a period of adventure and exploration that captivated the world from 1928 to the mid-1930s. Flying the Fokker Trimotor *Floyd Bennett*, named after his pilot (who died in 1928 of pneumonia, contracted while on a rescue flight in Canada), with Balchen and two other fliers, Byrd flew over the South Pole on November 29, 1928, setting yet another milestone in polar aviation.

Charles and Anne Morrow Lindbergh

The lives of Charles Lindbergh and his wife, Anne Morrow Lindbergh, have often been viewed as emblematic of America itself. Charles Lindbergh was probably the most famous person of his time, yet he was a retiring, contemplative man who hated publicity, even when he used it to further what he believed in. He became famous for a single heroic act, yet he influenced the development of commercial aviation through his continued efforts and flights, in a career that put him at the center of progress just as it put him at the center of controversy. He dropped out of the University of Wisconsin, yet he valued knowledge and supported the work of such researchers as Robert Goddard in rocketry and Alexis Carrel in biology. He spoke his mind, even when it threatened his fame and he was scolded by President Roosevelt, yet he continued to serve his country by flying combat missions in the Pacific through World War II. Anne Lindbergh, the daughter of a U.S. ambassador, became an accomplished pilot under her husband's tutelage, and became an author celebrated in her own right for elo-

ABOVE: *Charles Lindbergh in flying gear in 1927 (though not on the morning of the trans-Atlantic flight, as is often reported).* BACKGROUND: *Lindbergh inaugurating Pan Am mail service to the Panama Canal Zone in 1929.*

Douglas "Wrong Way" Corrigan

In 1927 Charles Lindbergh toured the Ryan Aircraft factory in San Diego and met a young mechanic working on his plane, later to be named *The Spirit of St. Louis.* The young man wiped his hands on his overalls and shook Lindbergh's hand. The mechanic never forgot that moment—he later said he would not have been more thrilled if he had shaken the hand of Abraham Lincoln. The young man's name was Douglas Corrigan, and from the moment Lindbergh completed his trans-Atlantic journey it became Corrigan's dream to retrace the flight.

In 1933 Corrigan bought a used Curtiss Robin for $325 and spent all his spare time repairing and improving it—a slow process. He obtained a used Whirlwind engine and fastened some of the electronic instruments together and onto the instrument panel of the plane with tape and wire. He flew his plane around Los Angeles, where it became known as the "Corrigan Clipper." In 1937, having outfitted the plane with fuel tanks that, as with Lindy's plane, obstructed his forward view, he applied to the Department of Commerce for a license to attempt a trans-Atlantic flight. The inspector took one look at the plane and told Corrigan the most he would do is grant him a license to fly from Los Angeles to New York, and he would permit him to fly back to Los Angeles only if he made the trip nonstop.

Corrigan told some friends in Los Angeles that he did not see how the inspector would know if he landed somewhere between Los Angeles and New York: in the mid-1930s, there was no way to check on whether a plane made an emergency or unscheduled stop at a small airfield along the way. Corrigan later admitted that the thought also occurred to him that the authorities had no way of knowing where he was heading at the time he took off. After arriving in New York and obtaining the license for the return trip, Corrigan bid the Department of Commerce inspector "Bon Voyage," and took off on the evening of July 16, 1938. Corrigan's plane was spotted heading over the Atlantic about an hour later. Landing in Ireland the next day, he claimed that his compass had malfunctioned and fog had prevented him from taking a visual reading.

Corrigan was given the name "Wrong Way," though nearly no one believed his story. He was made an honorary member of the Wisconsin Liars' Club and wrote an autobiography, *That's My Story*, in which he stuck to his story about flying across the Atlantic by mistake. He starred as himself in a film, *The Flying Irishman*, again presenting his "official version," but clearly with tongue in cheek. Corrigan earned quite a sum from all these activities—he even sold the plane to the San Francisco Golden Gate Exposition—and bought an orange farm, where he stepped out of the spotlight.

Douglas Corrigan in front of the Curtiss Robin in which he made his unauthorized 1938 flight to Ireland. After his brief moment in the spotlight, he retired to California to grow oranges. He died in 1995.

quently capturing the thrill of flight and the enigma that was her husband. The tragedy that engulfed them after the kidnapping and death of their child never left them.

Charles Augustus Lindbergh was born on February 2, 1902, in Detroit. His early career in aviation included barnstorming and mail delivery. When the Orteig prize was announced, he tried to obtain a Bellanca airplane, designed by the Sicilian designer Giuseppe Bellanca. But Bellanca had a champion flyer in Clarence Chamberlin, who was then working for the Wright Aeronautical Corporation. Chamberlin convinced his company to install their new Whirlwind engine in the plane for a try at the Orteig prize. The result was the *Columbia*, which Chamberlin was to fly across the Atlantic with Charles Levine after Lindbergh's flight, and which became the first plane to cross the Atlantic twice. But Lindbergh was not at all well known at the time and Wright was not about to risk the new plane on an unproven pilot. Anthony Fokker turned Lindbergh down for the same reason, though he suspected that Lindbergh might be able to win the prize.

With the help of some St. Louis businessmen (who insisted that the plane be named after their city), Lindbergh contracted with a small San Diego aircraft manufacturer, Ryan Aircraft, to modify their standard M-2 six-passenger, single-engine aircraft to his specifications. The plane, designated the NYP, bore a striking resemblance to the Bellanca. Its fuselage was cambered to give it added lift and its propeller was made of duralumin. Lindbergh's specifications stunned the workers at Ryan: he had them turn the plane into a flying gas tank, with no forward visibility and only a periscope giving the pilot any forward view at all. (Lindbergh figured that he

could depend on maintaining the correct flight path by keeping tabs on the few instruments he had aboard.) He had the workers round out all the rivets to reduce drag. There was no radio, no navigator, and no copilot—and the aircraft was highly unstable, requiring constant vigilance by the pilot. Amazingly, the plane was built in only two months at a cost of six thousand dollars (engine extra).

Lindbergh took off from Roosevelt Field, New York, in the early morning hours of May 20, 1927, when there was an unexpected clearing in the weather. He had been on his way to a Broadway show when he called the field from a pay phone on the way and got the word from the weatherman. He had not slept in nearly twenty-four hours when he took off, so fighting sleep was the most difficult part of the flight. Among the witnesses to the takeoff was Anthony Fokker, who was certain the Ryan would never make it over the telephone wires at the end of the field. He and Chamberlin stood at either end of the runway in case Lindbergh needed rescuing.

After thirty-three and a half hours of pinching himself and opening the side window to let in the cold air to stimulate him and keep him awake, Lindbergh landed in Paris. That made him the ninety-second person to cross the Atlantic, but he became internationally famous for being the first to cross the Atlantic alone and establishing in the process a distance record of 3,614 miles (5,815km).

In the subsequent goodwill tour, Lindbergh met Anne Morrow, daughter of the U.S. ambassador to Mexico. They were married in May 1929, and in 1930 the couple made three historic flights together: early in the year, they set a transcontinental speed record by crossing from Los Angeles to New York in fourteen hours and forty-five minutes, with only one refueling stop. They flew a Lockheed Sirius at fifteen thousand feet (4,572m), above the clouds and weather, where they believed the future of

flight lay. A similar flight took place in August of that year, as the Lindberghs flew from Maine to Tokyo, following a great circle route through Nome and Petroplavosk. Finally, in November, the Lindberghs inaugurated Clipper Ship service of Pan American Airways by flying the new Sikorsky S-40 Flying Boat, *Southern Clipper*, from Miami to the Panama Canal Zone.

The events in the lives of the Lindberghs from 1932 onward reflect the complications and malaise of the twentieth century. Their infant son was kidnapped and brutally murdered, and the sensational trial of the culprit was a strain that scarred them nearly as much as did the crime itself. In the late 1930s, Lindbergh became an isolationist and lent his name and prestige to causes that were tainted in the popular mind. He accepted citations from the German government as late as 1938, for which he was severely criticized. Anne Lindbergh found herself defending her husband in print, while at the same time putting forth her own, sometimes very different, views. Charles Lindbergh died in Hawaii on August 26, 1974.

Wiley Post

Because of the records set by Wiley Post in the Lockheed Vega, the plane became a favorite of distance fliers and record breakers, and for the most part these planes were available to any enthusiast. Wiley Post was born in Texas, but his family moved to Oklahoma when he was five and he was considered an Oklahoman his entire life. He began his aviation career in 1924 at the age of twenty-six as a parachutist for a flying circus, Burell Tobbs and His Texas Topnotch Fliers, and was soon a well-known performer on the barnstorming circuit. Post injured his left eye in an oil field accident, and when it seemed that an infection might spread to both eyes and deprive him of vision entirely, he had a surgeon remove his left eye. The gamble worked and he recovered normal sight in his right eye, but wore a patch over his false eye. He took the money he received from the workman's compensation for the accident and bought an old Canuck and repaired it himself.

In 1927, Post became the personal pilot of oilman F.C. Hall. In 1928 Hall, desiring a closed-cockpit plane, sent Post to the Lockheed factory in Burbank, California, to buy the best one the company produced. Post selected the Vega, and Hall named the plane the *Winnie Mae*, after his daughter. After Hall suddenly sold the plane back to Lockheed during a downturn in business, Post went to work for Lockheed as a salesman and test pilot. When Hall was again able to purchase a plane and hire a pilot, in 1930, he bought a new Vega (again calling it the *Winnie Mae*) and rehired Post, this time with the intention of letting Post carry out his plans for long-distance flights.

Post won the 1930 Men's Air Derby, a race from Los Angeles to Chicago that kicked off the National Air races. For the race, Post had Lockheed install a new Wasp engine capable of producing 500 horsepower. He used the Derby to test the plane and some modifications that he had made to raise its top speed to nearly two hundred miles per hour (322kph). He was ready to tackle the record for a round-the-world flight. Like most aviators, he was irked by the fact that the record for flying around the world was not held by an airplane, but by the *Graf Zeppelin*, which had been piloted by Hugo Eckener in a 1929 record-setting global circumnavigation of twenty-one days. Post engaged a marine navigator, Harold Gatty, for the flight. Gatty had developed several new navigational devices, including a combined ground-speed and wind-drift indicator. This was particularly important for Post because having only one seeing

ABOVE: *Wiley Post (left) and Harold Gatty (right) were considered the premier long-distance fliers of the Golden Age of flight. Here, they are greeeted in Moscow during their 1931 round-the-world flight.* RIGHT: *The* Winnie Mae *is among the most famous aircraft in aviation history.*

eye meant he lacked depth perception, which made it difficult for him to gauge distances and speed.

Post and Gatty took off from Roosevelt Field on June 23, 1931, and circled the globe west to east in just eight days, fifteen hours, and fifty-one minutes. (Naturally, they titled their memoir of the flight *Around the World in Eight Days*). They would have done better, but several times the *Winnie Mae* became stuck in soft sand or mud and the plane had to be moved to a new surface for take-off. In Edmonton, the plane was moved to a main street where it took off with a clearance of only inches for the wings. This was an astounding feat, and in appreciation Hall made a present of the plane to Post. The reception Post and Gatty received after their record flight rivaled Lindbergh's everywhere they went.

With other fliers attempting to break his record, Post immediately planned a new flight that he believed was well beyond the capabilities of any other flier: a solo flight around the world. On the face of it, this should not be more difficult than flying with a navigator since in neither case is anyone other than the pilot flying the plane. But not having a navigator puts an enormous strain on the pilot, who has to take readings and determine position while flying the plane. In an odd way, Post's injury actually helped him because he was accustomed to making calculations in his head all the time while flying, to compensate for his lack of depth perception. (He would often say that he would have to give up flying if they ever changed the height of two-story buildings.)

As he had for his flight with Gatty, Post trained like an athlete for the flight, becoming accustomed to taking short naps instead of sleeping through the night, and learning to focus his mind exclusively on flying. Post also had two new devices that would help him immeasurably: the automatic pilot and a homing radio receiver, both used for the first time on this record-setting flight. The automatic pilot, developed by the Sperry Gyroscope

Company, had expanded the technology developed by Jimmy Doolittle's "blind flights" of 1929 to include a servo-mechanism that adjusted the controls whenever the aircraft was out of trim or was rotating around any axis. Its main use was to allow the aircraft to cruise automatically while the pilot attended to the navigational chores. Although only an early prototype of the device existed, Post convinced Sperry to test it on the *Winnie Mae.*

The other device allowed a pilot to determine the direction a radio signal was coming from. This device was developed by the U.S. Army, which was eager to test it; Post was happy to oblige. By the time Post took off from Floyd Bennett Field in Brooklyn, New York, on July 15, 1933, his main challenger, Jimmy Mattern, had dropped out. But in spite of his rigorous training and the technological improvements, Post, who had seemed none the worse for wear after his earlier flight with Gatty, looked weary and exhausted when he landed at Floyd Bennett Field on July 22, to the cheers of the 50,000 New Yorkers there to greet him. Post had circled the globe in an astounding seven days, eighteen hours, and forty-nine minutes, more than twenty-one hours faster than his record pace in the flight with Gatty. Post credited the automatic pilot, but the fact was that the device did not work through much of the flight and had to be repaired several times. Post encountered more difficulties on this flight than on the first one, but he made up for lost time by cutting down on his sleep—he slept all of twenty hours during the entire flight. It was a feat that fliers to this day find unbelievable.

Post then considered entering the MacRobertson Race between England and Australia held in 1934. He believed the race could be won by flying very high, say above thirty thousand feet (9,144m), and for extended periods, to take advantage of one-hundred-mile-per-hour (161kph) winds in the upper atmosphere. Post designed a pressurized suit that would allow him to fly at forty thousand feet (12,192m) for long periods, but the

LEFT: *The beginning of the tragic August 1935 flight in which Wiley Post (left) and humorist Will Rogers were killed.* RIGHT: *The Orion Explorer onto which Post had installed pontoons rests upside-down in the shallow water of a lake near Point Barrow, Alaska.*

Amelia Earhart and husband George Palmer Putnam, an influential New York book publisher who made sure Earhart received much—and only the best kind of—publicity.

Winnie Mae was now obsolete and Post decided not to enter the MacRobertson Race. Instead, he worked with Lockheed designers to produce a hybrid plane that combined the wings of an Orion with the fuselage of an Electra. He hoped to set new altitude and speed records with the craft.

In 1932 Post met the famous humorist (and fellow Oklahoman) Will Rogers and the two became close friends. Rogers often flew with Post as a passenger and he contributed an introduction to the book Post had done with Gatty about their flight. In 1935, looking for new material for his newspaper column, Rogers asked Post if they could fly to Alaska. Post went to Lockheed and asked the engineers to add pontoons to the Orion-Electra aircraft, but they refused, telling him that pontoons would upset the aerodynamic of the plane. Post (believing Rogers' weight would compensate) had pontoons placed on the plane himself and flew Rogers up to Alaska. On August 15, the fears of the Lockheed engineers were realized and the plane stalled while taking off from a lake near Point Barrow. Post and Rogers died in the crash, sending the nation into mourning for two of its most popular cultural heroes.

Amelia Earhart

The stories and legends surrounding Amelia Earhart are so ingrained in the American psyche that one sometimes comes away from reading about her with the feeling that she is a fictional character, a larger-than-life American myth. She was, alongside Lindbergh (she was often called "Lady Lindbergh"), the most famous aviator of her time.

She virtually defined the strong presence women were to have in aviation, even though there were many great women aviators before and since. Even during her lifetime, many of the same people who idolized her regarded her as an enigma; it is somehow fitting that her death should constitute the greatest and most enduring mystery in the history of aviation.

Amelia Mary Earhart was born in Kansas in 1897. In 1919 she dropped out of Columbia University and began doing secretarial work in order to pay for flying lessons with Neta Snook. The two women became lifelong friends. Earhart's family's fortunes declined in the mid-1920s and she took employment as a social worker in Boston. In 1928 an extraordinary stroke of luck put Earhart in a position to be the first woman to fly the Atlantic, albeit as a passenger.

Mrs. Frederick Guest of London (née Amy Phipps of Pittsburgh) bought Richard Byrd's Fokker Trimotor and renamed it the *Friendship*. She intended to hire a crew to fly her over the Atlantic, but her family wouldn't hear of her taking such a risk. She insisted, however, that the plane be used to fly an American woman across the Atlantic, and formed a committee to find the woman who would take her place. On the committee was George Putnam, publisher of such aviation classics as Lindbergh's *We* and Byrd's *Skyward*. Putnam asked a friend if he knew of any likely candidates, and he was told to contact a woman working as a social worker at Dennison House in Boston. He did just that and invited Earhart to come to New York to be interviewed by the committee. It was in New York that she met George Putnam, whom she married in 1931.

The committee felt they had found the perfect replacement for Mrs. Guest. Earhart was attractive in an artless way, her tousled hair and boyish looks radiating a kind of purity that betrayed her midwestern origins. Yet she spoke emphatically and with a clear sense of independence. She was told that she was simply going to be a passenger on the flight, and that the plane would be piloted by veteran pilots Wilmer Stultz and Louis "Slim" Gordon. She asked whether there might come a time when she would be able to take the controls, however briefly; she was told perhaps.

On June 3, 1928, she secretly climbed aboard the *Friendship* in Boston for the first leg of the trip, to Newfoundland. A sailor in the harbor spotted her, however, and by the time the plane took off for Ireland on June 17, the word was out that a woman was in the process of crossing the Atlantic by airplane for the first time. When the plane landed in Wales (having overshot Ireland in the fog), the plane had been in the air twenty hours and forty minutes, and a great throng was ready to meet her. Earhart became world-famous, even though some women criticized her for accepting such a passive role on the flight. The fact was that Earhart simply did not have experience with multi-engine planes, and

LEFT: *Amelia Earhart's orange and silver Lockheed Electra soars over the Golden Gate Bridge as it heads toward Honolulu on the first stage of her first attempt at a round-the-world flight in 1937.* BELOW LEFT: *Fred Noonan and Earhart consult a map in Dakar, West Africa, in July 1937. Though Noonan was called the pilot and Earhart the navigator, both were accomplished in both tasks.* BELOW RIGHT: *Noonan and Earhart board their plane after a stop in Puerto Rico.*

another woman, Mabel Boll, was arranging to pilot a flight at the very time Earhart took off as a passsenger.

In the years that followed, Earhart made a determined effort to prove her piloting skills and to show the world that she could have flown the *Friendship* across the Atlantic. She worked to promote women's aviation and became an eloquent and forceful proponent of including women in exhibition and racing events. Although both men and women pilots questioned Earhart's flying abilities throughout her life, she proved her mettle in dozens of flights and in setting many records.

On May 21, 1932, Earhart flew a Lockheed Vega solo across the Atlantic, from Newfoundland to Northern Ireland. The flight encountered serious obstacles—a storm, a troublesome leak in the engine, a broken altimeter—and only a flier of skill would have made it. Later in the year, she set women's distance and speed records when she became the first woman to fly solo nonstop

across the United States. A series of trans-Pacific flights brought her fame, but her most important flying achievement was probably her solo flight from Hawaii to San Francisco in January 1935—she was the first person to make the flight, after many others had failed.

After Wiley Post's two flights around the world, aviators began looking forward to someone attempting a round-the-world flight along a route closer to the equator. Post had skirted the North American and Eurasian continents, which was not strictly a round-the-world trip. Earhart assembled a flight team consisting of two pilots—herself and Paul Mantz—and two navigators: Fred Noonan, Pan Am's chief navigator, and Harry Manning, a highly regarded maritime navigator. She also arranged with the Lockheed Company that she be lent an Electra for the flight.

On March 17, 1937, Earhart and crew took off from Oakland, intending to head westward and cross the

Pacific for the first leg of the flight. It is not known exactly what had happened, but the plane tilted and a wing scraped the ground. By the time the plane was repaired, only Noonan remained of the original crew. Since he was very familiar with the Caribbean from his work for Pan Am, the flight would now originate from Miami and head eastward. The plane took off on June 2 and headed out across the Atlantic, staying just a few miles from the equator.

The flight across the South Atlantic, Africa, and the Asian subcontinent went smoothly. The plane took off from Lae, New Guinea, on July 2, heading for a stop on Howland Island, about a third of the way to Hawaii. What happened next has been the subject of investigation and speculation for more than fifty years. The plane certainly went down at a location other than Howland Island. It does not seem reasonable to assume that the plane put down at sea since no floating wreckage was ever found. If the plane landed on an island in the vicinity, because it was lost or experienced some mechanical failure, then the most likely landing place would have been Gilbert Island, then under Japanese control. Relations between the United States and Japan were already strained during this period, and if, as some Lockheed employees said, spy cameras were mounted on the Electra for photographing the Japanese, then Earhart and Noonan might have been thought to be spies and eliminated.

The search lasted two weeks and involved hundreds of naval vessels and aircraft, as well as hundreds of personnel, but nothing was found (though search parties could not land on Gilbert Island). In the years since, many theories have been propounded about the fate of Amelia Earhart. Many natives of the South Pacific have testified that they saw Earhart a prisoner of the Japanese or that they saw a photograph of her amid Japanese boats or sol-

diers. Whatever the truth, her disappearance marked the untimely end of a career that promised to inspire many women to take active roles in many facets of American society, not just in aviation.

Howard Hughes

The curious turns Howard Hughes's life took in later years obscured the fact that the eccentric millionaire was, during the 1930s, a record holder and an important innovator in aviation. Hughes inherited the successful Hughes Tool and Die Corporation, which gave him an annual income of two million dollars with which he could indulge any interest. In 1930 he combined movie producing and aviation to produce the epic film *Hell's Angels*. The World War I aerial combat scenes were extremely realistic because Hughes spared no expense to use real planes and to shoot actual planes conducting aerial maneuvers. As a result, three stunt pilots died during the filming.

In the late 1930s, Hughes used his fortune to create specially outfitted airplanes that could set new records. In 1935 he equipped a Northrop Gamma H-1 with the newest 1000-horsepower Wasp engine, and broke the old air speed record of 314.3 miles per hour (505.5kph) by thirty-eight miles per hour (61kph). On June 14, 1936, Hughes set a transcontinental speed record by flying from Los Angeles to Newark Airport in nine hours and twenty-seven minutes, beating Roscoe Turner's 1934 record by two full hours. In January 1937, after further work on the Gamma H-1 (using the wind tunnel at Cal Tech, which he helped to fund), he cut yet another two hours off his own record, crossing the country in seven hours and twenty-eight minutes. Aviation professionals

LEFT: *Howard Hughes poses next to the red H-1 aircraft in which he set the transcontinental speed record in January 1937.* RIGHT: *Hughes (in flight cap) inspects the plane after a 1935 mishap in which he was forced to land with the retractable landing gear locked in the closed position. He had earlier set a speed record of over 347.3 miles per hour (559.2kph).* BACKGROUND: *A throng of twenty-five thousand greets Hughes in his New York World's Fair 1939 (a Lockheed 14-N Super Electra) at Floyd Bennett Field after he has completed a round-the-world trip in just under four days.*

The Lockheed Altair, developed from the Orion, was a favorite of explorers and distance fliers. It was in an Altair called The Lady Southern Cross *that Kingsford-Smith made his 1934 Brisbane-to-Oakland flight.*

regarded the feat as reckless because he flew much of the way at altitudes above fifteen thousand feet (4,572m) without any special oxygen equipment.

Hughes' crowning achievement came on July 14, 1938, when he shattered Wiley Post's round-the-globe speed record by circling the Northern Hemisphere (essentially Post's route) in three days, nineteen hours, and eight minutes (about half the eight days Post needed). When Hughes' Lockheed twin-engine 14-N Super Electra, which was equipped with two enormous Wright Cyclone engines, the most powerful available, landed at Floyd Bennet Field, a throng of twenty-five thousand New Yorkers rushed onto the field to the plane to congratulate him. The onrush of spectators was probably the only part of the flight that made the thirty-two-year-old Hughes at all apprehensive.

The flight was important not only for the record (which stood for nine years), but because it was conducted in such a routine and well-planned a manner. It demonstrated once and for all that long overseas flights were feasible for the average traveler and that electronic navigation had progressed to the point of offering a certainty that an aircraft could be guided unerringly to any destination.

Charles Kingsford-Smith and the Pacific Crossings

In 1927, 1928, and 1931, three historic crossings of the Pacific took place that underscored how the world was shrinking—and one trans-Pacific event took place in 1927 that aviators might just as soon have wanted to forget. The door to the Pacific was opened with the flight of U.S. Army Air Corps officers Lester J. Maitland and Albert F. Hegenberger, in a Fokker Trimotor called the *Bird of Paradise* (a virtual carbon copy of Byrd's plane, the *America*), from San Francisco to Honolulu, Hawaii. Unlike Bert Hinkler during his flight to Australia, Maitland and Hegenberger could not put down along the way and had no landmarks to guide them along the twenty-four-hundred miles (3,861.5km) of featureless ocean. The successful flight was a tribute to the piloting skills of Maitland, the navigating skills of Hegenberger, and the reliability of the Whirlwind engines and the Fokker aircraft.

That same year, James P. Dole, president of the Hawaiian Pineapple Company, issued a challenge offering prizes to the first two fliers to cross the Pacific from California to Hawaii nonstop. He intended to encourage a trans-Pacific flight as a prelude to eventual air transportation between Hawaii and the mainland. Dole, a member of the National Aeronautic Association, believed that the flight was well within the capabilities of the competitors for the Orteig prize, who had to fly a thirty-six-hundred-mile (5,792.5km) course. He hoped Lindbergh and Chamberlin would be induced into competing, but neither showed any interest. The authority that certified the race was appointed by the promoters, and therein lay the problem. Entrants with virtually no chance of making the flight were allowed in and, in Dole's words, the contest, dubbed the Dole Derby, became a free-for-all.

The Dole Derby was won by stunt pilot Art Goebel, flying a Travel Air called the *Woolaroc*; second place was taken by Martin Jensen, flying a Breese monoplane, the *Aloha*. But during the course of the race, four planes were lost and ten people died, including the only woman entrant, Mildred Doran (known as the "Flying Schoolmarm"), and the flying team of Scott and Frost

ABOVE: *The Fokker Trimotor* Bird of Paradise *in which Lieutenants Lester Maitland and Albert Hegenberger made the first flight across the Pacific—from Oakland, California, to Honolulu, Hawaii. The twenty-four hundred miles (3,840 km) represented the longest all-water flight made to that time.* LEFT: *Hegenberger (left) and Maitland in June 1927.* RIGHT: *Hugh Herndon (left) and Clyde Pangborn in England, preparing their plane,* Miss Veedol, *for the first nonstop trans-Pacific flight. Pangborn's experience as a barnstormer probably convinced him that discarding the landing gear after taking off (to save weight) and making a belly-skid landing upon reaching Wenatchee, Washington, was a good idea.*

(flying a prototype of the new Vega, the *Golden Eagle).* A number of sponsors of other races withdrew their support and the ban on uncertified transoceanic flights that was officially placed on the Atlantic was unofficially extended to the Pacific.

Into this dour environment stepped Charles Kingsford-Smith. "Smithy," as he was known, was precisely the wrong man to place in charge of an attempt to cross the Pacific. An average flier during the war, afterward Smithy demonstrated himself to be a reckless, hard-drinking, irresponsible thrill-seeker who had caused many accidents and injuries in the aftermath of his barnstorming stunts. In connection with the Dole Derby (which he passed up because it seemed foolhardy, even to him), it was unlikely that anyone would sponsor him or certify

any aircraft in which he wanted to attempt a Pacific crossing. In spite of all this, as a result of patience, careful planning, and a measure of luck he found himself in 1928 in possession of the Fokker Trimotor, now called the *Southern Cross,* that Sir Hubert Wilkins had flown in the Arctic. He also had a political sponsor—the Premier of New South Wales, who was coming up for reelection—and a new image—the result of a highly publicized record-setting flight around the perimeter of Australia that gave Kingsford-Smith and his partners, Charles Ulm and Keith Anderson, an air of respectability.

On May 31, 1928, the *Southern Cross* took off from San Francisco for Hawaii and then went on to Brisbane, a total of 7,316 miles (11,771.5km). The Fokker F-VIIB was tested on the flight by stormy weather and broken navigational equipment, and several times, Smithy reported, the aircraft came close to going down. But the crew of four made it, and Kingsford-Smith's past indiscretions were all forgotten as he became Australia's greatest hero (of the day, at least).

During the next five years, Smithy conducted a number of pioneering flights, including a record-setting solo flight from London to Australia in 1930, and a Brisbane-to-San Francisco crossing of the Pacific (a more difficult flight than flying the same route westward) in 1934. He was lost on November 8, 1935, in a flight over the Bay of Bengal during an attempt to regain the speed record for a London-Australia flight.

On October 5, 1931, Clyde Pangborn and Hugh Herndon, Jr. completed the first nonstop trans-Pacific flight, flying a Bellanca, the *Miss Veedol*. Pangborn's past as a celebrated wingwalker came in handy during this flight because he had to climb onto the wing to loosen the undercarriage that had failed to drop off after takeoff. The flight was unheralded at the time for several reasons. In the first place, the pair had started out trying to challenge Wiley Post in an around-the-world flight; crossing the Pacific was an afterthought when it was clear Post was too far ahead. Pangborn and Herndon had hoped to qualify for a twenty-five-thousand-dollar prize being offered by a Japanese newspaper for such a crossing, but the Japanese detained the fliers on suspicion of being spies when they photographed some of the Japanese shoreline. Then, when they landed in remote Wenatchee, Washington, not having any landing gear, the plane seemed to crash-land, possibly invalidating the flight. To top it off, the Japanese press reporting on the flight simply could not handle Pangborn's name, so that American newspapers were not certain just who had crossed the Pacific. (Then again, Pangborn's fame as a barnstormer may have led some editors to question the story at the outset.)

Amy Johnson and Beryl Markham

While Amelia Earhart captured the imagination and admiration of Americans, Europe had women aviators of its own to glory in, and two in particular became celebrated headliners during the 1930s. Amy Johnson and Beryl Markham were very different types of people in many ways, yet they became the source of endless fascination by a public that followed their personal lives as well as their exploits in the air.

Amy Johnson was born in the port city of Hull, England, into a modest fisherman's family. Early on she showed a fierce independence that took her through Sheffield University, then still a school largely for men. She became interested in flying at the age of twenty-five and used every bit of money she earned as a secretary to pay for flying lessons. She also showed a knack for

ABOVE: *Beryl Markham, the British socialite who made the first east-to-west nonstop solo trans-Atlantic flight in 1936. BACKGROUND: Markham with the Vega Gull at the RAF Field at Abingdon. She planned to land in New York City, but was forced down by mechanical failure and crashed into a peat bog in Cape Breton Island, Nova Scotia.*

mechanical devices and apprenticed with an airplane mechanic, becoming the first British woman to be granted an aircraft ground engineer's license. In 1930 she decided to become the first woman to fly solo from England to Australia, and was intent on breaking Bert Hinkler's record for the flight.

Johnson and her father managed to scrape together a small amount for the purchase of a Gypsy Moth, which she named *Jason*. The aircraft was entirely inadequate for so ambitious a flight, and "Johnnie," as she was called, did not have nearly enough flight experience. She took off from Croydon on May 3 and completed the early legs of the flight in record time, beating Hinkler's London-to-Karachi time by an amazing two days. But the last portions of the flight did not go well (largely because of the plane), and when she arrived in Australia she had taken four days longer than Hinkler to make the flight. She was disappointed, but all of Australia and England cheered her for being the first woman to complete so hazardous a solo flight.

The attractive aviator's life would never be the same. Amy Johnson inspired songs and fashions, and drew the admiration of her public with her direct manner of speaking. In 1932 she married one of England's most

celebrated aviators, James Mollison, providing a wealth of material for the front pages and the society pages. The marriage was a rocky one, though, partly because James was a flamboyant philanderer prone to bouts of drinking and partly because Amy turned out to be a more accomplished flier than her husband. Nearly every record James established was soon broken by Amy, sometimes flying the very same airplane (a de Havilland Puss Moth).

In an attempt to salvage their marriage, the couple attempted a round-the-world flight in a de Havilland Dragon biplane they called the *Seafarer*. The plane went down near the Connecticut coast (due, it seemed, to James' flawed flying) and was demolished by local souvenir hunters. James returned to England, but Amy stayed in the United States and became a good friend of Amelia Earhart. In 1938 the Mollisons were divorced and Amy sought anonymity. She died in a 1941 crash while ferrying airplanes for the RAF.

Beryl Markham was born Beryl Clutterbuck, an aristocratic (though the family was not wealthy) British name, in 1903 and was raised in British East Africa—now Kenya. She was smitten by flying when she was in her late twenties, soon logged a thousand hours and worked as a bush pilot out of Nairobi. Twice married and twice divorced, Markham was a woman with social graces and noble bearing, though she was a sportswoman and anything but snobbish.

Having flown, by her own calculation, hundreds of thousands of miles over the African jungle, she decided to fly a new Percival Vega Gull, which she named the *Messenger*, from England to New York. The flight westward over the North Atlantic was more difficult than a flight in the opposite direction because of the prevailing easterly winds of the jetstream. Markham made it to Nova Scotia, and when the engine cut out she landed the plane nose down in a bog. It was not the most elegant crossing of the Atlantic, but it made her famous nonethe-

less. Markham also showed a real talent for writing about flight and her works are still considered some of the most inspiring aviation literature ever written.

Though they had very different personalities, Johnson and Markham shared one very important quality—they competed and flew on equal terms with men, Johnson having the technical expertise and Markham the flight experience. Even Earhart, as accomplished as she was, could not match either of these aviators for sheer flying ability or know-how. It is inconceivable, for example, that either Johnson or Markham would have agreed to be only a passenger on the *Friendship*, as Earhart had. The next generation of woman aviators (such as Jean Batten) would look more frequently to Johnson and Markham as role models than to Earhart, Quimby, or Nichols.

Italo Balbo

While all the pathfinding was going on, very little attention was being paid publicly to military aviation. One European country, however, felt compelled to attend to its air forces in the early 1930s, and that was Italy. The Fascist dictator Mussolini had been in power since 1923 and it was clear to all of Europe that a future war was going to place Italy on the same side as Germany and against France and England. With the German air program crippled by the Treaty of Versailles, Mussolini hoped that developing an air force would give Italy a

Premier Mussolini (center) inspects the Caproni bomber fleet in a 1927 tour accompanied by generals Balbo (behind and to Mussolini's left) and Badoglio. The Italian premier was a steadfast proponent of air power and was himself an accomplished pilot.

In spite of the success of the Italian Formation Flight and his promotion, Balbo was sent off to be the governor of Libya. Possibly Mussolini regarded him as a threat and was suspicious of his overtly pro-British sentiments. Balbo was killed in 1940 by Italian gunners who claimed they mistook his airplane for a rebel fighter. Recent investigations have brought Balbo's support of Mussolini and the Fascist government further into question.

Jimmy Doolittle

The career of Jimmy Doolittle—from his service in World War I to his racing career to his leading the first bombing raid on Tokyo just weeks after Pearl Harbor, for which he was awarded the Congressional Medal of Honor—was a remarkable one. Doolittle was an accomplished pilot, he held a doctoral degree in engineering from MIT, and he retired a major general of the U.S. Armed Forces. From the point of view of aviation, Jimmy Doolittle's greatest contribution to the history of flight may well be his flight of September 24, 1929. What was remarkable about the fifteen-minute flight in the Consolidated NY-2 test plane was that he could not see out of the cockpit because of a hood that covered the windows. It was the first "blind flight" in which a pilot took off, flew a given course, and landed using only instruments.

The test was conducted at Mitchell Field on Long Island, New York, and the plane had dual controls. The other set was available to pilot Lieutenant Ben Kelsey in case anything went wrong. Kelsey did not have to touch the controls as Doolittle used his instruments to guide his flight. The three instruments most important for this test were the

valuable bargaining chip in dealing with Germany when the showdown came. (He turned out to be wrong. Germany had developed an air capability in secret and was not very much interested in the Italian air strength.)

In 1933 Mussolini's Minister of Air, Italo Balbo, planned and executed a display of Italian air strength that impressed the world. It involved building twenty-five specially equipped twin-hulled Savoia-Marchetti SM.55X flying boats and flying in formation across Europe and to the United States, to the Chicago World's Fair, then back to Rome. This was known as the Italian Formation Flight of 1933, and it was a stunning display of both airmanship and public relations. The planes flew in formation, in groups of three, descending on a city with a dramatic swoop. The Formation Flight began on July 1 and landed near Rome on August 12.

General Jimmy Doolittle in 1944. The series of Doolittle raids on Tokyo in 1942 was a public vindication of his belief that long-range bombing was going to be a decisive factor in the war.

The project required a full year of planning and the training of many pilots and mechanics. Only two planes of the original twenty-five were lost en route. Wherever the group flew, they were accorded welcomes reserved for dignitaries and were treated like heroes. Professionals in the field of aviation were impressed with the planes, but looked at the entire enterprise as childish. Nevertheless, Mussolini was pleased and Balbo was made Air Marshal of the Italian Air Force.

Sperry Horizon, a device designed by Doolittle himself, which instantly told the pilot the orientation of the plane with respect to the three axes of rotation (pitch, yaw, and roll); the Kollsman Precision Altimeter, a hypersensitive gauge that was designed by engineer Paul Kollsman and has been standard on virtually all aircraft since it was first introduced; and the Sperry Directional Gyro, which was used to measure turns and the direction of flight. With these tools, a pilot can fly in any weather or at night.

Chapter 7

The World Learns to Fly

Introduction

In the period between the wars, various means of transportation were improving steadily—automobiles, trains, and ships—so that flying was not the conveyance of choice for most travelers. Aside from being dangerous (when something went wrong with an aircraft, the results were often catastrophic), passengers were subject to cold air at higher altitudes, the constant nerve-shattering vibrations and deafening noise of the engines, air sickness and pressure on the ears during takeoffs and landings, cramped quarters, and the claustrophobic confines of the aircraft cabin.

The statistics comparing various means of transportation are a bit deceiving: the nearly 1.9 billion passenger miles logged in the air worldwide in 1934, one of the strongest years before World War II, represented a great increase from 1929 (sixty-six million passenger miles), but still represented less than 2 percent of all means of intercity transportation, and even less when considered on the basis of fare dollars or trips taken. By 1934 the people prepared to hazard flying had taken their first flight; the remainder were going to be hard to coax onto an airplane.

The industry's response was a technological one: planes had to become more comfortable, safer (and appear safer in design to the average person), and more stable; they had to be able to fly higher to avoid the turbulence of lower atmosphere weather, which meant sealing the passenger compartment and treating the air within it; and they had to develop many more safety systems, especially for takeoffs and landings, the most dangerous phase of most flights. Airplanes also had to vastly increase their speed and range to provide clear and obvious advantages over other long-range transportation

options if the benefits of flight were to be worth the risks. Virtually none of this was in place during the 1920s, and only the merest glimmer of light was apparent during the 1930s. It is therefore one of the remarkable aspects of the history of aviation during this period that the men and women of aviation, traditionally a hot-blooded and impatient lot, exercised great patience in solving each technological problem in turn. The impetuous character that had undermined the French in the first decade of the century was not apparent in these decades, at least not in the development programs of the airplane manufacturers.

This newfound sense of responsibility was the result of several factors. The industrialists had good reason to believe that they had the time and would have the resources to develop aviation slowly and carefully through the 1930s. For one thing, it was clear that governments were on their side. Legislation continually favored the industry over other means of transportation (just as the railroads and the road-builders and car makers had received government support). When it was clear that manufacturers and airlines would not be able to turn a profit for some time, ways were found to support them, either by providing contracts for services such as mail delivery or army transport, or by outright purchase of aircraft far in excess of the government's current needs. This latter form of support became so integral a part of the aircraft industry that it has lasted right to the present day, causing no end of problems even as it keeps the industry afloat.

Second, governments themselves undertook the research programs that were going to be necessary for the industry to grow. Ostensibly these programs were motivated by purely scientific and, to a lesser degree, military concerns, but the shape and size of the programs made it abundantly clear that it was civil aviation that was meant

Between the wars, civilian fliers looked for reliability, economy, and ease of handling. They found all three in the Waco planes, built not in Texas but in Ohio, by the Weaver Aircraft Company. (The company name was also borrowed—from a popular local test-pilot, Buck Weaver.)

to be the beneficiary. Very little of the research done by the National Advisory Committee for Aeronautics (NACA) or at the Institute Aerotechnique remained secret, especially not after it was applied to one of the aircraft produced by Lockheed or Breguet. With Germany forbidden from carrying out aeronautical research of any kind in secret (but getting around that by building aircraft that could be converted easily to military uses), a hope may have existed in American and British circles that open technological development would discourage military development of aviation. This turned out to be a false hope; after the war, the use made by the Germans and Japanese of data made public by NACA and other research facilities would be used as an argument against shared technology as an antiwar strategy.

The world of commercial aviation was to see its beginnings during the 1920s and have its first modest blossoming in the 1930s. The steps taken were halting ones, to be sure. The issue of airships had to be put to rest—as it finally was with the *Hindenburg* disaster, though the air transportation industry had already realized airships were not going to become a mainstay of air travel—and even the great flying boats had to run their course, though for a while they appeared to offer a feasible approach to the problems of air transportation. By the late 1930s, airports began to be designed that could accommodate the new transports, and airports like Idlewild and Croydon, built near water in anticipation of a great deal of flying boat traffic, adapted to land aircraft and provided the services both aircraft and passengers would need to make flying a safe and pleasant experience.

NACA and the Guggenheim Fund

At the end of World War I, the U.S. Congress commissioned a study by the Smithsonian Institution to evaluate the needs of the American aviation industry. The report asserted that the United States would continue to fall behind if the government did not step in, and recommended the establishment of a select committee with executive authority and a research facility to rival England's Royal Aircraft Factory at Farnborough. Congress concurred and established NACA in 1915. NACA's first act was to establish a research laboratory at Langley Field, Virginia (named after Samuel Pierpont Langley), which became the world's largest scientific research facility by the mid-1930s.

Through the use of wind tunnels and advanced photographic techniques, NACA scientists at Langley studied virtually every problem that might be presented by high-performing aircraft, in most cases years before American aircraft manufacturers could apply them to their own aircraft. The scientists at Langley investigated the airflow around a dizzying variety of airfoils at a wide range of speeds. They investigated the complex ways air acts around airfoils that are moving very quickly. In flight, the ends of wings, for example, create spinning vortices that trail backward and downward, which in turn support the wings along with the Bernoulli forces over the rest of the wing. These vortices were hypothesized at the turn of the century by F. W. Lanchester, but were not analyzed until the technicians in Langley devised techniques of photographing airflows by injecting smoke into their wind tunnel tests.

Out of these tests came a number of important innovations. Flaps and slats were appended to wings, allowing the aircraft to reach great speeds at reduced drag while being able to manage slower speeds with sufficient lift during takeoffs and landings. The NACA cowl was introduced, a collar that streamlined the area around the engine and greatly reduced drag; it was used first on the Lockheed Vega and by the early 1930s was a standard feature of all aircraft. NACA engineers also discovered

Called by some the "first modern commercial airplane," the Boeing 247-B was the first all-metal, low-wing, twin-engine air transport. It was also the first to use retractable landing gear, which made it impressive in flight. It became the model for configuration, crew, and service for decades of commercial aircraft.

The aerodynamicists theorize, the designers design, and the engineers test in wind-tunnels (or, of late, on computer screens), but someone still has to take the aircraft into the air and see if it will fly. This is the job of the test pilot, and it has been a crucial task throughout the history of aviation. Several test pilots have left a lasting mark on aviation—some by successfully demonstrating the airworthiness of a new aircraft, and some by showing an aircraft not fit to fly, and paying for that knowledge with their lives.

During the war years, Fritz Wendel, test pilot for the Luftwaffe, set records in the experimental Me 209, but his difficulty maneuvering kept the design off the production lines. Two sons of British aircraft designer-builder Geoffrey de Havilland test-flew de Havilland planes and both were killed in test accidents, one trying to break the sound barrier in a D.H. 108 Swallow. In 1946 NACA established a test site on Rogers Dry Lake at Muroc, in a remote area of the Mojave Desert. Muroc became a celebrated place where some of the greatest test pilots came to fly. It came complete with a bar, the Fly Inn, run by the barnstormer Pancho Barnes. It was at Muroc that Chuck Yeager became the first pilot to break the sound barrier in the Bell X-1. Another test pilot at Muroc at the time, Chalmers "Slick" Goodlin, had tested the X-1 at speeds just barely subsonic, paving the way for Yeager (who was chosen to be the pilot to break the sound barrier because he was an Air Force major and Goodlin was a civilian).

The dean of American test pilots was Edmund "Eddie" Allen, who tested more than eighty different aircraft before perishing in a crash of a B-29 in 1943. Allen taught that test pilots had a special responsibility not to take chances, to be sensitive to the most subtle idiosyncrasies of an aircraft, and to report them back to the designers—something a test pilot who crashes cannot do. Milburn "Mel" Abt broke Mach 3 in the X-2 in 1956, but then the aircraft spun out of control and crashed. Another X-2 pilot, Iven Kincheloe, was getting ready to test the X-15 when he crashed in a routine flight. (Kincheloe's name was used—as a sign of honor—in the television sitcom *Hogan's Heroes*, which was about American

pilots in a German POW camp.) The man who eventually flew the X-15, Joe Walker, died in a mid-air collision while flying an F-104.

The extraordinary handling abilities of the P-38 Lightning were first tested by Milo Burcham, and advanced experimental models of Northrop's Flying Wing planes claimed two great test pilots: Glen Edwards and the flamboyant Harry Crosby, a test pilot who was at the same time the most careful and the most daring. Jack Northrop once paid Crosby fifteen thousand dollars to make a single test-flight of a rocket-powered model of the Flying Wing in 1944.

ABOVE: *Geoffrey de Havilland (standing in the cockpit) was that rare breed of aircraft manufacturer who insisted on testing his planes himself. He died at the age of thirty-seven in a crash during a test flight of a Gloster Twin Jet Meteor in September 1946.*

the advantages of incorporating the engines into the wing structure itself, a feature of both the DC-3 and the Boeing 247 that every manufacturer subsequently adopted. Alloys were tested and refined; undercarriage configurations and equipment for de-icing the wings of planes at high altitudes were tested; electronic instruments for blind flying and for aerial navigation were developed, and manufacturing techniques for every material from balsa wood to stressed duralumin were devised and painstakingly tested.

In 1926 Daniel Guggenheim, a member of a prominent banking family who had only a slight connection to the world of aviation but who recognized the importance of aviation to the future of America, established the Guggenheim Fund for the Promotion of Aeronautics.

This huge endowment was devoted to funding education and research at many universities across America.

By the mid-1930s, a new generation of aerodynamic engineers, schooled in the theories of the Europeans at Guggenheim-funded universities, but with advanced diagnostic and experimental tools at its disposal, was ready to take America to the very frontier of aircraft design. By 1935 the aircraft developed by Guggenheim scientists using NACA data represented the leading edge of aviation, surpassing anything the Europeans could put in the air. NACA functioned as the spark behind the massive effort at Langley Field right up to 1958, when it was reorganized as the National Aeronautics and Space Administration—NASA—and placed in charge of the U.S. space program.

Pony Express of the Air

The story of how the delivery of the mail spawned commercial aviation in the United States is one of the remarkable chapters in the history of flight. After a rocky start on May 15, 1918, air mail runs became reliable, and the Post Office sought to expand its air mail operations. The fleet was expanded from the original seventeen planes, mostly Jennies, with the addition of Standard aircraft (manufactured by a Japanese company) and war surplus de Haviland D.H. 4 training planes dubbed "flying coffins," because the fuel tanks were right in front of the pilot. The first extension of the service would be to link Washington and New York with Chicago, but that required flying over the Allegheny Mountains, a treacherous flight in the old open-cockpit planes then in service. Between May 1919 and the end of 1920, the "graveyard run" between New York and Chicago was opened, though it claimed the lives of eighteen pilots—some crashing due to bad weather or mechanical failure, some crashing and being blown up while flying the JL-6, a Junkers aircraft bought by the Post Office that had serious fuel leakage problems.

Fearing that the Warren Harding Administration would cut the air mail service of the Post Office when it took power in March 1921, the Post Office Air Service, headed by Otto Prager, decided to stage a dramatic cross-country flight that would impress Congress and the president. On February 22 (Washington's birthday), two D.H. 4s took off from New York and two from San Francisco; the hope was that at least one would make it across the country. The event was followed by the entire country, with many along the route lighting bonfires to point the way. The two planes that set out from New York were grounded by bad weather in Chicago, and one of the planes flying eastward crashed in Nevada, which left only one plane still flying.

This plane landed in North Platte, Nebraska, and from there pilot James H. "Jack" Knight was to continue to Omaha, where another pilot would fly on to Chicago. A broken tail skid caused a three-hour delay, so by the time Knight arrived in Omaha, all the bonfire burners had gone home, figuring the flight had failed. The pilot who was to take over for Knight had been unable to come down from Chicago, and in what was to be described as one of the bravest (and most foolhardy) acts in the history of aviation, the exhausted Knight, who had never flown the Omaha-Chicago run, downed a quick cup of coffee and took off into the night for Chicago, with nothing but road maps to guide him. After seven hours in the air, Knight somehow found Checkerboard Field in Chicago, arriving at 8:40 A.M. The mail was transferred to another plane and the rest of the flight went off without a hitch. The mail had crossed the continent in an astounding thirty-three hours and twenty minutes, less than half the previous record. Jack Knight became a national hero (he would later become a celebrated pilot of the DC-3), and the air mail service was saved.

Harding's Postmaster General, Will H. Hays, addressed the entire issue of air mail service from a businesslike and professional point of view and instituted many innovations that benefited all forms of aviation, such as an electric-light directional beacon system, landing lights at airports, and regular broadcasts of weather conditions across the country. The routes were extended beyond the borders of the United States, and one such route, a "star route" (one handed over to a private contractor) between Seattle and Vancouver, brought William E. "Bill" Boeing into the aviation industry. Boeing, a member of a wealthy lumber family in Washington, had been nothing more than a hobbyist before 1919. When the opportunity arose, he and aviator Eddie Hubbard started building mail planes, intending to corner the air mail contracts from the United States to Asia. A similar star route run by Carl Ben Eilson (owner and one-man operator of the Farthest North Airplane Company) flew ski-equipped air mail planes to Alaska and initiated the legendary era of Alaskan aviation.

A young Bill Boeing (right) and Eddie Hubbard, after flying the first Canada-to-United States air mail flight in 1919. Behind them is the Boeing-built Curtiss Model C-700 navy trainer they flew.

The Post Office lost money on air mail service: between 1918 and 1925, its air mail service had cost $17 million to operate and had brought in less than a third of that. An odd alliance was forged between Pittsburgh Congressman Clyde Kelly and Postmaster General Harry New that resulted in the Kelly Act of 1925, which turned over air mail delivery to private contractors. Kelly believed that this would suppress the air transportation industry and thus help the railroads, the largest customers of Pittsburgh steel. Why, Kelly reasoned, would private air transporters stand any better a chance of making a profit than the Post Office? But New made sure that air mail carriers were permitted to keep 80 percent of the face value of the mail they carried, and this proved to be a windfall for the holders of the Contract Air Mail, or CAM, routes. Suddenly, there was a way to make big money with an airplane.

The holders of the CAM routes—only a handful of contractors were awarded routes at first, though more than 5,000 companies submitted bids—were among the biggest industrialists in America at that time. Henry Ford held two of the contracts—CAM-6 and 7 (Detroit–Cleveland and Detroit–Chicago). CAM-1 (New York–Boston) went to Colonial Air Transport, an outfit backed by Rockefeller, Vanderbilt-Whitney, and Fairchild money, and managed by Juan Trippe. Frank, Dan, and Bill Robertson, backed by powerful St. Louis business interests, were awarded

CAM-2 (Chicago–St. Louis), and featured Charles Lindbergh as its principal pilot. The Chicago–Dallas-Fort Worth route, CAM-3, was awarded to National Air Transport, a hastily assembled company headed by Clement Keys of the Curtiss Corporation and backed by Charles Kettering of General Motors and Howard Coffin of the Hudson Motorcar Company. CAM-4 (Los Angeles–Salt Lake City) was awarded to Western Air Express, managed by famed race car driver Harris "Pop" Hanshue and backed by Los Angeles *Times* publisher Harry Chandler; CAM-8 (Los Angeles–Seattle) was awarded to Pacific Air Transport, founded in 1912 by Vern G. Gorst and one of the few companies in operation before 1920 that received an air mail contract. Three smaller companies headed by Walter Varney, Clifford Ball, and Charles Dickinson were awarded CAM contracts for the more dangerous, less lucrative routes.

Having landed these potentially lucrative contracts, the companies put pressure on the manufacturers to create the planes that could fulfill them. Postmaster General New hoped that the opportunity to make a profit carrying mail would result in the carriers' building better aircraft that could also carry passengers. The better aircraft soon came, from such builders as Bill Stout, who built the Ford Trimotor, or "Tin Goose," which became a mainstay of early 1930s aviation.

The development of air mail services of other countries followed the American model. French airplane manufacturer Pierre-Georges Latecoere established the first air mail service between France and Morocco on September 1, 1919, with a fleet of fifteen Breguet 14 biplanes. The routes were even more hazardous than those flown by the Americans: pilots risked being cap-

Transcontinental Air Transport (TAT) offered luxury service, but the complicated plane-train (with buses to connect airfields and train stations) was expensive, required frequent transfers, and cut only a day off the railroad's 3-day coast-to-coast trip. Still, Lindbergh's promotion of TAT made flying a viable option to many—and resulted in the formation of TWA.

tured and held for ransom if their plane went down in a desert region. Like the Americans, French air mail pilots carried guns and frequently had to stand guard and fend off looters (sometimes while injured) if the plane went down for a crash or emergency landing. In May 1926 a celebrated flier for Latecoere, Jean Mermoz (who inspired Antoine de Saint Exupéry's 1931 novel, *Night Flight*) was captured by Moroccan nomads and imprisoned in a cage for three days until he could be ransomed by the company representative in Casablanca.

The Rise of Commercial Aviation: The Big Four and How They Got That Way

It remained for a Postmaster General even stronger than New to shape the commercial aviation industry. Stepping forth to fill this role, with a degree of ruthlessness that took the entire industry by surprise, was President Hoover's new Postmaster General, Walter Folger Brown, for many the quintessential Hoover Republican. Brown had been an attorney in Toledo, Ohio, and was a minor figure in Republican Party politics. Hoover's disinclination to regulate business led people to anticipate that at most Brown would continue the policies developed under the Kelly Act. Brown got Congress to pass the McNary-Waters Act in 1930, giving him virtually dictatorial power over how air mail contracts were to be awarded and how the industry should be developed "in the public interest." This act provided for carriers to be paid, not on the basis of how much mail they carried, but on the basis of the capacity of their aircraft, whether it was filled with mail or not. This was calculated to encourage (or force) the CAM carriers to use larger aircraft.

Requiring larger planes to turn a profit made it even more difficult for smaller companies to compete for the lucrative CAM routes. Brown used his office to force smaller companies to merge into larger ones by holding the CAM contracts over their heads. In a series of meetings that critics called the "Spoils Conferences," Brown manipulated the airlines like toy soldiers on a map, creating merged companies and shaping four major carriers that accounted for twenty-four of the twenty-seven CAM contracts. Even the aviation people who benefited resented Brown's autocratic dealings. Soon, however, four major companies were created that covered nearly the entire country—these became known as the Big Four.

The easiest merger was combining Boeing Air Transport, Varney, National, Stout, and Pacific into United Air Lines, since all these companies were controlled by Boeing in any case. More troublesome was forcing the sizable companies operating in the East and the Midwest—Robertson, Embry-Riddle, Colonial, Texas Air, and Thompson—to merge into American Airways. Still more difficult was forcing Transcontinental Air Transport (TAT)—known as the "Lindy Line" because it was backed by Lindbergh, and which was the only carrier devoted specifically to the transport of passengers—to merge with Western Air Express and other mail carriers to become Transcontinental and Western Air, or TWA. The rockiest road was that of the airlines that were merged to form Eastern Air Transport, because not only were there pressures from the government, but the company was tossed from crisis to crisis by a very active management led by the company president, the flamboyant Eddie Rickenbacker.

When Roosevelt took office in 1933, he addressed the issue of the airlines with typical New Deal zeal. A Senate committee headed by Senator Hugo L. Black (later to be appointed by FDR to the Supreme Court) conducted an investigation of Brown and the Post Office. Brown proudly claimed that he had acted in the public's best interest and had, in a very short time, turned an industry that in the early 1920s was little more than a barnstorming curiosity into a full-fledged, technologically sophisticated (profit-yielding and job-providing) American industry. The Black Committee's final report offered a mild rebuke of Brown and recommended that the entire CAM system be dissolved, and that the mail be flown by the U.S. Army. Postmaster General James A. Farley accepted the Black Committee's recommendation and, in an instant, on February 9, 1934, private carriers were out of the air mail business.

The army was ill-prepared to carry out air mail flights. In the first six months of the program, sixteen crashes resulted in eleven deaths, and only fourteen of the twenty-six main lines could be flown with any regularity. Although the record of the army fliers improved, the damage had been done and public opinion called for a return to the old system. Eddie Rickenbacker, a wartime hero (and later to become president and owner of Eastern Airlines) characterized the government's scheme as "legalized murder." The deadly beginnings of the Air Mail Service a decade earlier were forgotten by 1934, and the private airline people, many of whom despised Postmaster General Brown, now saw what the alternative might look like and banded together.

In returning to the CAM system, Farley, attempting to save face, decreed that none of the participants in the 1930 Spoils Conferences could be awarded contracts. The prevailing attitude was that this restriction would never hold up in court, so the government simply turned a blind eye when the same companies submitted bids under very mildly altered names. Eastern Air Transport became Eastern Airlines; Transcontinental and Western Air became Trans-World Airlines, retaining its TWA logo; and American Airways became American Airlines.

The only one of the Big Four that did not change its name was United Air Lines, partly because Bill Boeing

In the 1930s, cross-country flying became popular because of the Curtiss Condor (ABOVE), the first plane to feature sleeper berths. It was the determination to provide overnight coast-to-coast service that prompted American Airlines to approach Donald Douglas about building the magnificent DC-3 (BACKGROUND).

refused to be a part of the charade, but also because by then Boeing had undergone the most radical changes resulting from the New Deal "Trust-Busters." Taking a page out of the lumber industry notebook, Boeing assembled a series of companies that today is known as a "vertically integrated corporation." Boeing enterprises were manufacturing engines for aircraft being built by another Boeing company, which were then flown by a Boeing-owned airline. Antitrust laws like the Black-McKellar Act, passed as part of the New Deal, made such arrangements illegal and Boeing had to sever all connections between the manufacture of aircraft equipment and the delivery of air transportation services. Thus, Boeing Air Transport, and the layers of holding companies that served as umbrella corporations for diverse enterprises, were all dissolved, and no individual was affected as much as Bill Boeing. It was with no small measure of disgust that he suddenly announced his retirement from aviation in September of 1934, just a few days before the breakup of his various companies was to take place.

The same sort of government manipulation and conglomeration occurred in other countries. In France,

Latecoere was forced by the government to sell his air transport operation in 1927 to industrialist Marcel Bouilloux-Lafont, who renamed it Aéropostale and embarked on an ambitious plan of international aviation. The French had hoped the operation might at least break even, but it ran in the red for four consecutive years. In spite of a glamorous run with celebrated flights that momentarily revived French enthusiasm for aviation, Aéropostale shut down in 1931. France created a nationalized airline out of the remnants of Aéropostale and a union of four small operating airlines in 1933 and called it Air France. In 1926 the Germans, free from the antitrust restrictions of the United States and taking much more modest (and thus more reasonable) steps in building a commercial air industry, created Deutsche Luft Hansa (which became one word—Lufthansa—in 1934). Supplied with the latest aircraft produced in the Junkers factories, and making the first serious attempt to cater to the needs of the passenger, Luft Hansa established a strong market over all of Europe. The company wasted no time establishing a subsidiary in South America, VARIG, which supplanted Aéropostale as the major carrier between Europe and South America. Unlike the

French, who insisted that control of all Aéropostale operations remain in the hands of the home office, Luft Hansa encouraged the creation of locally managed airlines that were tied to the parent company to varying degrees. As a result, Germany, which was not overtly attempting to establish diplomatic footholds in South America, did just that to a far greater extent than any other European country.

An Airplane in Every Garage: General Aviation Between the Wars

If commercial and military aviation are the first two major categories of flying, general aviation is the third. Military organizations undertook distance flights that one would categorize as general aviation, and early commercial flights were little different from the flights of hobbyists or individual fliers. In the 1920s aircraft manufacturers, finding only a limited market for military aircraft, applied aviation to many other activities—crop dusting, advertising and skywriting, long distance transport of valuables, oil and timber surveys, forest fire patrol, and law enforcement.

The closest thing to a truly personal aircraft created before the war was Santos-Dumont's *Demoiselle*, dismissed at the time of its first introduction as irrelevant to the development of flight, but now studied once again as

a prototype of the "homebuilt"—the small aircraft that was simple and small enough to be built in one's garage or backyard. The first small private aircraft built after the war were European adaptations of military aircraft. England led the way with designs by Sydney Camm for Hawker, and by Geoffrey de Havilland for his own company. De Havilland's D.H. 53 Hummingbird monoplane became popular all over Europe, but was soon surpassed by his own D.H. 60 Moth, an elegant biplane that influenced many future aircraft.

Several extremely small aircraft—looking more like children's toys than legitimate aircraft—appeared on the scene: the Electric Wren, powered by a motorcycle engine; and the "Flying Flea" (the British translation of *Le Pou du Ciel*—"Louse of the Sky"), built by French mechanic Henri Mignet, and available in kit form for under five hundred dollars. Flying Flea sales soared in Europe and America, and governments were preparing to legislate them out of the air because they were a nuisance and a hazard, but did not bother when it became apparent that few mechanics could make heads or tails of the complicated French instructions.

Predictably, the man who had brought the automobile within the purchasing range of the ordinary driver, Henry Ford, took an interest in creating small, inexpensive aircraft. He put a young man, Harry Brooks, then in his early twenties, in charge of building and testing an aircraft that he hoped would be a flying "flivver." Brooks was the son of a good friend of Ford's, and Ford treated

The de Havilland D.H. 60 Gypsy Moth, first flown in 1925, represented a revolution in lightweight design. Powered by an ADC Cirrus engine with a mere 60 horsepower, it was the trainer of choice for the Allies in World War II and remained in production in some form for an astounding three decades.

him like a son. Brooks made headlines in 1927 when he flew Lindbergh's mother to Mexico City in a Ford Flivver (the name had become semi-official) so she could spend Christmas with her son. Brooks flew back to Detroit and then was heading down to Ford's winter home in Florida when he crashed into the Atlantic and was killed. Following the accident, Ford shelved his plane.

The first planes to find a receptive market in the United States were built by an Ohio company, the Weaver Aircraft Company, named after Buck Weaver, a popular local pilot who worked for the company. The planes produced by WACO, as the company was known, were much sturdier than the European planes and were equipped with powerful Whirlwind engines. The Waco Tapperwing and the Waco-10 replaced Jennies as the most widely used personal aircraft.

Meanwhile, a group of small aircraft manufacturers began to congregate around Wichita, Kansas, soon making it the private airplane capital of the United States. The names associated with Wichita aviation became legendary in the field of private general aviation. Clyde Cessna, an Iowa farmer, teamed up with a Tennessean, Walter Beech, and a Californian, Lloyd Stearman, to form Travel Air Manufacturing Corporation. Eventually, each man left the company to found a successful one of his own.

Sherman Fairchild built small aircraft to accommodate his aerial photographic equipment, which necessitated minimizing vibration, a selling point for a personal aircraft. Lockheed (the company name based on the phonetic pronunciation of the last name of the founders, Allan and Malcolm Loughead) built the Vega using Jack Northrop's design and data published by NACA. Guiseppe Bellanca's 14-9 was a dashing low-wing plane with striking lines. Eddie Stinson produced the popular Detroiter with generous backing from Detroit financiers.

During the 1930s, the Bureau of Aeronautics of the U.S. Department of Commerce, under the direction of Eugene L. Vidal, encouraged the creation of a "family airplane." The intent was to create a new industry (Vidal later admitted that the plan had not been all that well thought out) and to put people back to work. The only positive result of the program was the eventual creation of the most popular small aircraft of the 1930s, the Piper Cub.

The original Cub model had been designed in 1927 by G.C. Taylor in his small aircraft factory in Rochester, New York. Taylor was invited by the town of Bradford, Pennsylvania, to establish a factory there and was provided with a seed of fifty thousand dollars by the townspeople. Taylor began operations just before the stock market crash of 1929, and the company was driven into bankruptcy. William T. "Bill" Piper, a Bradford oil man who had been one of the investors, used his own money to reestablish the company in nearby Lock Haven. In 1937 Piper faced disaster a second time when the plant

The Piper Cub, first produced in 1930, was the most popular private airplane in the United States before the Second World War. Pilots became so adept at flying the light plane (able to land it virtually anywhere) that it was outfitted with a bazooka and became the L-4B "Grasshopper," an effective antitank weapon in World War II.

burned down. He got out the plans for the Taylor Cub, improved it, and banked the entire future of the company on this one design.

The Piper Cub was just the right size for personal flying and had a timeless design configuration. The Cub was determined to be an excellent training aircraft and more than three thousand of the eight thousand Cubs sold in its first two years were ordered by training programs across the country. Nearly half of the some thirty thousand pilots licensed by the end of the decade had been trained mainly in Piper Cub models.

Pan Am and the Age of the Clipper Ships

Juan Trippe was born into a wealthy banking family, descended from English seafarers who settled on the Maryland coast in the 1600s. He was educated in the finest schools (though he was, at best, an average student) and was graduated from Yale in 1919 after an active collegiate and extra-collegiate career that included playing on the football team, a brief stint as a navy flier in the war, reporting for the Yale newspaper on the NC flights of 1919, and starting a flying club.

As a businessman, Trippe regarded competition as an annoyance—he either joined forces with his competitors to create an even more powerful corporation or brushed them aside. Trippe was very comfortable in the world of high finance and the government movers and shakers, yet he did not hesitate to use the Spanish flavor of his name (even though he hated the name)—given to him by his mother, who had expected to give birth to a girl whom she had wanted to name after a favorite Aunt Juanita— to open doors for him in Latin America.

Trippe saw himself and his company as instruments of American foreign policy in Latin America and in the Pacific. He engaged Lindbergh as a technical advisor and rubbed elbows with virtually every power broker and politico of influence to further not only the interests of Pan Am, but also of the entire American presence in the air. Some admired him and considered him a patriot; at least as many despised him and viewed him a megalomaniacal cutthroat and robber-baron. But the entire aviation community had to acknowledge that Trippe created the largest and best-run distance airline in the world during the four decades of his stewardship.

His first effort in airline-building was a small ferry line that ran from Long Island, New York, to various mountain resorts; this airline used war surplus navy planes. He spent a great deal of time studying the history of the railroads and applied many of the techniques of the great railroad builders—fair and otherwise—to the air transport industry. In 1922 he formed Colonial Air Transport, which was awarded a CAM contract for carrying mail between New York and Boston. In 1927 Trippe won a contract for an air mail run from Florida to Havana, even though he had no planes to fly and two other airlines already operating in the Southeast were run by respected airmen like Eddie Rickenbacker and H.H. "Hap" Arnold. Trippe accomplished this magic by convincing the Cuban dictator Garado Machad to allow only his airline to land in Havana. Industry observers thought it particularly cheeky of Trippe to adopt the name of Arnold's operation, Pan American, when he forced that flier's company out of business and took over the company's airplanes.

Over the next decade, Trippe expanded farther out into Latin America and into the Pacific. At each step, he cultivated a friendship with aircraft builders and encouraged them to build better, more powerful, and more luxurious aircraft. He would make large purchases, for which the manufacturers were grateful. Yet Trippe dealt with a variety of manufacturers and kept all of them guessing (along with his Board of Directors) about which direction he was going to go. He viewed with alarm the inroads Luft Hansa and its parent company, Condor Syndicate, were making in Latin America, and overtly made his efforts to establish commercial air dominance in the region a geopolitical matter. Many flights and activities of Pan Am during the prewar period were nothing short of espionage or diplomatic missions carried out for the State Department.

Trippe first used Fokker Trimotor F-7s, equipped with the best Wright engines, for the Key West–Havana run in 1927. In 1928 these planes were joined by Sikorsky S-38 amphibian planes with Wasp engines. When Pan Am opened routes to Mexico and Central America in 1929, it used a fleet of Fort 5-AT-B Trimotors, the most expensive and advanced commercial plane of its day, and when Pan Am acquired Ralph O'Neil's New York–Rio de Janeiro–Buenos Aires Air Line (NYRBA, and known popularly as "Near Beer"), the new owner commandeered its fleet of fourteen Consolidated Commodore flying boats and flew them on the first Pan Am routes to South America beginning in 1930. Trippe's "secret weapon" in all the development of air routes was his chief pilot, Edwin C. "Eddie" Musick, a veteran Navy flier who built a training, communication, and weather forecasting and reporting system that was unmatched in aviation for decades. Musick flew ahead to stake out the best landing facilities, establish communication relays and weather stations, and plan the best routes and schedules. His contribution was acknowledged by Trippe to be the key to Pan Am's success in South America and the Pacific. (Musick died in 1938 while on a scouting mission for Pan Am near Pago Pago in the Pacific; he was flying the *Samoan Clipper*, a Sikorsky S-42B aircraft.)

It was clear by then that a leap in airplane design was going to be required if commercial aviation was to be extended further. Trippe worked closely with Sikorsky in creating the S-40, the first of the "Clipper" flying boats (so named by Trippe himself). The first of the S-40s, the *Caribbean Clipper*, began service in 1931 (it was christened by Mrs. Herbert Hoover in a ceremony on the Potomac River) and was followed by the *American Clipper*. These aircraft carried forty passengers and were equipped with four Pratt & Whitney Hornet engines that churned out 575 horsepower each and kept the seventeen-ton (15.5t) mammoth flying at a cruising speed of 117 miles per hour (188kph)—not very fast for so much horsepower, but the planes were built for luxury and safety, not speed. The plane looked like something assembled from different aircraft—the wing, the empennage (tail assembly), the engines, and the fuselage were held together by struts and wires—but it flew reliably and efficiently. In 1934 Sikorsky stunned the aviation world by building an even better and more luxurious clipper: the S-42. This time, the nacelles (the engine and propeller housings) were built into the wing so that the wing could be mounted just over the fuselage. The craft still relied on pontoons extending down from each wing for balance in the water, but the entire aircraft was sleeker, which accounted for its cruising speed's going up to 140 miles per hour (225kph).

Meanwhile Trippe had joined forces with the W.R. Grace Comapny, which had formerly been a bitter rival, to form a subsidiary airline, Panagra, that would service the west coasts of North and South America. Eyeing the

LEFT: *The Pan Am seaplanes (here, the Boeing Atlantic Clipper) were virtually flying luxury hotels, with spacious accommodations for fifty to seventy-five passengers (*ABOVE*), and the ultimate in service from a crew of eight. A clipper could make the nonstop New York to London flight in under twenty-four hours.* TOP: *Eventually, Pan Am encouraged Boeing to build large wide-body planes for land use: the Stratocruiser, inaugurated in 1949, made the New York–to-Paris flight in under ten hours, establishing once and for all the viability of the wide-body air transport.*

THE WORLD LEARNS TO FLY
147

How Big is Big?

Since the days of Henson and Stringfellow, aviation visionaries looked for larger and larger aircraft in which to transport passengers. Part of the motivation was to compete with other conveyances such as airships, ocean liners and railroads, each of which had large passenger loads. Both Dornier and Junkers built huge aircraft—the Junkers G38, with seats in the wings, and the Dornier Do X, a flying boat that represented the height of luxury—but though both performed well, neither was able to operate successfully.

Designers already knew that bigger did not automatically mean better. In 1921 Italian aircraft manufacturer Count Caproni, already world-famous for a series of large aircraft, decided the time had come for his masterpiece. His designers built the Ca 60, essentially a houseboat seventy-seven feet (23.5m) long with nine wings each one hundred feet (30.5m) long. In its first test flight on March 3, the Ca 60 lifted off the waters of Lake Maggiore, climbed to sixty feet (18m), and then crashed into the lake in a pile of struts and wires. Test pilot Federico Semprini walked (or swam) away from the wreckage, but the Ca 60 was scrapped.

The large size of the Pan Am Clippers was dictated by the sea-going requirements of the aircraft. These huge aircraft were among the most luxurious and successful commercial airplanes built. They were created by designers and builders whose names became synonymous with large aircraft—Sikorsky, Martin, Boeing—so that the feeling was that passenger aircraft had reached their size limit. However, in 1929 industrialist Norman Bel Geddes hired a staff of designers and instructed them to design an aircraft that could carry "a thousand luxury lovers from New York to Paris fast." The result was the Bel Geddes Airliner, a theoretical model (it existed on paper only; the plane was estimated to have a 1929 price tag of $9 million) of an airplane weighing seven hundred tons (635t), and capable of transporting 450 passengers (with 150 crew members) across the ocean at ninety miles per hour (145kph), or about three times as fast as the fastest ocean liner of the times. The giant pontoons on which the Airliner would rest were designed to contain lifeboats and two "life-planes" capable of cramming in all the passengers in case of emergency.

The Bel Geddes Airline was never built, but it reopened the issue of very large aircraft, and the designers of the Boeing 747 Jumbo Jet took note of it in approaching the designing of their aircraft.

The Dornier Do X over Lake Constance in 1930. Like the airships that flew from the same lake, the Do X was designed and operated more like an ocean liner than an airplane—the plush furniture, for example, was not attached to the floor. After a promotional tour of Europe and South America, the aircraft never flew commercially, and was retired to a museum.

Japanese expansion into the Pacific as yet another threat to the United States, he expanded Pan Am into the Pacific in 1935. For this, he needed yet another new Clipper: the M-130, built by Glenn Martin (who took Sikorsky's S-42 as his starting point). This aircraft was even larger than the S-42 and was more luxuriously appointed. Its main advantage, however, was that it more than doubled the nonstop range of the S-42—three thousand miles (4,827km) compared with twelve hundred miles (1,931km). It was an M-130, the *China Clipper*, that became the most famous of the Pan Am flying boats in the 1930s.

Pan Am ordered several smaller Clipper aircraft—some from Sikorsky, who manufactured the twin-engine "baby clippers," and others from Donald Douglas, who built the Dolphin, an eight-passenger flying boat that saw a great deal of service in the routes from the United States to China. The grandest Clipper was still to come in 1939, in the form of the Boeing B-314, the largest and most powerful of the Clipper aircraft, and the one that proved most profitable, with a passenger capacity of more than seventy (plus a crew of up to sixteen). The B-314, of which only a dozen were built, represented the pinnacle of flying luxury. It contained sleeping quarters, fine dining rooms and bar lounges, deluxe suites and powder rooms, and a walkway inside the wings that allowed engineers to make in-flight repairs. Another famous Pan Am aircraft, the *Yankee Clipper*, was a B-314.

The Europeans were hard pressed to keep up with Pan Am's aircraft builders. England's Short Company built the Empire, a clipperlike aircraft and a flying-boat–mail-carrying-seaplane combination that was intended to carry both mail and passengers across the Atlantic; it saw limited service in Europe and in the Atlantic before the late 1930s, when Pan Am finally turned its attention there. The Germans built ever larger flying boats, beginning with the Dornier Wals flying boats of the early 1920s and culminating in the gigantic Dornier Do X, an aircraft that dwarfed anything else then in the air. This plane had

The Russians produced the giant ANT-20, the Maxim Gorky *(with money raised by the Soviet writers union), an eight-engine aircraft that seemed to have had only propaganda value. It was destroyed when an escort plane (piloted by a flier showing off) crashed into it.*

twelve engines mounted in six pairs atop a 157-foot (48m) wing. It carried 169 passengers in unparalleled luxury. The maiden voyage of the Do X in the spring of 1931 took so long and was plagued by so many problems that support for the plane among investors dried up amid jokes the media made of the plane. Claude Dornier, builder-designer of the Do X, was forced to donate the plane to a museum.

The Do X was not the biggest of the 1930s aircraft to fly: that distinction goes to a Russian land-based aircraft, the Tupolev ANT-20, only one of which was built, the *Maxim Gorky*. Dubbed by Western journalists the "propaganda plane" (and called by some the *Maximum Gawky*), the ANT-20 was an immense needle of an airplane with a wingspan of 210 feet and powered by eight engines: six designed into the wing and a pair mounted above the fuselage. In flight, the *Maxim Gorky* was magnificent; it was also used effectively by the Soviets in many military parades. The *Maxim Gorky* crashed in May 1935 during a ceremonial flight, when an escort airplane crashed into its wing. The plane came apart in the air and none of the forty people aboard survived. The incident finally caused the aviation community to question the wisdom of building larger and larger aircraft.

The Great Airships

The two main technical problems faced by dirigibles were the high inflammability of hydrogen (the gas most commonly used to provide buoyancy) and the structural delicacy of a dirigible. The craft had to be light enough to float in the air, tight enough to retain the gas within its bags, and tough enough to endure winds and storms. The size of a dirigible made the drag caused by even a moderate wind significant; dirigibles crossing the Atlantic east to west, against the prevailing winds, typically took twice as long to cross as they did going the other way. Yet compared to the challenges presented in creating passenger planes, these problems didn't seem all that formidable.

The structural problems were deemed to be a matter of engineering, and the steady progress in design and alloy metallurgy offered promise that these problems would ultimately be solved. The hydrogen problem was another matter. The only apparent alternative to hydrogen was helium, which is just about eight percent heavier than hydrogen and completely inert—on the face of it, a perfect substitute. The problem was that helium was not nearly as abundant as hydrogen, and mining and refining it was a costly process. In the 1920s the principal source for helium in the world were a handful of locations in the United States—in Texas, Utah, and Colorado—and the cost of helium at that time was ten cents a cubic foot. The typical commercial dirigible required two to three million cubic feet of the gas, which sets the cost of helium at upward of $300,000 per craft. By 1925, after considerable government effort and support, the price of helium went down to a penny a cubic foot, but that was still a thousand times more expensive than hydrogen.

From 1919 to 1937, most problems experienced by dirigibles were caused by structural breakdowns caused by weather or wind stresses. The *Hindenburg* explosion was the most gruesomely public and spectacular disaster involving a dirigible, but it was not typical, which was why there was so much question about how the explosion happened and why theories that the ship had been sabotaged were taken seriously.

At the end of the war, the Zeppelin Company was headed by Dr. Hugo Eckener, protégé of Count Zeppelin, who had died of old age in 1917. The French had captured a single Zeppelin, the L49, intact during the war and permitted British and American airmen to inspect it. At war's end, only six Zeppelins were commandeered by the Allies before they could be destroyed by their German crews; one, the L72, the largest built to that time, was designed for the express purpose of bombing New York City. The Germans could only gnash their teeth as they watched the Allied nations using their blueprints to build record-setting airships, and when the leading German airship pilot, Ernst Lehmann, warned that simply copying

the plans without establishing a landing base experienced in the handling of these ships would lead to disaster, experts scoffed at what they regarded as a lame attempt to slow down foreign dirigible development.

The parade of airships that were built in the postwar period, only to be lost or destroyed, is remarkable. The ZR-2, built by England for the U.S. Navy, was to be housed at Lakehurst, New Jersey, in new hangars built especially for it and a companion dirigible, the ZR-1, to be built by the United States. Both were based on the blueprints for the German L72, the dirigible the Germans wanted to sail the Atlantic in, before being forbidden to do so by the British, who made the historic crossing in their R-34, a virtual carbon copy. During the final tests over Hull, England, the ZR-2 broke up and was destroyed, leaving the huge hangar in Lakehurst embarrassingly empty. In Washington, a pattern began that would be repeated many times in years to come: Admiral William A. Moffet, chief of the navy's Bureau of Aeronautics, staunchly defended the dirigible program and vowed to learn from the "lessons" of the ZR-2, so that the lives lost would not be in vain. (The illogic of this approach was one of the factors that eventually drove Billy Mitchell to criticize the navy. Richard Byrd

Louis H. Mayfield (ABOVE), commander of the ZR-2 when it broke up and crashed into the Humber River, near Hull. Because the airships often seemed to meet disaster in the midst of calm flying (as the Roma, *TOP, did during a carefully controlled test flight at Langley Field), the pilots were frequently unfairly blamed for the mishaps.*

had just missed being a passenger on the ill-fated flight, and one wonders if Moffet would have been so accepting of the loss and in such a learning mood had the celebrated explorer been among the fatalities.)

A similar fate was met by the *Roma*, a semi-rigid dirigible built in Italy by Umberto Nobile—it was destroyed during test flights at Langley Field, Virginia, in February 1921, when it crashed into high voltage lines after being forced down by a sudden downdraft. The U.S. Army's biggest dirigible, the C-2, exploded as soon as it left its hangar in October 1922. The L-72, renamed the *Dixmude* by the French, was on a flight to Africa in the winter of 1923 when it disappeared over the Mediterranean. The wreckage discovered a week later indicated that the ship had broken up in rough weather.

Thinking that there may have been something to Lehmann's warning, the Zeppelin factories and hangars at Lake Constance and Friedrichshafen, slated to be destroyed, were spared (though Eckener had to convert them so they could also produce kitchen utensils to keep them afloat). In 1923 a new company, the Goodyear-Zeppelin Corporation, was created to produce dirigibles, combining the newly developed alloy duralumin with German expertise and experience (much as German rocket scientists were pressed into service in the American missile and space programs after World War II). The two flagship U.S. dirigibles, the ZR-1 and the ZR-3, named the *Shenandoah* and the *Los Angeles*, were completed (in the factories in Akron, Ohio, and Friedrichshafen, respectively) and put into service in 1924. The C-2 explosion had made the navy reluctant to use hydrogen, and there was simply not enough helium for both ships, so it was decided that the two dirigibles would share the same helium and alternate flights.

The *Shenandoah*, which was built to military specification, toured the western states testing moorings and airfields. Then it returned to Lakehurst to transfer its helium to the *Los Angeles* for a more public tour promoting commercial dirigible flight. Technical problems with the *Los Angeles* forced it back to Lakehurst, and the navy decided to have the *Shenandoah* fulfill its sister ship's engagements. The airship's commander, Zachary Lansdowne, complained to his superiors that the ship was not prepared for the line squalls and thunderstorms that were common in the Midwest. The ship was sent anyway, and on September 3, 1925, the *Shenandoah* met a storm and broke up over the Ohio countryside. Lansdowne and thirteen of the crew were killed when the control car tore loose and fell. Several crew members sent into the hull earlier to secure one of the bags of gas, including Lieutenant Charles E. Rosendahl, clung to the bag while the rest of the craft peeled away, and landed safely twelve miles away.

It was the crash of the *Shenandoah* that prompted Brigadier General Billy Mitchell's intemperate remarks about the way the navy was handling its aircraft program. A Naval Court of Inquiry conducted a lengthy investigation, which included Lansdowne's widow testifying about her husband's misgivings, and Lieutenant Rosendahl, buttressed by Admiral Moffett, defending the navy's decision. The court blamed Lansdowne for the accident and made a great many self-serving pronounce-

ments about how the loss of the *Shenandoah* was the price to be paid for the lessons learned. After much debate, Congress caved in and approved the navy plan to build three replacements for the *Shenandoah*, two of them nearly twice its size and the other a smaller all-metal dirigible, the ZMC-2, the only dirigible that was still in active service during World War II.

The End of the Airship Era: The Hindenburg Disaster

With the building of the *Los Angeles*, the German dirigible industry was given a great psychological boost, which emboldened Eckener into building (with the help of funds donated by the German people) an even greater craft: the L-127, to be known as the *Graf Zeppelin*. Launched in 1928, the *Graf Zeppelin* conducted regular flights across the Atlantic to North and South America, as well as several trips around the world and to the Arctic region. On the ship's maiden voyage, Hugo Eckener had to use all his experience and piloting powers to maintain control when the *Graf Zeppelin* was caught in a storm over the East Coast of the United States. Lieutenant Rosendahl, the flier who had escaped death in the crash of the *Shenandoah*, was also on board.

In 1929 the British finally reentered the airship arena with two immense airships: the R-100 and the R-101. The R-100 was caught in a storm over the St. Lawrence Seaway during its maiden voyage to Canada; the dirigible barely made it back to England and was placed in its hangar as the authorities waited to see how the R-101, boasted to be safe enough to have an enclosed smoking room, would fare on its trip to India. Unfortunately, a new device that controlled the distribution of ballast water did not function properly, forcing the ship to fly at very low altitudes. As the airship passed over the French town of Beauvais, it struck a church steeple and exploded. Forty-eight passengers were burned almost beyond recognition. The British did not need any further evidence that the airships were unviable; the R-100, which was awaiting repairs, was summarily dismantled. But the United States was not swayed, and the ever-optimistic Admiral Moffet pointed to the U.S. supply of helium as the reason that no similar tragedy would occur with an American dirigible. The navy ordered two airships that were to be the largest yet produced: each nearly eight hundred feet (244m) long with a capacity of 6.5 million cubic feet (182,000 cubic m). In August 1931 the ZRS-4,

The poignant photos of eastern Ohio farm folk sadly viewing the twisted wreckage of the Shenandoah *stayed with many Americans and weakened popular support for dirigible flight a dozen years before the* Hindenburg *disaster.*

the *Akron*, took its place alongside the *Los Angeles* at Lakehurst. Earlier in the year, the Empire State Building had been completed and its roof structure was designed to be a mooring for the *Los Angeles* and later for the *Akron*. Although a test with a smaller dirigible made it clear that the system was not going to work, promotional photographs showing the *Los Angeles* docking at the top of the Empire State Building were published in newspapers around the country, sometimes without the photograph being identified as a "photographic composite."

On April 3, 1933, the *Akron* was on a flight off the Jersey shore, when it crashed into the Atlantic and sank quickly. Seventy-seven crew members were killed; the three survivors had to swim up from under the craft to the surface to save themselves. This disaster was the worst in the history of dirigible flight, and Admiral Moffett, who had called the *Akron* "the safest dirigible ever built" was not available to defend the program—he was among the fatalities. Lieutenant Rosendahl, who had been slated to captain the ship in the flight, had been replaced at the last minute, and thus escaped death in a dirigible disaster for the third time.

The navy's second great dirigible, the *Macon*, was a bit smaller and sleeker than the *Akron*; it was also faster, being able to cruise in still air at eighty-five miles per hour (137kph). On February 12, 1935, the *Macon* was practicing maneuvers off the California coast when it encountered a storm and crashed into the Pacific. This

time, eighty-one of the eighty-three crew members were rescued. The Naval Court of Inquiry rendered the same judgment about the *Macon* crash as it did of the *Akron*'s: the crashes were not caused by structural problems with the aircraft. But this time Congress suspended the program, and the United States did not build another dirigible until after World War II.

When Hitler came to power in Germany, neither he nor Hermann Göring, the head of the Luftwaffe (Germany's air force), believed that dirigibles had any value either as military or commercial aircraft. They allowed the propaganda minister, headed by Josef Goebbels, to take charge of the two mammoth Zeppelins then in service under German control: the *Graf Zeppelin* and the newly launched *Hindenburg*, the ultimate luxury airship, which was put in service in March 1936. Both ships were designed to be run with helium, but the United States had already placed a ban on exporting any of its helium supply, so hydrogen had to be used instead. The Germans used these ships as instruments of propaganda and espionage as the ships crisscrossed the globe during the 1936 season, flying north of the equator from May to September, and in the Southern Hemisphere the rest of the year. During the 1936 Olympics, which were held in Germany, the *Hindenburg* was everywhere, providing a sinister psychological edge for German athletes as it hovered over the games.

In May 1937, after a late summer run to Rio de Janeiro, the *Hindenburg* began its service to the United

OPPOSITE: *The Macon, launched in 1933 (seen here over Manhattan), was really a flying aircraft carrier, able to carry, service, and launch five fighters that could return and land.* LEFT: *In spite of the loss of seventy of the seventy-three aboard the Macon's sister ship, the Akron, when the latter crashed into the Atlantic off the New Jersey coast (here, rescuers survey the Akron's wreckage), the builders of the Macon believed that the ship was safer because it had multiple gas cells instead of one large cell. On February 12, 1935, the Macon also crashed (under the same captain), this time into the Pacific, with only three fatalities (among a crew of eighty-three).*

TOP RIGHT: *The Germans prided themselves in developing sophisticated controls for their Zeppelins. Captain Max Pruss, commander of the Hindenburg on its final voyage, is seen here at the controls of the airship on an earlier Atlantic crossing.* ABOVE: *Landing was a problem the great airships never solved. Ground crews had to pull the ship to its mooring in scenes that seemed to be out of films about Egyptian slaves. The great airship swayed gently, even in a light breeze, while passengers were disembarking.*

THE WORLD LEARNS TO FLY

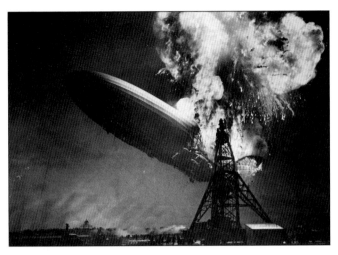

ABOVE: A sequence of news photos of the Hindenburg *disaster. Newspaper readers, seeing only the center photo, believed the airship had crashed into the mooring tower in the foreground or had exploded when a spark of static electricity from the tower ignited the hydrogen. The other photos show, however, that the center photo is misleading and that the craft was in fact well away from the tower at the time of the initial explosion. (Otherwise, the men seen at the top of the tower in silhouette would have to have been several stories tall.) Also, the ground lines are dangling from the airship's nose, while the explosion begins in the stern. So what did cause the accident? We'll never know.*
BACKGROUND: The LZ130—the Graf Zeppelin—the last hurrah of the airship era.

States with a flight from Berlin to New York. On May 6, as it approached Lakehurst, it waited for a squall to pass (as many other dirigibles had done in the past). At 7:20 in the evening, the *Hindenburg* headed for New Jersey and prepared to tie up at the mooring tower. What happened next has been the subject of many hundreds of hours of investigation and speculation. What was apparent to the eye and to the camera (and what was described by radio reporter Herb Morrison in one of broadcasting's most unforgettable moments) was that an explosion engulfed the rear of the dirigible and quickly spread to the entire ship, bringing it crashing to the ground in flames. The manifest listed ninety-seven passengers, unusually large because it included trainees for the *Graf Zeppelin II*, then under construction. Commanding the flight was Captain Max Pruss, one of the Zeppelin Company's most experienced pilots, and along for the flight (supervising the training program) was the company's premier pilot, Ernst Lehmann. Of the ninety-seven aboard, thirty-six died, including thirteen "civilian" (paying) passengers, the first passengers of this kind killed in a dirigible accident. (Past fatalities had been crew members and military personnel, never paying passengers.)

Captain Pruss was saved, but Captain Lehmann staggered out of the fire only to die in the hospital a few hours later. Before he died, however, he was interviewed by one of the investigators sent hastily to Lakehurst to determine what had happened—none other than Charles Rosendahl. As Lehmann lay dying, he muttered to Rosendahl that the explosion must have been caused by an incendiary bullet shot from the ground. Lehmann's dying words, "It must have been an infernal machine," were often quoted, though no one was quite sure what he meant.

The Germans conducted an elaborate Nazi funeral in New Jersey for the victims, milking the occasion for maximum propaganda and implying that the tragedy could have been averted if the United States had been willing to sell Germany some of its helium. When Secretary of the Interior Harold Ickes refused to let Germany have any helium, Hugo Eckener came to Washington to appeal to him personally. At first, Ickes relented, and tankers were dispatched from Germany. Before the pickup could be made, however, Hitler annexed Austria in March 1938, and Ickes, convinced that the Nazis were bent on war, rescinded the order. Right up to the invasion of Poland by Germany in September 1939, U.S. agencies pressured Ickes to let the Germans have the helium. When war came, Ickes gloated that he had been right all along.

The *Los Angeles* was dismantled and sold for scrap. In Germany, the two *Graf Zeppelin*s were stripped of anything that could be used in aircraft, and then the Germans did what the Allied countries had threatened to do since the end of World War I: they leveled the Zeppelin hangars at Frankfurt and closed down the factory at Friedrichshafen. The age of the great airships had come to an end.

The Court-Martial of Billy Mitchell and the Rise of U.S. Air Power

The prevailing attitude among U.S. military leaders regarding air power was a continuation of the prewar attitude, namely, that aircraft had only a supportive role to play in ground and naval actions. Even Billy Mitchell's spectacular military assault at St. Mihiel, which broke the German line at Verdun, did not convince the generals. Thus, when Mitchell was appointed Assistant Chief of the Army Air Service, he embarked on a campaign to have air power recognized as a key and independent element of the nation's defenses and military arsenal.

In the seven years during which he waged this campaign, Mitchell would point out the deficiencies of his superiors, he would be punished, and then the recommendations he made would be quietly carried out. Many American military leaders, such as Admiral Moffet, one of Mitchell's chief adversaries, were meanwhile admitting privately that Mitchell was right. In the hands of a more politically skillful officer, the battle could have been won without depriving the country of one of its most brilliant military tacticians, Mitchell, in the years prior to World War II.

Mitchell began his campaign with a series of record-setting flights and newsworthy maneuvers that piqued public interest in the continuing development of American air power. In 1923 Mitchell's Army Air Service department sponsored the first transcontinental nonstop flight of Oakley Kelly and John Macready, and the first Army demonstration of in-flight refueling. When the navy was given control of the dirigibles built using the blueprints the French had made from the captured German Zeppelin, Mitchell openly criticized the future use of dirigibles and urged that they be abandoned in favor of airplanes. He staged a nonstop flight by Russel Maughn designed to show that with an air force consisting of airplanes, a fighting force could be on either coast within a half-day, which was not possible with any foreseeable dirigible. Politicians and military leaders discounted Mitchell's claims as sour grapes for not being given charge of the dirigible program.

Mitchell then tackled two basic questions of military strategy: the need for an independent air force and the possible vulnerability of battleships to attack from the air. In the early 1920s the prevailing wisdom was that battleships were impervious to bombing from the air. Mitchell pointed out that for the cost of a single battleship one could build a thousand planes, and only a few were necessary to sink any battleship. Clearly influenced by Mitchell, the navy conducted a series of tests in 1920, during which they dropped dummy bombs on an obsolete battleship, the *Indiana*. The tests showed that an aircraft would have little trouble delivering bombs that would sink just about any naval vessel. The *Indiana* tests

were supposed to have been secret, but Mitchell revealed them when he was called to testify before Congress. The Navy countered with a report that claimed the tests showed the exact opposite.

In June 1921, the Navy offered to allow Mitchell to prove his contention once and for all by bombing and sinking a captured German battleship, the *Ostfriesland*. The test were held seventy-five miles (120.5km) off the Virginia coast, and not close to shore—one of the many ways the navy tried to undermine Mitchell's bomber crews. The navy would not permit the test to be delayed by bad weather and had selected as a target a battleship that was triple-hulled and which had withstood mines and torpedoes during the war. Mitchell rallied his troops, and they performed superbly, sinking the ship and leaving no doubt that battleships were vulnerable.

The import of Mitchell's success was not lost on the navy. The response was to go forward with a plan to build aircraft carriers. The first ship converted to accommodate aircraft was the *Langley*, nicknamed the "Covered Wagon" because of its landing platform covering the entire top of the ship. In 1927 two cruisers, the *Lexington* and the *Saratoga*, were converted into aircraft carriers. In 1934 the *Ranger* became the first aircraft carrier designed from scratch to join the fleet; the celebrated carriers the *Yorktown* and the *Enterprise* joined the fleet in 1939.

Meanwhile, Mitchell received support from an unexpected source. In 1919 the Secretary of War, Newton Baker, sent a group of advisers to Europe to study air defenses. This group, chaired by Benedict Crowell, toured Europe and then made its recommendations, one of which was that an independent air force should be organized on an equal footing with the army and the navy. Secretary Baker was not expecting this and tried to suppress the report, but Congress got hold of it and held hearings on the Curry Bill, proposing a Department of Aviation. It was during the Senate hearings on the Curry Bill that Mitchell first voiced his opinions publicly and, for five years, the general periodically made headlines with his brash testimony.

Mitchell's term as Assistant Chief of the Army Air Service was due to end in March 1925, and rumors were rampant that he would not be reappointed. When he testified that the United States was vulnerable to air attack from Japan against the Hawaiian Islands, he was not reappointed. He was demoted to his original rank of colonel and reassigned to Fort Sam Houston in San Antonio, Texas. When the *Shenandoah* dirigible disaster struck that September, at the same time that a navy attempt at a nonstop flight from San Francisco to Hawaii went awry, Mitchell launched his boldest attack. "These accidents," he said, "are the direct results of incompetency, criminal negligence and almost treasonable administration of the National Defense by the Navy and War Departments. . . . All aviation policies, schemes and

Admiral Moffet—Mitchell's Quiet Champion

While Billy Mitchell was stirring up the military, making powerful enemies in nearly every quarter, another military man was systematically accomplishing the same goals espoused by Mitchell, even while under attack by Mitchell and his supporters. Admiral William Moffett was famous for his steadfast support of the U.S. dirigible program, which ended disastrously for him in 1933 when he was killed in a dirigible crash. But less known were his behind-the-scenes efforts in bringing the U.S. Navy into the air age.

Even before Billy Mitchell demonstrated the potential of air power by sinking the *Ostfreisland* in 1921, Moffet was telling his colleagues in the navy that, without an air force to protect it, "the fleet would be a sitting duck." He was a talented diplomat who used the command structure of the navy to accomplish his goals. Convincing the navy brass that it was in the navy's interest to build larger and larger ships, he showed that aircraft carriers would be far larger than anything then on the boards. The creation of a separate Navy Air Force was probably the farthest thing from the minds of the politicians and the navy chiefs who approved the appropriations for the carriers, but that is exactly what those appropriations accomplished.

The first large carriers in the U.S. Naval Fleet, the *Saratoga* and the *Lexington*, were in service by 1927, and the construction of a series of carriers was well under way at the outbreak of World War II. This turned out to be very fortunate, because the U.S. Army Air Force would have had great difficulty mounting an attack on the Japanese without the ability to place attack aircraft in close proximity to the South Pacific. Did the U.S. military go along with Moffett because it anticipated this need, perhaps because intelligence reports indicated that the Japanese were building aircraft carriers? Possibly, but the naval commander placed in charge of the Pacific fleet and the Navy Air Force was Chester Nimitz, a naval commander who believed submarines, not aircraft carriers, were the key to naval warfare. Nimitz managed the air resources at his command very well, however, and became one of the celebrated heroes of the Second World War.

systems are dictated by the non-flying officers of the Army or Navy, who know practically nothing about it." The War Department had little choice but to bring Mitchell up on charges before a court-martial.

The court-martial of Billy Mitchell, which lasted from October 28 to December 17, 1925, was the longest and most widely followed and reported in U.S. history. Hoping to avoid media attention, the army held the trial in a shabby building, but this tawdry maneuver only made Mitchell's allegations seem all the more valid, and the trial yielded new headlines nearly every day it was in session. Mitchell delivered eloquent speeches regarding the state of the U.S. air forces, and spoke virtually without opposition. The chief judge of the twelve-member court, General Charles Summerall, was challenged on the grounds of bias because of a speech he had delivered a few months before the trial criticizing Mitchell; Summerall was forced to leave the court. Mitchell called as witnesses for the defense some of America's most celebrated heroes—Eddie Rickenbacker, Major Carl Spaatz, Representative Fiorello LaGuardia, and Rear Admiral of the Navy William Sims. During the testimony, one of the judges leaned over to a bailiff and, without realizing he could be heard throughout the courtroom, said the witness's testimony was "damn rot."

The most sensational testimony, however, came from the widow of Zachary Lansdowne, commander of the *Shenandoah*. She repeated the testimony she had already given regarding the misgivings her husband had had about the final mission of the airship, and then testified how the navy had tried to badger her into changing her testimony for the court-martial. The prosecution claimed throughout the trial that Mitchell's sole purpose in all his statements promoting an independent air force was to eventually become the head of it. Most people in the courtroom looked at one another and nodded that Mitchell seemed to be the most logical man for the job.

Two molders of U.S. air power: Admiral William A. Moffet (LEFT), who introduced air power by convincing the navy to convert battleships into aircraft carriers, and William "Billy" Mitchell (RIGHT), hero of the St. Mihiel offensive of World War I and abrasively outspoken proponent of air power.

Mitchell's performance during the trial elevated him even more in the public's estimation, and when the judges returned a guilty verdict, there was public outrage expressed in the press and in the halls of Congress. However, even when evidence surfaced that one of the judges, Douglas MacArthur, known to be a supporter of Mitchell, had voted for acquittal, Mitchell insisted that the matter not be reopened. Mitchell accepted the verdict and the punishment: a five-year suspension of rank, responsibility, and pay (later eased by President Coolidge to suspension of half his pay). Mitchell's response was to resign his commission. He lived out the last ten years of his life as a country gentleman on his Virginia estate, periodically going on lecture tours, promoting the idea of an independent air force and criticizing the navy's dirigible program and management of the nation's air defenses. Billy Mitchell died at the age of fifty-six on February 19, 1936, of heart failure in a New York hospital.

While the Mitchell court-martial was in progress, an Aircraft Inquiry Board appointed by President Coolidge and headed by Dwight Morrow submitted its report to the president. It contained generous helpings of Mitchell's testimony (though he refused to testify further once his trial began). The report's conclusion was that a separate air force was not necessary, but that some independence for the air service was of potential benefit and, in any case, the corps should be run by experienced fliers, preferably those with combat experience. The Air Service was upgraded to the Air Corps and the post of Assistant Secretary of War for Aeronautics was created. The Corps's budget and personnel were greatly increased, and five-year plans were drawn up for its development, making it clear that the air forces of the United States were not going to be dependent on the plans of the army or the navy. In effect, all that Mitchell had tried to accomplish slowly came to pass. Just a few days before Billy Mitchell was buried in his native Wisconsin, the Air Corps placed its first order for the B-17 Flying Fortress bomber, which was to become the mainstay of the American air effort in the coming war.

Chapter 8

World War II: The Aerial War

Introduction

More than fifteen hundred years ago, the Chinese strategist Sun-tzu wrote: "Every battle is won before it is ever fought." The superiority of one side over the other (he meant) can be determined before the actual conflict; more often than not, superior forces will vanquish inferior. This was never so clearly demonstrated as in the air war of World War II. Both sides made very clear decisions that took them in one direction or another, and with the benefit of hindsight it is possible to determine which of those decisions proved advantageous and which proved disastrous.

The outcome of the war, in both the European and the Pacific theaters, was determined by certain decisions and their outcomes—in a very real sense, World War II was an air war, and it was in the air that it was won by the Allies and lost by the Axis powers. This is not to diminish the heroism and sacrifice of the soldiers and sailors who also fought, but supremacy on the ground and at sea were determined by supremacy in the air. The ability to bomb targets with minimal resistance, the ability to sink battleships and carriers, the ability to secure beachheads and forward positions—all these were made possible by one air power vanquishing the other, with armaments and instruments that were not available (or even dreamed of) in World War I.

The preparations for the war began several years earlier, and it was apparent from the very beginning that a major portion of the conflict would be fought in the sky. On March 10, 1935, Hermann Göring, Air Minister of the Luftwaffe, the German Air Force, called the military attachés of England and France to his opulent offices in the Air Ministry building in Berlin. He informed them that Germany no longer considered itself bound by the restrictions placed on its development of military aircraft by the Treaty of Versailles. To underscore his point, he drew aside the tall drapes of his office window and displayed a sky filled with all manner of aircraft, flying over the Ministry just for the benefit of Göring's visitors. It was the first of many incidents before and during the war in which the Germans tried to convince their adversaries that their power was greater than it actually was. Had those attachés been competent (or inclined) to look a bit closer at the several hundred planes that flew overhead, they would have noticed that many of them were not military aircraft, but old Junker trimotors painted with military colors.

The ruse (conducted consistently and elaborately) worked both for and against the Germans. It convinced England and France that the Germans were too powerful to challenge when Hitler annexed Austria, and that (along with reports from Lindbergh, who toured many German factories and had been fooled himself) in turn prompted Chamberlain's policy of appeasement. It also sent the British and the Americans scurrying back to the drawing board and the factories to overcome the head start the Germans seemed to have. The shock of Göring's display hit particularly hard in England, where the government had sworn by the "ten-year rule"—the idea that England would have a ten-year warning before the next war, and thus plenty of time to develop any weaponry required—and had thus allowed its weapons research program to languish.

Throughout the war, the Allies were convinced that the Germans were developing, and on the verge of unleashing, super weapons—from jet aircraft to intercontinental rockets to the atom bomb. There was plenty of evidence that could not be dismissed: the Germans had actually deployed V-2 rockets from Peenemunde on the Baltic, and

The Curtiss P-40 Tomahawk was a modified version of the earlier P-36 Hawk. Inferior to their Japanese counterparts in almost every way, Tomahawks nevertheless saw much action in the Pacific and were effective because the Flying Tiger pilots flew missions in packs.

Nearly thirteen thousand B-17 Flying Fortresses—the mainstay of the Allied bombing campaign—were built by Boeing. Yet Congress feared that appropriating funds for such a plane would create fear among the public of cross-oceanic bombing. The start of a goodwill flight to South America (ABOVE) in February 1938 was designed to allay such fears and promote the plane.

they had all the necessary brainpower in many other areas of science. But what the Allies did not know was that the Germans had a time rule of their own: they did not commit any resources to a weapons project that could not be reasonably expected to yield a field weapon within a year. This rule grew partly out of the belief that the war would not last longer than two years, and partly out of a belief that the industrial capacity of Germany could not sustain a development program for that long. The Nazis were right about the second premise, but wrong about the first, and they mistakenly scuttled the programs for the jet aircraft and the atom bomb virtually in the bud.

Meanwhile the Allies continued to develop aircraft that could overcome the advantages of the earliest German fighters, as well as long-range bombers that were unchallenged and unmatched by the Luftwaffe. This did not happen easily or automatically: the battles that Billy Mitchell fought and lost had to be waged over again and with greater cunning if an independent U.S. air force was to be created. As for the Germans, they had learned some lessons from Mitchell and ignored others. Mitchell believed strongly in the development of large, fast, high-flying bombers that were beyond the range of ground fire and faster than fighter aircraft. His first attempt at build-

ing such a bomber, designed by Walter Barling in 1919, was an expensive experiment that came to known as "Mitchell's Folly." Over the next decade, Glenn Martin provided the Navy with a series of bombers, beginning with the MB-1 that Mitchell had used to sink the *Ostfriesland* and culminating in the MB-10. The MB-10 and similar fine planes produced in England and France were not going to be adequate if the United States ever found it necessary to fight a war in Europe. This set Boeing's chief designer, Clairmont Egtvegt, to work and resulted in the Boeing B-17 Flying Fortress, arguably the plane most responsible for the defeat of the Germans.

In the face of defeatist talk from Lindbergh (who, in fairness, flew combat missions in the Pacific, paid dearly for his isolationist beliefs, and placed his entire knowledge of the German aircraft industry, distilled of German misdirection, at the disposal of General H.H. "Hap" Arnold, chief of the Army Air Corps), aviation pioneer and Russian exile Alexander de Seversky, who had lost a leg flying for the czar in World War I and was one of the world's most gifted aircraft designers, encouraged the development of air power and promoted a program that exploited the many weaknesses he saw in the Luftwaffe. In the final analysis, the air war was won as much by what the Luftwaffe failed to do as by what the Allies succeeded in doing.

The German approach (which had its roots in the Red Baron's Flying Circus of World War I) was to provide air support for ground troops in the actual field of battle. The Junkers JU 87 Stuka dive-bombers that descended on Poland in 1939 and were used so effectively as a component of the *Blitzkrieg* ("lightning war") were still operating as independent agents in the air, attacking targets with the same kind of spontaneity of the armor and infantry. This was exactly what made the strategy so effective. But once the lines were drawn, the Germans had no way of maintaining control of the air or extending destruction beyond the immediate battle line. Göring had taken note of Mitchell's actions at St. Mihiel, but he was unaware of how coordinated an operation it was and how much of his resources Mitchell had devoted to monitoring and directing the planes.

The entire practice of dive-bombing was an American invention that World War I ace Ernst Udet witnessed while on tour in the United States and which he brought back with him to his native Germany. The amiable Udet was not a Nazi (he reportedly had a picture of Hitler in his Berlin apartment that he used for target practice) and was not much of an administrator. When he was appointed technical director of the Luftwaffe after Göring took power as Air Minister, many eyebrows were raised. Ernst Heinkel, one of Germany's great airplane builders, had several large bombers on the drawing boards; Udet

Herman Göring (left) and Ernst Udett, the famed World War I ace who was placed in charge of Luftwaffe development, confer in 1938.

summarily canceled the program, telling Heinkel that there would be no need for long-range bombers.

Analysis of what transpired more than fifty years ago has raised many questions. Udet returned to the United States, now as a high Nazi official, yet the United States encouraged his pursuit of dive-bombing as a technique and even sold him two planes, the Curtiss F8C "Hell-Diver," which had been developed by the Navy specifically for dive-bombing. By temperament, Göring was not a man to relinquish glory or power to anyone, least of all Udet, whom he privately regarded as nothing more than a stunt flier. Yet this is what he did, giving Udet all the credit for the Stuka's success in the invasions of Poland and Norway. It is possible that Udet was a pawn of both sides: the Americans, who knew that dive-bombing was effective in the short run but a losing strategy in the long run, and Göring, who needed a scapegoat if the war took any longer than originally planned or if the Allied production capacity buried the German war machine (which is exactly what happened).

Udet committed suicide in November 1941, scrawling on the wall, "Reichsmarschall, why have you forsaken me?" Göring had wanted to court-martial Udet posthumously, but instead he presided over a lavish state funeral for the hero of the First World War. Udet's successor, Hans Jeschonnek, was even less qualified than Udet; not surprisingly, he too committed suicide when blamed for the failure of the Nazi air war. The irony of ironies is that the judgment of history places a large measure of blame for the fall of the Third Reich at Göring's doorstep. The vaunted Luftwaffe, which wreaked so much destruction on Europe and was hailed as the chief instrument of Hitler's conquests, proved in the end to be an inadequate instrument of empire.

Rehearsals for War: Ethiopia, Spain, and China

Before the outbreak of World War II, several of the major combatants had opportunities to test their equipment, especially their combat aircraft and air tactics. The first such test came when the Italians invaded Ethiopia (then known as Abyssinia) in May 1936. The use of bombers against tribal soldiers with pre–World War I equipment outraged the world and gave a clear indication what Italian Fascist dictator Mussolini was made of. It left little doubt that if Germany declared war, Italy was likely to side with the Germans and use the opportunity to grab anything within the flight range of its aircraft. The Italian Caproni bombers used dive-bombing techniques taught them by German flight instructors, and the battle for Ethiopia was over in just a few months.

A more serious test that pitted plane against plane was the Spanish Civil War of 1937–1938. To many observers,

the war was promoted by Germany, Italy, and Russia for the express purpose of providing an opportunity for these nations to test their weaponry in combat situations— at least that was how the wavering support on both sides was interpreted. Germany and Italy backed the Nationalists led by Francisco Franco, while the left-wing Republicans were supported by the Soviet Union. Both sides provided their latest aircraft and insisted that their own pilots fly them, ostensibly to prevent them from falling into enemy hands. Expensive and secret Junkers JU52s were used to transport troops when simple trucks would have served. And several operations were entirely gratuitous, such as the saturation bombing of the inconsequential town of Guernica on April 26, 1937, by the elite Kondor Legion of the Luftwaffe. The bombing was decried around the world and became the subject of a celebrated antiwar mural by Picasso.

The most telling indication of the German motive for entering the conflict, however, was the introduction of its most advanced fighter plane, the Messerschmitt Bf 109B. This aircraft was to become a mainstay of the Luftwaffe, and it had its first test runs in Spain in 1937. The plane had been designed by a young airplane builder, Willy Messerschmitt, whose name was to become virtually synonymous with the German fighter aircraft of World War II. Messerschmitt, born in 1898, was too young to have been involved in World War I, but he spent much of the postwar years learning to glide and building, first gliders, and then light aircraft. He was a particularly ambitious young man and joined the Nazi Party as soon as it came to power. Messerschmitt became a close friend of Hermann Göring and was unofficial technical advisor to the Luftwaffe throughout the war (which was another reason a weak man like Udet filled the post officially).

The basic design principle behind the Bf 109 was a simple, if coldly calculating, one. Until World War II, designers had little hard information on the strength of material or manufacturing techniques, and since it would not do to have a plane come apart in flight, engineers took no chances. The planes were thus better armored

and better constructed than they needed to be. (A similar reason accounts for the incredible longevity of the early DC and Boeing transports of the 1930s: they were much better built than their expected lifespan required, and that kept them in service for decades longer than their designers intended.) Messerschmitt, accustomed to the transitory construction of gliders, believed that there was no reason for fighter aircraft to have this safety factor built in—so he eliminated it. The fighter pilot should survive by virtue of his flying, Messerschmitt thought, and not at the expense of the aircraft. As a result, the Messerschmitt planes were lighter and faster than comparably designed and powered fighters.

Messerschmitt (and his chief designer, Walter Rethel) could get away with this as a manufacturing policy only if he knew he had the unwavering support of the Air Ministry and that Göring would allow that some planes and pilots would be lost when planes came apart in a dive or too sharp a turn. This policy was equivalent to a "trading of like pieces" in the chess game of the battlefield, a strategy Germany could afford early in the war, but for which they paid dearly in the Battle of Britain and in the latter stages of the war.

The final rehearsal for World War II was the Japanese invasion of China in 1937. During the 1930s the attitude of the United States toward Japan was ambiguous. On the one hand, the State Department liked having an irritant to Russia on its eastern border, and the Japanese were certainly that, seizing Manchuria in 1931. On the other hand, the United States supported the government of Chiang Kai-shek in China and supplied him with (meaning, sold him) Curtiss Hawk fighter aircraft to defend his country against Japan. There was little doubt that when Japan invaded China in 1937, it was using aircraft that were designed by Jiro Horikoshi, who had been taught his craft at the Curtiss-Wright plant and who was the principal designer for Mitsubishi.

In its invasion of China, the Japanese used the Mitsubishi 96, an aircraft designed to be launched from an aircraft carrier. This was deemed unnecessary for invading China and indicated larger goals for the Japanese. When fighting broke out with Russia, the Russians brought in their best fighter, the Polikarpov I-16, teaching the Japanese that they were going to have to continue fighter development if they were ever to fight

ABOVE: The 1937 air war between China and Japan saw the final transition from World War I open-cockpit planes (used by the Japanese in 1933), in which armament was hand-controlled, to the closed cockpit, featuring automatic armaments, of World War II aircraft.
BELOW: The Sino-Japanese conflict also gave the first indication that ground canon might be effective anti-aircraft devices (even against advanced fighters), particularly in protecting airfields.

an air war with the Soviet Union. The hostilities were ended in June 1940 with the signing of the Russo-Japanese Pact. The Japanese saw from early in the 1930s that its main rival in the Pacific was not China or Russia, but the United States. For fourteen years prior to the outbreak of war in the Pacific, the single question on the final examination in the Japanese aeronautical military academy was how one would plan an aerial attack on the U.S. Naval Base at Pearl Harbor.

Blitzkrieg: War Breaks Out in Europe

In spite of the demonstration of the Blitzkrieg in Spain, and the role the Stukas played in it, the Poles were completely unprepared for the German onslaught—it took only twenty-seven days, from September 1 to 27, 1939, for Poland to be conquered. The Junkers JU52 Stuka was not a particularly fast or agile plane; it did not even have a retractable undercarriage, and it did not carry much of a bomb load. The Stuka did, however, provide the pilot with great control when it dove, and it pulled out of the dive easily. The secret was in the "inverted-gull-wing" design—the fact that the wings left the fuselage aimed downward and then turned upward.

The plane was equipped with sirens that blared loudly as the plane dove in on its target, making the Stuka an effective psychological weapon. Reports from the front, in fact, indicated that the best way to counteract the Stuka was to ignore it. Most planes could deliver only one bombload per sortie, which meant the plane would have to return to base after each strike. This also meant that the Stuka's range was very small and the plane could be used only at the front lines of battle.

An assessment of the resources of the German ground forces at the outset of the war indicates that, in spite of

The Germans developed the JU-87 Stuka dive bomber and turned some of its weaknesses—its low speed and sluggish handling—into useful components of their blitzkrieg tactics. Stukas were never a factor when opposed by nearly any of the Allied fighters of the war.

its boasts, it was very much outdated when compared with the armies of France and England. It relied mainly on horses for transportation, and much of its weaponry dated back to World War I. But Poland's armed forces were even more archaic—the cavalry units dated back a century and the air force had fewer than three hundred planes.

It is also worthwhile to note that when Germany invaded Poland from the west, the Soviet Union invaded from the east seventeen days later, according to the terms of the secret agreement between Germany and the Soviet Union signed in August. When the hostilities ended on October 6, the Soviet Union had occupied eastern Poland, an area coveted and sometimes held by the czars in the previous century. The Soviets did not stop there. Believing they were insulated from the west by the Germans, Stalin launched air attacks on Finland in December. The Finns had a larger air force than Poland, but it was no match for the planes the Soviets had tested in the Far East.

An immediate consequence of the Soviet invasion of Finland was the withdrawal of the Soviet planes and pilots that were protecting the Chinese from the Japanese. Stepping into the breach was General Claire Chennault, who organized a mercenary force to fly the planes the Soviets left behind. Chiang Kai-shek was content to leave the flying to the Soviets, but with the pilots gone he suddenly welcomed any advice Chennault had about creating an air force for China. The Japanese seemed to have taken Chennault more seriously than the Chinese and soon launched raids against the Chinese airfields that destroyed nearly all the planes China owned. It would be a year and a half before Chennault would be able to resurrect the idea of a Far East air force, with planes supplied by the United States.

The British declared war on Germany on September 3; the French followed suit the same day. In spite of the success of the Blitzkrieg strategy and the important role the Stukas played in it, the Germans had a very limited understanding of the role of air power and even less of

the need for continual development of new designs and weaponry. Looking at the incredible development of fighters between 1939 and 1940, one is struck by the following: new designs and models were continually flowing from the factories in America, England, and Russia (and even Japan), but not those in Germany. The Germans improved the Bf 109 ten times, and by the end of the war had manufactured some thirty-five thousand of them, but the Allies maintained the advantage over the Germans by constantly producing new and improved aircraft.

Even the best aircraft has weaknesses and a fighter can win against a superior machine, given enough time to learn what those weaknesses are. This was exactly the approach taken by Hugh Trenchard in World War I and was how the Americans in the Pacific dealt with the superior Japanese Zero fighters in the early days of the Pacific conflicts during World War II. Once the capabilities of a fighter aircraft are known, designers can create aircraft that can beat it, even though they cannot outperform it. The head of the RAF's Fighter Command during the war was Sir Hugh Dowding (his nickname, "Stuffy," could hardly have been more apt), a supporter of the development of radar who had worked directly with the inventor, Robert Watson Watt, and of the tactical approach for fighter aircraft. During the Battle of Britain, the inferior Hurricanes used their advantage in being able to make tighter turns and engaged the Bf 109s at close range.

The only other fighter the Germans built in any number (about twenty-thousand) was the Fock Wulf Fw 190, a twin-engine airplane that was not introduced until 1941 and underwent continual change throughout the war. At its most developed, it could hold its own against the best fighters the Allies could put in the air, but it arrived on the scene too late and in too few numbers to affect the course of the war.

Another Messerschmitt fighter, the Bf 100, intended as a companion-successor to the Bf 109, proved a failure. It was designed in 1934 and underwent little change before being test-flown in 1936 and then again in 1939. An improved model, the Bf 110 G-4, equipped with radar, was introduced in 1942, but it fared no better against the much improved Allied fighters then being deployed. Only 6,000 BF 110s were manufactured, and most saw very limited duty in the war.

The Allied Response in the Air: The Battle of Britain

The first fighters to confront the Messerschmitts were British: the Hawker Hurricane, already deployed by the RAF in 1937, and the Supermarine Spitfire, a plane developed from the Supermarine seaplanes that won the Schneider Trophy but which was not produced in great numbers until the war was underway.

The Hurricane had begun on the drawing board of Sidney Camm as early as 1934. Camm's intention was to replace the Gloster Gladiator, then being built as the ultimate biplane fighter. Camm was convinced that the era of the biplane fighter was past and that the next war would see dogfights between much faster and better-performing single-wing aircraft. The way had already been shown in the United States with the creation of the Seversky P-35. As the fighter role of the Hurricane was taken over by the Spitfire, the Hurricane was found to be a versatile aircraft that could be used for many other missions, including night bombing, ground support, and as a carrier-based aircraft.

The British fighter airplane that became the most celebrated during the war was the Spitfire, based on the designs of Reginald J. Mitchell in the late 1920s. The Spitfire benefited not only from Mitchell's intuitive genius about aerodynamics, but also from the close association with Henry Royce, who developed the Merlin engine specifically for the Spitfire. The development of the Spitfire took time, and improvements were made throughout the war that kept the aircraft a step ahead of its adversaries. But the fact that only a few Spitfires were involved in the Battle of Britain, and that the brunt of the battle was borne by the Hurricanes, points to another strategic error the Germans made in conducting the air war: they waited too long, giving England and the United States the opportunity to develop fighters and bombers that could challenge the Nazis in the air.

This was evident in the nine-month "phony war" that took place between Germany and France, during which the Allies initiated a crash program, and in the hesitation Hitler showed at Dunkirk, allowing a large portion of the British ground forces to escape. It was also evident in the hesitation the Germans showed in invading England and beginning the air war over British skies that came to be known as the Battle of Britain. Why the Germans hesitated at key moments when their entire strategy depended on swiftness is grist for the historian's mill, but the results were clear enough. The Germans did not cut off development and deployment of advanced aircraft in England the way they had in France, and this was a critical factor in the outcome of the war.

In May 1940, the Germans invaded the Low Countries (Belgium, Netherlands, and Luxembourg) as a prelude to the "end run" invasion of France. The tech-

Above left: The remarkable Focke-Wulf FW 190, Germany's answer to the British Spitfire, was a masterpiece of fighter design and one of the most versatile planes ever built. The Focke-Wulf plant in Bremen was a high-priority Allied bombing target. Above right: The Messerschmitt Me 109 was the backbone of the Luftwaffe—some thirty-five thousand were produced. Mistaken sometimes for the RAF Spitfire (background), it was enlarged into the Me 110, a plane that proved to be a dismal failure. Left: In the Second World War, the Germans continued the World War I practice of lionizing their fighter pilots. Here, nine German aces of the "Spades" Squadron—with the spade insignia on the plane—are photographed in 1940 after 2,008 sorties and 112 kills.

nique was the by-now terribly familiar Blitzkrieg, with a new wrinkle in that Stukas were used to airlift supplies to forward ground troops, which allowed the troops to move across the countryside even faster. With a speed that made the conquest of Poland leisurely by comparison, France—and with it the French aircraft development program—fell in June 1940. Most observers at the time believed the French program had great promise, and two fighters in particular—the Dewoitine 520 and the Arsenal VG-33—were believed capable of one day becoming fighters of the first rank. These were produced in French factories under German management during the occupation of France, but either because of sabotage of the production or the German belief in the superiority of the Messerschmitt planes, they were not deployed in large numbers.

The key aerial confrontation between Germany and England came early in the war, during the summer of 1940. At the time, the fighter force of the RAF stood at about six hundred planes, about a third the size of the Luftwaffe. The only way the RAF stood a chance against a force so superior in numbers and capabilities was by using the latest communications and electronic technology to mount a coordinated defense. The Operations Room of Fighter Command HQ was connected to airfields, communications stations, radar installations, and observation posts all over England through a telephone, radio, and teletype network that allowed all movements of the fighter planes to be coordinated. The Germans had attempted to discover these electronic secrets of the British before the war, but were unsuccessful. Though they did not fully appreciate how powerful an instrument radar was, they knew that destroying British radar installations would be an important step in winning the war.

On July 21, Göring, acting on direct orders from Hitler, announced to the commanders of the Luftflotten (air fleets) the plans for Operation *Adler Angriff*—Eagle Attack—aimed at the destruction of the RAF. The day on which the air invasion was to take place, called *Adler Tag* (Eagle Day), was August 10. The strategy was simple: on day one the radar stations would be taken out; on day two, the airfields; on day three, the planes and hangars. All that would be necessary, Göring believed, were three days of clear weather in which to fly.

ABOVE: *During World War II, the Spitfire became the dominant fighter in the European sky. A key to its success was its ability to continue to perform well when increasingly powerful engines were installed. The Rolls-Royce Merlin engines that powered the plane eventually doubled their output in the course of the war, allowing the Spitfire literally to save England from invasion during the Battle of Britain.*
LEFT: *The Heinkel He-111 was based on a 1935 plane that the Germans claimed was designed for commercial transport. When Lindbergh visited Germany in 1936, he took one look at the He-111 and knew he was looking at a bomber.*

The Flight of the Spruce Goose

The "Spruce Goose" is famous for being the largest airplane ever built; it was converted into a museum piece in 1977 after exactly one flight of about a mile (1.5km), only seventy feet (21m) above the waters of Long Beach Harbor in New York. Periodically, stories surface about plans to resurrect the Spruce Goose and actually put it (or a facsimile) into service. More than a few aviation buffs would buy a ticket to that.

In the spring of 1942, the U.S. government approved a plan put forward by industrialist Henry J. Kaiser to build immense "Liberty ships" that could supply England with war materials and be out of the range of the German U-boats prowling in the Atlantic. Kaiser brought in millionaire Howard Hughes (then-owner of TWA) to build the H-4 Hercules, first of the HK-1 flying boats. How serious the government ever was about this project is open to question: the government insisted that the H-4 be constructed of nonstrategic materials. Possibly the government hoped that this announcement would discourage the use of U-boats (it did not).

Kaiser might have been enthralled with the very idea of "an aerial freighter beyond anything Jules Verne could have imagined," but Hughes was a longtime aviator and a shrewd businessman, and so was unlikely to make such an effort (and sink $8 million of his own money) into the project without some hope of a return. Had the H-4 fulfilled its promise, it would indeed have opened an entirely new age in commerce. As it turned out, however, the plane was not finished before the end of the war, and the military promptly forgot about it. But Hughes couldn't. Putting an additional few million into the project and completing the prototype in June 1946, he placed it in Long Beach Harbor in preparation for a test flight. The plane was dubbed the "Spruce Goose" because it was made of chemically treated wood (not spruce, in fact, but birch). The final prototype was seventy-nine feet (24m) high and 218 feet (66.5m) long, with a wing span of 320 feet (97.5m); it had eight Wasp engines and was capable of carrying a payload of 130,000 pounds (59,020kg).

Just before Hughes was to take the Spruce Goose for a test spin, the city of Long Beach refused to grant him a permit to fly the plane. (They were probably fearful that the plane would break up on take-off and shower the city with flaming debris.) Hughes promised only to taxi the plane on the water to test its sea-worthiness; he would address flying it later. On November 2, 1947, Hughes took the plane out of its specially constructed hangar and taxied on the harbor. Then, after gaining a little speed, he nosed the plane up and the Spruce Goose flew briefly. After landing, Hughes told the none-too-pleased city officials that the controls had gotten away from him (in other words, it had been an accident). Hughes thought it funny; the officials did not, and they impounded the aircraft in its hangar, where it remained unused for the next thirty-five years.

The scale of the Spruce Goose can be seen when one realizes that in this photo Hughes and his assistants are standing atop the fuselage in the middle of the wingspan, which is as long as a football field.

The initial attempts to knock out the radar stations at Dover, Pevensey, and Rye were unsuccessful for the simple reason that the British radar system gave the defenders ample warning and permitted them to marshal their forces. It became immediately apparent that the only way the Germans would have a chance of gaining mastery of the air was to conduct a total onslaught of the British skies, so that Britain could not use its sophisticated detection and communications systems to move its forces into the most advantageous position. If the RAF were engaged everywhere, they would be outmatched everywhere.

The renewed onslaught began on August 13, 1940, and in the three weeks that followed the skies above England became a battlefield in which the true capabilities of the aircraft fighting each other became apparent.

It also became clear what advantages could be gained by engaging in an air battle over one's own territory (lessons that would be useful when the air war was taken to Germany). The Messerschmitt Bf 109s were very poorly armored, which meant that the slightest hit brought down a plane, usually killing the pilot. The British planes may have been slower, but they were much better protected. (Dowding had even fought to have bulletproof glass used for the cockpits.) A Hurricane or a Spitfire could take many blows and keep fighting. The Bf 109s used 75 percent of their fuel just getting to the theater of battle and returning. This meant that a British plane had two to three times the useful flight combat time that a German plane had. A damaged British plane could land in a field or at a nearby airbase, be repaired, and be in the air again within a few hours. A German flier whose plane was damaged in battle could only hope to make it back over the English Channel; most did not.

By early September, the RAF had fought the Luftwaffe to a stalemate, an incredible achievement given the advantages enjoyed by the Germans. When it appeared that a strategic victory over the RAF was not going to be possible (or come as quickly as promised), Hitler, claiming he was acting out of revenge for British bombing raids on Berlin, changed policy and attempted to intimidate the British into submission by directing his bombing attacks at London and other British cities instead of at the RAF airfields. The tactic had worked in the past, and it appealed to the Fuhrer's sense of the dramatic. (The sound effects that were added to the Stukas were said to appeal to Hitler more than the dive-bombing techniques that made them so effective. In early discussions about the possibility of an atom bomb, Hitler supposedly mused about what a magnificent noise it would make, and was disappointed when told that there would be no survivors of a bomb blast left to hear anything.) It was considered another major blunder in the conduct of the air war, and the British were grateful for the respite.

On September 8, 1940, the "Blitz" of London began, driving most of the city underground as the battle waged overhead. Now the major weapons the Germans threw at the British were their bombers: the Dornier Do 17 and the Heinkel He-111. These planes were designed primarily as medium-range bombers with ranges of about one thousand miles (1,609km), and they were no match for the British fighters. Hitler had grossly underestimated the resolve of the British and their determination to win the war, no matter the cost. By the end of October, the Battle of Britain was over. The British had lost more than nine hundred planes, but the German toll was twice that, and most of their losses were costly bombers with crews of three or four.

It was during the Battle of Britain that the first aces of the war emerged (and the reader will note that names of individual fliers are absent in this air war). The RAF had always been reluctant to single out individual pilots, believing it contradicted the team approach to air combat. But two of the top three pilots in the Battle of Britain were not RAF officers, and the government believed that singling them out would make for good public relations at home and with other countries. The top ace was Czech pilot Josef Frantisek; next came Eric Lock, an RAF officer; and then James "Ginger" Lacey, a noncommissioned pilot who shot down the He-111 that bombed Buckingham Palace.

The air war over England was by no means over. The Germans were to continue bombing for many months, and a November 14 bombing raid on Coventry was one of the most severe of the war. But by then it was clear that a German invasion of England was not going to be possible, and that mastery of the skies over England belonged to the RAF. England was committed to defeating the Nazis and liberating the nations of Europe; the Germans, however, could have been content to leave England alone for the moment and solidify their hold on Europe. Hitler was already making plans to invade the Soviet Union—Operation Barbarossa—and spurring on production of munitions for the campaigns ahead.

The great unknown factor in the war was the United States. Throughout 1941, it became increasingly clear that the United States would come into the war on the side of England, if it entered the war at all. The passage of the Lend-Lease Act of March 12, 1941, put the United States into the war as a chief supplier of goods to England. A provision of the Lend-Lease program was that England could procure from any U.S. manufacturer any aircraft it produced, once a superior aircraft by any other manufacturer was delivered to the U.S. Army Air Corps. This meant that the entire air force of the United States was placed at the disposal of England and the Army Air Corps would not lose a single plane in the process.

The United States even started supplying squadrons of pilots to fly the planes: they were called the Eagle Squadrons and they distinguished themselves through the latter half of 1941, winning three Distinguished Flying Crosses. They risked loss of citizenship, a consequence of fighting for a foreign power, but none were so punished, and in September 1942 the squadrons were placed under American command as part of the Fourth Fighter Group. As 1941 drew to a close, the United States found itself already in a sea war with the German U-boats that had tried to prevent the delivery of the Lend-Lease materials. It was now only a matter of time until the United States would enter the war.

War in the Pacific: From Pearl Harbor to Midway

The United States was caught by surprise on the morning of December 7, 1941, when 365 aircraft—bombers, fighters, and torpedo aircraft—attacked the U.S. Naval Base at Pearl Harbor, Hawaii, and sank or severely damaged eighteen warships, destroyed or damaged 347 aircraft, and left 2,403 dead on the ground. The reaction of the United States was outrage at this undeclared act of war, and the United States declared war on Japan the next day. Three days later, Hitler and Mussolini declared war on the United States, making the conflict truly a world war.

At the time of Pearl Harbor, the U.S. aircraft carrier fleet was out on maneuvers and thus escaped attack. However, the effect of the Pearl Harbor attack was to bring the United States and Japan into a closer state of military parity. Although the attack, and the December 13 attack on the U.S. airfields in the Philippines (which somehow also came as a surprise), gave Japan the momentary edge, and the United States would be involved in a theater of war on the other side of the

globe, the industrial output of the United States would clearly make up the shortfall in a year or so. The strategy of the Japanese government in 1941, as it had been twice before in the century, was to fight a limited war until it gained its objectives, and then dig in. The attacks on Pearl Harbor and the Philippines were designed to buy the time needed to create new boundaries in the Pacific. That the war turned into a contest to the death was due in part to the unwillingness of the Japanese military and the American political leadership to think in such equivocal terms.

The fighter aircraft that Japan used to achieve early control of the skies were, as has been pointed out, derived from American and British designs (the Germans were much more circumspect about sharing their technology with their Japanese allies), but the designers at the chief manufacturers—Aicihi, Kawanishi, Kawasaki, Mitsubishi, and Nakajima—took those ideas and pushed then in new directions that astounded aircraft designers the world over. Moreover, unlike the Germans, the Japanese kept developing their aircraft and creating innovative designs. In fact, sometimes new models of older fighters (like the A6M3, a new model of the A6M) were given new designations because they looked like new airplanes even to trained observers.

The greatest of these fighters, on a par with the Spitfire and the Bf 109, was the Mitsubishi A6M Reisen, identified officially by the Allies as "Zeke," but known throughout the war as the Zero. The Zero had a maneuverability that seemed physically impossible to American

TOP LEFT: In the early morning hours of December 7, 1941, Japanese bombers and fighters took off from six carriers sailing just 230 miles (370.3km) north of Hawaii. About an hour later, the attack on Pearl Harbor was in full swing. TOP RIGHT: The Zeros were actually sent to protect the G-97 "Kate" torpedo planes, which did most of the damage. ABOVE: The attack was so sudden that the Japanese encountered nearly no resistance. The major portion of the Pacific fleet was sunk or rendered useless, and the Naval Air Station at Wheeler Field on Ford Island (BACKGROUND) was destroyed. Ironically, the Japanese considered the Pearl Harbor attack a purely naval operation, expecting the rest of the war to be fought on the high seas.

pilots; finding its weakness became a top priority. Painstakingly (and sometimes heroically), pieces of downed Zeros were recovered and brought to Wright Field in Dayton, Ohio, and pieced together. The engineers found that the engine was modeled on an old Pratt & Whitney model that had been abandoned because of difficulty it had in diving, and that the plane had virtually no protective armor. The strategy developed for fighting Zeros was to avoid engagements at close range, to attack from above, forcing it to dive, its most vulnerable flight

ABOVE: The Battle of the Coral Sea in May 1942 was the first air battle fought exclusively between aircraft carriers that never saw each other. The United States lost the USS Lexington (shown, with the crew abandoning ship as ordered) with thirty-three planes aboard, but the Japanese were thwarted in their attempt to capture Port Moresby, New Guinea, which would have cut off Australia from the American fleet.
RIGHT: Three key aircraft of the Japanese air war: the very light but nimble Zero ("Zeke"), vulnerable to any sort of fire from the ground or air, was the most successful Japanese bomber of the war; by the time the Tonys were developed, Japan was fighting a defensive war, which made the plane's armor and self-sealing tanks all the more important.
BACKGROUND: The USS Yorktown is hit by a torpedo during the Battle of Midway, really a series of air-sea battles in early June 1942, in which the U.S. forces led by Admiral Chester Nimitz achieved victory over Admiral Yamamoto's Imperial Navy.

phase, and to use wide-area explosives that would disable the aircraft with even a glancing hit.

The key to the defeat of the Japanese air force was not in the tactics used against the Zero, but in the limited capacity of Japan to manufacture planes to replace those downed. Of the five important Japanese fighters deployed during the war, the Zero was produced in the greatest numbers by far, but production reached only about 10,500. The other planes—Nakajima's Ki 43 Hayabusa ("Oscar") and Ki 84 Hayate ("Frank"), Kawasaki's Ki 61 Hien ("Tony"), and Kawanishi's N1K1 J Shiden ("George")—totaled fewer than fourteen thousand units, for a total first-line fighter output of fewer than twenty-five thousand. Compare that to the U.S. fighter plane output: seven major models and seventy thousand planes were manufactured (about the same number of Allied fighter aircraft deployed in the European theater).

Mitsubishi A6M "Zero"

Nakajima Ki 27 "Nate"

Kawasaki Ki 61 "Tony"

Outnumbered in the air three-to-one, the Japanese were fighting a losing battle the minute the United States entered the war.

Two different philosophies informed the production of Japanese planes during the war. That the Japanese military supported both and gave proponents of each free rein to develop, make their mistakes, and come back with new machines showed intellectual fortitude, during what was, after all, a time of war. The one approach had its roots in the ancient martial disciplines in which the weapon was an extension of the warrior. The pilots of these aircraft were all steeped in the martial art of Kendo and practiced as much with bamboo Shinai as with their training aircraft. The Nakajima Ki 27 ("N\ate"), built in the mid-1930s, was a paradigm of economy and miniaturization: a wing span of only thirty-seven feet (11m), a length of less than twenty-five feet (7.5m), and virtually nothing between the pilot and the air save a thin metal skin so loosely riveted that pilots felt the draft of the onrushing air while in flight. The Ki 27 was maneuverable as few fighter aircraft before or since, and it remained in production throughout the early stages of the war.

The design approach of the Ki 27, the brainchild of Hideo Itokawa and Yasumi Koyama, was carried forth into the Ki 43, a larger aircraft that maintained its predecessor's agility, but at higher speeds. The plating protecting the plane was still tissue-thin and the weaponry was still minimal, but the plane had a larger cross-sectional area, all of which made the Ki 43 vulnerable (to some, more so than the Ki 27). The two Nakajima planes became the mainstays of the Japanese Army and were used throughout the Pacific for most of the war.

Meanwhile, the success of the navy's A6M Zero, a decidedly Western airplane in conception, fostered the second design path the Japanese followed. The Zero gave rise to the Ki 61 Hien, a plane that melded the features of the Zero with those of the Polikarpov I-16 used by the Soviets against the Japanese in 1939. The basic problem with the Ki 61 was its engine, a modified version of an outdated Daimler-Benz engine supplied by the Germans. The Ki 61 was most useful in defending Japanese targets against Allied bombers and fighters and in any area where it was likely to encounter ground fire or fire from enemy aircraft, resistance the other Japanese fighter could not withstand.

The two basic approaches came together in the Ki 84 Hayate, a Nakajima fighter designed by Yasumi Koyama that combined adequate protection and structure; significant armament, and as much of the agility that the design could incorporate. "Frank" fighters entered the fighting in 1943 and some thirty-five-hundred were built, but it was too little too late to alter the course of the war significantly. The Hayate was seen by experts as the best Japanese fighter of the war.

In May and June of 1942, two battles, fought at great cost to both sides, marked the turning points in the war: the Battle of the Coral Sea (fought May 2-8) and the Battle of Midway (fought June 4-7). Both were called naval battles, but they were fought by ships that never saw one another and never, in fact, fired directly on an enemy naval vessel. In both battles, the objectives were very similar: the Japanese were seeking a foothold that would allow them to isolate Australia from the American fleet, and the Allies were determined to stop them. Both battles ended with the Japanese being forced to retreat, but whereas the Japanese claimed victory at the Battle of the Coral Sea because the Americans sustained greater losses, no such claim was possible at Midway. The Japanese lost four aircraft carriers and more than 330 aircraft to the Americans' losing only the *Yorktown* and 150 aircraft. Midway was also the first battle for the CV 6 *Enterprise*, a name that was to become synonymous with excellence in naval aviation.

The American Fighter Planes of World War II

At the time of the attack on Pearl Harbor, the fighter aircraft in the U.S. Army Air Corps were outclassed by both their Japanese and German counterparts, but the industry had been developing at a rapid pace for peacetime and had the momentum, the industrial base, the economic foundation, and the will and talent to catch up. The key individuals in bringing this about were Alexander P. de Seversky and his chief designer, Alexander Kartveli. Throughout the war, they would be at the forefront of fighter design, urging the government and the military to make the greatest demands of, and place the greatest reliance on, the nation's aircraft.

The two prewar aircraft produced by the de Seversky-Kartveli team at Republic Aviation were the P-35, the plane that took America into the modern age of fighter aircraft, and the P-43 Lancer, more heavily armed than the P-35, but paying for that armament with poorer performance. Both planes were sent to air forces overseas and became the stopgap foundation of later fighter fleets. Another prewar fighter that excited the U.S. military was the Bell P-39 Airacobra, a sleek and agile aircraft that had the remarkable addition of a 37mm cannon that shot rounds through the propeller's disc. With four machine guns and the ability to carry five-hundred pounds (227kg) of bombs, the Airacobra in all its many versions was a versatile and formidable weapon. Some ten thousand of them were produced during the war and many were shipped to air forces overseas.

The U.S. Air Corps kept having problems with the plane because Bell kept changing the engine specifications and thus its performance. The Airacobra became the basis of other successful fighters, but it was not a favorite of the Army Air Corps. (In June 1941 Congress established the

Curtiss P-40 Warhawk

Grumman F6F Hellcat

U.S. Army Air Forces, virtually an independent branch of the U.S. Armed Forces, under the direction of Major General H.H. "Hap" Arnold. The USAAF was made into the totally autonomous U.S. Air Force—USAF—via the National Security Act of 1947 in September of that year.)

The most important fighter of the early years of the war was the Curtiss P-40 Warhawk, designed by Donovan Berlin as an extension of the old Curtis Hawk of the early 1930s. The P-40 was important not because it was a very good fighter—it was not particularly fast or agile and performed poorly at high altitude—but because it was very reliable and sturdy, which was important if the plane were to see action far from suppliers of spare parts. More than 13,700 P-40s were produced during war. Built primarily as a defensive fighter for patrol of the American coastline, it was ill-suited for the aggressive open-sky dogfighting it would encounter in war.

It was the P-40 that was used by Claire Chennault in China in early 1942 when he commanded the American Volunteer Group known as the "Flying Tigers." The plane lent itself to being painted with menacing shark's teeth (which inspired the group's original name, the "Flying Tiger Sharks," which was later shortened). The Flying Tigers, under Chennault's gritty leadership (seldom has the field of battle witnessed so forceful a jaw as Chennault's), downed 286 Japanese airplanes while losing only twenty-three of their own. The experience gained in these encounters, many with superior Zeros and other fighters, proved helpful in creating fighter tactics and the next generation of American fighters.

The first American fighters to enter the war comparable to enemy aircraft then in the sky were the "Cat" fighters produced by Leroy Grumman and his chief designer, William Schwendler, beginning with the Grumman F4F Wildcat. The Wildcat was not a fast plane either —in fact, it was among the slowest fighters in the air during the war—but it had other features that made it useful. It was extremely durable and very short (shorter

even than the old P-39). This, and the fact that its wings folded at its sides, made it perfect for aircraft carrier use. An American carrier could hold nearly twice the aircraft of a comparably sized Japanese carrier. (During some early encounters, the Japanese sent out patrols looking for the other carriers all these aircraft must surely be coming from.)

As the size and capacity of carriers grew, so did the Wildcat, and it eventually inspired the F6F Hellcat, introduced in 1942: the plane that outfought the Japanese fighters. The Hellcat was the fullest expression of the American approach to meeting the Zeros and turning the battle to their advantage. In a typical dogfight, a Zero would have to score a direct hit to knock out a Hellcat; a Hellcat's six machine guns had only to strike a Zero to disable it. Since the Hellcat was faster than the Zero in straight flight, it could easily pursue and finish off its adversary. Some eight thousand Wildcats and nearly 12,300 Hellcats were manufactured during the war, making Grumman the largest producer of American fighters and the Cat series the most prolific of the war.

America took the forefront of fighter aviation with the Lockheed P-38 Lightning, an airplane of astonishingly original design. This aircraft, first deployed in January 1939, was fast, agile, durable, and reliable, and could stay in the air longer than any fighter then in use. To prove its advantages, during tests it flew coast to coast in seven hours and two minutes, and would have broken the record then held by Howard Hughes had it not stopped twice along the way to refuel and test its equipment. The essence of the Lightning's innovation was the twin boom that housed the engine and propellers, leaving the center component free for control, armament, and whatever else was needed. Giving speed, agility, and a solid reliable landing mechanism to an aircraft this heavy (heavier than some bombers) was no easy task.

Hap Arnold was a firm supporter of the Lockheed P-38, and its designers, H.L. Hubbard and Clarence

"Kelly" Johnson, adapted the plane to many uses, including bombing; this aircraft clearly inspired the effective night-fighter, the Northrop P-61 Black Widow. Some ten thousand P-38s were built, and this plane was credited with being used to shoot down more enemy aircraft—including the plane that carried Admiral Isoroku Yamamoto, the commander of the attack on Pearl Harbor—than any other American fighter over the course of the war.

The best American fighter of the war, and arguably the best fighter of any nation and even the best propeller-driven fighter ever flown, was the North American P-51 Mustang. Its beginnings, however, were anything but auspicious; it was one of the few planes whose very designing made news. The RAF, frantic to procure more aircraft in 1940, offered a contract to North American to build the Curtiss P-40 with Allison engines. The president of the company, J.H. "Dutch" Kindelberger, did not care for this arrangement (mainly because the licensing fee to Curtiss-Wright was too high), and offered to build a fighter for the RAF that would surpass the P-40. The RAF accepted the offer on the condition that a prototype of the aircraft be ready 120 days later.

On October 4, only 102 days after accepting the challenge, the prototype, designed by Raymond H. Rice and Edgar Schmued, was ready—except for the engine. Allison never believed that North American would meet the impossible deadline and dawdled on delivery of their V-1710 engines. The first test flights were held on October 26, but the prototype was damaged when the pilot hastily took off with an empty fuel tank and the plane cut out shortly after take-off. It was clear from the outset that the Mustang had a clean line and performed better than the P-40, but it did not climb well and performed poorly at higher altitudes, where it could be expected to see much action.

It turned out to be fortuitous that the designers of the P-51, not having actual engines to install, had been careful to allow a bit of extra space for the engines. In September 1942 British engineers noticed that the engine casing of the Mustang could accommodate the new Rolls-Royce Merlin engine. With the Merlin powering it, the Mustang was a new plane. Its top speed jumped to 440 miles per hour (708kph), tops for a single-engine fighter, and it climbed to twenty-thousand feet (6,096m) in half the time. The performance of the plane at all altitudes was virtually the same and uniformly spectacular, and production of the hybrid aircraft was stepped up. The P-51 Mustang became the most produced fighter of the war, with just under 15,700 made. The model P-51D had a streamlined fuselage and a cockpit canopy that provided the pilot a full 360-degree view; the P-51D was thought by pilots to be the ultimate propeller-driven fighter.

If the Mustang had a challenger to these titles, it was from another American airplane: the Vought F4U Corsair, a fighter good enough to remain in production for ten

Lockheed P-38 Lightning

Northrop P-61 Black Widow

North American P-51 Mustang

The American air armada: the early, outmatched Warhawks (OPPOSITE LEFT) held off the superior Zeros and accounted for 75 percent of U.S. air-to-air kills until the Hellcats (OPPOSITE RIGHT) appeared; the P-38 Lightning (TOP), created from rough designs some twenty years old, was a plane of unequaled performance; the twin-fuselage concept achieved its greatest development in the Northrop P-61 Black Widow (CENTER), a night fighter-bomber that wreaked havoc on the enemy in both theaters; the P-51 Mustang (BOTTOM) was only a fair aircraft until it was outfitted with the Merlin engine—it then became the best long-distance fighter escort of the war.

ABOVE: The Vought F4U Corsair's "inverted-gull-wing" allowed for a larger propeller. This plane was the only carrier-based fighter that performed as well as any land-based aircraft. The Japanese called the plane "Whistling Death."

ABOVE: The P-47 Thunderbolt was small but rugged, said to be the plane that could "take a punch" better than any other wartime fighter.
LEFT: A Focke-Wulf FW190 goes down after a bullet hits its fuel tank, a hit that the Thunderbolt survived many times during the war.

years after the war. The concept behind the Corsair, designed by Tex B. Beisel, was to marry the most powerful engine then available, the Pratt & Whitney Double Wasp, the first 2,000-horsepower engine, with the smallest possible airframe. In all the early designs, the size of the engine demanded a large fuselage, a large wing structure, and the largest propellers of any fighter in the war. The combination fell apart when a large undercarriage was necessary to support everything. Beisel's ingenious solution was to design the wings in an inverted-gull-wing configuration and put the landing gear in the wings. This not only saved space in the fuselage, but also allowed for smaller, lower-to-the-ground landing gear. The result was another distinctive fighter design, but the aircraft was beset with many problems in the early going. The large and bulky fuselage cut down on pilot visibility, and the plane had trouble landing on the tightly confined surface of an aircraft carrier. The Corsair operated from land bases for three years until it was ready in 1943 to become a part of the carrier-based fleet of fighters. Nearly 12,700 F4U Corsairs were produced during the war; most flew over a Pacific theater that had already been cleared by the Mustangs, its own numbers thinned in the process, but the Corsair's dominance of the sky, especially when it carried two one-thousand-pound (454kg) bombs, was unchallenged in the last phases of the war.

One other fighter was developed in the latter stages of the war, made important contributions to American air supremacy, and became a part of postwar air forces around the world, but would probably not have been built in such numbers had the performance of the Mustang and the Corsair been well established earlier. It was the Republic P-47 Thunderbolt, produced by the de Seversky-Kartveli team that started the entire enterprise. Still committed to packing the most power in the smallest package, the duo took its turn at designing a fighter around the Double Wasp engine. The result was a fighter that was an excellent performer at mid to low altitudes, but at the difficult higher altitudes (above twenty thousand feet [6,096m]) was far and away the best fighter in service. The "Jug," as it was known, had a stubby appearance, but that was appreciated by the carrier commanders.

The Thunderbolt also had excellent diving capabilities, and this made it an extremely effective fighter-bomber, which was its primary use. Over 15,600 Thunderbolts were built (second only to the Mustang among U.S. fighters), 80 percent of which were the model D, with the elevated see-all cockpit, a 2,535-horsepower Double Wasp engine, and a bombload capacity of twenty-five hundred pounds (1,135kg). It was said that a pilot flying a P-47D at forty-thousand feet (12,192m), untouchable by any aircraft then flying, was the closest thing to being a god.

The Bombers of World War II—
The Early Campaigns

The bombing campaigns of World War II were the one element of the air war that had a strategic significance on a par with the ground movements of infantry and the blockade-related activities of both sides on the high seas. It was this use of air power, first deployed to a significant extent in the 1940s, that was to have a lasting influence on geopolitics for decades to come. Previously, bombing from the air was looked upon as a form of sabotage—an irritant and a hindrance, but not a map-changing strategic factor in the course of a war. However, once bombing was carried out extensively against industrial, military, and civilian targets, it had the power to change battle lines, and ultimately to determine the outcome of a war.

The first use of bombing in the war was as a tactical weapon, by the Germans in the invasion of Poland. The early bombers were converted transports that were originally designed to be transformed into bombers: the Junkers JU86 and JU88, the Dornier Do 17, and the Heinkel He-111, all used in the invasion of Poland. All these aircraft had been tested in the Spanish Civil War

and had been found to be vulnerable to attack from the aft and forward directions. The remedy was to create gunner's nests in "greenhouse" type nests, which were to become common in later bombers of both sides.

The bombers in service in France, Poland, and the Netherlands at the outbreak of World War II were antiquated, certainly compared with the German aircraft. Some, like the French Bloch 131, were so unreliable that the Germans preferred to destroy captured ones rather than use them or even turn them over to their allies. Two captured planes did see service in back areas (the North Sea and North Africa): the Dutch Fokker T VIII, a seaplane (unusual for a bomber) that was also used by England when some Dutch pilots escaped the German invasion; and the Polish PZL P-37, an excellent plane that was produced in small numbers and was capable of delivering a bombload of a whopping fifty-seven hundred pounds (2,588kg).

Most British bombers at the outbreak of the war were only a little better developed. The Fairey Battle was used extensively during the Battle of France, but it fell so easily that production was halted suddenly and the factory allowed to stay idle while new planes were designed. A bit better was the Bristol Blenheim Mk 1, a plane designed from a private passenger plane commissioned

JACK NORTHROP AND THE FLYING WING

Jack Northrop gave many technical reasons why a "flying wing"—a plane in the shape of a single, large wing—was the best of all, but his lifelong fascination with the flying wing was probably prompted by something deeper, perhaps a feeling that it was the true fulfillment of the human dream of putting on a pair of wings and taking flight. Others had considered the flying wing but recognized that, for all its elegance, it was not a very stable configuration. To understand this, simply let a narrow strip of paper go in mid-air and you will see that the strip twirls as it drifts to the ground. This meant that the aircraft would have to be fitted with powerful and sophisticated control surfaces if it was to be controllable in the air. The most serious problem, though, was one of bulk: in order to take full advantage of the streamlining afforded by a flying wing, the engine—be it rotor or jet—had to be small enough to fit inside the wing without creating a drag-inducing bulge.

In 1923 Northrop built his first balsa-wood model of an all-wing aircraft, and for the next three decades he promoted the idea while producing some of America's most important fighter aircraft. The first near-flying wing aircraft to fly took to the air in 1929; it had a minor tail assembly which Northrop claimed served only "cosmetic purposes." Northrop was still apprehensive about presenting a strict flying wing in 1940, so he had his designers droop the wing tips. Wind tunnel tests indicated this feature was not necessary, so it was eliminated, and in 1942 the first pure flying wing, the N-9M, was tested. It served as the scale model for the 1942 XB-35 bomber, a plane that was (because of its streamlined design) faster than any comparably powered bomber in the U.S. fleet.

The flying wing then went through its most difficult test: a political one. A number of military aircraft manufacturers, led by Convair's Floyd Odlum, were fearful that either Northrop would demand payments on certain patents he took out, or that all the standard configurations they were developing would be rendered obsolete overnight. After ordering a fleet of XB-35s, the U.S. Air Force canceled part of its order in favor of the B-36 Vultee, an aircraft already obsolete the day it was delivered. The Air Force claimed it was canceling the XB-35 project because it was concerned that the planes would not be able to accommodate jet engines or atom bombs. Northrop continued developing the aircraft at considerable risk (his only possible customer had, after all, already told him they were not interested). Outfitted with jet engines and mock bombs, his new flying wing bomber, the YB-49, performed even better than Jack Northrop could have hoped. But the Air Force would not budge (in spite of threats of FBI and congressional investigations, which forced the USAF to swallow the eleven planes already built.)

Northrop was vindicated in 1989 when the B-2 Stealth Bomber was unveiled (it was probably operational as early as 1981). The advanced aircraft was the spitting image of the YP-49, and the U.S. government ordered 132 of them at half a billion dollars each. The passenger versions of the YP-49, created in mock-up, placed the passengers in the leading edge of the wing behind a glass-enclosed greenhouse front. Taking off and landing as a passenger in such a plane would probably have been the thrill of a lifetime—so the government might well have been doing Jack a favor.

by newspaper magnate Lord Rothermere for his personal use. It was an extremely fast plane for the day (and was specifically designed for speed), but adapting it to bomber duty turned it into a mediocre bomber at best.

The main bombers of the RAF were classic aircraft that owed their designs to the state of the art in the early 1930s, but were adaptable to new developments and situations and remained useful through the war. The Handley Page Hampden, for example, was relatively fast and could carry a very large load, but it had meager defenses, so it saw most of its use as a night bomber later in the war. The Armstrong-Whitworth Whitley accommodated a large fuel tank, which gave it a long flight time, making it perfect for antisubmarine patrol. The Vickers Wellington was the bomber with the most promise, using a geodetic frame that gave it great strength without great weight. It would surely be the bomber that would see the most service for the RAF and was produced in the greatest number—about 11,460 by war's end.

The British finally managed to field a modern generation of bombers that became important elements in the bombing of Europe and the softening of the Germans in preparation for the Allied ground assault. The Short Stirling was the first British four-engine bomber and may be viewed as England's first modern bomber. Its main deficiency was an inability to maintain performance at high altitudes. It soon gave way to the two planes that became the core of the British Bomber Command: the Handley Page Halifax and the Avro Lancaster. Both relied heavily on the Rolls-Royce Merlin engines manufactured in England and the United States, and on the most sophisticated electronics available. An important factor in the success of the British bombing campaign was the use of the Norden bombsight, developed by the American Carl Norden, who had worked with Elmer Sperry on gyroscopic equipment and then went on to manufacture his own version in a secret factory in New York. In 1939 a German-American employee at the factory handed over a working model of the bombsight to the Luftwaffe, who copied it and used it, but the technology that went into the model remained secret and the Allies were able to stay a step ahead of the Germans in bombsight technology throughout the war.

The one plane produced by the RAF that distinguished itself in particular as both a bomber and a fighter (and was used for everything else from reconnaissance to submarine patrol), though it defied classification and broke all the rules, was the de Havilland Mosquito. The Mosquito came about as a result of a "what-if" experiment conducted by designer R.E. Bishop, who wondered about the effect of marrying an advanced Merlin engine to the lightest possible airframe, one made of wood. The notion found a surprisingly receptive ear in the RAF; a prototype was ordered in November 1940 and was flying by May 1941. The Mosquito was supposed to outrun any fighter pursuit by flying at its maximum speed of four

TOP: The workhorse of the Allied bombing campaign of Nazi-occupied Europe was the Avro Lancaster, a plane with a bombload of a whopping fourteen thousand pounds (6,356kg). ABOVE: The de Havilland Mosquito, a plane that defied all the rules, was made of wood and was so simple that it could be constructed anywhere; the eight thousand Mosquitos built placed nearly no strain on British manufacturing and the planes were in almost constant use toward the end of the war. LEFT: A line of Mosquitos takes off from a base in Scotland in 1945 to bomb German shipping in the Norwegian fjords.

hundred miles per hour (643.5kph) at a height of thirty-nine thousand feet (11,887m), higher than any fighter could go. The plane performed so well that the experimenting continued and machine guns were added. The result was to turn the Mosquito into an effective fighter capable of diving onto any fighter and thus attacking from an advantageous position: above. Even the addition of cannon did not adversely affect the plane's performance. Nearly sixty-five hundred Mosquitos were built during the war, and the plane continued to be built and placed in service until 1951, a testament to its utility and brilliant design.

The country with the most experience with large bomber-type aircraft was Italy, and the war gave the Italians many opportunities to develop their bomber fleet. Mussolini's practice of going after lightly defended areas, however, gave these planes little challenge, and there was, therefore, little incentive for the Italian air force to progress. As a result, the SIAI-Marchetti bombers that were first-rate in the late 1930s were still the bulk of the bomber fleet in 1942, by which time they had become obsolete. The only bomber the Italians produced that could compete with those of other air forces (and the only four-engine plane Italy made) was the Piaggio P-108B, held up in production and not placed in service until June 1942.

In contrast to the Germans, who tested their fighters and dive bombers in the Spanish Civil War, but not, to any great extent, their heavy bombers, the Japanese developed and tested their bombers in China in 1937 and prepared for war by developing their bomber fleet as much as their fighters. Yet the Japanese only reluctantly accepted Admiral Yamamoto's insistence that the bomber was also an important weapon for ground and naval support. More bombers were developed and built by the Japanese than would have been built without Yamamoto, but even so, only between one thousand and twelve hundred of each of the seven most important Japanese bombers were built during the war, as compared with more than eighteen thousand B-24s alone.

The key bombers in the first year of the war were the Mitsubishi G3M and G4M planes (identified by the allies as "Nell" and "Betty," respectively). In the earliest stages of the war, these aircraft had little need of protective armor or armament. As this changed, the deficiencies of these bombers became apparent and the Japanese (characteristically) devised solutions to the problems. The result was the Aichi D3A1 ("Val"), a single engine dive-bomber that had the built-in protection of three machine guns and maneuvered comparably to a fighter (at least at this stage of the war). The efforts to improve the fighter component of the bomber resulted in an improved dive-bomber, the Kawasaki Ki 48 ("Lily"), but its inadequacy made it clear that bombers would have to be developed independently.

The bombers deployed by the Japanese between 1942 and 1944 betray the half-hearted way the designers approached the issues of bomber design. The "Lily," for example, was a fast and agile airplane, but no match for an Allied fighter and without even rudimentary defenses. The only four-engine bomber produced by the Japanese in this period was the Nakajima G8N1 Renzan ("Rita"); only four were ever built and none saw active service.

Failing to create a bomber fleet, yet desperately in need of impeding the Allied forces making their way toward Japan, the Japanese formed the kamikaze corps. In conscious emulation of ancient samurai warriors (and named after the "divine wind," or storms, that drove the Mongol invaders away from Japan in the thirteenth century), pilots volunteered for suicide missions, first flying dive-bombers loaded with explosives, then flying outdated fighters to elude ground fire and Allied fighters. Toward the end of the war, 852 Yokosuka MXY7s, known as "Ohka flying bombs" and code-named Baka ("fool"), were built with rocket engines and short airfoils. These were launched at ships, and were virtually unsteerable. (It was unclear to the Allies why they required pilots at all.) An aerial explosion anywhere near an Ohka in flight assured a miss (except on the rare occasion that a deflection forced the Ohka back on target). Kamikaze attacks accounted for half the Allied naval vessels lost in the last two years of the war.

The American Bombers Conquer the Sky

The key factor in the Allied victory in World War II in both theaters was the bombing campaigns that crippled the Axis powers and paved the way for the Allied armies and navies. The metaphor of conquering the sky had become a literal truth at the hands of the American air forces. The triumph of the American bomber program was as much a tribute to American industry as to the fliers and support troops. Intercepted German espionage reports on American production capacity—which grew from producing fifty-five hundred aircraft a year in 1939 to fifty-five hundred aircraft a month in 1942—show that plane production was the single most telling factor in convincing the Germans as early as 1942 that the war was lost.

The first bomber to arrive in Europe immediately elevated the bombing program and indicated clearly what was yet to come. It was the North American B-25 Mitchell, named after Billy Mitchell, with qualities so apparent that it was one of the few large planes ordered right off the drawing board. Although only a two-engine plane, and thus a medium-range bomber, it was remarkably powerful and maneuverable, and was the first bomber to offer serious protection against fighter attack in the form of as many as fourteen machine guns distributed throughout the plane. The basic form of the bomber, with gunnery nests from glasshouse vantage points, was proven in the Mitchell and became standard for the

BENJAMIN DAVIS AND THE TUSKEGEE SQUADRON

The fighters that accompanied the bombers that flew missions over Europe were responsible for the lives of the fliers in those bombers, since the only defense the Germans could mount was from fighter aircraft of their own. The dogfights of the previous war returned as the Luftwaffe concentrated its efforts on pushing back the bombers that pounded German targets day and night. One of the fighter squadrons of the 332nd Fighter Group, the 99th, was an all-black unit, the first to fly for the USAAF.

Under the command of West Point graduate Lieutenant Colonel Benjamin O. Davis, Jr., the 99th Squadron, known as the Tuskegee Squadron because all the pilots had been trained at the AAF Flight Training Center at Tuskegee, Alabama, saw its first action in North Africa in May 1943. The challenges to the Tuskegee flyers were formidable, because bomber crews operated under the prejudice that blacks were not capable of flying. As often happened in other areas, the 99th had to prove itself by outperforming other squadrons, and in this Ben Davis was the right man to lead them. By July the Squadron had shot down German fighters over Sicily; soon three additional all-black squadrons joined the 332nd—the 100th, the 301st, and the 302nd—flying P-40 Warhawks and P-51 Mustangs, and bomber fliers came to realize they could not be in safer, more capable hands than those of the Tuskegee Airmen.

By the end of the war, the Tuskegee fliers had downed more than four hundred enemy aircraft and were the mainstay of the Allied air war in northern Italy. On March 24, 1945, Davis led an attack group of seventy-two Mustangs on a mission escorting the Fifteenth Air Force's bombing run on Berlin. Despite the fact that the Luftwaffe sent its most advanced jet fighters to meet them, including the new Me 262, the bombers reached their target and three attack planes were shot down. The 301st lost two planes, one of them flown by squadron leader Captain Armour G. McDaniels, who was captured by the Germans. McDaniels was freed by the advancing Allies near the end of the war, and the 301st was awarded the Distinguished Unit Citation for their valor on that mission.

Benjamin O. Davis, Jr. was eventually promoted to Brigadier General in 1954, making him only the second African American to achieve that rank. The first had been his father, in 1940.

The American bombing campaigns during the war were part of a thorough, methodical plan of bringing the enemy to submission with a minimum of Allied casualties. The planes that carried out the bombing became legends: the Martin B-26 Marauder (OPPOSITE BACKGROUND), which gave way to the Boeing B-17 Flying Fortress (RIGHT) and the North American B-25 Mitchell (BELOW), the plane used by Doolittle for his raids on Tokyo.

bombers that followed. Some eleven thousand B-25s were built, second only to the B-29 among American bombers.

On April 21, 1942, General James Doolittle led a squadron of 16 B-25 Mitchell bombers on a bombing raid of Japan. The squadron took off from the carrier *Hornet* and bombed Tokyo, Yokohama, and three other cities before continuing on to land in China. The raid came as a shock to the Japanese, who had come to believe their island was invincible. The Doolittle raid did not have great strategic significance, but it did demonstrate the effectiveness of the Mitchell bombers and was a great psychological boost to American soldiers and to Americans back home. A month later, the RAF, under Bomber Command Air Marshal Arthur Harris, conducted the first of the one-thousand-or-so bomber raids on German cities, this on Cologne. The two raids of Doolittle and Harris made it clear to the Allies that the most effective way of conducting the war was to place great emphasis on the saturation bombing of Japanese cities and military targets. This was accomplished under the direction of General Curtis LeMay, who had initiated the Allied bombing runs on "Fortress Europe" with the new B-17 Flying Fortresses.

The first long-range American bomber to enter the war proved to be a classic: the Boeing B-17 Flying Fortress, one of the most famous planes ever built. The B-17 first appeared in 1937, and some military analysts believed its mere existence might deter Hitler from starting a war. The B-17 was heavily armored with self-sealing fuel tanks and armament that made attack by anything but a

squadron of fighters pointless. The Germans, however, soon learned that they had to attack this plane with entire squadrons to defeat it, and a third of the B-17s flown were downed. Still, B-17s conducted most of the forward bombing of Germany. Some B-17s, such as the *Memphis Belle*, named after the fiancée of Captain Robert Morgan, became individually famous.

Realizing that bombers were only going to be getting bigger and more complicated, the USAAF paid much attention to the flight systems that would allow the duties to be performed on a multicrewed bomber to function independently, yet in coordination with other crew members. This was an unheralded achievement, and proved to be essential not only for the B-17, but for all later bombers. The United States used its production capacity during the war to replace the aging and battered bombers of England with newer, better-protected, and better-performing aircraft. The Martin B-26 Marauder series replaced the old Blenheims and the Douglas A-20 Invader (known as the Havoc in England) replaced the old Whitley bombers. In each case, American designers continued working on these designs and produced a second generation of bombers that took their place alongside them: Martin produced the Baltimore Mk series (a plane more reliable and controllable than the Marauder, which came to be known by flight crews as the Widow Maker); Douglas had the Boston series. These aircraft were far better built and armored than anything the British had put in the air, and their entry into every phase of the European theater altered the course of the air war.

The British used these planes to conduct nightime bombing raids on German cities and were aided by a combined flare and electronic beacon system developed by Robert Dippy, a British electronics researcher. Known as the Gee system, it was put in place by an RAF bomber unit, the Pathfinder Force (PFF), led by Captain Don Bennett. The PFF missions were dangerous: they attempted to fly in silently, drop the Gee devices discreetly, take bearings, and then leave without engaging the enemy or even alerting them to the fact that the British had been there.

Even the B-17 soon had company. The Consolidated B-24 Liberator was the bomber produced in the greatest numbers during the war—more than eighteen thousand—requiring factories other than Consolidated's to meet the needs for the plane. The B-24, designed by Isaac M. Laddon, was not the fighting machine that the B-17 was, but it had a longer range, which was vital in the Pacific, and a larger bombload capacity, and was a better flying machine at higher altitudes. It proved to be the perfect bomber for both the European and the Pacific theaters once the Allies had control of the skies. The B-24s were mechanically durable and were used to conduct endless bombing runs on targets in both theaters. The B-24 Liberator was the chief bomber used in the August 1, 1943, raid on the oil refineries at Ploesti.

As the Pacific war progressed, it became apparent that the United States was going to need two kinds of aircraft it had not yet developed: a dive-bomber and a long-range bomber. An earlier effort to build a dive-bomber, the Vultee A-35A Vengeance, was not considered adequate, even though over a thousand of them were used successfully by the British in North Africa and Burma. The solution took the form of the Douglas SBD-3 Dauntless, a single-engine plane that had to its credit the critical sinking of the Japanese aircraft carriers *Akagi*, *Kaga*, and *Hiryu* at the Battle of Midway on June 4, 1942.

The Dauntless was soon joined by the Curtiss SB2C Helldiver, an aircraft of such forward-looking design that it remained in production well into the 1950s. The Helldiver had a longer range than the Dauntless and, by carrying its bombload externally under its wings, was capable of more accurate pinpoint targeting. The Helldiver and the Dauntless were manufactured in large numbers—thirteen thousand combined—and saw a great deal of action, especially once the tide had turned and the Allies controlled the skies.

Another class of bomber developed by the Allies (and somewhat by the Japanese, but not by the Germans at all) was the torpedo-bomber: an aircraft that would launch a torpedo in the water at a naval vessel. The most successful of these was the American Grumman TBF-1 Avenger, which replaced the earlier Douglas TBD-1 Devastator. The Avenger was an important weapon in the Battle of Midway, and continued as a versatile aircraft performing many duties in all theaters. Nearly ten thousand Avengers were built, and many became important in postwar air forces (including, paradoxically enough, Japan's).

The most important strategic bomber of the war was the Boeing B-29 Superfortress, the only true long-range bomber deployed during the war. This plane was so advanced and complicated a machine that Boeing had to enlist the industrial capacity of the Bell and Martin companies to complete the project. The plane was equipped with the most advanced electronics then available, such as a General Electric remote ranging and firing system

Heavily armed and armored American planes saw important service in the Pacific and established American dominance in the Pacific skies: the Grumman TBF-1 Avenger (TOP) reverted to the through-the-propeller shooting mechanism that had been favored in World War I; the Douglas SBD-Dauntless (ABOVE) was a dive-bomber that supported ground troops as much with its smoke bombs as with explosives.

that allowed gunners to aim and fire the plane's machine guns and cannon from within the plane; gone were the bubbled gunner's nests that were so dangerous in the B-17. The B-29's main use was in the Pacific theater, where the island-to-island advance of the American marines toward Japan did not yield closer air bases from which to launch bombing raids (as it did in Europe). The 3,970 Superfortresses built constituted the most formidable bombing force assembled to that time, and under the command of General Carl "Tooey" Spaatz and directed in the field by General LeMay, the B-29s systematically destroyed Japanese industry and its military infrastructure.

The B-29 Superfortress known as the *Enola Gay* was inscribed in the annals of history when, on August 6, 1945, it dropped an atom bomb on the Japanese city of Hiroshima. The blast of the uranium bomb, known as "Little Boy," was the equivalent of twenty thousand tons (18,140t) of TNT, about an eighth of the bombs the B-29s had already dropped on Japanese targets. More than 100,000 people died in the blast, and the city was laid waste. On August 9, a second atomic bomb, this time a plutonium bomb named "Fat Man," was dropped from the B-29 called *Bock's Car* on the city of Nagasaki, killing more than thirty thousand people. The two blasts prompted Japan to surrender unconditionally to the Allies on August 14, 1945.

Heroes and Aces of World War II

Although the emphasis in flying during the war had shifted from individual feats to the accomplishments of the group—be it a squadron or an entire division—and to the designers, builders, commanders, and inventors, there were still heroes and remarkable acts of flying that became part of the history of aviation. Often these were flights and missions in remote areas, where the actions of one or a few aviators played a crucial role in the progress of the war.

RIGHT: Colonel Paul W. Tibbits was the commander and pilot of the Enola Gay, *the B-29 Superfortress that dropped the atom bomb on Hiroshima.* BELOW: *The* Enola Gay *lands at Tinian Air Base in the Marianas Islands after completing its historic mission in August 1945. The Superfortress was the most advanced bomber of the war, developed specifically for the final onslaught on the Japanese islands.*

The leading American ace of the war was Richard Bong, a Wisconsin farm boy who was remarkably skilled at flying the P-38 Lightning. He flew 146 missions and shot down forty Japanese aircraft, for which he received the Congressional Medal of Honor. He was killed in a test flight of the P-80 Shooting Star jet airplane in 1945. Another farm-raised ace was Joe Foss, who shot down most of his 26 kills while flying an F4F Wildcat, sometimes during severe bouts of malaria. He also was awarded the Medal of Honor and later became governor of South Dakota. Another Wildcat pilot who became a hero in the war was Edward Butch "Five-in-One" O'Hare, who shot down five Japanese bombers about to attack his aircraft carrier, the *Lexington*. A similar act of flying heroism, this one involving leading a group of Hellcats in intercepting a squadron of more than a hundred planes bearing down on the *Essex*, resulted in a Medal of Honor for Captain David McCampbell, who became one of the best group commanders of the war.

Two aerial operations that became celebrated during the war were the May 1943 "dambusting" exploits of RAF 617 Squadron, in which nineteen Lancaster bombers, under the command of Guy Gibson, dropped specially designed "bouncing bombs" and blew up the dams supplying power to German war factories in the Ruhr valley (but not without enduring heavy ground fire); and the decisive victory of Marc Mitscher's Task Force 58 (TF58) over Japanese aircraft above Guam and the Marianas Islands in June 1944, which was such a rout that it became known as the "Marianas Turkey Shoot." The top RAF ace of the war, with twenty-three kills, was Pat Pattle, whose achievement is particularly astounding since for most of the war Pattle flew an antiquated Gladiator biplane. On April 22, 1941, while destroying three German Bf 109s, Pattle's plane crashed into the Aegean Sea and he disappeared. An RAF hero of the May 1942 campaign to prevent the Germans from taking control of the strategic island of Malta was George "Screwball" Beurling, the greatest Canadian ace of the war. An Australian RAF hero, Clive Caldwell, earned his nickname, "Killer," by downing twenty-eight enemy aircraft in Australia's Western Desert in 1941.

The Germans had their aces, too, as one would expect: the greatest Luftwaffe ace of the war (and possibly of all time) was Erich "Bubi" Hartmann, who between November 1942 and the end of the war shot down 352 planes, most of them Russian. His black-nosed Bf 109 earned him the nickname the "Black Devil," and the Soviets placed a bounty on his head during the war. He was one of the few fliers the Soviets

LEFT: *Lieutenant Edward "Butch" O'Hare, who won the Medal of Honor in 1942, was also known as "Five-in-One O'Hare" for downing five Zeros in a single run.* MIDDLE: *Lieutenant Joe Foss, who also received a Medal of Honor, later became governor of South Dakota.* RIGHT: *Richard Bong, top-scoring ace of the war. Also a Medal of Honor winner, Bong was killed in 1945 while testing a jet aircraft.*

THE FINAL MISSION OF JOE KENNEDY, JR.

The Kennedys were always a competitive family—Joseph Kennedy, Sr., would hire tutors to train his children in ordinary childhood games and activities (which may have been a factor in the later Kennedy reliance on experts in political life). Kennedy's eldest son, Joe Jr., was being groomed for the presidency, almost from the cradle. He was a robust, intelligent, and handsome young man who learned much about politics from his father and his maternal grandfather, a mayor of Boston with legendary political acumen.

Joe enlisted in the U.S. Navy Air Force in World War II and fully expected that his career as a war pilot would enhance his political career after the war. While he was training on the new Liberator bombers, his frail and shy younger brother, John, was gaining glory in the Pacific as the hero of PT-109. This was intolerable to Joe, and he was determined to outshine his brother in war heroics. After months of frustrating flying over England and over the Channel, during which time he saw no action, Joe volunteered for a mission to fly a Liberator loaded with high explosives and blow up the concrete-bunkered V-bomb rocket installations at Mimoyecques on the coast of France. If successful, it would have allowed Joe to claim that it had been a Kennedy who had stopped the dreaded Buzz-Bomb attacks on London, and it probably would have launched his political career toward the presidency.

The mission was a tricky one, however. It required Joe and his copilot (Lieutenant Bud Willy) to aim the Liberator at the target and bail out as they approached it. The plane would then be guided by remote control (through a television camera in its nose) to the tar-

Lieutenant Joe Kennedy, Jr., is seen here in England before taking off on his dangerous (and ultimately fatal) mission.

get. Tests of such drones by both the army and the navy had never been successful, though the navy believed it had most of the bugs worked out. So with more than twenty-one thousand pounds (9,534kg) of Torpex high explosives crammed on board, the Liberator, accompanied by a squad of seven planes (some to guide the flying bomb to the target, some to defend the plane or to draw ground fire, and some simply to observe and photograph the mission) took off from Framingham on the afternoon of August 12, 1944. The mission was clearly perceived as important, because in one of the escort planes was General Jimmy Doolittle, and in another was Elliott Roosevelt, there just to photograph what he believed would be a history-making event.

About twenty minutes after taking off and forty minutes from the target, while over Blythburgh on the English coast, something went terribly wrong. The Liberator blew up in a huge fireball, killing Kennedy and Willy instantly; two planes flying nearby were nearly forced into the ground by the blast. There was very little to go on in the ensuing investigation, and the navy was concerned that Joseph Kennedy would be upset that his son was allowed to go on so risky a mission. (It also turned out that the British did not consider the V-rockets strategically important weapons.) Over the years, a great deal of misinformation was issued by the navy about the mission (for example, that the target was the U-boat pens at Helgoland, against which the Liberator would have been ineffective), but there was no doubt that the accident deprived America of a man who stood an excellent chance of one day becoming president.

pursued after the war; once they captured him, they made him serve ten years in a Soviet prison camp. Two other Luftwaffe heroes were Adolf Galland, a flier who modeled himself on Roscoe Tanner but who proved to be an able Luftwaffe general once his flying days had passed; and Hans-Joachim Marseille, the most decorated Luftwaffe ace of the war, with 158 kills to his credit and celebrated for downing seventeen RAF aircraft in one day. He died during a bail-out.

The Japanese were not given to lionizing individual fliers, so it was only after the war that Hiroyoshi Nishizawa was acknowledged as Japan's leading ace in the war.

The Women of the World War II Air War

Women aviators had had a difficult time breaking into the field of aviation from the very beginning, but that situation changed during the war. The contributions that women made—which turned out to be significant—were usually the result of determined effort against a wall of prejudice that was even stronger in the military than among civilians. In 1937 Jacqueline Cochran set a new women's speed record by flying a Beech D-17W at over 203 miles per hour (326.5kph). When she won the 1938 Bendix Trophy flying a Seversky AP-7 against a field of men, she had to endure vicious, unfounded rumors that a man impersonating her had flown her plane.

Cochran was the flier who convinced the British to establish the Air Transport Auxiliary (ATA) that would have qualified women pilots ferrying planes to the theater

of battle. Hap Arnold, commander of the USAAF, resisted a similar plan for the United States, believing it risky to entrust the advanced American planes to female pilots. Cochran finally convinced him in May 1941 to try the idea with the fifty most qualified American women pilots, and so the USAAF Ferrying Command, under veteran pilot Nancy Love, was born.

The service established so solid a record that in October 1943 the Women's Air Force Service Pilots, or WASP, was established under Cochran's command for the purpose of transporting aircraft and for other noncombat missions. These missions kept expanding during the war and included reconnaissance and transporting personnel. Missions (even just ferrying) had a habit of becoming dangerous—because of sudden weather shifts or surprise enemy patrols—and WASP pilots, members of the Women's Auxiliary Flying Squadron (WAFS), the flying unit of WASP, frequently had to show a flying competence of which any combat flier would be proud. In all, women flew over 12,500 missions, transporting everything from fighters and seaplanes to B-17 bombers; only twenty-six

The two women aviators most active in pressing women into flight service during the war were Jacquelin Cochran (TOP, in the cockpit of the plane in which she set a nonstop speed record in a flight to Miami in 1938) and Pauline Gower (ABOVE, AT LEFT, commander of the British Air Transport Auxiliary [ATA]), seen here in this 1940 photograph of the first ATA squadron.

pilots were killed in the line of duty. ATA pilots, led by Commander Pauline Gower, were even busier (since they transported planes once they were delivered from the United States), flying more than 300,000 missions during the course of the war. One of their pilots was the celebrated aviator Amy Johnson, who was killed in January 1941 while on an ATA ferrying mission.

In spite of the record, the USAAF was not quick to acknowledge the contribution made by women fliers to the war effort (perhaps fearing that pilots like Cochran would push to have women accepted as Air Force combat pilots). The United States did acknowledge, however, the importance of the Women Ordnance Workers (WOW) who made up nearly a third of the factory working force responsible for the incredible plane production—360,000 aircraft produced during the war—that led to an Allied victory.

The Germans had a much more accepting attitude toward women pilots, possibly because several women pilots (Thea Rasche and Elly Beinhorn, to name two) had distinguished themselves in international competition throughout the 1930s. A proponent of German women entering aviation was Marga von Etzdorf, the first woman to earn a commercial flying license in Germany. Her death in 1933 was a cause for national mourning, and she was given a military funeral by the Nazis. The woman who achieved the most in military aviation during the war for Germany was Hanna Reitsch, a racer and record-setter known and admired the world over. Reitsch was made an honorary flight captain in the Luftwaffe and flew several dangerous missions during the war for which she was awarded the Iron Cross.

The nation that had the most accepting view toward women as combat pilots was the Soviet Union, but the conduct of that country in World War II deserves to be examined separately.

Women played important roles in the German and Russian air forces. Here, Hannah Reitsch receives a medal from Hitler (Göring is in the background) for missions that would have earned any flier the same accolades.

The Soviet Air Force in World War II

At first, the Soviet Union found itself out of the war, shielded by a nonaggression pact made between Hitler and Stalin, and then in the thick of it when Germany opted to ignore the agreement and attack Russia, on June 22, 1941. (The Soviet Union did not declare war on Japan until six days before Japan surrendered.) The role

of air power in Russia was difficult to determine: the areas involved were too vast to permit either side to claim air superiority, and the weather often made the entire issue moot, as the war was sometimes fought strictly on the ground and by artillery. Aviation had developed in Russia along active and parallel lines to its development in Europe and in America. The father of Russian aviation, Nikolai Zhukovsky, had established a wind tunnel research station in Moscow in 1914, beginning a deep tradition of aeronautical research in Russia. The designer who became the most prolific in the years following World War I was Andrei Nikolaevich Tupolev. It was in a Tupolev plane, the ANT-25, that three Russian fliers made their 1937 nonstop flight from Moscow to California over the North Pole, a flight of 6,750 miles (10,861km) completed in sixty-two hours and seventeen minutes. Tupolev continued the Russian fascination for large aircraft begun by Sikorsky and his *Ilya Mouremetz*, and eventually built the *Maxim Gorky* and the ANT-25bis.

Meanwhile, the Soviets realized that its air force would have to include fighters as well. This effort was led by Nikolai Polikarpov, who was to design many of the best Russian fighters through World War II. The two men who developed the pilot corps of the Red Air Force were Yakov Smushkevich, who coordinated the Soviet air activities during the Spanish Civil War, and General Alexander Novikov, commander of the Soviet Air Force during World War II.

The planes that the Soviets deployed in the war formed the foundation of the air force that afterward would vie with the Western powers for superiority in the sky. The plane that became the cornerstone of the Russian air campaign was the Ilyushin IL-2m-3 Shturmovik, a two-man fighter-bomber dive-bomber with a powerful 1,770-horsepower engine and armor to withstand scores of direct hits. The Shturmovik was known as the "Flying Tank," and the Soviets built and deployed an incredible thirty-six thousand of them during the war. Its two cannons and two machine guns, combined with a bombload capacity of 1,320 pounds (660kg), made it a powerful weapon and support for ground troops.

The only Soviet bomber of consequence in the war was the Petlyakov PE-8, a bomber with a range adequate for targets inside Germany. In the category of fighters, the Soviet Air force relied on four planes, each with strengths and weaknesses that Russian fliers came to know intimately. The first was an American plane: the

Bell P-39 Airacobra, five thousand of which were given to the Soviets when the plane was spurned by American pilots. The Russians used it as a low-altitude fighter and for ground support; fitting it with a more powerful cannon made it an effective antitank weapon.

The Mikoyan-Gurevich MiG-3 was a fighter with poor maneuverability and meager armament, yet it proved an irritant to German planes because it climbed and dove as no other fighter. A Messerschmitt could, if not alert, suddenly find itself being swooped down on from above by a MiG-3 that cruised at forty thousand feet (12,192m) waiting for the perfect opportunity to strike. The need for a fighter that could engage the Luftwaffe at close range was met by the Yakovlev YAK-3, introduced in 1943 and comparable in performance to the Spitfire. The YAK-3 neutralized the German fighter and Stuka attacks, and that was all that was necessary, given that Germany did not have a long-range bomber program to speak of. The most advanced Soviet fighter produced during the war was the powerfully elegant Lavochkin LA-7, a fighter introduced in 1944 that was superior to anything the Luftwaffe flew; with fifteen thousand produced, the LA-7 gave the Soviets the edge in a theater Germany believed it dominated right to the end.

The long tradition of flying in Russia, coupled with its continuing awareness that it would likely be involved in wars from both the east and the west, resulted in a strong corp of aviators, and thus of war aces. The Red Air Force's top ace was Ivan Kozhedub, with sixty-two kills in a Lavochkin fighter purchased for him by private donations. Many other pilots endured great tests during the sieges of Russian cities and there were aces duly decorated, but no tale compares to that of Alexei Maresyev.

With nineteen kills to his credit already, Maresyev crash-landed behind enemy lines and in the process crushed both his legs. He dragged himself through the snow, surviving on berries and ants, until he was rescued nineteen days later. Both his legs had to be amputated, but within a year, walking on artificial legs, he returned to service and scored seven more victories.

Women pilots found their greatest acceptance in the Red Air Force, partly out of egalitarian ideology and partly because the one thousand women who volunteered were excellent pilots. An impressive thirty Citations of Hero of the Soviet Union went to women pilots, twenty-three to members of the 588th Night Bomber Regiment—the so-called Night Witches, who flew whatever planes they could find (even if they were slow PO-2 biplanes) to bomb the enemy. Three entire regiments of the Air Force were made up entirely of women, and some became legendary combat pilots.

The most famous of them was Lilya Litvyak, known as the "White Rose of Stalingrad," a pilot with twenty-two kills to her credit before she was shot down. Other women whose exploits were hailed both in Russia and throughout the world were Anna Yegorova, one of the most proficient Shturmovik pilots (previously thought to be too difficult a plane for a woman to fly); Natalya Meklin, a teenage member of the Night Witches who flew 840 missions in less than three years; Valeria Khomyakova, a member of the 566th Fighter Regiment who became famous for being the first woman to down a German bomber, a JU88, in 1942; and Olga Yamschikova, the top woman ace of the war with seventeen kills, who volunteered for combat after serving as a flight instructor preparing many men to fly fighter aircraft.

The Russian Air Force played an important part in the air war of World War II, and two of its planes—the YAK-3 (ABOVE), a light fighter that was considered a match for the Spitfire, and the Shturmovik IL-2, a dive-bomber that was virtually invulnerable to ground fire—were among the best produced during the war years.

Chapter 9

Fire in the Sky: The Jet Age

Introduction

World War II was over. There were many aircraft in the Allied arsenals that were still active and still usable; most would not go to waste. For there began a phenomenon that was to have an overriding and defining influence on the latter half of the twentieth century and would play a pivotal role in the development of aviation during that period: the Cold War between the Communist countries, led by the Soviet Union, and the nations of the "Free World," led by the United States (and, to a much lesser extent, Great Britain and France).

As far as aviation was concerned, the Cold War was similar to a conventional war: over a half-century, the major powers developed ever newer military aircraft at a pace reminiscent of wartime and with an urgency and determination born of the heat of battle. There were two reasons for this. First, there were to be occasions when states representing both sides of the Cold War would, in fact, engage in actual battle on battlefields, and the armaments supplied by East and West would be pitted against each other and tested in the field. Second, the advent of atomic weapons and the possibility of delivering war-ending (even civilization-ending) bombs with bomber aircraft made the struggle to keep producing the best airplanes a life-and-death matter.

The technological development that defined the aviation of the postwar period was the creation of jet-powered aircraft. Not that the jet replaced the propeller (or "prop")—far from it. An extremely small percentage of aircraft are purely jet driven; nearly all aircraft that we now regard as jet aircraft are propelled by engines that are in reality a combination of jet and propeller. This can happen in a number of ways: the engine might be a

turbojet, in which the propeller component feeds incoming air into the combustion chamber where it is mixed with fuel and burned, so that it is sent rearward with even greater speed, thus propelling the aircraft forward. The engine might be a turboprop, in which the propulsion is provided by a propeller that is driven, not by an internal combustion engine, but by a jet engine that turns a turbine connected to the propeller shaft. The engine might be a turbofan, in which the propeller uses some of its energy to feed the jet engine, which in turn rotates the propeller—a sharing of the propulsion duties. Or the engine might be a propfan (one of the most fuel-efficient of these configurations, which is why it has found wider use in the 1990s), in which the jet engine is used to turn a specially designed pair of propellers that provide most of the aircraft's propulsion. In all of these, there is a marriage of propeller-driven propulsion and jet propulsion—sometimes visible to the eye and sometimes taking place within the large so-called jet engines on the wing of the plane (or in the fuselage, as in an F-15 fighter).

The principle behind jet engines was known long ago (it is related, but not identical, to rocket propulsion), and the technical requirements of a jet engine were spelled out in detail in 1928 by Frank Whittle, then an RAF cadet. Whittle even took out a patent, but no one showed any interest because the metals the jet engine would require had not yet been developed, and the patent lapsed. (Rockets, however, were well along in development by 1930, and were developed during the war to frightening levels by the German scientists at Peenemunde, which should indicate that the two technologies are not identical.) Whittle later renewed his patent, but did not get a chance to build a model of his engine until 1937, when he was supplied with Stayblade steel and a new nickel-chrome alloy by the Thompson-

After World War II, the development of military aircraft boomed as jet propulsion opened up an entirely new realm of aviation. At left, an F117 Stealth Fighter—a plane that has seen a surprising amount of combat action in the 1980s and 1990s—is refueled.

Huston Company of Lutterworth, England. In the intervening years, a young student from Göttingen, Pabst von Ohain, brought a similar idea to airplane builder Ernst Heinkel, who was already supporting the research of an ambitious young man named Werner von Braun. (It now appears virtually certain that Ohain knew nothing of Whittle's patent or his work, but developed the idea independently.)

The first test of a jet-driven airplane took place at Rechlin on July 3, 1939, when test pilot Erich Warsitz flew the Heinkel He-176 jet plane for Hitler, Göring, Udet, and the entire Luftwaffe High Command. The test went swimmingly—so well, in fact, that the Nazi hierarchy thought the device was a hoax or a joke. When Warsitz landed perfectly and climbed out of the aircraft beaming, Hitler and the generals looked at him stone-faced, turned on their heels and left. The Luftwaffe, Heinkel understood, was not inclined to sponsor further research. (Heinkel and Messerschmitt, both astute judges of technology, pursued the research on their own.)

The British were not able to fly a jet aircraft until May 15, 1941, when Jerry Sayer flew the Gloster-Whittle E.28/39. This test flight was also a success, and Frank Whittle was knighted as a result, but no one knew how to incorporate the new engine into a fighter aircraft or how to enable the aircraft to fly for longer than the few minutes the E.28/39 had. The answer, ironically, lay in the fact that Whittle's engine used propellers in a grossly inefficient way.

Before the war was over, both the Germans and the Allies put jet aircraft in the air: the Messerschmitt Me 163 and Me 162, and the Heinkel He 162; and the Gloster Meteor and the Bell P-59A Airacomet. These were impressive, but they were of very limited usefulness, came too late, and played virtually no role in the course of the war, let alone its outcome.

The Rise of Commercial Aviation

The effect of the war was to telescope decades of development in aviation—in materials and structure, navigation and communication, flight procedures and ground support—into half a decade. There was, at this point, nothing unusual about flying, even if the experience of flight did not get any less unsettling. It was clear that landing mechanisms and procedures developed during the war had made the flying boats unnecessary; the luxuriant British Saunders-Roe "Saro" Princess flying boat was obsolete the day it was unveiled in 1952. The importance to a city of having an international airport nearby caused city governments to build striking airports as a stimulus to business and as symbols of status.

At first, airlines used converted and enhanced World War II planes and prewar models, such as the Douglas DC-3s (which flew in the war as the C-47 transport), and

Jet aircraft did not play a significant role in World War II, but the earliest applications of jet propulsion were in military aircraft. TOP: The Volkjaeger ("People's Fighter")—officially designated the Heinkel He 162—was used briefly in the latter stages of World War II to break up bomber formations. CENTER: The Messerschmitt Me 262A is considered the first jet fighter, and would certainly have prolonged the war if it had been used strictly as a fighter interceptor and not (as Hitler insisted) also as a bomber. BOTTOM: The British response to the German jets was the Gloster Meteor, the first of which was tested in 1941. The British, with typical thoroughness, spent three years perfecting the airframe that could best control such power.

the four-engined Lockheed Constellation (the "Connie") and the less refined, but still serviceable DC-4. Boeing developed a four-engine competitor to the Connie based on the B-29 Superfortress, the Boeing 377 Stratocruiser, and Lockheed came back with the Super Constellation in 1950. This gave the United States three sizeable prop aircraft, richly appointed with comfort and convenience, yet with sizeable passenger loads, which met the newly-created demand for long-distance air travel.

Great Britain, after some careful but misguided analysis by the Brabazon Committee, which met during the war to plan postwar development of commercial aviation, countered by plunging into the development of jet-powered commercial airliners. The first offering, the Vickers Viscount, a turboprop, was popular with carriers for short distances. Two other efforts inspired by the Brabazon recommendations—the Saro Princess and the Bristol Brabazon, an ambitious attempt at creating a huge turbojet that had to be abandoned after eight years of fruitless development—were not as fortunate. The problem seems to have been that the Brabazon Committee tried to guess what the market would be like a decade hence and to plan accordingly. The American approach was to listen to what the market was saying right now and meet those needs. The result was that the British kept building aircraft no one asked for, while the seats on the American planes were full.

When the British did create a fully jet-powered passenger aircraft, the de Havilland Comet, it was a sleek, elegantly streamlined and appointed four-engine plane with a respectable passenger load. The first Comet model was put in service in 1949, and it went through four models, each lengthening the fuselage to allow a larger passenger load. In 1954 two of the earlier models crashed in the Mediterranean and service on the plane was suspended. An investigation determined that the problem lay in metal fatigue around the square-cut windows, a problem easily correctable, but the shock caused by the crashes could not be so easily assuaged and the entire program was put on hold while new fuselages could be designed with round window holes.

At the time, the United States enjoyed 80 percent of the commercial airplane market and more than half of that was from the Douglas Company. The DC-6 had replaced the DC-4 and it was in turn replaced by the DC-7, the definitive prop model of the line. Donald Douglas watched and waited to see how the Comet fiasco would be resolved before leaping into jet transport. This was the opening Boeing was looking for. In 1954 Boeing introduced its new passenger jet aircraft, the Boeing 707, an airplane that used the same basic design specifications as the B-52 the company was building for the U.S. Air Force. The initial reaction to the 707 was not enthusiastic; its first orders were not received until a year after the prototype was unveiled. But with the support of a large

Monty Montieth and Ed Wells: The Boeing Tradition

Bill Boeing's name may have been on the factories, but the planes were the creations of gifted designers who established a tradition of excellence at the company. Two Boeing designers who left their imprint on the history of aviation are virtually unknown to people outside the industry. Charles N. "Monty" Montieth was a talented pilot, as well as an accomplished artist, musician, and photographer. Trained at the Massachusetts Institute of Technology, he became chief of the aeronautics division at McCook Field in Dayton, and later wrote the standard textbook in aeronautical engineering used by the USAAF. He went to work for Boeing in 1925 and was chief engineer by 1927. He designed the first American fighter plane to use flaps, the P-26.

Montieth introduced a conservative design philosophy that seems impossible to argue with today, but was innovative for his time. In his view, the designer's primary purpose was to ensure the safety of the pilot and the passengers, and while this sometimes sacrificed the performance of the aircraft, it was a necessary step in making flying acceptable to a wary public. He actually eliminated an advance in aerodynamic design, the variable pitch propeller, from the Boeing Monomail because he felt it gave the pilot too many opportunities to try reckless maneuvers. In 1940, despairing at the prospect of going blind, Montieth killed himself. He was forty-eight years old.

One of the designers Montieth recruited was Edward C. Wells, who served as the company's chief designer from 1935 to 1969. Ed Wells' first plane was the B-17, a plane that virtually set in concrete the configuration of the passenger aircraft for the rest of the century. Wells was a firm believer in the use of flaps and slats as control surfaces on his planes, and while these devices had been pioneered by Douglas, it was Wells who adapted them to the fullest in giving the B-17 the maximum lift and a low-enough landing speed to be safe. These control surfaces permitted larger wings, which in turn required a more intricate and better designed fuselage. The mechanisms of the wing became standard and were the basis of the design of the 707, the first successful commercial jet aircraft, and on the 727, described by observers as "the airplane whose wing comes apart."

Wells was an integral member of the design team that developed the Minuteman Missile and the X-20 "Dyna-Soar," forerunner of the Space Shuttle. He retired after the successful unveiling of the 747, a plane that violated all the design rules established by Wells himself but which became a prestige plane for many private and national airlines.

By always looking to develop its planes further, Douglas stayed in the forefront of the market in the years following the war. Here, four generations of Douglas airliners are parked at the Douglas factory in Santa Monica, California (from the rear): the DC-3, the four-engine DC-4, the DC-6, and the DC-7, the last of the prop line.

The Europeans remained a step behind the American manufacturers, creating the Vickers Viscount (LEFT), a turboprop that found wide use as a short-haul airliner. BELOW: The Fokker F-27 Friendship, a fifty-passenger short-distance aircraft, remained in production longer than virtually any other commercial airplane. But the long-distance market belonged to Boeing, makers of the 707, which was produced in the most variations and for more applications (here, BOTTOM, as an in-flight refueler) than any other airplane.

order from Pan Am, by the time the 707 began commercial service in 1959, the orders had rolled in, and Boeing took the lead in the market. Douglas countered with the DC-8, and the British Convair Company entered the market with the 880/990 series built for Delta Airlines and TWA, but neither could shake Boeing's dominance of the market. A new generation of jet airliners arrived in 1963 using the fuel-saving technology of the turbofan engine; again Boeing led the way with the Boeing 727, the most successful series of passenger jetliners of the past fifty years. The 707/727 not only has outsold any other single model, but also has been adapted into the most number of models (more than a thousand) and applications of any commercial jet in history.

Not being able to compete with Boeing and Douglas in the long-haul market, other builders in the 1950s looked to create better airplanes for the short-haul carriers. Several models produced in Europe and the United States found popular support in the market: the much admired French Caravelle, based on the Comet fuselage but with engines attached to the rear of the fuselage and not built into the wing (which was both a positive and a negative for the Comet); the British Aerospace Corporation's BAC 111 and its close rival, the DC-9; and the Boeing 737. Two aircraft that proved popular for very short trips and for commuter routes were the Fokker F-27 Friendship, produced under license after 1955 by Fairchild, and the de Havilland Twin Otter.

In 1969 Boeing again struck out into the unknown by producing the 747 Jumbo Jet, a wide-body commercial jet based, as before, on a Boeing military aircraft, the C-5 Galaxy, and powered by four Pratt & Whitney JT9D turbofan engines. This time, Boeing was so certain of its reception in the market that it did not bother with a prototype but used its first production models for test flights. The 747 can seat five hundred passengers, though it usually holds 385. It cruises at about six hundred miles per hour (965.5kph) and has a nonstop range of seventy-two hundred miles (11,585km). It often is designed to have a

forward first-class (or "business class") section and a second level on which the cockpit and a lounge are located. The 747 is an expensive airplane, and the cost overruns on the engines, borne by Boeing, nearly bankrupted the company. But twenty-five years of service have proven it to be a durable plane, and it has paid the airlines that use it—and thus Boeing—handsome returns.

Boeing's chief American rivals, Lockheed and McDonnell Douglas (the amalgamated company taking shape in 1967), responded to the 747 with large planes of their own. The Lockheed L-1011 TriStar is a somewhat smaller airplane (four hundred-passenger limit) with three Rolls-Royce turbofan engines. (The cost overruns of the L-1011 engines bankrupted Rolls-Royce.) The McDonnell Douglas DC-10 is smaller still and uses three General Electric turbofan engines. Although cheaper than the 747, these planes have never mounted a serious challenge to Boeing's dominance in the passenger airline

Britain's entry into the high-stakes long-distance sweepstakes was the de Havilland D.H. 106 Comet (ABOVE), a jet aircraft of incomparable design and performance that was years ahead of its time when unveiled in 1952. Were it not for a fatal flaw, it might have established England as a major manufacturer of large jet transports. The two courses followed by the American giants are the tail-jet design, represented by the DC-10 (LEFT TOP) and the Lockheed L-1011 Tristar, and the wing-jet Boeing 700-series, the latest of which, the 777 (LEFT MIDDLE) is reputed to be the most advanced large transport jet ever built. The British-French gamble to recapture the forward position in air transportation with the SST Concorde (LEFT BOTTOM) proved a public-relations success but an economic failure.

market. The only rival that has emerged is the Airbus A300 series, built by a consortium of French, British, and German government and industrial interests.

Smarting from having lost the early rounds in the commercial airplane building market, BAC and the French firm Aérospatiale joined forces in 1962 and planned a supersonic transport (SST) to be called the *Concorde*. Americans had been through this before with the Brabazon Committee, and they settled back to watch. Their studies indicated that without large government support, the market would not make an SST profitable, and lengthy hearings in the U.S. Congress indicated that such support was not forthcoming. American builders also anticipated protest from environmentalists over noise and air pollution that would result from any SST.

The *Concorde* was built (there are actually fourteen models in existence, with rarely more than two in use at any one time), and, as predicted, it failed to make anything close to a profit. The French and British governments maintain the service strictly for the prestige value. In the late 1970s the Soviet Union had built an SST of its own, the Tupolev Tu-144 (dubbed the "Concordki"). It briefly saw limited service between Moscow and Vladivostok and was promptly mothballed after it was involved in a disastrous crash at the 1973 Paris Air Show.

Periodically, there has been talk of creating a National Aerospace Plane (which President Reagan called the "Orient Express") based on the experimental X-30 aircraft, which would be able to make the San Francisco–Tokyo trip in two hours by following a suborbital route.

The inroads made by the Airbus A340 in the wide-body passenger jet market have prompted Boeing to forge ahead again and develop the 777, reputed to be the first commercial passenger airplane created completely by computer and without paper. The 777 uses the most sophisticated electronic communications, navigation, and digital display, and provides a higher standard of passenger comfort (but is still impoverished compared to the airliners of the 1930s).

The important issue in the 1990s in commercial aviation is the management crisis that plagues many airlines and the industry as a whole. Twenty years of labor difficulties, mismanagement, airport congestion, rising fuel costs, and government interference, as well as questions raised concerning safety and protection from aircraft failure, terrorism, and even on-board pollution, have put the commercial air transportation industry in an extreme state of crisis, causing financial analysts to wonder whether anyone can still make any money flying people from one place to another.

The Cold War

The rivalry between the United States and the Soviet Union was fraught with many tense moments, but it also brought out the best in aircraft research, design, and development. Without the stakes of the Cold War, real or imagined, it is difficult to see what could have inspired an aviation program such as the one undertaken by both sides in the decades from the end of World War II to the fall of Communism.

The first airplane that the United States added to its arsenal after the Korean War was the ten-engine (six piston, four jet) Consolidated B-36 Peacemaker, a bomber that replaced the Boeing B-29 and B-50 bombers of World War II and the Korean War, but which did not have the capability to reach and deliver bombs to every spot in the world. This became a high priority of the USAF, as indicated by the formation of the Strategic Air Command (SAC) with the Air Force, and several possible aircraft—the Douglas XB-43, the Martin XB-51, and the North American XB-45—were rigorously tested and found wanting. A bomber that almost met this criterion (requiring only one in-flight refueling) was the B-57, developed by Martin from an aircraft originally commissioned by the RAF, the Canberra. Similarly, Boeing's improved model of the B-29, the B-50, was a fine aircraft, but short of the goal.

While SAC was waiting for the right plane to come along, it endured the Convair B-36, an aircraft that was so large that a small railway had to be installed running down the length of the fuselage just so the crew could move from one end of the plane to the other. The B-36 was large enough to carry in its body a McDonnell F-85 fighter that could protect the bomber from other fighters and then return to the aircraft. The problem with the B-36 was that it was very slow: it had a maximum speed of 435 miles per hour (700.4kph), well within the range of even World War II fighters.

Two bombers were selected by SAC: the Boeing B-47 Stratojet, a six-engine swept-wing decendent of the B-29, and soon after the B-52 Stratofortress, the classic eight-engine version of the B-47, one of the most remarkable military aircraft ever flown. Both Boeing aircraft were fast (cruising at 600 and 660 mph [966 and 1,062.6kph], respectively), with high ceilings, good range (4000 and 10,000 miles [6,440 and 16,100km]), and good maneuverability. The key design element of these planes was

ABOVE: *The backbone of the U.S. strategic bomber fleet through the 1960s was the Boeing B-47 Stratojet, which was eventually replaced by the B-52 Stratofortress. Both planes were designed in the mid-1940s in case Germany had to be bombed from the United States. BELOW: The rapid development of fighter-bomber aircraft culminated in the remarkable delta-winged Convair B-58 Hustler, the first supersonic bomber-fighter deployed by the United States Air Force.*

ABOVE: *This unusual photograph shows the rapid development of bomber aircraft in the postwar period. The transition from the prewar Douglas B-18 (wingspan of eighty-nine feet, top) to the B-17 Flying Fortress (wingspan of 103.7 feet, bottom left) and the B-29 Superfortress (wingspan of 141 feet, top left) was considered meteoric. But it paled next to the jump to the Convair B-36H (wingspan of 230 feet, right), the giant in the U.S. air arsenal.*

ED HEINEMANN AND THE SKYHAWK

The experience of fighter pilots in the Korean War—they found the more primitive Soviet-built MiG-15s capable of outperforming their more sophisticated American planes—led American designers to focus on speed, agility, and performance. At Lockheed, this resulted in Clarence "Kelly" Johnson's F-104 Starfighter, a plane that held every speed record but was difficult to control. The Starfighter, with its small wings, was called the "missile with a man in it," and was a mainline fighter-bomber in several European air forces from the late 1950s to the 1960s.

At Douglas, Johnson's counterpart was a designer named Gustav H.E. "Ed" Heinemann. Born in Michigan in 1908, Ed moved to California with his family in 1915, and it was there that he saw Lincoln Beachey's barnstorming flights. He became a student of Jack Northrop and was the principal designer of the SBD-3 Dauntless, the decisive aircraft at the Battle of Midway in World War II. When the navy gave Heinemann the specifications for a plane it wanted, the result was the A-4F Skyhawk, a light bomber with the agility and speed of a fighter. Heinemann's approach had a classic barnstormer flavor to it: take the best engine one could find, stick a wing under it, put a cockpit on top for the pilot—and cut out everything else.

Heinemann's simple design allowed the plane to be upgraded each time an advance was made in the power plant. The original Skyhawks of 1954 weighed a bit more than ten thousand pounds (454kg) with an engine providing ninety-three hundred pounds (4,222kg) of thrust. This meant nearly a 1:1 thrust-to-weight ratio, unheard of in attack aircraft of the day, and making supersonic speeds possible. By the 1970s, however, with the plane amazingly still in production and in service, the weight had grown to twenty-five thousand pounds (11,350kg) with an engine providing eleven thousand pounds (4,994kg) of thrust; it still performed beautifully at subsonic speeds and, anyway, there were other aircraft available for supersonic flight.

Heinemann was famous for providing outstanding attack aircraft in record time. He was given overnight to come up with a design for which he had asked nine months to develop—and he delivered. The plane eventually became the AD-1 Skyraider, the "flying dumptruck" that saw extended bombing service during the Vietnam War. But the Skyhawk remains Heinemann's masterpiece. This plane was so agile that in 1974 it became the principal aircraft for the navy's aerobatics squad, the famous Blue Angels.

LEFT: *The A-4 series Skyhawks were among the most versatile and durable carrier-based aircraft in the U.S. arsenal, and were in continuous service for nearly three decades before they were retired.* RIGHT: *The Douglas Skyraider, another hastily assembled Heinemann design, became the basis of fighter aircraft used in the air forces of many nations during the last decades of the twentieth century.*

that their wings were extremely thin, which cut down on drag and gave the plane greater lift. Special alloys had to be devised to maintain the wing integrity, and they were so thin that they could not support landing gear. The landing gear on the B-52 consists of only fore and aft double bicycle tire assemblies, forming the trickiest element in the entire design. The B-52 was also electronically sophisticated so that it could be flown with a crew of three. As central as the B-52 was in SAC's overall plan, the plane was used as a tactical field weapon in the Vietnam War. The B-52 first flew in 1952 and remains in service over forty years later, a tribute not only to its original design, but to its ability to adapt new systems and design elements.

The only plane type that SAC was interested in considering as a replacement for the B-52 was a supersonic bomber, but efforts to create such a plane have proven difficult. The Convair B-58 Hustler, a Mach 2 bomber, was dropped after four years in service because of very high maintenance costs. North American produced two prototypes of the experimental XB-70 Valkyrie Mach 3 bomber, a stainless steel aircraft with a sophisticated refrigeration system, but one crashed during a test and the other was built mainly as a test craft. The most promising model, the Rockwell B-1 swing-wing, was dropped during production because of feared cost overruns, but the project was eventually resumed under a modified design as the B-1B.

The B-2 Stealth Bomber, modeled on the Northrop YB-35 Flying Wing of World War II and designed to penetrate enemy radar without being easily detected or identified, has been produced and has tested well, but it has been a costly aircraft. Stealth technology uses a combination of absorptive alloys and electronic scrambling of radar echoes, all dependent on showing a minimal surface to incoming radar beams.

The Soviet Union, less able to afford an advanced aircraft development program than the United States, was nevertheless driven to keep up by a fear that the capitalistic West had murderous designs on the nation of the Revolution, just as the West evinced the same paranoia about the evil intentions of the Reds. They matched the West plane for plane, improving on them whenever possible and using every opportunity to mislead the West regarding the true capabilities of their aircraft (although modern electronic espionage techniques made such subterfuge increasingly more difficult to pull off).

After a slow start recuperating from World War II, the Soviets were assisted by a downed B-29 bomber retrieved off the eastern coast of the Soviet Union during the war. The Soviets spent two years patiently disassembling the plane and studying everything about it, from its electronic systems to its metallurgy. This formed the basis of their bomber development program. At the height of the Cold War, the Soviet arsenal included the jet-powered TU-16 Badger and the Myasishchev M-4 Bison, equivalents to the B-47 and B-52. The Soviets have even developed, ahead of the United States, the backfire bomber (the TU-26), the equivalent of the B-1B. Since the war, the importance of these bombers has been a matter of doubt, because it is not known how effective they would be against anti-aircraft defenses, or how necessary they would be in the event ICBMs or cruise missiles are used.

Both sides that participated in the Cold War also produced an amazing array of jet-powered fighter aircraft. The earliest jet fighters were adaptations of World War II aircraft: the Lockheed P-80 Shooting Star was the first jet used by the U.S. Air Force; the McDonnell FH-1 Phantom was the U.S. Navy's first jet fighter; and the North American FJ-1 Fury was the first fighter to see combat during the Korean War. The Fury inspired the F-86 Sabre, the favorite of USAF pilots confronting MiG-15s in the air over Korea. American pilots discovered the disadvantages of fighter air combat conducted far from home base (something the British had demonstrated during the Battle of Britain) when most engagements with the MiGs took place in an area near the North Korean border known as MiG Alley.

In 1953 a new crop of fighters appeared: North American improved on its Sabre formula to produce the F-1000 Super Sabre. Britain produced the Convair F-102 Delta Dagger and the F106 Delta Dart. These sparred occasionally with the chief Soviet fighter of the period, the MiG-19. The art of fighter design reached a high point in the 1960s with the building of the McDonnell Douglas F4H Phantom, one of the most versatile fighter-bombers produced by the United States since World War II, and the Dessault Mirage III, a fighter the French sold to everyone, making it a main component of fifteen of the world's air forces.

The principal instruments of the U.S. strategic policy in the latter years of the Cold War: the B-52G (LEFT); the swing-wing Rockwell B-1B bomber (BELOW LEFT), the controversial Mach-2 aircraft developed during the Reagan administration; and the Northrop B-2 Stealth Bomber (BELOW RIGHT), unveiled in 1989 and said to be the most sophisticated airplane ever built. (It is important to note that the Soviets had excellent strategic bombers of their own, but could not support a fleet of them financially.)

North American F-86 Sabrejet

Chance-Vought RF-8G Crusader

McDonnell Douglas F4C Phantom II

Soviet MiG-15

The Vietnam era produced yet a fresher crop of fighters, now with "Coke bottle" design to enhance their speed to the supersonic range: the Republic F-105 Thunderchief, a fighter that was able to deliver an awesome six thousand rounds of cannon fire per minute; the Grumman A6E Intruder, a slow fighter that had the advantage of being able, because of super-sophisticated electronics, to fly even in stormy weather; and the Chance-Vought F-8 Crusader, a Navy fighter that was used extensively during the Cuban Missile Crisis of 1962. All used advanced electronics and, for the most part, missiles instead of cannons, although the success enjoyed by the Israeli Air Force flying Phantoms during the Six Day War of 1967 convinced many that there was still a place for fixed-barrel armament in a fighter. Their main adversary in the air was the Russian-built MiG-21, a delta-wing jet that carried air-to-air missiles and was configured mainly for aerial combat and not for ground support or bombing. As a result, the MiGs were a significant factor in control of the skies over Vietnam, but the North Vietnamese never benefited from other ways in which fighter aircraft can be used in war. The MiG-21 was exported by the Soviets to more than thirty other nations who learned only later that its excellent flight characteristics were achieved at the cost of its versatility.

Largely because of support from Secretary of Defense Robert McNamara, the Convair F-111, a swing-wing (or "variable-geometry") fighter-bomber, saw a great deal of action during the Vietnam War and continued to be an important fighter during the U.S. air attack on Libya in 1986 and again during "Operation Desert Storm"—the Gulf War—in 1991. In addition to the F-111 and the Phantom, the U.S. fighter arsenal contains the General Dynamics F-16A Fighting Falcon, the Lockheed F-104 Starfighter, and, most important, the McDonnell Douglas F-15 Eagle.

Looking at the Soviet side, we find that nearly every type of aircraft in the U.S. fleet has a directly corresponding answer in the Soviet fleet, often an aircraft that has taken advantage of being second in the air to create specifications that make it first in performance. The F-111's counterpart is the Su-24 Fencer, which is faster and has a larger range. The Phantom is met by the MiG-27 Flogger, also a swing wing (the Phantom is not) that is identical to the light dogfighting MiG-23. The F-16 has two Soviet counterparts: the MiG-21 and the MiG-29 Fulcrum. And the F-15 Eagle is matched in the air by the MiG-25 Foxbat. Not surprisingly, the USAF did not allow the Soviet supremacy in any of these models to go unchallenged, and improvements eventually put the aircraft out of the Soviets' reach, particularly in the F-15, the premier USAF fighter.

The same technology—a combination of material science and electronics—that created the Stealth Bomber was used to create the Stealth Fighter, the F-117A, an airplane first delivered in secret in 1983, but which proved itself during the American invasion of Panama and during the Gulf War, when it used laser-guided missiles to knock out Iraqi targets.

An aircraft developed by the British and adopted by the American Air Force, but which the Soviets were hard pressed to duplicate, is the Hawker-Siddeley Harrier, a jet fighter that allows the thrust to be directed downward so that the plane can hover or take off vertically. The "Jump Jet" is particularly useful in confined-area engagements, where noncombatant borders and geographical boundaries, coupled with the increased ability of army units to "disappear" in an area using camouflage, force a fighter aircraft to be in the thick of battle virtually at a moment's notice from any position. The Harrier saw extensive and effective action during the Falklands crisis in 1982 and has become an important ground-support aircraft of the U.S. Marines.

The war between the U.S.-led coalition and Iraq following the latter's invasion of Kuwait in 1991, known as the Gulf War or "Operation Desert Storm," pitted the air capabilities of the United States against the ground capabilities and largely Soviet-supplied air arsenal or Iraq. The objective of U.S. operations seems to have been to win the war most expeditiously through the use of air power while endangering as few American lives as possible. The air war over Iraq was not supported by Russia, so that much of the equipment used by the Iraqis, including the MiG-21 Fulcrum fighters they flew, were not in the best battle-ready condition and enjoyed virtually no ground support. As a result, the American F-15 Eagles, aided by the E-3 AWACS radar aircraft, had little trouble clearing the skies.

The main assault aircraft used in this war was the Panavia Tornado, a low-altitude fighter developed by England, Germany, and Italy that was the mainstay of the Saudi Arabian Air Force, the other major combatant. The Panavia is a variable-geometry aircraft that is designed to fight well at high speeds when contending with other fighters, and at low speeds when its wings are extended. The Panavia was instrumental in the entrance of a new word into the military vocabulary: interdiction. An aircraft is carrying out an interdiction when by virtue of its bombing and ground support it is cutting off a military unit (of whatever size) from its main headquarters. A feature of the Panavia that makes it an ideal interdictor is its terrain-following radar, allowing it to fly low and anticipate enemy ground fire. Interdiction became an oft-used word in the Gulf War and has become an important goal in the design of fighter aircraft.

Two classes of new weapons were used during the Gulf War: the Lockheed F-117A Stealth Fighter, used sparingly but effectively in the early stages of the conflict, when Iraq had a semblance of an air defense; and the laser-guided missiles that provided pinpoint accuracy (and impressive video footage) in conjunction with the Forward-Looking Infra-Red (FLIR) system.

Convair F-111

McDonnell-Douglas F-15 Eagle

Soviet MiG-29 Fulcrum

Lockheed F-117A Stealth Fighter

The Smaller Hot Wars

In an age of mass communication, it seems the times are more barbaric than days gone by, but a sober look at history shows (just as depressingly) that not very much has changed in the way people and nations conduct their affairs. Skirmishes, conflicts, battles, and full-scale wars are continually breaking out in one place or another in many corners of the globe and, in many of them, air power plays an important role.

In the period immediately following World War II, two crises underscored the continuing role aircraft would play in the military. One, the Berlin Blockade, initiated in 1948 by the Soviets, who cut off the isolated city of West Berlin, was addressed by the Berlin Airlift, a massive operation code-named "Vittles" in which tons of food and supplies were brought into the besieged city by C-54 transports and virtually any large aircraft available. By the time the operation ended in September 1949, with the blockade broken, nearly 300,000 flights (about seven hundred each day) had been made.

The other crisis was the rather more serious Korean War, which began in 1950. American helicopters played an important role in moving the wounded and transporting supplies over the rough terrain. The role of the helicopter on the battlefield was developed further during the Vietnam War, where airfields were few and far between and helicopters had to be relied upon as much for their armament as for transportation. The Sikorsky HO3S and the Bell Model 40 (known as the "Korean Angel") became famous for rescuing twenty-three thousand wounded soldiers from front-line positions and transporting them to Mobile Army Surgical Hospital (MASH) units for medical care. French Alouette helicopters set records and were used for extraordinary exploratory missions, but Alouette did not become a financially successful company.

The Sikorsky and Bell helicopters continued to develop new military and civil applications in the decades to follow: the Sikorsky S-51 became a popular commercial transportation helicopter, serving as the backbone of services between many American cities; the S-55 became an important seagoing tool for rescue and naval operation; and the S-64 Flying Crane was the first of the crane helicopters capable of transporting heavy cargo to and from inaccessible areas. The Bell helicopters became critical during the Vietnam War. The UH-1 Iroquois were armed with machine guns and became known as Huey gunships; by 1967 the aircraft had grown into the AH-1G Huey Cobra, the key mover of personnel through the jungles during the war. Military helicopters have continued to develop—Sikorsky was contracted in 1995 to develop a Stealth helicopter—and by the 1990s the Hughes AH-64 Apache, loaded with missiles, cannon, and machine guns, became a particularly lethal weapon in the U.S. arsenal, as has the Soviet-built Hind D in the Russian.

Boeing Vertol CH47 Chinook

Hawker-Siddeley Harrier

Hughes OH-6A Cayuse Scout

Bell UH-1 Huey Cobra

The area of the world where air power played the most significant role in the decades after World War II was in the Middle East. Air power was recognized early by the Israelis as one of the few means by which they could address the numerical advantage of the Arab armies that surrounded them. Throughout its history, therefore, the Israeli Air Force (IAF, or Chel Ha'Avir) has pursued a program of technical superiority that has at times overshadowed similar efforts of even the superpowers. Israeli technicians have modified nearly all aircraft given them, becoming so familiar with them that they have been recruited by American manufacturers for special briefings, and developing special armaments and missile systems suited to the terrain and the mission profiles (and to the capability of carrying atomic weapons, which the Israelis have never acknowledged having).

The most resounding victory of the IAF was in June 1967, when Israeli Dessault MD 42 Mysteres and Mirage IIIs swooped down on and destroyed Soviet-supplied MiG-17s and MiG-19s while they were on the tarmac at Egyptian air bases. This establishment of air superiority led directly to the Israeli victory in the Six Day War of 1967. The situation was different in 1973, when the Egyptian Air Force was equipped with first-line MiG-21 fighters and could support the air war from the ground with Soviet SAM-6 missiles. By then, the IAF was equipped with American F-4 Phantom and A-4 Skyhawk fighters, with support from the A-4 Hawk missile—an arsenal that did not represent the American state-of-the-art in the air. Only an emergency airlift, ordered by President Nixon, with C-4 transports delivering all manner of war materials, and a fresh supply of Phantoms flown directly (and in some cases, with only enough time to have their American identification whitewashed over), averted an Israeli defeat. During the Yom Kippur War of 1973, the United States also used the SR-71, its super-fast spy plane, to provide detailed and instantaneous intelligence on Arab troop movements and aircraft deployments.

Two other operations involving the IAF became the focus of the world: the July 4, 1976, rescue of more than one hundred hostages from the Entebbe Airport in Uganda by commandos flying two C-130 Hercules transport planes; and the June 7, 1981, bombing of the Iraqi atomic reactor at Osirak by a squadron of IAF-flown General Dynamics F-16 and McDonnell Douglas F-15 fighters, the newly acquired core of the IAF. Although both missions brought the Israelis simultaneously under criticism and praise, both were later seen to be admirable uses of air power and were emulated by other nations. One of the immediate consequences of the fall of Communism and the cessation of the aggressive development programs at Russian fighter aircraft plants has been to give the IAF an even greater dominance in the area. Since 1992, Russia, formerly the chief supplier of fighter aircraft to the Arab states, has not supplied them with a single aircraft, forcing the Arab states to turn to the

ABOVE: *A formidable ground-support weapon, the Hughes Advanced Attack Helicopter (AAH) Apache YAH-64 boasts four weapon mountings.* BACKGROUND: *The poor communication between MiG pilots and Egyptian ground troops hampered Arab military operations during the 1967 Mideast War. Israelis concentrated on destroying aircraft aloft and on the ground, knowing the Russians would not replace them.*

United States (as well as adopting a more conciliatory attitude toward the Israeli government).

The advent of the Stinger missile, a device that can be launched from a shoulder-held bazooka-like launcher, and which uses heat-seeking technology to find its target (so that the shooter need not even have very good aim), and of other highly mobile surface-to-air anti-aircraft systems, has cast doubt on the entire premise of the decisiveness of air superiority in a confined area of battle. After the frustrations experienced in Bosnia in 1995, where NATO air strikes were able to clear the skies but had little effect on the ground, military planners are again discovering that while there is a close supporting element that air power can give to ground troops, the two are not interchangeable—ground forces are not replaceable by air power.

The Speedsters

With the development of jet-powered flight, a new series of record-breaking speed flights began as soon as the planes were available. The first achievement was to fly faster than the speed of sound (760 miles per hour [1,223kph] at sea level, although that number falls as the altitude is increased until it is 659 miles per hour [1,060.5kph] at thirty-six thousand feet [10,973m]), designated Mach 1—meaning compared as a ratio to the speed of sound—after Ernst Mach, the nineteenth-century physicist who worked out some of the physics involved in "transonic" flight.

On October 14, 1947, Charles E. "Chuck" Yeager, a decorated American ace, became the first flyer to "break the sound barrier" by flying at Mach 1.015 (or 670 miles per hour [1,078kph]) at forty-two thousand feet [12,801.5m]) in the experimental Bell X-1. Yeager named the airplane the *Glamorous Glennis*, after his wife. Pilots in Korea who took their aircraft near Mach 1 experienced a violent buffeting, and several lost their lives when their planes broke up. Yeager had encountered the same thing as he neared Mach 1, but once past it, he experienced an eerie quiet as he raced ahead of the noise and shock wave his airplane was creating.

In 1951 famed test pilot Bill Bridgeman flew a Douglas Skyrocket to Mach 1.88, demonstrating that several existing engines would be capable of taking an aircraft above Mach 1, and establishing Mach 2 as the next goal of the speed fliers. Meanwhile, research at NACA at Langley Field had reached an obstacle: airplane designs that were supposed to be able to break Mach 1 were falling consistently short. There had been speculation in the late 1940s that it might be impossible to break the sound barrier (that was why it was called a barrier), and the early tests of the Convair F-102 gave some credence to this fear. Then NACA aerodynamicist Richard Whitcomb reasoned that the smoothest airflow over an aircraft would be achieved if the cross-section of the craft increased smoothly from front to back. This would be a problem once the wings started to protrude from the plane. The solution was to pinch the fuselage in at the wings: the result was the classic "Coke bottle" design of supersonic aircraft. The revised design of the F-102 yielded a fighter that achieved speeds of Mach 1.2 with no other change in the plane.

Jacqueline Cochran became the first woman aviator to break the sound barrier on May 18, 1953, flying a Canadian F-86E Sabre jet. Later that month an American F-100 Super Sabre became the first jet fighter to fly above Mach 1, and later that year test pilot A. Scott Crossfield flew a B-29 at Mach 2.01. Chuck Yeager ended the year with a record flight of 1,650 miles per hour (2,655kph)—Mach 2.44—though he was just barely able to regain control of the aircraft when it went hurtling earthward in a tailspin.

In the years that followed, a corps of exceptional test pilots working at Boscombe Down in England and at

LEFT: Charles E. "Chuck" Yeager standing next to the Bell X-1, Glamorous Glennis, *in which he broke the sound barrier in 1947.*
BELOW: Yeager set another record—Mach 2.44 (1,650mph)—in the Bell X-1A in December 1953, barely managing to land safely.

Edwards Air Force Base in California became celebrated for "pushing the envelope" of flight. In 1958 Major Howard C. Johnson, one of those pilots with the "right stuff," set an altitude record (91,243 feet [27,811m]) and then a speed record (1,403 miles per hour [2,257.5kph]), flying a Lockheed F104A Starfighter each time. The seven original Mercury astronauts were chosen from among this group of pilots. Speed flying took a quantum leap with the building of the North American X-15, designed by Harrison Storm. The X-15 was designed to fly as fast as Mach 7; when it was flown in July 1962 by Robert White at an altitude of fifty-nine miles (95km) above sea level, it was seen as a step toward putting an astronaut into space.

The next phase in speed flying came about because of the downing of a U-2 spy plane piloted by Francis Gary Powers over Russia in May 1960. The U-2 had been designed by Kelly Johnson at the "Skunk Works," Lockheed's secret plant in Burbank, California. The plane used a very high aspect-ratio (long, narrow wings) and a powerful Pratt & Whitney jet engine to fly very high and very fast over targets that it would then photograph. The Russians had found a way of hitting the plane with surface-to-air missiles (possibly with the help of a Marine defector who had worked on the project—Lee Harvey Oswald), and the ensuing scandal was one of the major crises of the Eisenhower administration.

The military turned to Lockheed again, and this time the Skunk Works, under the direction of Johnson and Ben Rich, produced an aircraft that was too fast even for missiles: the SR-71 Blackbird. The SR-71 began its life as the YF-12, a high-speed interceptor fighter—from certain angles, in fact, an SR-71 looks to be two aircraft melded together down the middle. The plane has been modified and improved many times since its introduction in 1964—new materials, new systems, and, most importantly, new fuels have allowed the aircraft to reach its potential speed of Mach 7-plus. However, the world's airplane speed record is held by William J. "Pete" Knight, who flew an X-15-2A over Edwards Air Force Base at 4,535 miles per hour (7,297kph), or Mach 6.72—a record set on October 3, 1967. Aviation observers point out that several U.S. military aircraft (even some later models of the SR-71) may be capable of greater speeds and that the USAF may well have established new records in secret since.

In addition to high speed, designers of fighters are always on the lookout for high maneuverability. The newest experimental aircraft—one that may prove to be more agile than even a human-computer combination can control—is the X-29, a forward swept-wing that appears to be flying backward. This configuration creates hot spots on the skin of the aircraft that requires special heat-dissipative metals. It is feared that during some sharp turns at high speed pilots in this aircraft may be subject to G-forces that will kill them.

Airships and Balloons: Rising from the Ashes

After the *Hindenburg* disaster, one would have thought that the airship was forever dead as a possible means of air transportation. The attempts by the Germans to keep the airships aloft soon failed, and after the war dirigibles became strictly an advertising tool—something to fly above a sporting event so that television cameras could record a bird's-eye-view of the event while the broad side of the airship was used for advertising. Such blimps sponsored by Goodyear, Fuji film, and Met Life have become ubiquitous at college and professional sporting events.

In 1973 an attempt was made by Cameron Balloons, a British firm headed by E.T. Hall, to revive the airship as a means of transportation. The effort failed because of a combination of underfunding and overdesigning, but the episode sparked interest on both sides of the Atlantic. In 1984 another attempt to establish an airship service in England failed after a few months of service, with two airships, the Skyship 500 and 600, ferrying passengers between London and Cardington. The U.S. Navy has

The Lockheed SR-71 Blackbird, developed by Clarence "Kelly" Johnson's team at the Skunk Works, is the only aircraft capable of cruising at Mach 3 (its top speed is still classified) for extended periods (two or three hours). Its chief design element is the way it directs heat away from the cockpit, beginning with the remote placement of the engines.

used airships for long-duration surveillance of Soviet trawlers and for maintenance of antisubmarine sonar nets, but the great body of aerodynamic research conducted over the past two decades has yet to result in a practical commercial venture.

For many aviation purists, flight in a dirigible or balloon is the most legitimate form of human flight—especially ballooning, because it is powered completely by the wind. Yet if one were to consult any history of aviation, one would find many references to ballooning early in the book and then a lonely reference toward the end, with nothing in between. That final reference would more than likely be to the August 17, 1978, crossing of the Atlantic in a balloon, accomplished at long last by Captain Ben Abruzzo and his crew in the *Double Eagle II.*

Slower (and Quieter) Record-Breaking Flights

Flying higher and faster is not the only frontier in flight, and it does not represent the only progress made in aviation in recent times. Engineers have taken renewed looks at the foundations of aerodynamics and aeronautics and have attempted to solve problems in flight, combining modern computer and other technologies with the age-old method of trial and error. Three problems have received the most attention: flying by power supplied by a human being, solar-powered flight, and very long distance nonstop flight.

In recent times, some old dreams of flight were revived. A trans-Atlantic crossing by balloon (ABOVE) was finally accomplished in August 1978. BACKGROUND: Brian Allen piloted Paul MacCready's Gossamer Albatross *across the English Channel in 1979, marking the first such flight by a human-powered aircraft.*

THE FRONTIERS OF FLIGHT

The importance of big aircraft as commercial transports and bombers, and of fast aircraft as fighters, has created the impression that the age of innovation is past; in fact, innovation in aircraft design continues to this day, and the variations are every bit as wild and creative as in the early days of flight. Two aircraft have advanced the concept of Vertical Take-off and Landing (VTOL), which allows an airplane to operate without an airfield (formerly a vulnerable point in any air force). They are the Harrier, a jet-powered VTOL, and the rotor Bell XV-15 Osprey. Both aircraft hold the promise of eliminating the major safety concern for aircraft: take-off and landing.

The engineering required for variable-wing design has progressed steadily, so that now it is possible to think beyond the simple extended wings of the F-111 or the B-1 bomber to "switchblade" designs in which the wing disappears altogether and the fuselage provides all the lift required, or helicopters with rotors that can be locked and turned into fixed, X-shaped wings that provide lift. Periodically, new designs are created on the drawing boards and even tested in the wind tunnels, but thus far they have not proven to be cost-effective.

Designers have also discovered that, rightly or wrongly, certain configurations are deemed unsafe and risky by ordinary fliers and they simply will not set foot in them if they can avoid it. This is particularly true of double-fuselage designs and has also been the case with flying-wing transports. As a result, the most promising new designs have been those based on the older 707 configuration, such as the new computer-designed Boeing 777, and the similar aircraft of Airbus.

Paradoxically, the one new design that may find a receptive public is a variation of the old Pan Am Clippers—the Wing-In-Ground, or WIG, aircraft developed and used in Russia. These aircraft use the extra lift provided by updrafts from the ground in order to cut down on fuel and provide safe transportation. Whether or not these aircraft find a use in the West, it is clear that the flight parameters of the next generation of passenger aircraft will have to include "passenger tolerances" as well as speed and fuel economy. There seems little point in getting a passenger from point A to point B in one hour when the trip to and within the airport takes five, and when not enough passengers can be transported to make the operation profitable.

Human-powered flight had been replaced by hang gliding in the last century, and people did not pursue the matter until well after World War II. In 1962 John Wimpenny, an aerodynamical engineer for Hawker-Siddeley, constructed a balsa-wood airplane with a propeller driven by a bicycle wheel. Wimpenny and the fellow members of HMPAC (the Hatfield Man-Powered Aircraft Club) were at the time attempting to win a five-thousand-pound prize offered by industrialist Henry Kremmer to the first human-powered aircraft that could fly a figure-eight over a half-mile course. Kremmer was to offer several prizes during the 1960s and 1970s for human-powered flight achievements. The *Puffin*, as Wimpenny's plane was called, managed a straight flight of more half a mile (0.8km), but was not able to complete the difficult course laid out by the Kremmer rules.

The Kremmer prize went unclaimed for fifteen years, during which time it grew to a fifty-thousand-pound prize. In August 1977 sailplane designer Paul MacCready used light materials—carbon-composite poles and Mylar sheets for the wings—to construct the *Gossamer Condor*. This plane was piloted by cyclist Bryan Allen around a Kremmer course laid out at Shafter Field, California. In June 1979 MacCready, Allen, and the *Gossamer Albatross* teamed up to stage a human-powered flight across the English Channel. The trip took just over three hours and the team was awarded another Kremmer Prize, this one for 100,000 pounds.

Kremmer was to offer one more prize: twenty thousand pounds to the first human-powered circular flight of a mile (1.6km) in under three minutes. The prize was claimed by a team at the Massachusetts Institute of Technology who designed the *Daedalus* and staged a flight from Crete to the island of Santorini, piloted by Greek champion cyclist Kanellos Kanellopoulos. The wing span had grown from ninety-seven feet (29.5m) for the MacCready aircraft to 112 feet (34m). (After flying for nearly four hours and coming within sight of its destination, the *Daedalus* ditched in the Aegean Sea and the pilot had to swim the final few yards to shore.)

England also was the site of the first successful flight by a solar-powered airplane, on December 19, 1978, when the *Solar One*, designed by Freddie To and piloted by David Williams, made a brief flight—more like the hops of the pre–Kitty Hawk aviators. A full, sustained solar-powered flight took place in August 1980, when ninety-nine-pound (45kg) Janice Brown piloted MacCready's *Gossamer Penguin*, a modified version of the *Gossamer*

Albatross. The flight was powered by solar panels and Brown did not pedal the propellers. A similar flight the previous May began with the plane being towed to cruising speed so that the takeoff was assisted, which caused some engineers to dismiss the flight. Finally, on July 7, 1981, MacCready's *Solar Challenger*, piloted by Stephen Ptacek, became the first solar-powered airplane to cross the English Channel.

The flight of the *Voyager*, the two-seat, twin engine airplane that circumnavigated the globe, taking off from Edwards Air Force Base on December 14, 1986, and landing there nine days later without stopping for mid-air refueling, captured the world's attention as few flights had done in fifty years. The plane was designed by Burt Rutan and flown by his brother, Dick Rutan, and Jeanna Yeager. The aircraft was just big enough for the pilots to take turns popping his or her head into the raised bubble while the other lay flat and slept or ate. The pair had oxygen for flights higher than sixteen thousand feet (4,877m), but the *Voyager* was not pressurized, so they could not fly higher than twenty thousand feet (6,096m), which meant that they could not fly above harsh weather. Rutan reported later that they had to make so many detours en route to avoid storms that he did not believe they would have enough fuel for the flight.

The plane weighed 2,680 pounds (1,217kg) with empty fuel tanks; with fuel, the *Voyager* weighed in at 11,680 pounds (5,303kg). When the plane took off, the tips of the wings scraped dangerously along the runway on the desert floor; at least a few observers thought it reminiscent of the historic takeoff of the Wright *Flyer* at Kitty Hawk nearly a century before.

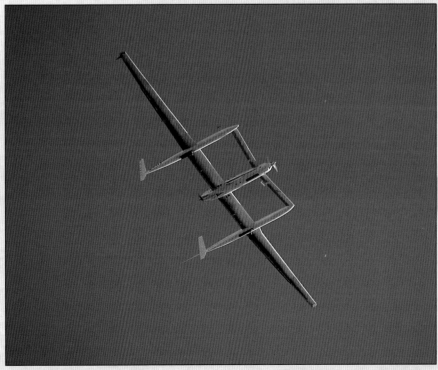

The Voyager *was the result of yet another collaboration between brothers. Burt Rutan's innovative configuration (owing much to the glider designs of the 1930s) was tested, refined, and perfected in test flights conducted by his brother, pilot Dick Rutan.*

Bibliography: The Flying Five-O

In an effort to utilize this valuable space well, I list just fifty works about aviation—five general titles and five for each chapter. Several of these works (marked with an asterisk) are so well done that it pays to seek them out—even if the search involves a few trips to used-book stores.

Aside from the titles listed, the twenty-six-volume Time-Life series *The Epic of Flight* is well-written and authoritative (if at times thin) and features lavish picture treatments covering every aspect of the history of aviation. These books are also worth rummaging for.

General
Anderson, John D. *Introduction to Flight*. New York: McGraw-Hill, 1985. A beautiful blend of science and history by a respected professor of aeronautical engineering.

Bilstein, Roger E. *Flight in America: From the Wrights to the Astronauts*. Revised. Baltimore: Johns Hopkins University Press, 1994. A serious study of the place of aviation in U.S. history with a bibliographic essay that's worth the price of admission.

Boyne, Walter J. *The Smithsonian Book of Flight*. Reprint, New York: Crown, 1994. A grand tour by a great aviation historian and former Director of the National Air and Space Museum.

* Chant, Christopher. *Aviation: An Illustrated History*. Edison, N.J.: Chartwell, 1978. A careful look at the technology of aviation, with some remarkable illustrations and ephemera by one of the great aviation writers.

Josephy, Alvin M., Jr, ed. *The American Heritage History of Flight*. New York: American Heritage, 1962. The full AH treatment by a first-class historian, with special attention paid to the personalities involved.

Dreams of Flight
Alexander, John. *Conquest of the Air*. New York: Wessels, 1902. With a marvelous preface by Hiram Maxim.

Gibbs-Smith, Charles H. *The Inventions of Leonardo da Vinci*. New York: Scribners, 1978. No bibliography should fail to list this author of many of the landmark works in the field.

* Hart, Clive. *The Prehistory of Flight*. Berkeley, Calif.: University of California Press, 1985. A beautifully produced tour-de-force.

Murchie, Guy. *Song of the Sky*. New York: Riverside, 1954. A rhapsody about the sea of air we live in and about our efforts to explore it.

Soderberg, Henry. *Swedenborg's 1714 Airplane: A Machine to Fly in the Air*. Westchester, Penn.: Swedenborg Foundation, 1988. A charming, privately published (but widely distributed) booklet on an interesting ongoing investigation.

From Dream to Plan to Reality
Crouch, Tom D. *A Dream of Wings: Americans and the Airplane, 1875–1905*. Washington, D.C.: Smithsonian Institution Press, 1989. An engrossing account of the race to be the first to fly.

———. *The Eagle Aloft: 300 Years of Ballooning in America*. Washington, D.C.: Smithsonian Institution Press, 1989. A monumental study that will give the reader a profound respect for ballooning.

Gibbs-Smith, Charles H. *The Invention of the Aeroplane, 1799-1909*. New York: Taplinger, 1965. The British view, which is where many of the interesting events were taking place.

Penrose, Harold. *An Ancient Air: The Biography of John Stringfellow of Chard, the Victorian Aeronautical Pioneer*. Washington, D.C.: Smithsonian Institution Press, 1988. A biography of John Stringfellow and his colleague William Henson that presents a more serious side than the one presented in this book (the truth probably lies somewhere in between).

Pritchard, John L. *Sir George Cayley: The Inventor of the Aeroplane*. London: Horizon Press, 1961. A sympathetic and very readable biography, though it makes some questionable claims about successful flights.

The First to Fly
Combs, Harry. *Kill Devil Hill: The Epic of the Wright Brothers, 1900-1909*. Boston: Houghton-Mifflin, 1969. A careful, detailed look at how the Wrights managed at Kitty Hawk, with drawings and photos.

* Crouch, Tom D. *The Bishop's Boys: The Life of Wilbur and Orville Wright*. New York: Norton, 1989. A definitive, engaging biography.

Harris, Sherwood. *The First to Fly: Aviation's Pioneer Days*. New York: Simon & Schuster, 1970. Year-by-year through the first fifteen years of the century, with many nifty photos.

Serrano-Villard, Henry. *Contact! The Story of the Early Birds*. Reprint, Washington, D.C.: Smithsonian Institution Press, 1987. An exciting rendering of the early years of aviation on the other side of the Atlantic.

Wykeham, Peter. *Santos-Dumont: A Study in Obsession*. New York: Putnam, 1962. A careful and compelling telling of a poignant story.

World War I: The Airplane Goes to War
Clark, Alan. *Aces High*. New York: Putnam, 1973. A classic work on the extraordinary aviators of the WWI air war.

Hegener, Henri. *Fokker—The Man and the Aircraft*. Letchworth, Herts: Harleyford, 1961. Not as flattering as the biography Fokker would have authorized. Interesting glimpses into the creative processes in the "labs."

Hudson, James J. *Hostile Skies: A Combat History of the American Air Service*. Syracuse, N.Y.: Syracuse University Press, 1968. Includes stirring descriptions of combat in the skies over Europe.

Jablonski, Edward. *Warriors with Wings: the Story of the Lafayette Escadrille*. New York: Doubleday, 1961. A great and interesting chapter in military aviation history by a premier historian.

* Wohl, Robert. *A Passion for Wings: Aviation and the Western Imagination, 1909-1918*. New Haven, Conn.: Yale University Press, 1994. An engrossing look at how thoroughly Western culture embraced flight.

Barnstormers, Trailblazers, and Daredevils
Corn, Joseph J. *The Winged Gospel: America's Romance with Aviation, 1900-1950*. New York: Oxford University Press, 1983. An entertaining look at America's romance with aviation during its formative years.

* Dwiggins, Don. *The Barnstormers: Flying Daredevils of the Roaring Twenties*. New York: Grosset & Dunlap, 1968. By the author of several wonderful can't-put-'em-down books on the period.

Foxworth, Thomas. *The Speed Seekers*. New York: Doubleday, 1974. The serious matter of speed racing as undertaken by people who were not always that serious. A splended evocation of the period.

Gilpatrick, Guy. *Guy Gilpatrick's Flying Stories*. New York: Dutton/Signet, 1946. Exciting recollections of stunt flying at air shows and for early films.

Glines, Carrol V. *Jimmy Doolittle: Daredevil Aviator and Scientist*. Indianapolis: Macmillan, 1972. A thorough biography that highlights Doolittle's contribution to the advancement of aviation science.

The Pathfinders: Aviators of Flight's Golden Age
Bilstein, Roger E. *Flight Patterns: Trends of Aeronautical Development in the United States, 1918-1929*. Athens, Ga.: University of Georgia Press, 1983. A scholarly presentation, with valuable material on the cultural and social impact of aviation in the United States.

De la Croix, Robert. *They Flew the Atlantic*. New York: Norton, 1959. Conveys the international drama of the quest to cross the Atlantic by air.

Gill, Brendan. *Lindbergh Alone: May 21, 1927*. New York: Harcourt Brace Jovanovich, 1977. A celebrated writer's appreciation of Lindbergh's historic flight, with many judiciously selected photos.

Lovell, Mary S. *The Sound of Wings: The Life of Amelia Earhart*. New York: St. Martin's, 1989. A wonderful biography free of the nonsense and rumor that has contaminated the story of Earhart's life, by the author of an equally fine biography of Beryl Markham.

* Roseberry, C.R. *The Challenging Skies: The Colorful Story of Aviation's Most Exciting Years, 1919–1939*. New York: Doubleday, 1966. A rollicking ride that will make you sorry to see the back cover approaching.

The World Learns to Fly
Biddle, Walter. *Barons of the Sky*. New York: Simon & Schuster, 1991. A penetrating portrait of the founders of the American aerospace industry.

* Coleman, Ted. *Jack Northrop and the Flying Wing: The Real Story Behind the Stealth Bomber*. New York: Paragon, 1988. Not really about the stealth bomber at all (except for a mere fifteen pages), but a wonderful history by a Northrop associate, with a bonus lecture by Northrop.

Josephson, Matthew. *Empire of the Air: Juan Trippe and the Struggle for World Airways*. Orlando, Fl.: Harcourt Brace, 1944. A thoughtful biography about a murky figure (despite later, longer biographies).

McKee, Alexander. *Great Mysteries of Aviation*. Lanham, Md.: Madison Books, 1982. Not as lurid as the title suggests, but great fun and filled with episodes that have become part of aviation lore.

Soberg, Carl. *Conquest of the Skies: A History of Commercial Aviation*. Boston: Little, Brown, 1979. Told well in a journalistic style and covering more than half a century of a complex community and enterprise.

World War II: The Aerial War
Boyne, Walter J. *Clash of Wings: Air Power in World War II*. New York: Simon & Schuster, 1994. A masterful summary, with Boyne's usual flair.

Gurney, Gene. *The War in the Air: World War II*. New York: Crown, 1962. More than three hundred pages of wall-to-wall black-and-white photos covering every aspect of the aerial war.

Jablonski, Edward. *Airwar*. New York: Doubleday, 1979. Published as four-volume and two-volume sets, and finally in one large volume; a monumental work with photos, text, and a kitchen-sink analysis of every aspect of the WWII air war.

Overy, R.J. *The Air War, 1939-1945*. Lanham, Md.: Madison Books, 1981. A British view, with interesting material on the technological background and the RAF development program by a great aviation historian.

Verges, Marianne. *On Silver Wings: The Women Air Force Service Pilots of World War II, 1942-1944*. New York: Ballantine, 1991. Covers many aspects in an engrossing way, but points to the need for more on the topic.

Fire in the Sky: The Jet Age
Christy, Joe, and Page Shamburger. *Summon the Stars: The Advance of Aviation from the Second World War*. South Brunswick: A.S. Barnes, 1970. A sequel to an earlier history of prewar aviation; filled with interesting material and many well-captioned illustrations that focus on the planes.

Hallion, Richard P. *Supersonic Flight: Breaking the Sound Barrier and Beyond*. Indianapolis: Macmillan, 1972. A first-rate account with many insights into the future development of flight.

————. *Test Pilots: The Frontiersmen of Flight*. New York: Doubleday, 1981. A singular book by the outstanding historian of the USAF.

Higham, Robert. *Air Power: A Concise History*. New York: St. Martin's, 1972. An engaging and sweeping view of the role air power has played in international politics.

* Wolfe, Tom. *The Right Stuff*. New York: Farrar, Straus & Giroux, 1979. An extraordinary work of reportage that is as fresh today as it was when it first appeared.

Photo Credits

Index